Petrarch's Lyric Poems

Celesti Page Morgan

Durham, N.C.   March 1981

The beginning of "Vergine Bella," as it appears in Petrarch's hand in Vat. Lat. 3195 *(Courtesy of Vaticana Apostolica Vaticana)*

Petrarch's Lyric Poems

The *Rime sparse* and Other Lyrics

Translated and edited by
ROBERT M. DURLING

HARVARD UNIVERSITY PRESS
Cambridge, Massachusetts, and London, England

Copyright © 1976 by Robert M. Durling
All rights reserved
Publication of this volume has been aided by a grant from
the Andrew W. Mellon Foundation
Printed in the United States of America
Second printing 1979

Library of Congress Cataloging in Publication Data

Petrarca, Francesco, 1304-1374.
    Petrarch's lyric poems.

    English and Italian.
    Bibliography:
    Includes index.
    I. Durling, Robert M.   II. Title.
PQ4496.E23D8   851'.1   76-3716
ISBN 0-674-66345-4

For Kenneth, Rachel, Sarah, and Ruth

Preface

Petrarch's achievement as a lyric poet is particularly complex.
He combines matchlessly rich expressiveness with a sometimes
empty formalism, critical self-awareness with sentimentality and
narcissism, daring originality with conservative respect for tradition. The mannerisms are readily available for vacuous imita-
tion, and Petrarch's first imitator, his fervent admirer Boccaccio,
was guilty of it, like many later ones (bad imitations are often an
indication that the greatness is genuinely appreciated). The
history of Petrarch's influence is obviously beyond my scope
here, but it may be well to point out that to identify Petrarch's
influence with Petrarchism narrowly conceived—the sonnet-
eering vogue, the cult of conceits, the fashion of wordplay—
is an error. In England, France, Germany, Spain, Portugal, and
elsewhere Petrarch's influence meant the abandonment of out-
moded medieval forms, the introduction of the sonnet and other
Italian forms, of the ten-syllable (or eleven-syllable) line as
normative. It meant a new conception of the music possible in
verse; it brought new ways of reading Virgil and Ovid.
Petrarch's example aroused in poets all over Europe the hope of
achieving classic expressiveness in the mother tongue. The deepest tributes to Petrarch's influence are in poets great enough to
make his lessons their own, poets like Ariosto, Michelangelo,
Ronsard, Garcilaso de la Vega, Góngora, Camoëns, Sidney,
Donne. He stood for a new sensibility that could combine aristocratic reserve and elegance, wit, allusiveness, Virgilian evoca-
tiveness and emotional depth, symbolic complexity—in classi-
cally balanced, perfected form. All over Europe the very
emergence of Renaissance style was inseparable from the influence of the *Rime sparse* and the *Trionfi*. Virgil and Ovid are

perhaps the only other poets whose influence on European poetry has been so all-pervasive.

Ezra Pound once remarked that there are two kinds of translations, "interpretative translation," which he claimed to be attempting in his first translation of Cavalcanti's "Donna mi prega," and "the other sort," "where the 'translator' is definitely making a new poem." Pound apparently used the term "interpretative translation" to mean one without poetic pretensions, meant to accompany and point to the original text. I suppose the "other sort" of translations from the *Rime sparse* have tended to come into being through the translator's having been particularly struck by an individual poem or groups of poems; there exist many admirable verse translations of individual poems, by Thomas G. Bergin, Morris Bishop, Dwight L. Durling, to mention only Americans. When one translates the entire *Rime sparse*, however, one can no longer pick and choose.

And there are special problems with Petrarch. One symbol of them could be the animus Pound expresses. "The Italian of Petrarch and his successors," he wrote, "is of no interest to the practising writer or to the student of comparative dynamics in language, the collectors of bric-a-brac are outside our domain." When one considers some of the affinities between Pound and Petrarch—their fascination with Propertius, Ovid, and the Provençal poets, with the broodings of memory, with the fragmentation of experience and of poetic form—Pound's animus may seem the more surprising. It seems clear that he never accurately gauged Petrarch's greatness. His hostility toward Petrarch is part of his general hostility toward the genteel rhetorical tradition, and he was certainly accurate in identifying the sonnet as a form preeminently compromised in the crisis of traditional literary culture. Reacting against his own bric-a-brackish Pre-Raphaelitism, Pound moved entirely away from rhyme. And certainly today there is hardly a single aspect of poetic form that is more difficult to manage in English, more likely to reveal falsity, than rhyme, especially in traditional forms like the sonnet or canzone. And there is truth in Pound's irritated strictures against Petrarch: he *is* formal, rhetorical, decorative, cerebral, artificial; his cult of form is deeply problematic. That he is also, at his best, precise, difficult, even profound, has escaped readers who have depended on the rhymed verbosities of the Bohn Library.

It is the interrelation of these various qualities that makes Petrarch interesting today, and for the translator the question is not whether Petrarch's play with form is meaningful or trivial but whether there is any point in trying to reproduce it in sonnet or canzone or ballata form. What is the point of a mere approximation? The gyrations of one's sonnet would have to be different from Petrarch's gyrations, and they would have the added factitiousness of having only—or primarily—an *external* justification, not whatever inner justification the ingenuities of the original may have.

Therefore I have chosen to translate Petrarch's poems into prose. In translating all of the *Rime sparse* I have needed a medium that would accommodate all the poems, not only the greatest. And of the greatest a literal prose translation can at least convey the sense straightforwardly and show that much of Petrarch's interest as a poet does reside in the sense. In short, it is because the formal elaboration of the *Rime sparse* is both so integral to their greatness and so problematic that I have chosen prose. I hope the absence of rhyme will continually remind the reader to look across at the Italian. My translation is meant to be a guide to the original, not an equivalent.

Having said "literal prose translation," of course I am immediately in difficulties. Can there be any such thing? Granted that one omits the expressiveness of rhyme and the play of forms, granted that one often has to disentangle periodic, subordinating syntax into simpler, coordinating structures, there are three other principal difficulties. Petrarch is obscure, he is ambiguous, and he is refined and even precious in his diction. There are many passages where the meaning is doubtful (no one has satisfactorily explained the last line of poem 138) or disputed (in poem 43, to whose eyes does line 13 refer?). The translator must make up his mind, choose a meaning, and perhaps discuss the passage in a footnote. Petrarch's diction is a more basic problem. In his brilliant essay on Petrarch's language, Gianfranco Contini has stressed the extreme narrowness of Petrarch's vocabulary in comparison with Dante's; in comparison with the literary vocabulary of the nineteenth and twentieth centuries it is even narrower. At the same time, however, many of Petrarch's words bring with them a wealth of associations—and often a technical precision—derived from their earlier use. These associations can almost never be conveyed in English, and sometimes there is no English word with even a reasonably similar denotation. For words like *leggiadro, vago, fera, vaneggiare,* and *favola* there are no English equivalents.

Not only do Petrarch's words enter the *Rime sparse* laden with associations, they occur again and again, forming a sharply delimited, intensely reflexive system. The whole range of their meanings is exploited, now one aspect, now another, with elusive overtones. This quality of the book is particularly hard to convey, for the translator may have to use five different words to indicate the meaning of the same Italian term in different contexts (for instance, *fine, legno, porto,* and *vela* in poem 85). And, finally, what to do with words like *dolce* or *bello*? *Bello* occurs in almost every poem, often several times; it glides urbanely by, without attracting much attention, as in "i be' vostr' occhi, Madonna." Not so *beautiful* or *lovely*—they splash and call out and embarrass. There is no help; the English is only an approximation. It is printed on the left to leave the place of honor to Petrarch's own words.

The Italian text of the *Rime sparse* is edited from Ettore Modigliani's flawless diplomatic edition (Rome, 1904) of Petrarch's definitive copy of the *Rime sparse,* the Vatican Library's codex Vat. Lat. 3195. Vat. Lat. 3195 is partly in Petrarch's hand and incorporates his last revisions of individual poems and of their order. The principles of editing this text have been established by Carducci, Chiòrboli, and Contini, and I have followed in their footsteps.

Ordinarily there is no question about the readings of the manuscript, since Vat. Lat. 3195 was prepared with extraordinary care. At times, however, Petrarch's spelling or punctuation is ambiguous. For instance, in poem 285 one must decide whether the punctuation of the last line indicates that the last *o* is to be understood as *or* (*o*) or as *I have* (*ò*). One must frequently decide whether *che* means *that* (either pronoun or conjunction) or *because* (*ché*). One might follow the manuscript in not distinguishing between the two Italian words; indeed, the ambiguity is to some extent unavoidable in fourteenth-century Italian. But in English the ambiguity is not possible, and in translating I have been forced to choose.

Most editions of the *Rime sparse* have modernized spelling, some of them inconsistently. At the other extreme is Gianfranco Contini's superb edition, which meticulously reproduces the spelling of Vat. Lat. 3195; every student of Petrarch should own it. I have closely followed the text of Vat. Lat. 3195, but I have lightly modernized it with a view to the needs of American readers. Thus I have not kept many of the Latinisms of orthography; I have followed the spelling of the manuscript when it is for the ear rather than for the eye only. Thus for *intellecto* I print *intelletto*, for *obgecto*, *oggetto*; but for *obiecto*, I print *obietto*. I have followed Petrarch when he spells with a single consonant words that in modern Italian have doubled consonants, and I have retained his various spellings of *and* (*e*, *ed*, *et*), regularly expanding the Tironian symbol ⊤ to *et*, his usual spelling, even when that might—it is debatable—produce a hypermetric line. I have not introduced diaereses, and I have made no attempt to normalize the text; Petrarch clearly wished the same word to be pronounced differently in different contexts.

The punctuation of Vat. Lat. 3195 is heavy and inconsistent, and it follows principles and uses symbols that have only limited correlation with modern ones. I have to a large extent followed American principles of punctuation, keeping in mind the difficulties American readers are likely to have with Petrarch's elaborate syntax. I have been sparing of punctuation, but when meaning is involved I have been guided by the manuscript. I have freely added quotation marks and parentheses.

Ballata and canzone stanzas are printed in a format that indicates their parts. In ballate, the *ritornello* is indented. In canzoni, *fronte* and *sirma* are indented when the stanza follows the Italian pattern with *concatenatio*, whether or not the rhymes of *fronte* and *sirma* overlap (as they do in poems 135 and 366); identical *piedi* are indented; there is no indentation in stanzas that follow Provençal models (29, 70, 206)—the sestinas of course also belong to this last category.

This is the first complete translation into English prose of all of the *Rime sparse*, and of Petrarch's uncollected lyrics, not to mention the poems addressed to him. I have not attempted to include all of the poems that have been attributed to Petrarch, but only those whose attribution is beyond doubt, and I have omitted fragments. "Donna mi vene" is edited from Vat. Chigi L.V. 176. The poems of Vat. Lat. 3196 are from the diplomatic edition by M. Pelaez, "Abbozzi autografi di Francesco Petrarca," *Bulletino dell'archivio paleografico italiano*, no. II (Perugia, 1910), pp. 163–216. The poems of Casanatense 924 are from the facsimile in the *Archivio paleografico italiano*, III (Rome, 1892–1910).

Other poems are reprinted from modern editions with the generous permission of the publishers. "Ingegno usato a le question profonde," "Antonio, cosa à fatto la tua terra," "La santa fama, de la qual son prive," "O novella Tarpea, in cui s'asconde," "Io non so ben s' io vedo quel ch' io veggio," and "L'arco che in voi nova sita disserra" are from E. Chiòrboli's edition of the *Rime sparse e i Trionfi* (Bari: Laterza, 1930); Dante's poems from Dante Alighieri, *Rime*, edited by Gianfranco Contini, 2nd ed. (1946; reprint ed., Turin: Einaudi, 1970).

E. H. Wilkins' translation of Petrarch's note on Laura is quoted by permission from his *Life of Petrarch*, © 1961 by The University of Chicago. J. J. Parry's translation of Andreas Capellanus is quoted by permission of Columbia University Press from *The Art of Courtly Love*. The frontispiece has been graciously supplied by the Biblioteca Apostolica Vaticana, with whose permission it is reproduced.

It is a pleasure to express my gratitude to those who helped and encouraged my work on this project. My oldest debt is to my father, whose gift of a copy of Guinguené's *Oeuvres amoureuses de Pétrarque*, with its facing prose translation, first aroused my interest in Petrarch. My teacher Charles S. Singleton, Robert Hollander, Norman Rabkin, Max Bluestone, Ephim G. Fogel, Rachel Jacoff, Claudio Guillen, Jonathan Saville, Victoria Kirkham, Harry Berger, Jr., and Joseph H. Silverman read different portions of the manuscript, encouraged me generously, and made valuable suggestions. My assistant, Roberta Cairney, caught a number of errors in proof. Joseph B. Dallet years ago lent me his copy of Modigliani (formerly belonging to George B. Weston), on which this edition is based; he has patiently waited for its return. My work has been supported by grants from the Department of English, Cornell University, and the Humanities Institute of the University of California, and by a University of California Faculty Research Grant. I am especially and deeply grateful to the dean of Petrarch translators, Thomas G. Bergin, who—in the midst of pressing commitments and in a period of difficult health—generously encouraged me and read through the entire text and translation, criticizing them in detail. He saved me from many errors and infelicities.

Contents

Introduction   1

The *Rime sparse*   35

Poems Excluded from the *Rime sparse*   585

Appendix One
    Poems Addressed to Petrarch   601

Appendix Two
    Dante's *Rime petrose* and *Canzone montanina*   611

Bibliography   637

Index of First Lines   647

Introduction

Ser Petracco (or, as he sometimes spelled it, Petrarcha) of
Florence was exiled from his native city in 1301, at the same time
as his friend Dante Alighieri; but his later life was much more
prosperous than Dante's. Along with many other Italians he
eventually moved to Avignon, the new seat of the papacy,
where he became one of the most successful members of the legal
profession, thanks partly to the patronage of powerful Italian
clergymen. His eldest son, Francesco, who had been born in
Arezzo on July 20, 1304, was eight when the family moved to
Provence; with his mother and brother Francesco lived near
Avignon, in Carpentras. Francesco was given every educational
advantage. As a boy he had a distinguished tutor, the grammar-
ian Convenevole da Prato, and as a young man he was maintained for ten years as a law student at two of the foremost uni-
versities of the day, first Montpellier and then Bologna.

After Ser Petracco's death in 1326, Francesco and his brother,
Gherardo, returned to Avignon, now the most cosmopolitan
cultural center in Europe, and lived for a time as wealthy young
men about town. Whether the two squandered their considerable inheritance or whether they were swindled by their father's
executors and their own servants, as Francesco later related, or
both, it eventually became necessary for them to seek some
means of support. The idea of practicing law seems to have been
repugnant to Francesco from the outset; he decided to take the
path of clerical preferment, which would allow him the leisure to
continue his studies, and at some time he probably took minor
orders so that he could legally hold benefices.

Already a great classical scholar in his early twenties,
Francesco came to the attention of a powerful Roman family,

the Colonnas, and in 1330 he formally entered the service of
Cardinal Giovanni Colonna as a private chaplain (this may have
meant no more than that he occasionally sang prayer services in
the chapel), remaining more or less loosely under the family's
patronage until 1347–48. From 1330 on Petrarch lived essentially
in a scholarly semiretirement guaranteed for him by his connec-
tions with the great, carrying on a voluminous correspondence
with learned and princely friends all over Europe, and frequently indulging his love of travel. Thanks to the patronage of the
Colonnas and other prominent friends, he was able to accumu-
late benefices (most of them in Italy) that assured him a modest
financial independence. Although throughout his life he willing-
ly served on special diplomatic missions for popes and other
rulers, he repeatedly refused preferments—for instance as a bishop or as papal secretary—that would have meant the end of his
devotion to study.

Between 1326 and 1337 Petrarch lived mainly in Avignon; in
1337 he moved to the wild, romantic source of the Sorgue River
at the fountain of Vaucluse, twenty miles east of Avignon. The
1340s brought momentous events in Petrarch's life. On Easter
Sunday, 1341, Petrarch's celebrated coronation as poet laureate
took place on the Capitol in Rome; skillfully dramatized by
Petrarch, this event added considerable luster to his fame,   ·
especially in Italy, and led to his spending increasing amounts of
time there. Petrarch's coronation oration, in form a sermon on a
text from Virgil's *Georgics*, calls for a rebirth of classical wisdom
and poetry and develops in some detail the idea of the laurel as
symbolic of poetry and literary immortality.

In 1342 Gherardo became a Carthusian monk after the death
of his beloved, and except for brief visits to Montreux in 1347
and 1353, Petrarch never saw him again. Petrarch's daughter,
Francesca, was born in 1342 (his son, Giovanni, had been born
in 1337); she lived with him until the end of his life. It is not
known who the mother of these illegitimate children was. In
1345 Petrarch made his most notable philological discovery,
that of the manuscript of Cicero's letters to Atticus, Quintus,
and Brutus, in the library of the cathedral of Verona; these were
the models for his collections of his own letters. In 1347 Cola di
Rienzo's attempt to revive the Roman Republic at first evoked
Petrarch's sympathy. His feelings changed, however, as it be-

came increasingly antipatrician and several members of the Colonna family were killed in bloody uprisings. In 1347 the Black Death appeared in Sicily and began to make its way up the peninsula; during 1348 and 1349 Petrarch lost to it a number of friends and relations, including Cardinal Giovanni Colonna, the poet Sennuccio del Bene, so frequently addressed in the *Rime sparse*, and, he tells us, his beloved Laura.

In October 1350 Petrarch visited Florence for the first time (while on a pilgrimage to Rome) and there made acquantance with his devoted admirer, Giovanni Boccaccio, beginning a friendship that lasted until Petrarch's death. To what extent Petrarch's much-debated religious conversion took place in the late 1330s, in the late 1340s, or in the early 1350s will probably never be determined fully. There is no doubt, however, that after 1350 he rewrote much of his earlier work and composed poems and letters with fictitiously early dates.

In 1353 Petrarch left Provence for good, accepting first the patronage of the Visconti in Milan, who were emerging as the most powerful dynasty in Italy. Boccaccio and other Florentine republicans were scandalized by this apparent condoning of what they regarded as tyranny. Petrarch maintained that he had complete independence, but it seems clear that the Visconti were able to take advantage of his prestige as an ambassador by manipulating his vanity. In 1361 Petrarch left Milan, perhaps because of the increasing gravity of the plague there (his son died of it that year), and gravitated toward the Venetian sphere of influence, while continuing to maintain friendly relations with the Visconti. After long periods of residence in Venice, Pavia, and Padua, he retired in 1370 to a modest house (still standing, though much altered) that he built on land given him by Francesco da Carrara, lord of Padua, at Arquà in the Euganean Hills, where he lived until his death on the night of July 18, 1374.

Boccaccio once accused Petrarch of having spent his life with princes, and the charge has considerable weight in spite of Petrarch's reply that it was the princes who had sought him and that he had preserved his independence. His friends were princes, prelates, and their servants. His identification with privilege was unquestioning, and his quietism amounted to tacit consent in the political arrangements of the day. It can be claimed for him that he did not seek political power for himself (although he does seem to have cherished the hope that Clement VI would make him a cardinal, which may help explain his strange mixture of adulation and denunciation of that pontiff), that when he was manipulated it was because he was naive, and that he actively sought to promote Christian virtue (including the ideal of crusade against the Moslems) and to prevent war among the Christians. But he set a style of ambiguous relation of humanist to prince that in the later Renaissance was to degenerate into subservience.

The glory of the Italian communes was a thing of the past, and it was inevitable that in a society increasingly dominated by princely courts Petrarch's effort to create a secular role for the man of letters should be aristocratic in orientation. After 1350 both Petrarch and Boccaccio threw the weight of their influence on the side of aristocratic culture in Latin; their audience was learned and international, not peninsular, let alone municipal. But both are beloved for the other side of their genius and for their writings in Italian.

LAURA

To immortalize Laura is an avowed purpose of the *Rime sparse*, as of the *Trionfi* and many verse epistles and eclogues in Latin. We do not know who she was, however, or even whether she really existed. One of Petrarch's closest friends, Giacomo Colonna, seems to have doubted that she was anything but a symbol and a pretext for poetry. At the other extreme are the sixteenth-century commentators who, like Vellutello, imagined a biographical basis for each poem, or the abbé de Sade, who in the eighteenth century discovered what he thought was archival evidence for Laura's being an ancestress of his who died in 1348. Outside of the poetry, however, evidence is slight. Petrarch answered Giacomo Colonna's charges in a letter, asserting that Laura was only too real, his passion all too unfeigned. But the letter by itself is very inconclusive evidence, since it was clearly written for publication (at least in the limited sense of circulation among the poet's friends and wealthy patrons) and since it serves just as much to call Laura's reality into question as to prove it.

More interesting are the references to Laura in Petrarch's *Secretum*, probably first written around 1342 and revised after

Laura's death. Although the *Secretum* is as dominated by
Petrarch's reflexive irony as any of the works intended for publication, he never published it, and there is no evidence that he
ever intended to. This dialogue between Francesco and his
spiritual mentor, Saint Augustine of Hippo, imagined as taking
place in the presence of Truth, consists of the saint's efforts—
sometimes resisted, often successful—to bring his charge to the
realization of his sinfulness and of the inadequacy of his earlier
efforts to change. The first two books analyze Francesco's pre-
ference for a state of sinfulness and measure his varying subjection to each of the seven capital vices. In the third book,
Augustine singles out what he regards as the two greatest obsta-
cles to Francesco's repentance—his "virtuous" love for Laura
and his immoderate desire for glory. Francesco argues heatedly
against the saint's critique, but he is outmaneuvered by
Augustine to the point of acknowledging that his love for Laura
must have a basis in sensuality, since he would not have fallen in
love with an equally virtuous woman in an ugly body. At one
point, in a passage that was probably added in revision, the
saint points out that one must expect a woman "worn out with
frequent childbearing" to have limited life expectancy. The precision of this indication, in a work presumably not intended for
publication (and in none of Petrarch's Italian or Latin poetry or
other published works is there any reference to Laura's being
married or having children), may be regarded as strong evidence
of her existence.

Another piece of evidence is furnished by a note on the flyleaf
of Petrarch's copy of Virgil. Throughout his life, Petrarch used
the flyleaves of various books for personal notes (lists of his
favorite books, gardening enterprises, and so forth). On the flyleaf of his Virgil—a magnificent codex apparently commissioned
by Petrarch and his father, stolen at some time but recovered in
1347, when Petrarch commissioned a frontispiece by his friend
the famous painter Simone Martini—Petrarch wrote obituaries
of relatives and friends. One of the notes refers to Laura.

> Laura, illustrious through her own virtues, and long famed
> through my verses, first appeared to my eyes in my youth, in
> the year of our Lord 1327, on the sixth day of April, in the
> church of St. Clare in Avignon, at matins; and in the same
> city, also on the sixth day of April, at the same first hour, but

in the year 1348, the light of her life was withdrawn from the light of day, while I, as it chanced, was in Verona, unaware of my fate. The sad tidings reached me in Parma, in the same year, on the morning of the 19th day of May, in a letter from my Ludovicus. Her chaste and lovely form was laid to rest at vesper time, on the same day on which she died, in the burial place of the Brothers Minor. I am persuaded that her soul returned to the heaven from which it came, as Seneca says of Africanus. I have thought to write this, in bitter memory, yet with a certain bitter sweetness, here in this place that is often before my eyes, so that I may be admonished, by the sight of these words and by the consideration of the swift flight of time, that there is nothing in this life in which I should find pleasure; and that it is time, now that the strongest tie is broken, to flee from Babylon; and this, by the prevenient grace of God, should be easy for me, if I meditate deeply and manfully on the futile cares, the empty hopes, and the unforeseen events of my past years. (Translated by E. H. Wilkins, in his *Life of Petrarch* [Chicago: University of Chicago Press, 1961], p.77)

This note suggests some of the respects in which the *Rime sparse* are an expression of genuinely held attitudes—the sense of the connection between grief and *contemptus mundi*, of the liability of earthly existence, of the passage of time—all amply substantiated in Petrarch's repeated experience of bereavement. It suggests also some insights into the indirection, not to say evasiveness, of the *Rime sparse.*

For the *Rime sparse* avoid the factual. There is no mention of Laura's being a married woman (if such she was) or having children, just as there is no mention of Petrarch's two illegitimate children or their mother. There is no mention of Saint Clare's Church—in fact, there is no mention of any encounter with Laura taking place indoors (the inference is possible in several cases, but not imposed by the text). The *Rime sparse* transpose all "events" to the level of recollection and reflection, bring them into a zone where the dividing line between fact, illusion, and fiction is obscured. This is partly a literary elegance, partly a serious theme—again, the line is hard to draw. Not one external event involving Laura is related in a literal, straightforward, factual manner. Did he actually see her bathing naked in the Sorgue? Did he first see her in Avignon and then later fall in love with her in Vaucluse? That is possible, but for the purposes of the *Rime sparse* it is assumed that the first encounter and the decisive encounter are the same. Furthermore, April 6, 1327, was not Good Friday; it was the historical anniversary of the Crucifixion, as its date was calculated in Petrarch's day. But poem 3 says he fell in love amid "the common grief," which clearly implies the liturgical date. (The solution would seem to be that he did not expect the reader to remember the difference.) As Aldo S. Bernardo and Bortolo Martinelli have recently pointed out, April 6, 1348, the date of Laura's death, was Easter Sunday. The coincidence of the two anniversaries comes to involve both the penitential implication for the lover and the assurance of Laura's salvation.

The figure of Laura emerges in the *Rime sparse* with a concrete vividness, rich with at least implied incident, quite different from the hieratically stylized or philosophically abstract manner of the dolce stil or the *Vita nuova*, justifying De Sanctis' formula that in comparison with Dante, Petrarch brought woman down from Heaven to earth. Still, Laura herself is not the central focus of the poetry. Her psychology remains transcendent, mysterious (perhaps even miraculous, but that is evaded), the subject of conjecture and bewilderment except at moments represented as virtually total spiritual communion. Rather it is the psychology of the lover that is the central theme of the book.

EVOLUTIONS

Although Petrarch was accustomed in later life to disparage poetry in the vernacular, he lavished intense if intermittent care on his own over more than forty years. It does not consitute a large proportion of his entire literary output—some 10,000 lines of Italian verse (the *Rime sparse*, the *Trionfi*, the uncollected poems, a few fragments), as opposed to thousands of pages of verse and prose in Latin—but it has been accepted as his greatest achievement. He apparently began writing the poems that were to form the *Rime sparse* in the early 1330s; perhaps by 1335 he had decided to make a collection; by the mid-1350s most of the 366 poems had been drafted. Working papers of various kinds, from first drafts to fair copies, have come down to us for sixty-five poems and for several of the *Trionfi* in the Vatican Library's codex Vat. Lat. 3196. Many of these papers have dated marginal notations, and on their basis the great Petrarchan scholar Ernest

Hatch Wilkins built a series of hypotheses about the development of the collection. The first version of the collection that actually survives is a preliminary, incomplete one that Petrarch allowed to circulate in 1359. It is found in a manuscript (the Vatican's Chigi L.V. 176) that includes an anthology of poems by Dante and others, and an important version of Boccaccio's life of Dante; it is now generally thought to have been transcribed by Boccaccio himself. This version of the *Rime sparse* consists of 215 poems (1–120, "Donna mi vene," 122–156, 159–165, 169–173, 184–185, 178, 176–177, 189, 264–304; in that order).

In 1366 Petrarch began intensive work on a definitive version of the *Rime sparse*. He replaced "Donna mi vene" with 121, drastically revised the order of poems after 156, and added 151 other poems, many of which he revised just before they were transcribed into his definitive copy. Abandoned by his copyist late in 1366, Petrarch continued to revise, transcribe, and rearrange the poems well into the last year of his life. The definitive manuscript of the *Rime sparse*, Petrarch's own copy, is the Vatican's codex Vat. Lat. 3195; poems 121, 179, 191–263, and 319–366 are in Petrarch's handwriting. Wilkins inferred reliable dates of transcription into Vat. Lat. 3195 from notations in Vat. Lat. 3196, from variations in the handwriting and ink of Vat. Lat. 3195, and from fairly detailed knowledge of Petrarch's whereabouts from 1366 on. Some time after the transcription had been completed in 1374, Petrarch renumbered the last thirty poems, thereby sharpening the focus of the conclusion. The final version of the *Rime sparse* is the basis of this edition.

Both the Chigi version and the post-1366 versions (Petrarch allowed several copies to be made from Vat. Lat. 3195 while it was in progress) have two parts, often referred to, somewhat inappropriately, as poems *in vita* and *in morte*. The second begins with the great canzone of inner debate, "I' vo pensando" (264). In Vat. Lat. 3195 the division between the two parts is indicated by an elaborate initial for poem 264 and by the presence of seven blank pages before it; whether Petrarch meant to add more poems there has been debated.

In the Chigi version and in manuscripts deriving from it, in Vat. Lat. 3196, and in Vat. Lat. 3195 it is possible to trace the process of revision of individual poems, in some cases from the first draft through several versions to the final one. Some of these materials have been assembled by Carl Appel and Angelo Romanò in their editions of Vat. Lat. 3196, but there has been no reliable codification of all the variant readings, and a truly critical edition of the *Rime sparse* is still awaited.

Petrarch's themes are traditional, his treatment of them profoundly original. From Propertius, Ovid, the troubadors, the *Roman de la rose*, the Sicilians, the dolce stil novo, Dante, Cino da Pistoia there comes to him a repertory of situations, technical vocabulary, images, structures. Love at first sight, obsessive yearning and lovesickness, frustration, love as parallel to feudal service; the lady as ideally beautiful, ideally virtuous, miraculous, beloved in Heaven, and destined to early death; love as virtue, love as idolatry, love as sensuality; the god of love with his arrows, fires, whips, chains; war within the self—hope, fear, joy, sorrow. Conceits, wit, urbane cleverness; disputations and scholastic precision; allegory, personification; wooing, exhortation, outcry; praise, blame; self-examination, self-accusation, self-defense; repentance and the farewell to love. These elements of the world of the *Rime sparse* all exist in the tradition. Petrarch's originality lies in the intensity with which he develops and explores them, in the rich, profoundly personal synthesis of divergent poetic traditions, in the idea of the collection itself.

Although Petrarch's wide familiarity with troubador poetry is evident on every page of the *Rime sparse*, the way in which he assimilated and made use of its influence—at all levels—was shaped by the example of Dante. The study of Provençal poetry, in particular the poems of Arnaut Daniel, had had a profound effect on Dante, provoking (around 1296) a series of radical experiments, the *rime petrose* (stony rhymes), so called because the central theme is the hard, unyielding cruelty of the lady. The way Petrarch learned to adapt to his own purposes what he found in the *rime petrose* was a key moment in the clarification of his attitude toward both the *Vita nuova* and the *Commedia*. The *rime petrose* are so important for an understanding of the *Rime sparse* that I have included them, along with a translation, in Appendix Two (also included there is another late canzone of Dante's that Petrarch often echoes, the so-called *canzone montanina*).

One of Petrarch's greatest originalities lies in the idea of the collection itself. C. S. Lewis once wrote that Petrarch invented the sonnet sequence by omitting the prose narrative found in the *Vita nuova*, and it ought to be kept in mind that, as Wilkins established, before the *Rime sparse* it was the custom to keep different metrical forms separated, in different sections of manuscripts. (The Verona manuscript of Catullus separates short poems in lyric meters from long poems in lyric and other meters and from poems in elegiacs; Italian manuscripts regularly separate sonnets, ballate, canzoni; the same principle applies in Provençal collections.) The *Rime sparse* are arranged *as if* they are in chronological order, and most modern opinion holds that they are in fact more or less, and with certain notable exceptions, in the order of composition. But this cannot be determined with much reliability, since the anniversary poems, which used to be thought of as anchors of the "real" chronology, could have been written years later or even years earlier, and we have evidence in Vat. Lat. 3196 that a number of the poems of the first part were written long after 1348. The work presents a *fictional* chronology that should not be confused with a real one, and the ordering of the poems derives from artistic principles.

As a collection the *Rime sparse* have a number of models. Some are classical: Horace's *Odes*, Virgil's *Eclogues*, Propertius' and Ovid's elegies are collected in works that form composites, made up of separate units arranged in complex, obliquely symmetrical patterns. In the *Vita nuova*, the retrospective prose narrative explains the circumstances of composition of the poems and provides some technical commentary; the assumption is that the poems express the most intimate experience of the poet, the meaning of which becomes apparent only later, not at the time of writing. This becomes an important principle in the *Rime sparse*: the meaning of experience is qualified in retrospect, and the passage of time becomes a structural principle as well as a major theme. It is discernible both in the recurrence of the anniversaries and in the succession of separate poems. Presented as if the products of distinct occasions, the poems are arranged as if deposited by the passage of time. Omitting the prose narrative means that there is no mediation between poems, that the reader must supply the narrative and psychological inferences. Successive poems often may or may not have been written on the same day (in the fictional chronology). The passage of time may cast altogether new light on earlier poems, as the second anniversary poem (62) does on the first one (30), or as Laura's death does on the whole first part.

The *Vita nuova* provided another structural principle for the *Rime sparse*. It has thirty-one poems in the following order: ten sonnets or short poems, *one canzone*, four sonnets, *one canzone* (prophetic of Beatrice's death), four sonnets or short poems, *one canzone*, ten sonnets or short poems. Petrarch derived from this arrangement the idea of placing canzoni and groups of canzoni as structural nodes or pillars at varying intervals among the short poems. The arrangement of the second part of the *Rime sparse* is a particularly clear allusion to the symmetry of the *Vita nuova:* it has *three groups* of canzoni, separated by long stretches of sonnets, standing at the beginning (264, 268, 270), the middle (323, 325, 331, 332), and at the end (359, 360, 366); the first group of sonnets is exactly twice as long as the second, but the midpoint of the second part falls in poem 331. Laura's death is announced in poem 267, which gives exactly one hundred poems from there to the end.

Wilkins accepted Ruth S. Phelps' view that the poems added in the post-Chigi versions were less carefully arranged than those in the Chigi version. It is increasingly clear that this view was based on utterly inadequate criteria and is untenable. Rather what emerges from recent studies is that Petrarch's notion of what he was seeking to achieve in the arrangement of the poems grew clearer as he neared the end of his work on them. His renumbering of the last thirty poems is a striking instance.

MEASURES AND NUMBERS

Petrarch was less an inventor of new forms than an untiring explorer of the possibilities of existing forms. More than anyone before him, he demonstrated the remarkable range of the sonnet; he developed a new flexibility, sinuousness, and variety in the canzone; he made the sestina peculiarly his own. Some discussion of forms here is vital to an understanding of the interrelation for him of form and the other aspects of poetry.

The formal principle of the sonnet is closely related to that of the Italian canzone stanza. The Italian sonnet consists of two parts (octave and sestet) theoretically governed by a different "melody"; its divisions are marked by the rhymes, which do not overlap between the two parts. The rhythmical, formal contrast between the parts is between double-duple movement (2 x 4 lines, four appearances each of two rhymes) and double-triple (2 x 3 lines, two appearances each of three rhymes, or vice versa). Petrarch explores the possibilities of symmetry and contrast among the parts of the sonnet with endless ingenuity, and the self-conscious technical mastery is integral to his expressiveness. It is commonly said that the Petrarchan sonnet presents a situation, event, image, or generalization in the octave and in the sestet a reflection, result, or application. Many do follow such a scheme, but the range of possibilities is broad, and it is characteristic of Petrarch to capitalize, in the sestet, on the division between first and second tercet—to introduce a qualification or reversal, often epigrammatically coming to focus in the very last line. I shall discuss one example in order to suggest some of the subtlety of what may seem to modern readers merely formal or cerebral.

An extreme case of Petrarch's artificiality, the fifth poem in the *Rime sparse*, puns on the meaning of each syllable of Laura's name (Laurette, adapted to high style in a Latinate form, Laureta). In the octave, after a pair of introductory lines, each of the three syllables receives two lines of comment:

> Quando io movo i sospiri a chiamar voi
> e 'l nome che nel cor mi scrisse Amore,
> LAU-dando s'incomincia udir di fore
> il suon de' primi dolci accenti suoi;
>
> vostro stato RE-al che 'ncontro poi
> raddoppia a l'alta impresa il mio valore;
> ma "TA-ci!" grida il fin, "ché farle onore
> è d'altri omeri soma che da' tuoi."

$$(5.1–8)$$

> When I move my sighs to call you and the name that Love wrote on my heart, the sound of its first sweet accents is heard without in LAU-ds.
> Your RE-gal state, which I meet next, redoubles my strength for the high enterprise; but "TA-lk no more!" cries the ending, "for to do her honor is a burden for other shoulders than yours."

The regularity of the pattern (two lines per syllable) is connected with the idea of slow pronunciation of the name. What is said about each syllable, in addition to being a pun (though that is not strictly true in the case of the first, since according to traditional etymology *laurus* was derived from *laudare*, to praise), also plays on the position of the syllable in the name: praise, he says, *begins* with the first syllable; next, the energy is *redoubled*; and the ending calls for *silence*. Even more: the position of the syllables in the lines corresponds to their position in the name—beginning, middle, and—but just when the structure is becoming mechanical, the urgency of anxiety brings the third syllable back to the beginning of the line.

In the sestet the positioning of the syllables is different. The first two appear immediately and together, while the third is delayed until the last line of the poem (thus the promise of the octave is obliquely fulfilled):

> Cosi LAU-dare et RE-verire insegna
> la voce stessa, pur ch' altri vi chiami,
> o d'ogni reverenza et d'onor degna;
>
> se non che forse Apollo si disdegna
> ch'a parlar de' suoi sempre verdi rami
> lingua mor-TA-l presuntuosa vegna.
>
> (5.9–14)

Thus the word itself teaches LAU-d and RE-verence, whenever anyone calls you, O Lady worthy of all reverence and honor; except that perhaps Apollo is incensed that any mor-TA-l tongue should come presumptuous to speak of his eternally green boughs.

The first tercet sets up a neat chiastic relation between line 9 and line 11; it leads up to *degna* as establishing the explanation of the strange efficacy of the name. *Degna* is thus the hinge of the sestet; juxtaposed with it is the forbidding and enigmatic *disdegna*, and the last lines bring in a more serious anxiety than the finitude of the poet's gifts—the finitude of his existence itself. The silence of line 7 is now connected with the idea of death.

Is this merely precious, trivial play? What is the relation between the urbane, witty, complimentary surface and the recurrence of the anxiety, a recurrence dictated by the last syllable of the name, inherent in the formal "perfection" itself? The last word of the poem, *vegna*, may seem a curiously weak one in view of the emphasis on the last syllable of the name. But that emphasis in fact gives it a relief, and it is to be connected with line 12 of the next poem: "a morte mi trasporta; / sol per *venir* al lauro"—to *speak* the name is itself to reenact the myth of Apollo and Daphne. That Petrarch found this an interesting poem may be inferred from his giving it such a prominent place at the beginning of the *Rime sparse*: it is the first poem that refers to the myth of Apollo and Daphne.

Brief mention will suffice for the other short forms Petrarch uses. The term *madrigal* has no precise formal meaning. All of Petrarch's (52, 54, 106, 121) are experiments in three-line groups (their schemes are, respectively, *A B A, B C B, C C; A B A, C B C, D E D E; A B C, A B C, D D; A B B, A C C, C D D*). The principle of *ballata* form is that after an initial statement of a *ritornello* (a melodic unit that recurred, originally, thus a rhyme scheme, not a refrain) one or more stanzas follow, each of which ends with the ritornello; the first rhyme(s) of these later ritornellos must be attached to the rhymes of the individual stanzas, and the last rhyme repeats the last rhyme of the original ritornello, thus (11): *A B B A* (ritornello), *C D E D C E, E F F A* (stanza). When there is more than one stanza, each starts afresh. Most of Petrarch's ballate have only one stanza; two (55 and 59) have two stanzas.

The longest poems in the *Rime sparse* are canzoni, a form in which Petrarch's greatness as a poet reaches its fullest expression. In both the Provençal and the Italian type, a canzone consists of several stanzas of identical form, the form being devised by the poet: he is free to make the stanza as short or as long as he pleases (Petrarch's shortest stanza is seven lines long; his longest, twenty), to arrange the rhymes as he pleases, and to mix long and short lines as he pleases. (Petrarch's long lines are always the normal Italian eleven-syllable line, corresponding to iambic pentameter; his short lines all have seven syllables.) The canzone usually ends with a *commiato* or *congedo* (farewell) that repeats the scheme of the last few lines of the stanza.

It is integral to Petrarch's cult of technical refinement that (except for the sestinas) he devises a new stanza for each new canzone. There are two exceptions to this rule, each involving successive poems. One is the sequence of three canzoni in praise of Laura's eyes (71–73), all in the same stanza form. The other is the pair 125 and 126, discussed below. As one might expect, the interplay in the *Rime sparse* of the different stanza forms and different lengths of poems is carefully planned.

Most of Petrarch's canzoni are of the Italian type, in which the stanza has two "melodies," two rhyme schemes that are separate, except that the first line of the second part rhymes with the last line of the first part. As Dante had pointed out, either or both the parts of the Italian canzone stanza could be symmetrically subdivisible (into two or three parts) or not. Petrarch's stanzas are always divisible in the first part, indivisible in the second. Here is a stanza in which there is a clear division of sense between the first and second parts:

In quella parte dove Amor mi sprona	A
conven ch' io volga le dogliose rime	B
che son seguaci de la mente afflitta:	C
quai fien ultime, lasso, et qua' fien prime?	B
Collui che del mio mal meco mi ragiona	A
mi lascia in dubbio, sì confuso ditta.	C
Ma pur quanto la storia trovo scritta	C
in mezzo 'l cor che sì spesso rincorro	D
co la sua propria man de' miei martiri	E
diro, perche i sospiri	e
parlando an triegua et al dolor soccorro.	D
Dico che perch' io miri	e
mille cose diverse attento et fisco,	F
sol una donna veggio e 'l suo bel viso.	F

(127.1–14)

Like the overwhelming majority of Petrarch's stanzas, this one has a first part of six lines; most rhyme like this one, some rhyme *A B C A B C*. Second, most of the stanzas end, like this one, with a *rima baciata* (two consecutively rhymed lines). Third, in almost all his stanzas, as here, the second part begins with some variant of *C D E E D*, and the longer ones even repeat it (the second part of poem 23 is *C D E e D F G H H G F F I I*). In other words, in Petrarch's usage, the two parts of the stanza tend to be "melodically" related in a way similar to the two parts of the sonnet: in the first part of the canzone stanza the double-triple rhythm, similar to the sestet of the sonnet, governs; in the second part, within the basic asymmetrical indivisibility, there is usually a recurrent sense of double rhythm in the groups of four lines and in the paired lines.

Petrarch used the Provençal type of stanza, which has no division, much less frequently, and in such poems as 70 and 206 there is still a strong feeling for division. The stanza of 135 is a hybrid:

Qual più diversa et nova	a
cosa fu mai in qualche strania clima,	B
quella, se ben s'estima,	b
più mi rasembra: a tal son giunto, Amore.	C
Là onde il dì ven fore	c̄
vola un augel che sol, senza consorte,	D
di volontaria morte	d
rinasce et tutto a viver si rinova.	A̲
Così sol si ritrova	a
lo mio voler, et così in su la cima	B
de' suoi alti pensieri al sol si volve,	E
et così si risolve,	e
et così torna al suo stato di prima;	B
arde et more et riprende i nervi suoi	F
et vive poi con la fenice a prova.	(f) A
	(135.1–15)

This stanza has a symmetrically divided first part and seems to
move into the ordinary division with line 9; instead it rein-
troduces both the *a* and *B* rhymes. Thus *a* and *B* occur at the
very beginning of the stanza; *A*, *a*, and *B* at the center; and *B*
and *A* at the end. The connection with the theme is clear: the
form is renewing itself, finding itself again (lines 8 and 9), ending
with its beginning (line 15), in a cycle like that of the phoenix.

The sestina, which was probably invented by Arnaut Daniel,
is technically a canzone with undivided stanza, of a type that
Arnaut particularly cultivated—one in which rhymes do not
occur within stanzas but only between them (*canso a coblas
dissolutas*—poems 29 and 70 are of this type) and in which the
same rhymes are used throughout the poem (*coblas
unissonans*—29 is an example). More than half of Arnaut's
poems are of this difficult type. The sestina has two further
refinements: instead of rhymes, entire rhyme-words are repeated, and the order of the rhyme-words is changed according
to a fixed rule, called *retrogradatio cruciformis* (cruciform retro-
grade motion): *a B C D E F, f A E B D C*, and so forth. This
procedure would in a seventh stanza bring back the original
order; instead Arnaut closes the poem with a three-line envoi in
which each line ends with *two* of the rhyme-words. Arnaut's
sestina, "Lo ferm voler q'el cor m'entra," is a brilliant poem in
which the technical daring is the tense victory of an expressiveness combining obsession, warmth of intimacy, angry frustration, and ironic self-awareness.

Dante's sestina, "Al poco giorno e al gran cerchio d'ombra," is an important part of the *petrose* group (Appendix Two, poem 2). Both Dante's and Arnaut's sestinas are almost by definition unique—one would be surprised to see either poet repeat the form, devised and conquered in an individualized act of expression. Dante—who had changed Arnaut's form by making all six lines the same length—went on to invent an even more elaborate and difficult form, sometimes called a double sestina, though it is not properly a sestina at all ("Amor, tu vedi ben"; Appendix Two, poem 3). The *rime petrose* are consciously *microcosmic;* "Io son venuto" is based on (1) a parallelism between the cycles governing the cosmos and the cycles governing the life of the self; (2) the traditional parallelism between the realms of nature and the parts of the human body. The sestina is a particularly clear example of a cyclical form expressing the embeddedness of human experience in time.

Petrarch assimilated, codified, and diluted the intensities of Dante's sestina and the other *rime petrose* in order to fit them into his own poetic universe. That he wrote nine sestinas (or ten, if you count 332 as two) is indicative of the process. His theme is not the victorious ascent out of time, though the number six has in the *Rime sparse* an importance analogous to that of the number three in the *Commedia*. As medieval readers knew, God created the world in six days, and on the sixth day (Friday) He created man. According to many medieval authorities, including Dante, man fell on Friday also; and Christ redeemed man on a Friday. Six was, then, the number of the created world, of man's earthly existence, of man's excess, and of time. Seven, corresponding to the day God rested, and eight, corresponding to Easter, were the numbers of eternity, of life beyond the world and beyond time. In Petrarch's sestinas the recurrence of the six rhyme-words expresses the soul's obsession with its inability to transcend time. The rhyme-words recur cyclically but with changing meanings, and the form reflects the nature of the mutable world, governed by cycles in which all things change but recur: *omnia mutantur, nil interit (Metamorphoses* 15.165). The *commiati* of Petrarch's sestinas, furthermore, usually have a function related to the figural significance of the number seven: they allude to the intensity of contemplation (30), to conversion (42, 214), to death (22, 332), to the end of time (22). It is not accidental that the vast majority of Petrarch's canzone stanzas have a first part of six lines. Petrarch made the number six peculiarly his own, as can be seen also in the number of poems in the entire *Rime sparse*, 366 (6 x 60 + 6), probably a solar number (the number of days in a leap year), and in the importance assumed by that anniversay of anniversaries, *feria sexta aprilis*: the sixth day of the fourth month. Recent studies suggest that numerological principles also govern the arrangement of the *Rime sparse* to a hitherto unsuspected degree.

LOVE AND MEMORY

The theme of the first sight of Laura derives much of its importance from the fact that Petrarch accepts the traditional conception of love as an obsession with the mental image of the lady, imposed on the fantasy at the moment of falling in love. For the image to take effect, the force with which its arrow reaches the heart must derive from both a special sensuous intensity and a predisposition to love in the observer. Under the right conditions, just as in perception the mind—the imagination—assumes the form of a lady as mental image, so the will assumes her form as its goal; when the two coincide, the image of the lady is always before the mind's eye, the will always moves toward her. So mind and will cooperate to inflame each other. Here is Andreas Capellanus' description of the typical process of amorous meditation:

> only from the reflection of the mind upon what it sees does this passion come. For when a man sees some woman fit for love and shaped according to his taste, he begins at once to lust after her in his heart; then the more he thinks about her the more he burns with love until he comes to a fuller meditation. Presently he begins to think about the fashioning of the woman and to differentiate her limbs, to think about what she does, and to pry into the secrets of her body, and he desires to put each part of it to the fullest use. Then after he has come to this complete meditation, love cannot hold the reins, but he proceeds at once to action . . . This inborn passion comes, therefore, from seeing and meditating. Not every kind of meditation can be the cause of love, an excessive one is required (*immoderata cogitatio*); for a restrained thought does not, as a rule, return to the mind, and so love cannot arise from it. (*The Art of Courtly Love*, trans. J. J. Parry [New York: Columbia University Press, 1941], pp. 28–29)

Andreas is describing the process of a natural love that proceeds to a natural goal, but Petrarch's subject is the possibility of a sublimated, virtuous love, and the different forms of his fantasies are expressions of the conflict inherent in sublimation. Insofar as his love is a form of sexual desire, it consists in sexual fantasies, but these are seldom of the explicit kind Andreas describes. The most nearly explicit ones emerge almost against the lover's will, either when he is off his guard or when his obsession has reached a particularly intense phase (as in 22 or 237). A major theme is the way the lover's meditation on the lady's virtue and on her virtuous influence paradoxically leads to the emergence of the sensual basis of his love. A clear instance is poem 37, closely related to Dante's *canzone montanina*, "Amor, da che convien pur ch' io mi doglia" (Appendix Two, poem 5). The subject of both poems is the destructiveness of the obsession with the lady's image as the lover deliberately evokes it. Dante states the theme directly (lines 16–28); Petrarch's poem enacts the principle dramatically: it is the very composition of the poem, a self-pitying meditation on his absence from Laura, that instead of consoling him causes the image to emerge to consciousness and makes his suffering worse. Just before the midpoint of the poem, he states his realization that, since it is in his power not to prolong the process, the composition of the poem is a perversity (lines 49ff). As he describes the psychological mechanism of this self-indulgence he simultaneously enacts it, and thus the activity of introspective poetic composition results in the emergence to dominance—both in his consciousness and in the poem—of an image of Laura that becomes gradually more sensuous. The poem ends with the cycle completed, with the failure of hope all the more exacerbated.

The fullest exploration of the self-destructiveness of this process is in poems 71–73, where the desire to praise the beauty of Laura's eyes and their power to guide him to virtue is shown dramatically to lead into an uncontrollable negative spiral. He is led to say what he does not wish to say—that he is unhappy—and the poem culminates in a thinly veiled sexual fantasy:

> così vedess' io fiso
> come Amor dolcemente gli governa
> sol un giorno da presso
> senza volger giamai rota superna,

né pensasse d'altrui né di me stesso,
e 'l batter gli occhi miei non fosse spesso!

(73.70–75)

Might I see thus fixedly how Love sweetly governs them, only
one day, up close, without any supernal wheel ever turning,
nor think of any other nor of myself, and the blinking of my
eyes not be frequent!

There are two kinds of expression in the *Rime sparse* of the
fantasy of sexual fulfillment. The direct form avoids sensuous
particularity (for example, poem 22); the indirect form, as here,
is veiled, but the link with poems 22 and 237 is provided by the
optative past subjunctive. Even more important is the presence
behind all these passages of the fantasy of fulfillment in Dante's
"Così nel mio parlar voglio esser aspro," lines 53–78 (Appendix
Two, poem 4). Dante's fantasy asserts the passage of time as
constitutive of a prolonged sexual encounter, but Petrarch calls
for time to stand still. Petrarch's model is the Beatific Vision of
God; the more sensuous the content, the greater the tendency to
assimilate the fantasy toward the safe religious category of contemplation. The stasis Petrarch desires is both an intensification
of the fantasy and an evasion of the idea of activity. This critical
tension between contemplative form and sexual content is a
major theme of the *Rime sparse*, and not least in the second part.

Petrarch's exploration of the experience of love thus derives
considerable depth from his use of Augustinian psychology and
metaphysics. The most important Augustinian concepts under-
lying his analysis are (1) the power and deceptiveness of the
images of desire; (2) the instability of man's nature, fluctuating
among inconsistent desires and multiple loves, spiraling downward toward nonbeing unless upheld, integrated (*collected*, to
use the Augustinian term favored by Petrarch) by grace; (3) the
opposition of eternity and time (eternity represents fullness of
being, unchanging stability; time represents succession, change,
instability).

Petrarch represents the experience of love in terms of these
oppositions, but he does not resolve them unambiguously, as
Augustine does. In the Augustinian view, sexual desire is love
directed outward and downward toward mutable lesser goods;
it is doomed to frustration and subjects the soul to its own
habitus ad nihilum, its tendency toward nothingness. In this

view sexuality is not a source of integration but of disorder, and the Augustinian answer to it is denial. The *Rime sparse* do demonstrate the lover's subjection to the fluctuating instability of his will, as in the juxtaposition of contradictory poems represented as written on the same day, often an anniversary (poems 60–63, for example). Caught in the inconsistency of his desires, wandering in the labyrinth of his illusions, the lover is only intermittently capable of identifying the erotic source of even his most sacrosanct fantasies. Laura's death does not solve the problem; rather it frees his fantasy all the more, and he imagines her coming down from Heaven to sit on his bed in all her beauty (359), a kind of fantasy earlier identified as dangerous nonsense (345). The lover must pray for grace to heal the split in his will and clear the clouds from his understanding. But the unambiguous experience of grace never comes, and the *Rime sparse* end not with victory achieved or assured but with the longest and most poignant of the many prayers for help.

Although Petrarch's pessimism accepts the Augustinian critique of love of the mutable, the other pole of his ambivalence asserts its value. Two of the longest canzoni (264 and 360), placed at the beginning and near the end of the second part, dramatize the impossibility of simple judgments about love; they are closely related to the debates of book 3 of the *Secretum*. For the experience of love makes possible the only integration the lover does in fact achieve, however temporary or imperfect it may be. Absence is an experience of scattering, presence one of synthesis; the image of Laura in the memory is a principle of integration. This can be seen with particular clarity in the central group of canzoni in the first part, 125–129, most of them explorations of different aspects of the dominance in his fantasy of the image of Laura.

Poems 125 and 126, which form a unit, show clearly the identity in Petrarch's mind of the problematics of poetry and love, both seen in terms of Augustinian categories. In 125 the intensity of the poet's frustration has created a split between the inner poignancy of his feelings and his capacity to express them. If he could express them adequately he would surely win her love, he says, but his frustration has so accumulated with time that he has become blocked even from the kind of outpouring of feeling that formerly gave him relief though it did not succeed in winning her love (stanzas 1–3). There may seem to be a characteristic Petrarchan paradox in these beautiful verses discussing the poet's inability to write beautiful verses. The paradox has a point, for it focuses the problem of the relation of outer and inner, of form and content: it is resolved by the poem's being dramatic, of *representing* the simultaneity of love and poetic inspiration as *in process.*

The initial situation in 125 is one of impasse, split, alienation, resulting from the fact that Laura, the source of integration and inspiration, is absent. The block can only be broken by an upsurge of energy that will free the sources of feeling and resynthesize the existential situation, reunite inner and outer. A way must be found to make Laura present, and it will consist in eliciting the full power of her image. At the moment there seems no way to accomplish this.

In the fourth stanza the focus of attention is the setting of the meditation (we are meant to identify it as Vaucluse), and the gesture of addressing the landscape is represented as a defeated renunciation of direct address of Laura. Actually this is a first step toward evocation of her presence, but it begins as a demonstration of her absence. The lover's eye interrogates the scene, running discursively over it for the signs of her former presence. The poem ends on a note of provisional satisfaction afforded by imagining her "scattered footprints," which evoke the memory of disconnected moments—not synthesized—of the experience of the first day. In this, poem 125 is recapitulating and gathering up a series of scattered recollections that began around poem 85, and includes especially 90, 100, 108, 112, 116 (all sonnets).

In poem 126 the lover's meditation continues the despairing indulgence in alienation: he imagines his death and hopes to be buried here; after his death, Laura will return to seek him, but he will be dust, and she will weep for him. Here the mixture of despair and displaced wish fulfillment—a low point in terms of any real future but for that very reason safe for fantasy, disinterested and therefore laden with affect—triggers the release called out for in 125, and the image of the first day abruptly emerges with a greater intensity than in any other poem of the book.

This release has a magical intensity partly because its stanza form is identical with that of 125 except that the last line of each stanza has eleven syllables instead of seven, a difference that is stunningly effective in suggesting the overcoming of the halting inhibition of 125. The difference between the two poems is signalized also at the beginning of 126 by the prominence given the image of water (never directly mentioned in 125) and of Laura's body. Poem 126 begins where 125 leaves off, with a discursive interrogation of the place: it looks back to the unsynthesized past, then to the blocked, defeated present, then to the transcendent—and useless—future (in which Laura will interrogate the place); finally comes the ecstatic image, and the synthesis reintegrates both the lover's sense of Laura and the poet's evocative power.

The image itself (stanzas 4 and 5) derives its categories from the Beatific Vision. It is a suspended moment, its immobility evoked by the motion of the falling flowers, Laura's nimbus or glory. It is a contemplative rapture that is utterly engrossing, from which the lover can no more turn away than the blessed can from God. The rain of flowers is a direct reference to the appearance of Beatrice in *Purgatorio* 30:

> Tutti dicean, *'Benedictus qui venis!'*
>   e, fior gittando di sopra e d'intorno,
>   *'Manibus o date lilia plenis!*
>   . . . . .
> Così dentro una nuvola di fiori,
>   che dalle mani angeliche saliva
>   e ricadeva in giù dentro e di fuori,
> Sovra candido vel cinta d'uliva,
>   donna m'apparve, sotto verde manto
>   vestita di color di fiamma viva.
>   (*Purgatorio* 30.19–21, 28–33)

All were saying, "Blessed is he who comes" and, throwing flowers above and around, "O give lilies with full hands!" . . . So within a cloud of flowers that rose up from the angels' hands and fell back again within and without, girt with an olive branch over her white veil a lady appeared to me, under a green mantle clothed in the color of living flame.

Petrarch's flowers are natural flowers, expressive of the culminating but transitory moment of the springtime, as opposed to angelic flowers; Laura is sitting, not standing like Beatrice; the flowers touch Laura, falling first on her lap, while Beatrice is within the cloud and there is no mention of the flowers' touching her. Dante will eventually cross the river and see Beatrice unveil herself: for him the moment is a circumscribed, provisional goal soon to be transcended; for Petrarch it is an almost mythic *original* synthesis that is a goal in itself. The release, in 126, is both sublimated and orgasmic, and consciously so. The sowing of seed is displaced from the lover to the tree; the lover may not acknowledge the wish, and the tree contains and isolates Laura, protects both lover and poet, and permits the symbolic release, the moment of grace.

A major emphasis of the last stanza of the poem is the difference between the image of Laura treasured in the lover's mind and the "true image," from which the lover says he was "divided." By definition the memory has been transfigured by desire. It is an image from the distant past—eighteen years back, according to the fictional chronology (see 120). To what extent is it an accurate memory even of his own experience, to what extent refashioned? The question hovers over the vision: the incessant falling of the flowers is the sign both of the present urgency and of the passage of time—the barrier that separates the present from the unrecoverable past. Thus in the *Rime sparse* memory is reevocation and resynthesis, it must be constantly renewed. The recurrences of space and time—revisiting of the consecrated place, commemoration of the recurrent anniversary (a kind of secularization of the Christian year), a new interest in the milestones of experience, personal anniversaries, memorials—express also the anxiety of a reflexiveness clearly aware of the willed, even arbitrary, element in each of its self-assertions.

Poems 125 and 126, then, provide a model of the Petrarchan-Augustinian dialectic of dispersal and reintegration that governs the entire *Rime sparse*. As the fullest evocation of the original synthesis, the climax of 126—emerging from the alienation of 125 (and the sonnets)—provides essential support to the three other canzoni in this central group. The appearance of 125–129 as a group (in violation of chronological order and geographical logic) is an enactment of relative psychological integration around the image of Laura; it is also an important formal node, a poetic integration, of the book. That "Italia mia," Petrarch's most important patriotic poem, is part of this group is not accidental: surrounded by the great love canzoni, with which it has many structural and poetic similarities, it is meant to be related to the critical psychological insights of these poems. The dialectic of 129, where the ascent of the mountain is accompanied by increasing awareness of the lover's actual situation, culminates in a measurement of distance which brings release because of the sense of exalted clarity. Poem 127, a rich exploration of the theme "all things remind me of Laura," gradually intensifies the nature images to the superb effect of stanza 5, where the static image of roses in a vase indoors is suddenly given life in the image of the wind moving across a meadow. But that intense—if indirect—evocation of the *imago* is not the culmination of the poem, for in the sixth stanza the summation suddenly brings to the fore the theoretical models on which the poem has been based.

> Ad una ad una annoverar le stelle
> e 'n picciol vetro chiuder tutte l'acque
> forse credea, quando in sì poca carta
> novo penser di ricontar mi nacque
> *in quante parti* il fior de l'altre belle
> *stando in se stessa à la sua luce sparta,*
>   *a ciò che mai da lei non mi diparta;*
> né farò io, *et se pur talor fuggo,*
> *in cielo e 'n terra m'à racchiuso i passi.*
>
> (127. 85–93)

> Perhaps I thought I could count the stars one by one and enclose the sea in a little glass when the strange idea came to me to tell in so few pages *in how many places* the flower of all beauties, *remaining in herself, has scattered her light*
>   *in order that I may never depart from her;* nor shall I, and *if at times I flee, in Heaven and earth she has circumscribed my steps.*

The idea of a supreme source of beauty which though transcendent fills all things with its omnipresence, which cannot be escaped by any flight, mirrors the relation of God to the universe and to the human soul, as described in the Wisdom of Solomon 7:26–27 and Psalm 138:2–13, passages repeatedly echoed by Augustine in the *Confessions* (see especially 1.2–4, 7.16–19, 10.33–38), not to speak of Dante in the opening lines of the *Paradiso.*

The remarkably original and innovative structure of the *Rime sparse,* with its mixture of symmetries and looseness, with its structural pillars—groups of canzoni where what is scattered among the short poems is gathered and brought to fuller development—this form reflects the provisional, even threatened nature of the integration of experience possible for natural man. Perfect integration of a life or a book comes only when the mutable and imperfect is caught up into eternity. That ultimate gathering, that binding of the scattered leaves, comes only on the anagogical Sabbath. The force of Dante's claim to have the *Commedia* stand as a perfectly integrated poem rests, as Dante understood, in its claim to derive from God, the ultimate unifier of all things:

> Nel suo profondo vidi che s'interna,
> legato con amore in un volume,
> ciò che per l'universo si squaderna.
>
> (*Paradiso* 33.85–87)

> In its depths I saw internalize itself, bound with love in one volume, what through the universe is scattered unbound.

This is the point of Petrarch's title for his collection, *Rerum vulgarium fragmenta* (Fragments of vernacular poetry), for which the Italian is given in the first poem: "rime sparse" (scattered rhymes). This may well be the first use of the term *fragment* to describe a kind of work of art. There is, however, a scriptural precedent in the story of the miracle of the loaves and fishes (John 6:12), where Jesus says "Colligite fragmenta quae supersunt ne pereant" (Collect the fragments that remain lest they perish). Bede and Alcuin interpreted the words as referring to the gathering together in exegesis of the prophecies and allegories scattered through the Bible. For Petrarch the term expresses the intensely self-critical awareness that all integration of selves and texts is relative, temporary, threatened. They flow into multiplicity at the touch of time, their inconsistencies juxtaposed as the successive traces of a subject who dissolves and leaves only words behind.

METAMORPHOSIS

Metamorphosis is, then, a dominant idea in the *Rime sparse*. It is seen in the psychological instability of the lover, the ontological insufficiency of human nature, in time, in death. It is an idea that governs the relation of the poems to their sources or to the broader tradition: they transform it. It governs the relation of the individual poems, themes, motifs, forms, even individual words, to each other. Ovid is omnipresent. The first and basic metamorphosis in the *Rime sparse* reenacts the myth of Apollo and Daphne: when the lover catches up with the object of his pursuit, she has turned into the laurel tree. It is merely the change of a letter that turns *Laura* into *lauro* (laurel), and since Petrarch did not have the apostrophe as part of his punctuation, but simply ran elided words together, there was for him hardly an orthographic distinction between *Laura* and *l'aura* (breeze) or *lauro* and *l'auro* (gold). The deployment of these various kinds of metamorphosis is so ingenious that many critics have been blinded to the poetic seriousness that lies behind them.

Transformation into the laurel is a figure of sublimation, in which desire accepts an object other than its natural one; instead of Laura, the lover gets (or becomes, it amounts to the same thing) the laurel of poetic achievement and glory. The longest poem in the *Rime sparse* is the canzone "Nel dolce tempo de la prima etade" (23), which a marginal note in Vat. Lat. 3196 calls "one of my earliest" ("est de primis inventionibus nostris"). In a highly artificial, elaborately rhetorical style, the poem narrates the "events" of the lover's experience as reenactments of six Ovidian myths of metamorphosis. He falls in love with Laura and turns into a laurel tree like Daphne; because his overreaching hope, like Phaeton, was struck down by a thunderbolt, he turns into a swan and mourns like Cygnus; because, misled by deceptive appearances, he spoke of his love after having been forbidden, he turns to stone, like Battus; because all his pleading for mercy is to no avail, he turns to a fountain of tears, like Byblis; though mercifully restored to his own shape, he begs for mercy once more and therefore is divided into stone and a wandering voice, like Echo; finally, one day while out hunting, when the sun is hottest, he stands gazing at Laura naked in a fountain, whereupon she sprinkles his face with water, like Diana, and he is transformed into a fleeing deer, like Actaeon.

The theme of the poem is the incomprehensible changeability of the self in love, which is so violent as to call its very identity into question. The myths succeed one another in a brilliant, surrealistic superimposition of images. There is a baffling coexistence of abrupt, radical instability and of permanence and cyclicality. It is obvious that the myths were not chosen at random, and Petrarch expects the reader to know Ovid and to be alert to subtle changes. None of the myths is reenacted in its entirety or without some significant change. Petrarch's lover completes three times a cycle that takes him through falling in love, hoping and wooing, being rejected and rebuked, and finally (Cygnus, Byblis, Echo) lamenting and writing poetry. Poem 23 ends with the Actaeon myth for many reasons: it is the most violent episode in "Nel dolce tempo"; it is the least metaphorical, the least disguised; it allows the fullest emergence of sexual affect and acknowledges most fully the fear resulting from a sense of taboo. Furthermore, it is significant that Petrarch ends the series of transformations with one that is in process: he is still in flight.

> ch' *i' senti' trarmi de la propria imago*
> et in un cervo solitario et vago
> di selva in selva ratto *mi trasformo*
> et ancor de' miei can fuggo lo stormo.
>
> (23.157–160)

> for *I felt myself drawn from my own image* and into a solitary wandering stag from wood to wood quickly *I am transformed* and still I flee the belling of my hounds.

"Ch' i' senti' trarmi de la propria imago" echoes the words describing the first transformation into the laurel (lines 41–45); the unusual turn of phrase of the second two lines quoted here is richly ambiguous, the shift in tenses startling.

What Petrarch has *omitted* from Ovid's myths is also part of the meaning of the poem. He has left out Daphne's sexual fear and her flight from Apollo. In Ovid's account of Actaeon, as the dogs begin to tear Actaeon to pieces he tries to call them by name, to reveal his identity; but, since he is now a stag, that is impossible, and all he can do is weep. In Ovid the myths (with the exception of that of Battus, which Petrarch skillfully adapts) are about frustrated love, about loss and refusal. With the exception of the Battus myth they take place near a body of water into which at least one of the characters gazes. With the exception of the Daphne myth they involve characters who are punished for something they have seen. All of them concern frustrated—or even disastrous—speech or writing, and in each case the speech involves deception or confusion or some question about the identity of one of the protagonists.

As Petrarch saw, the myth of Actaeon is an inversion of the myth of Daphne. In one, it is the beloved who flees, in the other the lover. In one, the end result is speech: poetry and fame; in the other, silence. In one, there is evergreen eternizing; in the other, dismemberment. Daphne, as she runs, looks into the water and becomes a tree, takes root; Actaeon, who is standing still, branches into a stag, grows hooves, flees, sees his reflection and flees the more. These extremes are also connected in the myth of Orpheus, who was able to move rocks and trees and tame beasts; he both recalled Eurydice from death and was dismembered after losing her again (Virgil, *Georgics* 4.522: "discerptum latos iuvenem sparsere per agros"—tearing the youth apart, they scattered him across the wide fields). By beginning and ending "Nel dolce tempo" with Daphne and Actaeon, Petrarch paired myths that are related to the deepest preoccupations of the *Rime sparse:* dismemberment or scattering versus integration; poetic immortality versus death; the creation of poetry as an expression of the impossibility of speech resulting from sexual fear.

Thus the myths of Daphne and Actaeon are intimately connected with Petrarch's other great mythic symbol, the Medusa (Ovid's account is in *Metamorphoses* 4.617ff), whose sight turns men to stone—indeed, into marble statues, something like works of art. Traditionally, the Medusa had been variously interpreted: as a symbol of the fear that blinds the mind (Fulgentius), of lust (*Ovide moralisé*), of the power of memory (Fulgentius). Dante's *rime petrose* are based on the idea of a young woman whose heart is hard as stone; she is a "stone that speaks and has sensation as if it were a woman." This lady is associated with the influence of the cold planet, Saturn, and with the freezing of all nature in the depths of winter. If her cruelty continues long enough, she will turn the lover into a marble statue; in other words, she will be a Medusa for him, an implicit though never stated reference. A celebrated incident in the *Inferno* has Dante, outside the gates of Dis, threatened with the sight of the Medusa and only saved by turning away and covering his eyes. The interpretation of the passage is debatable; clearly the threat of despair—a fear that blinds the soul to God's mercy and deprives it of hope—is involved. Whether, as John Freccero has recently argued, a rejection by Dante of the *petrose* is also implied, there is no doubt that Petrarch did connect the *petrose* with the traditional interpretations of the Medusa, and that his countless allusions to the *petrose* are to be connected

with his references to the Medusa. The Medusan transformation
most frequently alluded to is that of Atlas. Petrarch combines
references to Ovid's account with allusions to Virgil's description (*Aeneid* 4.246–251), a projection of Aeneas' immobile fixa-
tion on Dido, as in 366.111–112, where the dripping tears are
suggested by the rivers in Virgil's anthropomorphic description.
Petrarch's allusions to the Medusa are often implicit, as in poem
129, where they are related to the themes of memory and
writing; the parallels with 125 and 126 are perhaps more obvious
than the equally important connection with the myths of
Daphne and Actaeon:

> I' l'ò più volte (or chi fia che mi 'l creda?)
> ne l'acqua chiara et sopra l'erba verde
> veduto viva, et nel troncon d'un faggio
>   e 'n bianca nube, sì fatta che Leda
> avria ben detto che sua figlia perde
> come stella che 'l sol copre col raggio;
>   et quanto in più selvaggio
> loco mi trovo e 'n più deserto lido,
> tanto più bella il mio pensier l'adombra.
> Poi quando il vero sgombra
> quel dolce error, pur lì medesmo assido
> me freddo, pietra morta in pietra viva,
> in guisa d'uom che pensi et pianga et scriva.

> (129.40–52)

> I have many times (now who will believe me?) seen her
> alive in the clear water and on the green grass and in the trunk
> of a beech tree
>   and in a white cloud, so beautiful that Leda would have said
> that her daughter faded like a star covered by the sun's ray;
>   and in whatever wildest place and most deserted shore I
> find myself, so much the more beautiful does my thought
> shadow her forth. Then, when the truth dispels that sweet de-
> ception, right there in the same place I sit down, cold, a dead
> stone on the living rock, like a man who thinks and weeps and
> writes.

It is not merely the idea of petrifaction that establishes the
connection with the *rime petrose* and the Medusa, it is such
phrases as "sopra l'erba verde" (compare "Al poco giorno e al
gran cerchio d'ombra," lines 28, 39), "stella che 'l sol copre col
raggio" ("Io son venuto al punto de la rota," lines 5–6); "quando
il vero sgombra / quel dolce error" ("Io son venuto," lines 10–
11); "pur lì medesmo assido / me freddo, pietra morta in pietra

viva" ("Amor, tu vedi ben che questa donna," lines 33–34, 57;
"Al poco giorno," line 34). The central idea of the passage, that
meditation on Laura's image is in tension with the wildness of
the surroundings, is related to the situation of "Io son venuto,"
just as the theme of the projection of the image of the lady onto
the external world is related to "Amor, tu vedi ben che questa
donna," lines 40-43:

> per che ne li occhi sì bella mi luce
> quando la miro, ch' io la veggio in petra,
> e po' in ogni altro ov' io volga mia luce.

> so beautiful into my eyes she shines
> when I gaze on her, that I see her in stones
> and in everything else, wherever I turn my sight.

The lover is fascinated with the complexity of his own
psychological processes; the image that turns him to stone in the
Rime sparse is a projection of them onto the outside world. The
idea that the lover's fixated gaze on the beloved turns him into a
statue is emphasized in Ovid's account of Narcissus, who stares
at his image in the pool:

> . . . vultuque immotus eodem
> haeret, ut a Pario formatum marmore signum.
> (*Metamorphoses* 3.418–419)

> he stares unmoving on that one face, like a statue formed of
> Parian marble.

This is an ultimate form of the Medusa, a perception that hovers
over the *Rime sparse*, that endlessly polished mirror of the poet's
soul. The charge of a fundamental narcissism in the collection
(as in Petrarch's entire output) would be only partially answered
by the undeniable intensity of his self-criticism. He rather tends
to avoid making explicit the presence of Narcissus in the mythic
networks he weaves. But the two extremes of poem 23, Daphne
and Actaeon, like the other myths in the poem, converge on and
point toward the figure of Narcissus: at the midpoint of 23 there
is a curious breakdown and a decision to omit certain things (the
break occurs exactly at line 89, in the midst of the Battus
passage, where the lover is turned to stone), and soon after he
recounts how he has reenacted the myth of Echo. But Echo, after
all, wasted away because of her love for Narcissus, and the
implicit connection (Petrarch = Echo means Laura = Narcissus;

if Laura's image = Narcissus' image, Petrarch = Narcissus) is both established and evaded. In the working papers of poem 23 there is evidence that completing the poem was difficult for Petrarch. On the recto of leaf 11 of Vat. Lat. 3196 lines 1–89 are written in a book hand as a fair copy; on the verso of leaf 11 are lines 90–169, in a cursive hand as a working draft. The verso has seven major instances of revision; the recto has two. The marginal notes indicate that work on the poem continued over a number of years. It may well be that the sensitivity of the nexus Battus-Medusa-Narcissus-Echo (in a poem beginning with Daphne and ending with Actaeon) caused Petrarch's difficulty.

In any case, the myths constantly blend into one another, and Petrarch expects us to bring a detailed knowledge of them to his poems. Poem 23 is echoed and balanced by poem 323, which describes six emblematic visions of Laura's death—a deer with a human face is killed by dogs, a ship sinks suddenly, a laurel is struck by lightning, the phoenix dies, a fountain is swallowed up by the earth, a lady is bitten in the heel by a snake—all instances of abrupt mutability. These myths and their order are related to those of poem 23. Poem 323 begins with an emblem similar to Actaeon, has the laurel at the center, and ends with a more realistic though not less symbolic emblem (the death of Eurydice), in which, as in the last myth of 23, the pathos is allowed to come through less masked. Each of the major emblems for Laura thus at some time or other also stands for the lover, and vice versa. If Laura is the laurel, the lover turns into a laurel; if she is the beautiful deer he is hunting, he is an Actaeon (and, again, in 323 she is torn by dogs); if he becomes a fountain of tears, she is a fountain of inspiration (but is it Narcissus' pool?); if like Echo he becomes merely a voice, she dies, and he is left to imagine her voice in dreams. The myths are constantly being transformed.

To see one's experience in terms of myth is to see in the myth the possibility of the kind of allegorical meaning that was called tropological. Petrarch knew and used freely the traditional allegorical interpretations of the Ovidian myths. But he dissociated them from clear-cut moral judgments, and in this he was closer to the Dante of the *petrose* than of the *Commedia*. To say that falling in love and becoming a love poet is a transformation into a laurel tree involves the sense that the channeling of the vital energy of frustrated love into the sublimated, eternizing mode of poetry has consequences not fully subject to conscious choice or to moral judgment. For Petrarch the perfection of literary form, which exists polished and unchanging on the page in a kind of eternity, is achieved only at the cost of the poet's natural life. His vitality must be metamorphosed into words, and this process is profoundly ambiguous. If on the one hand Petrarch subscribes to—even in a sense almost single-handedly founds—the humanistic cult of literary immortality and glory, on the other hand he has an acute awareness that writing poetry involves a kind of death. This recognition has something very modern about it; it gives a measure of the distance that separates Petrarch from Dante, who gambled recklessly on the authority his poem would have as a total integration. Petrarch is always calling attention to the psychologically relative, even suspect, origin of individual poems and thus of writing itself. His hope is that ultimately the great theme of praise will redeem even the egotism of the celebrant.

The *Rime sparse*

1

You who hear in scattered rhymes the sound of those sighs with which I nourished my heart during my first youthful error, when I was in part another man from what I am now:

for the varied style in which I weep and speak between vain hopes and vain sorrow, where there is anyone who understands love through experience, I hope to find pity, not only pardon.

But now I see well how for a long time I was the talk of the crowd, for which often I am ashamed of myself within;

and of my raving, shame is the fruit, and repentance, and the clear knowledge that whatever pleases in the world is a brief dream.

2

To take a graceful revenge and to punish in one day a thousand offenses, Love took up his bow again secretly, like a man who waits for the time and place to hurt.

My vital power was concentrated in my heart, to make there and in my eyes his defense, when the fatal blow fell where every previous arrow had been blunted;

therefore, confused in the first assault, he lacked both strength and time to take up arms in this need,

or to lead me up the weary high mountain away from the slaughter, out of which now he would wish to help me, but cannot.

---

mountain: traditional for Reason.

1

Voi ch' ascoltate in rime sparse il suono
di quei sospiri ond' io nudriva 'l core
in sul mio primo giovenile errore,
quand' era in parte altr' uom da quel ch' i' sono: 4

del vario stile in ch' io piango et ragiono
fra le vane speranze e 'l van dolore,
ove sia chi per prova intenda amore
spero trovar pietà, non che perdono.   8

Ma ben veggio or sì come al popol tutto
favola fui gran tempo, onde sovente
di me medesmo meco mi vergogno;   11

et del mio vaneggiar vergogna è 'l frutto,
e 'l pentersi, e 'l conoscer chiaramente
che quanto piace al mondo è breve sogno.   14

2

Per fare una leggiadra sua vendetta
et punire in un dì ben mille offese,
celatamente Amor l'arco riprese,
come uom ch' a nocer luogo e tempo aspetta.   4

Era la mia virtute al cor ristretta
per far ivi et negli occhi sue difese
quando 'l colpo mortal là giù discese
ove solea spuntarsi ogni saetta;   8

però turbata nel primiero assalto
non ebbe tanto né vigor né spazio
che potesse al bisogno prender l'arme,   11

o vero al poggio faticoso et alto
ritrarmi accortamente da lo strazio
del quale oggi vorrebbe, et non po aitarme.   14

3

It was the day when the sun's rays turned pale with grief for his Maker when I was taken, and I did not defend myself against it, for your lovely eyes, Lady, bound me.

It did not seem to me a time for being on guard against Love's blows; therefore I went confident and without fear, and so my misfortunes began in the midst of the universal woe.

Love found me altogether disarmed, and the way open through my eyes to my heart, my eyes which are now the portal and passageway of tears.

Therefore, as it seems to me, it got him no honor to strike me with an arrow in that state, and not even to show his bow to you, who were armed.

---

day...Maker: the anniversary of Christ's crucifixion. According to poem 211 and a note in his copy of the works of Virgil, Petrarch first saw Laura on April 6, 1327.

4

He who showed infinite providence and art in His marvelous workmanship, who created this and the other hemisphere, and Jove more mild than Mars,

who, coming to earth to illuminate the pages that for many years had hidden the truth, took John from the nets and Peter, and gave them a portion of the Kingdom of Heaven;

He, when He was born, did not bestow Himself on Rome, but rather on Judea, so beyond all other states it pleased Him always to exalt humility.

And now from a small village He has given us a sun, such that Nature is thanked and the place where so beautiful a lady was born to the world.

---

village: Laura's birthplace is unknown. Other poems seem to indicate that it was on a low hill in the plain between Vaucluse and Avignon, visible from the cliff above the fountain of Vaucluse.

3

Era il giorno ch' al sol si scoloraro
per la pietà del suo fattore i rai
quando i' fui preso, et non me ne guardai,
ché i be' vostr' occhi, Donna, mi legaro.   4

Tempo non mi parea da far riparo
contr' a' colpi d'Amor; però m'andai
secur, senza sospetto, onde i miei guai
nel commune dolor s'incominciaro.   8

Trovommi Amor del tutto disarmato,
et aperta la via per gli occhi al core
che di lagrime son fatti uscio et varco.   11

Però al mio parer non li fu onore
ferir me de saetta in quello stato,
a voi armata non mostrar pur l'arco.   14

4

Que' ch' infinita providenzia et arte
mostrò nel suo mirabil magistero,
che criò questo et quell'altro emispero,
et mansueto più Giove che Marte,   4

vegnendo in terra a 'lluminar le carte
ch' avean molt'anni già celato il vero,
tolse Giovanni da la rete et Piero
et nel regno del ciel fece lor parte;   8

di sé nascendo a Roma non fe' grazia,
a Giudea sì, tanto sovr' ogni stato
umiltate esaltar sempre gli piacque.   11

Ed or di picciol borgo un sol n'à dato,
tal che natura o 'l luogo si ringrazia
onde sì bella donna al mondo nacque.   14

5

When I move my sighs to call you and the name that Love wrote on my heart, the sound of its first sweet accents is heard without in LAU -ds.

Your RE -gal state, which I meet next, redoubles my strength for the high enterprise; but "TA -lk no more!" cries the ending, "for to do her honor is a burden for other shoulders than yours."

Thus the word itself teaches LAU -d and RE -verence, whenever anyone calls you, O Lady worthy of all reverence and honor;

except that perhaps Apollo is incensed that any mor- TA -l tongue should come presumptuous to speak of his eternally green boughs.

The poem plays on the syllables of Laura's name, in a Latinized version, Laureta, of the French Laurette.

eternally green boughs: the evergreen laurel, with an allusion to the myth of Apollo and Daphne. Daphne, daughter of the god of the river Peneus in Thessaly, was pursued by Apollo. She prayed to her father to preserve her virginity, and when Apollo caught up with her she was transformed into a laurel. Apollo adopted the tree as his own and crowned himself with a wreath from it. (Ovid, *Metamorphoses* 1.452–567.) The laurel was supposedly immune from lightning. Its Latin name, *laurus*, was thought to derive from the verb *laudare* (to praise). Petrarch considered it the crown both of poets and of triumphing emperors.

6

So far astray is my mad desire, in pursuing her who has turned in flight and, light and free of the snares of Love, flies ahead of my slow running,

that when, calling him back, I most send him by the safe path, then he least obeys me, nor does it help to spur him or turn him, for Love makes him restive by nature;

and when he takes the bit forcefully to himself, I remain in his power, as against my will he carries me off to death;

only to come to the laurel, whence one gathers bitter fruit that, being tasted, afflicts one's wounds more than it comforts them.

5

Quando io movo i sospiri a chiamar voi
e 'l nome che nel cor mi scrisse Amore,
LAU-dando s'incomincia udir di fore
il suon de' primi dolci accenti suoi;   4

vostro stato RE-al che 'ncontro poi
raddoppia a l'alta impresa il mio valore;
ma " TA-ci," grida il fin, "ché farle onore
è d'altri omeri soma che da' tuoi."   8

Così LAU-dare et RE-verire insegna
la voce stessa, pur ch' altri vi chiami,
o d'ogni reverenza et d'onor degna;   11

se non che forse Apollo si disdegna
ch'a parlar de' suoi sempre verdi rami
lingua mor-TA-l presuntuosa vegna.   14

6

Sì traviato è 'l folle mi' desio
a seguitar costei che 'n fuga è volta
et de' lacci d'Amor leggiera et sciolta
vola dinanzi al lento correr mio,   4

che quanto richiamando più l'envio
per la secura strada men m'ascolta,
né mi vale spronarlo o dargli volta
ch' Amor per sua natura il fa restio;   8

et poi che 'l fren per forza a sé raccoglie,
i' mi rimango in signoria di lui,
che mal mio grado a morte mi trasporta;   11

sol per venir al lauro onde si coglie
acerbo frutto, che le piaghe altrui
gustando affligge più che non conforta.   14

7

Gluttony and sleep and the pillows of idleness have banished from the world all virtue, and our nature, conquered by custom, has almost ceased to function;

and so spent is every benign light of heaven by which human life should be shaped, that whoever wishes to make a river flow from Helicon is pointed at as a strange thing.

What desire for the laurel is there? or for the myrtle? "Philosophy, you go poor and naked!" says the mob, bent on low gain.

You will have few companions on the other way: so much the more I beg you, noble spirit, do not abandon your magnanimous undertaking.

The recipient of this poem has not been identified.

make a river flow from Helicon: bring about the renewal of poetry, which would come from the Hippocrene, the fountain on Mount Helicon, sacred to the Muses, that sprang from the blow of Pegasus' foot.   myrtle: sacred to Venus.

8

At the foot of the hills where she first put on the lovely garment of her earthly members—that lady who often wakens weeping from his sleep him who sends us to you—

free and in peace we were passing through this mortal life, which every living thing desires, without fear of finding on the way anything to snare us.

But for the miserable state to which we have been brought from that other untroubled life, and for our death, we have only one consolation,

which is vengeance on him who brings us to it: for he remains in the power of another, near his end, bound with a greater chain.

The poem seems to have accompanied a gift of game. The recipient has not been identified.

7

La gola e 'l sonno et l'oziose piume
ànno del mondo ogni vertù sbandita,
ond' è dal corso suo quasi smarrita
nostra natura vinta dal costume;   4

et è sì spento ogni benigno lume
del ciel per cui s'informa umana vita,
che per cosa mirabile s'addita
chi vol far d'Elicona nascer fiume.   8

Qual vaghezza di lauro, qual di mirto?
"Povera et nuda vai, Filosofia,"
dice la turba al vil guadagno intesa.   11

Pochi compagni avrai per l'altra via:
tanto ti prego più, gentile spirto,
non lassar la magnanima tua impresa.   14

8

A pie' de' colli ove la bella vesta
prese de le terrene membra pria
la donna che colui ch' a te ne 'nvia
spesso dal sonno lagrimando desta,   4

libere in pace passavam per questa
vita mortal, ch' ogni animal desia,
senza sospetto di trovar fra via
cosa ch' al nostro andar fosse molesta.   8

Ma del misero stato ove noi semo
condotte da la vita altra serena
un sol conforto et de la morte avemo,   11

che vendetta è di lui ch' a ciò ne mena,
lo qual in forza altrui presso a l'estremo
riman legato con maggior catena.   14

9

When the planet that marks off the hours returns to dwell with the Bull, from his flaming horns falls virtue which clothes the world in fresh color.

And not only that which opens to us without, the riverbanks and the hills, he adorns with flowers, but within, where day never dawns, he makes the earthly moisture pregnant of himself,

that it may yield such fruit as this and others like it. Thus she who among ladies is a sun, moving the rays of her lovely eyes, in me

creates thoughts, acts, and words of love; but however she governs or turns them, spring for me still never comes.

The poem seems to have accompanied a gift of truffles.
planet . . . Bull: the sun is in Taurus from mid-April to mid-May.

10

Glorious Column on whom rests our hope and the great renown of Latium, whom even the ire of Jove in the windy rain has not yet turned aside from the true path:

here are no palaces, no theater or gallery, but in their stead a fir tree, a beech, a pine—amid the green grass and the nearby mountain where we climb and descend poetizing—

all these lift our intellects from earth to Heaven; and the nightingale that sweetly in the shadow every night laments and weeps

burdens our hearts with thoughts of love. But so much good you alone cut short and make imperfect, for you keep yourself, my Lord, far from us.

Addressed to Stefano Colonna the Elder, head of a powerful Roman family, probably from the estate of his son Giacomo, bishop of Lombez (France), near the foot of the Pyrenees, where Petrarch spent the summer of 1330.

9

Quando 'l pianeta che distingue l'ore
ad albergar col Tauro si ritorna,
cade vertù da l'infiammate corna
che veste il mondo di novel colore.   4

Et non pur quel che s'apre a noi di fore,
le rive e i colli, di fioretti adorna,
ma dentro, dove giamai non s'aggiorna,
gravido fa di sé il terrestro umore,   8

onde tal frutto et simile si colga.
Così costei, ch' è tra le donne un sole,
in me movendo de' begli occhi i rai   11

cria d'amor penseri atti et parole:
ma come ch' ella gli governi o volga,
primavera per me pur non è mai.   14

10

Gloriosa Columna in cui s'appoggia
nostra speranza e 'l gran nome latino,
ch' ancor non torse del vero camino
l'ira di Giove per ventosa pioggia: 4

qui non palazzi, non teatro o loggia;
ma 'n lor vece un abete, un faggio, un pino—
tra l'erba verde e 'l bel monte vicino
onde si scende poetando et poggia—   8

levan di terra al ciel nostr' intelletto;
e 'l rosigniuol che dolcemente all'ombra
tutte le notti si lamenta et piagne,   11

d'amorosi penseri il cor ne 'ngombra.
Ma tanto ben sol tronchi et fai imperfetto
tu che da noi, Signor mio, ti scompagne.   14

11

Lady, I have never seen you put aside your veil for sun or for shadow since you knew the great desire in me that lightens my heart of all other wishes.

While I carried my lovely thoughts hidden (with desire they are bringing death into my heart) I saw you adorn your face with pity; but since Love has made you aware of me, your blond hair has been veiled and your lovely gaze kept to itself.

What I most desired in you has been taken from me; thus the veil controls me and to cause my death shades the sweet light of your lovely eyes in both warm and icy weather.

12

If my life can withstand the bitter torment and the struggles for so long that I may see, Lady, the light of your lovely eyes dimmed by the power of your last years

and your hair of fine gold made silver, see you abandon garlands and clothes of green, and see your face lose its hue, which in my misfortunes makes me slow and reluctant to lament;

then at least Love will give me so much boldness that I shall disclose to you what have been the years and the days and the hours of my sufferings;

and if time is hostile to my sweet desires, at least it will not prevent my sorrow from receiving some little help of tardy sighs.

11

   Lassare il velo per sole o per ombra,
Donna, non vi vid' io
poi che in me conosceste il gran desio
ch' ogni altra voglia d'entr' al cor mi sgombra.   4

Mentr' io portava i be' pensier celati
ch' ànno la mente desiando morta,
vidivi di pietate ornare il volto;
ma poi ch' Amor di me vi fece accorta,
fuor i biondi capelli allor velati
et l'amoroso sguardo in sé raccolto.   10
   Quel ch' i' più desiava in voi m'è tolto,
sì mi governa il velo
che per mia morte et al caldo et al gielo
de' be' vostr' occhi il dolce lume adombra.   14

12

Se la mia vita da l'aspro tormento
si può tanto schermire, et dagli affanni,
ch' i' veggia per vertù degli ultimi anni,
Donna, de' be' vostr' occhi il lume spento,   4

e i cape' d'oro fin farsi d'argento,
et lassar le ghirlande e i verdi panni,
e 'l viso scolorir che ne' miei danni
al lamentar mi fa pauroso et lento,   8

pur mi darà tanta baldanza Amore
ch' i' vi discovrirò de' miei martiri
qua' sono stati gli anni, e i giorni, et l'ore;   11

et se 'l tempo è contrario ai be' desiri,
non fia ch' almen non giunga al mio dolore
alcun soccorso di tardi sospiri.   14

13

When among the other ladies now and again Love appears in her lovely face, by as much as each is less beautiful than she, by so much grows the desire that enamors me.

I bless the place and the time and the hour that my eyes looked so high, and I say: "Soul, you must give great thanks that you were found worthy of such honor then.

"From her comes the amorous thought that, while you follow it, sends you toward the highest good, little valuing what other men desire;

"from her comes the courageous joy that leads you to Heaven along a straight path, so that already I go high with hope."

14

My weary eyes, while I turn you toward the lovely face that has slain you, I beg you, be cautious, for already Love defies you, for which I sigh.

Death alone can cut off my thoughts from the amorous path that leads them to the sweet port of their healing; but your light can be hidden from you by a lesser obstacle, for you are formed less perfect and of lesser power.

Therefore, sorrowing, before the hours of weeping have come that are already near, take now finally brief solace for so long a martyrdom.

13

Quando fra l'altre donne ad ora ad ora
Amor vien nel bel viso di costei,
quanto ciascuna è men bella di lei
tanto cresce 'l desio che m'innamora.   4

I' benedico il loco e 'l tempo et l'ora
che sì alto miraron gli occhi mei,
et dico: "Anima, assai ringraziar dei
che fosti a tanto onor degnata allora.   8

"Da lei ti ven l'amoroso pensero
che mentre 'l segui al sommo ben t'invia,
poco prezzando quel ch' ogni uom desia;   11

"da lei vien l'animosa leggiadria
ch' al ciel ti scorge per destro sentero,
sì ch' i' vo già de la speranza altero."   14

14

Occhi miei lassi, mentre ch' io vi giro
nel bel viso di quella che v'à morti,
pregovi siate accorti,
che già vi sfida Amore, ond' io sospiro.   4

Morte po chiuder sola a' miei penseri
l'amoroso camin che gli conduce
al dolce porto de la lor salute,
ma puossi a voi celar la vostra luce
per meno oggetto, perché meno interi
siete formati et di minor virtute.   10
Però dolenti, anzi che sian venute
l'ore del pianto che son già vicine,
prendete or a la fine
breve conforto a sì lungo martiro.   14

15

I turn back at each step with my weary body which with great effort I carry forward, and I take then some comfort from your sky, which enables my body to go onward, saying: "Alas, woe's me!"

Then, thinking back on the sweet good I leave behind, on the length of the road and the shortness of my life, I stand in my tracks dismayed and pale and lower my eyes weeping to the ground.

At times in the midst of my sad laments a doubt assails me: How can these members live far from their spirit?

But Love replies to me: "Do you not remember that this is a privilege of lovers, released from all human qualities?"

16

The little white-haired pale old man leaves the sweet place where he has filled out his age and his fear-stricken little family, who watch their dear father disappear;

thence dragging his ancient flanks through the last days of his life, as much as he can he helps himself with good will, broken by the years and tired by the road;

and he comes to Rome, following his desire, to gaze on the likeness of Him whom he hopes to see again up there in Heaven.

Thus, alas, at times I go searching in others, Lady, as much as is possible, for your longed-for true form.

---

likeness of Him: the Veronica, said to be the kerchief with which Saint Veronica (*Verum ikon*, true image) wiped the face of Christ on the way to Calvary, retaining the image of His features. It is preserved in Saint Peter's basilica.

15

Io mi rivolgo indietro a ciascun passo
col corpo stanco ch' a gran pena porto,
et prendo allor del vostr' aere conforto
che 'l fa gir oltra, dicendo: "Oimè, lasso."   4

Poi ripensando al dolce ben ch'io lasso,
al camin lungo, et al mio viver corto,
fermo le piante sbigottito et smorto,
et gli occhi in terra lagrimando abbasso.   8

Talor m'assale in mezzo a' tristi pianti
un dubbio: come posson queste membra
da lo spirito lor viver lontane?   11

Ma rispondemi Amor: "Non ti rimembra
che questo è privilegio degli amanti,
sciolti da tutte qualitati umane?"   14

16

Movesi il vecchierel canuto et bianco
del dolce loco ov' à sua età fornita
et da la famigliuola sbigottita
che vede il caro padre venir manco;   4

indi traendo poi l'antico fianco
per l'estreme giornate di sua vita,
quanto più po col buon voler s'aita,
rotto dagli anni, et dal camino stanco;   8

et viene a Roma, seguendo 'l desio,
per mirar la sembianza di colui
ch' ancor lassù nel ciel vedere spera.   11

Così, lasso, talor vo cercand' io,
Donna, quanto è possibile in altrui
la disiata vostra forma vera.   14

17

Bitter tears rain from my face with an anguished wind of sighs, when it happens that I turn my eyes to you for whom alone I am divided from the world.

It is true that your sweet mild smile quiets my ardent desires and withdraws me from the fire of my torments, as long as I am intent and fixed on watching you,

but my spirits turn cold later, for at parting I see my fated stars—your eyes—turn away from me their gentle motions.

Finally, let loose with the key of love, my soul leaves my heart to follow you; and with much care does it uproot itself thence.

18

When I am all turned toward the place where shines my lady's lovely face, and in my thought the light remains that burns and melts me within bit by bit,

since I fear for my heart, which is breaking, and see my days near their end, I go without light like a blind man who does not know where to go and still departs.

Thus I flee before the blows of death, but not so quickly that my desire does not come with me, as it is accustomed;

I go silent; for my dead words would make people weep, and I desire my tears to be shed in solitude.

17

Piovonmi amare lagrime dal viso
con un vento angoscioso di sospiri,
quando in voi adiven che gli occhi giri
per cui sola dal mondo i' son diviso.   4

Vero è che 'l dolce mansueto riso
pur acqueta gli ardenti miei desiri
et mi sottragge al foco de' martiri
mentr' io son a mirarvi intento et fiso;   8

ma gli spiriti miei s'agghiaccian poi
ch' i' veggio al departir gli atti soavi
torcer da me le mie fatali stelle.   11

Largata al fin co l'amorose chiavi
l'anima esce del cor per seguir voi,
et con molto pensiero indi si svelle.   14

18

Quand' io son tutto volto in quella parte
ove 'l bel viso di Madonna luce,
et m'è rimasa nel pensier la luce
che m'arde et strugge dentro a parte a parte,   4

i' che temo del cor che mi si parte,
et veggio presso il fin de la mia luce,
vommene in guisa d'orbo, senza luce,
che non sa ove si vada et pur si parte.   8

Così davanti a' colpi de la morte
fuggo, ma non sì ratto che 'l desio
meco non venga, come venir sòle;   11

tacito vo, ché le parole morte
farian pianger la gente, et i' desio
che le lagrime mie si spargan sole.   14

19

There are animals in the world of sight so audacious that it withstands even the sun; others, because the great light harms them, do not come out except toward evening;

and others, with their mad desire that hopes perhaps to enjoy the fire because it shines, experience the other power, the one that burns; alas, and my place is in this last band.

For I am not strong enough to look on the light of this lady, and I do not know how to make a shield of shadowy places and late hours;

therefore my destiny leads me, with tearful and weak eyes, to see her: and I know well I am pursuing what burns me.

20

At times, ashamed that I do not speak in rhyme, Lady, about your beauty, I recall the time when I first saw you, such that there will never be another who pleases me;

but I find a weight that is not for my arms, a work not to be polished with my file; therefore my wit, judging its strength, becomes all frozen in its workings.

Many times already have I opened my lips to speak, but then my voice has remained within my breast: but what sound could ever rise so high?

Many times have I begun to write verses, but my pen and my hand and my intellect have been vanquished in the first assault.

19

Son animali al mondo de sì altera
vista che 'ncontra 'l sol pur si difende;
altri, però che 'l gran lume gli offende,
non escon fuor se non verso la sera;   4

et altri, col desio folle che spera
gioir forse nel foco, perché splende,
provan l'altra vertù, quella che' ncende,
lasso, e 'l mio loco è 'n questa ultima schera.   8

Ch' i' non son forte ad aspettar la luce
di questa donna, et non so fare schermi
di luoghi tenebrosi o d'ore tarde;   11

però con gli occhi lagrimosi e 'nfermi
mio destino a vederla mi conduce,
et so ben ch' i' vo dietro a quel che m'arde.   14

20

Vergognando talor ch' ancor si taccia,
Donna, per me vostra bellezza in rima,
ricorro al tempo ch' i' vi vidi prima,
tal che null' altra fia mai che mi piaccia;   4

ma trovo peso non da le mie braccia,
né ovra da polir colla mia lima;
però l'ingegno che sua forza estima
ne l'operazion tutto s'agghiaccia.   8

Più volte già per dir le labbra apersi,
poi rimase la voce in mezzo 'l petto:
ma qual son poria mai salir tant'alto?   11

Più volte incominciai di scriver versi,
ma la penna et la mano et l'intelletto
rimaser vinti nel primier assalto.   14

21

A thousand times, O my sweet warrior, in order to have peace with your lovely eyes, I have offered you my heart; but it does not please you to gaze so low with your lofty mind;

and if some other lady has hopes of him, she lives in weak and fallacious hope; mine—since I disdain what does not please you—mine he can never be as before.

Now if I drive him away, and he does not find in you any help in his sad exile, nor can stay alone, nor go where some other calls him,

his natural course of life might fail, which would be a grave fault in both of us, and so much the more yours as he loves you the more.

22

For whatever animals dwell on earth,
except the few that hate the sun,
the time to labor is while it is day;
but when the sky lights up its stars
some return home and some make a nest in the wood
to have rest at least until the dawn.

And I—from when the lovely dawn begins
to scatter the shadows from about the earth,
awakening the animals in every wood—
I never have any truce from sighs with the sun;
and then when I see the stars flaming
I go weeping and longing for the day.

When the evening drives away the bright day,
and our darkness makes elsewhere a dawn,
I gaze full of care at the cruel stars
that have made me out of sensitive earth;
and I curse the day on which I saw the sun,
for it makes me seem a man raised in the woods.

21

Mille fiate, o dolce mia guerrera,
per aver co' begli occhi vostri pace
v'aggio proferto il cor, m' a voi non piace
mirar sì basso colla mente altera;   4

et se di lui fors' altra donna spera,
vive in speranza debile et fallace;
mio, perché sdegno ciò ch'a voi dispiace,
esser non può giamai così com' era.   8

Or s' io lo scaccio, et e' non trova in voi
ne l'esilio infelice alcun soccorso,
né sa star sol, né gire ov' altri il chiama,   11

poria smarrire il suo natural corso;
che grave colpa fia d'ambeduo noi,
et tanto più de voi quanto più v'ama.   14

22

A qualunque animale alberga in terra,
se non se alquanti ch' ànno in odio il sole,
tempo da travagliare è quanto è 'l giorno;
ma poi che 'l ciel accende le sue stelle
qual torna a casa et qual s'annida in selva
per aver posa almeno infin a l'alba.   6

Et io, da che comincia la bella alba
a scuoter l'ombra intorno de la terra,
svegliando gli animali in ogni selva,
non ò mai triegua di sospir col sole;
poi quand' io veggio fiammeggiar le stelle
vo lagrimando et disiando il giorno.   12

Quando la sera scaccia il chiaro giorno,
et le tenebre nostre altrui fanno alba,
miro pensoso le crudeli stelle
che m'ànno fatto di sensibil terra,
et maledico il dì ch' i' vidi 'l sole
che mi fa in vista un uom nudrito in selva.   18

I do not believe that there ever grazed in any wood
so cruel a beast, either by night or by day,
as she whom I weep for in the shadow and in the sun,
and I am not slowed by the first sleep or the dawn,
for although I am a mortal body of earth
my firm desire comes from the stars.

Before I return to you, bright stars,
or fall down into the amorous wood
leaving my body which will be powdered earth,
might I see pity in her, for in but one day
it could restore many years, and before the dawn
enrich me from the setting of the sun.

Might I be with her from when the sun departs
and no other see us but the stars,
just one night, and let the dawn never come!
and let her not be transformed into a green wood
to escape from my arms, as the day
when Apollo pursued her down here on earth!

But I will be under the earth in dried wood,
and the day will be lit by the tiny stars,
before the sun arrives at so sweet a dawn.

---

amorous wood: according to Virgil's account of the underworld (*Aeneid* 6),
those who die for love are assigned to wander in a dark wood.   green wood:
see note to poem 5.

Non credo che pascesse mai per selva
sì aspra fera, o di notte o di giorno,
come costei ch' i' piango a l'ombra e al sole;
et non mi stanca primo sonno od alba,
ché ben ch' i' sia mortal corpo di terra
lo mio fermo desir vien da le stelle.   24

Prima ch' i' torni a voi, lucenti stelle,
o tomi giù ne l'amorosa selva,
lassando il corpo che fia trita terra,
vedess' io in lei pietà, che 'n un sol giorno
può ristorar molt' anni, e 'nanzi l'alba
puommi aricchir dal tramontar del sole.   30

Con lei foss' io da che si parte il sole,
et non ci vedess' altri che le stelle,
sol una notte et mai non fosse l'alba,
et non se transformasse in verde selva
per uscirmi di braccia, come il giorno
ch' Apollo la seguia qua giù per terra!   36

Ma io sarò sotterra in secca selva,
e 'l giorno andrà pien di minute stelle,
prima ch' a sì dolce alba arrivi il sole.   39

23

In the sweet time of my first age, which saw born and still almost unripe the fierce desire which for my hurt grew— because, singing, pain becomes less bitter—I shall sing how then I lived in liberty while Love was scorned in my abode;

then I shall pursue how that chagrined him too deeply, and what happened to me for that, by which I have become an example for many people; although my harsh undoing is written elsewhere so that a thousand pens are already tired by it, and almost every valley echoes to the sound of my heavy sighs which prove how painful my life is. And if here my memory does not aid me as it is wont to do, let my torments excuse it and one thought which alone gives it such anguish that it makes me turn my back on every other and makes me forget myself beyond resistance, for it holds what is within me, and I only the shell.

I say that since the day when Love gave me the first assault many years had passed, so that I was changing my youthful aspect; and around my heart frozen thoughts had made almost an adamantine hardness which my hard affect did not allow to slacken:

no tear yet bathed my breast nor broke my sleep, and what was not in me seemed to me a miracle in others. Alas, what am I? what was I? The end crowns the life, the evening the day. For that cruel one of whom I speak, seeing that as yet no blow of his arrows had gone beyond my garment, took as his patroness a powerful Lady, against whom wit or force or asking pardon has helped or helps me little: those two transformed me into what I am, making me of a living man a green laurel that loses no leaf for all the cold season.

23

Nel dolce tempo de la prima etade,
che nascer vide et ancor quasi in erba
la fera voglia che per mio mal crebbe,
perché cantando il duol si disacerba,
canterò com' io vissi in libertade   5
mentre Amor nel mio albergo a sdegno s'ebbe;
   poi seguirò sì come a lui ne 'ncrebbe
troppo altamente e che di ciò m'avenne,
di ch' io son fatto a molta gente esempio;
ben che 'l mio duro scempio   10
sia scritto altrove, sì che mille penne
ne son già stanche, et quasi in ogni valle
rimbombi il suon de' miei gravi sospiri,
ch' acquistan fede a la penosa vita.
E se qui la memoria non m'aita   15
come suol fare, iscusilla i martiri
et un penser che solo angoscia dàlle,
tal ch' ad ogni altro fa voltar le spalle
e mi face obliar me stesso a forza,
ch' e' ten di me quel d'entro, et io la scorza.   20

   I' dico che dal dì che 'l primo assalto
mi diede Amor, molt' anni eran passati,
sì ch' io cangiava il giovenil aspetto,
e d'intorno al mio cor pensier gelati
fatto avean quasi adamantino smalto   25
ch' allentar non lassava il duro affetto;
   lagrima ancor non mi bagnava il petto
né rompea il sonno, et quel che in me non era
mi pareva un miracolo in altrui.
Lasso, che son? che fui?   30
La vita el fin, e 'l dì loda la sera;
ché sentendo il crudel di ch' io ragiono
infin allor percossa di suo strale
non essermi passato oltra la gonna,
prese in sua scorta una possente Donna   35
ver cui poco giamai mi valse o vale
ingegno o forza o dimandar perdono;
ei duo mi trasformaro in quel ch' i' sono,
facendomi d'uom vivo un lauro verde
che per fredda stagion foglia non perde.   40

What I became, when I first grew aware of my person being transformed and saw my hairs turning into those leaves which I had formerly hoped would be my crown, and my feet, on which I stood and moved and ran, as every member answers to the soul,

becoming two roots beside the waves not of Peneus but of a prouder river, and my arms changing into two branches! Nor do I fear less for having been later covered with white feathers, when thunderstruck and dead lay my hope that was mounting too high; for, since I did not know where or when I would recover it, alone and weeping I went night and day where it had been taken from me, looking for it beside and within the waters; and from then on my tongue was never silent about its evil fall, as long as it had power; and I took on with the sound of a swan its color.

Thus I went along the beloved shores, and, wishing to speak, I sang always, calling for mercy with wondrous voice; nor was I ever able to make my amorous woes resound in so sweet or soft a temper that her harsh and ferocious heart was humbled.

What was it to hear? for the memory burns me. But much more than I have already said I must tell about my sweet and bitter enemy, although she is such that she surpasses all speech. She, who with her glance steals souls, opened my breast and took my heart with her hand, saying to me: "Make no word of this." Later I saw her alone in another garment such that I did not know her, oh human sense! rather I told her the truth, full of fear, and she to her accustomed form quickly returning made me, alas, an almost living and terrified stone.

---

prouder river: the Rhone or the Durance, in Provence.   white feathers: an allusion to the myth of Cygnus. Phaeton persuaded his father, the sun god, to let him drive his chariot. When he lost control of it, Jupiter struck him down with a thunderbolt; he fell near the river Po, on the banks of which the nymphs built a tomb for him. His friend and relative Cygnus turned into a swan for grief. (Ovid, *Metamorphoses* 1.747–2.380.)   stone: an allusion to the myth of Battus. Battus saw Mercury stealing Apollo's oxen and for a reward promised Mercury not to reveal the theft. Later Mercury returned disguised and promised Battus a greater reward; Battus then disclosed it and Mercury made him into a stone. (Ovid, *Metamorphoses* 2.676–707.)

Qual mi fec' io quando primier m'accorsi
de la trasfigurata mia persona,
e i capei vidi far di quella fronde
di che sperato avea già lor corona,
e i piedi in ch' io mi stetti et mossi et corsi,   45
com' ogni membro a l'anima risponde,
  diventar due radici sovra l'onde
non di Peneo ma d'un più altero fiume,
e 'n duo rami mutarsi ambe le braccia!
Né meno ancor m'agghiaccia   50
l'esser coverto poi di bianche piume
allor che folminato et morto giacque
il mio sperar che tropp' alto montava;
che perch' io non sapea dove né quando
me 'l ritrovasse, solo, lagrimando,   55
là 've tolto mi fu, dì et notte andava
ricercando dallato e dentro a l'acque;
et giamai poi la mia lingua non tacque
mentre poteo del suo cader maligno,
ond' io presi col suon color d'un cigno.   60

  Così lungo l'amate rive andai,
che volendo parlar, cantava sempre,
mercé chiamando con estrania voce;
né mai in sì dolci o in sì soavi tempre
risonar seppi gli amorosi guai   65
che 'l cor s'umiliasse aspro et feroce.
  Qual fu a sentir? ché 'l ricordar mi coce.
Ma molto più di quel ch' è per inanzi
de la dolce et acerba mia nemica
è bisogno ch' io dica,   70
ben che sia tal ch' ogni parlare avanzi.
Questa che col mirar gli animi fura
m'aperse il petto el' cor prese con mano,
dicendo a me: "Di ciò non far parola."
Poi la rividi in altro abito sola,   75
tal ch' i' non la conobbi, o senso umano!
anzi le dissi 'l ver pien di paura;
ed ella ne l'usata sua figura
tosto tornando fecemi, oimè lasso!
d'un quasi vivo et sbigottito sasso.   80

She spoke, so angry to see that she made me tremble within
that stone, hearing: "I am not perhaps who you think I am!"
And I said to myself: "If she there unrocks me, no life will be sad
or noisome to me: come back, my Lord, to make me weep!"
   How, I do not know, but I moved my feet thence, blaming no
one but myself, a mean, all that day, between living and dead.
But because time is short, my pen cannot follow closely my good
will; wherefore I pass over many things written in my mind and
speak only of some, which make those who hear them marvel.
Death was wrapped about my heart, nor by being silent could I
draw it from her hand or give any aid to my afflicted powers.
Words spoken aloud were forbidden me; so I cried out with
paper and ink: "I am not my own, no; if I die, yours is the loss."

   I thought well thus to make myself in her eyes from unworthy, worthy of mercy, and this hope had made me bold. But
sometimes humility quenches disdain, sometimes inflames it,
and that I learned later clothed long time in darkness,
   for at those prayers my light had disappeared, and I, not
finding anywhere a shadow of her, nor even a trace of her feet,
like a man who sleeps on the way threw myself tired onto the
grass one day. There, blaming the fleeing ray, I loosed the rein
to sad tears and let them fall as they willed; nor did ever snow
under the sun disappear, as I felt myself entirely melt and
become a fountain at the foot of a beech; long time did I keep
that damp journey. Who ever heard of a spring being born from
a real man? And I am saying things obvious and known.

---

fountain: an allusion to the myth of Byblis. After a long struggle with herself,
Byblis confessed her love for her brother in a letter to him. After his angry rejection she wooed him until he fled to a foreign land, whereupon, grief-stricken,
she was transformed into a fountain. (Ovid, *Metamorphoses* 9.454–665.)

Ella parlava sì turbata in vista
che tremar mi fea dentro a quella petra,
udendo: "I' non son forse chi tu credi."
E dicea meco: "Se costei mi spetra
nulla vita mi fia noiosa o trista;   85
a farmi lagrimar, signor mio, riedi."
  Come non so, pur io mossi indi i piedi,
non altrui incolpando che me stesso,
mezzo tutto quel dì tra vivo et morto.
Ma perché 'l tempo è corto   90
la penna al buon voler non po gir presso,
onde più cose ne la mente scritte
vo trapassando, et sol d'alcune parlo
che meraviglia fanno a chi l'ascolta.
Morte mi s'era intorno al cor avolta   95
né tacendo potea di sua man trarlo
o dar soccorso a le vertuti afflitte;
le vive voci m'erano interditte,
ond' io gridai con carta et con incostro:
"Non son mio, no; s' io moro il danno è vostro."   100

  Ben mi credea dinanzi agli occhi suoi
d'indegno far così di mercé degno,
et questa spene m'avea fatto ardito;
ma talora umiltà spegne disdegno
talor l'enfiamma, et ciò sepp' io da poi,   105
lunga stagion di tenebre vestito;
  ch' a quei preghi il mio lume era sparito,
ed io non ritrovando intorno intorno
ombra di lei né pur de' suoi piedi orma,
come uom che tra via dorma,   110
gittaimi stanco sovra l'erba un giorno.
Ivi accusando il fugitivo raggio
a le lagrime triste allargai 'l freno
et lasciaile cader come a lor parve;
né giamai neve sotto al sol disparve   115
com' io senti' me tutto venir meno
et farmi una fontana a piè d'un faggio;
gran tempo umido tenni quel viaggio.
Chi udì mai d'uom vero nascer fonte?
e parlo cose manifeste et conte.   120

The soul, which only by God is made noble, for from no one
else can come such grace, keeps a state like to its Maker;
therefore it is never sated with forgiving whoever with humble
heart and face, after any number of offenses, comes for mercy.

And if, contrary to her custom, she allows herself to be
begged long, she mirrors Him, and does it that sinning may be
more feared, for he does not repent well of one sin who prepares
himself for another. Since my lady, moved with pity, deigned to
gaze on me and recognized and saw that the punishment was
equal to the sin, benignly she reduced me to my first state. But
there is nothing in the world on which a wise man may rely; for,
when I prayed again, she turned my sinews and bones into hard
flint, and thus I remained a voice shaken from my former
burden, calling Death and only her by name.

A wandering sorrowful spirit, I remember, through desert
ravines and strange, I bewailed for many years my unleashed
boldness, and still later found release from that ill, and returned
again to my earthly members, in order, I believe, to feel more
pain there.

I followed so far my desire that one day, hunting as I was
wont, I went forth, and that lovely cruel wild creature was in a
spring naked when the sun burned most strongly. I, who am not
appeased by any other sight, stood to gaze on her, whence she
felt shame and, to take revenge or to hide herself, sprinkled
water in my face with her hand. I shall speak the truth, perhaps
it will appear a lie, for I felt myself drawn from my own image
and into a solitary wandering stag from wood to wood quickly I
am transformed and still I flee the belling of my hounds.

---

flint...voice: an allusion to the myth of Echo. With her garrulity Echo once
prevented Juno from discovering Jupiter making love with one of the nymphs.
Juno punished her by making it impossible for her to speak except by echoing
others. Rejected by Narcissus, who had fallen in love with his own image in a
forest pool, Echo wasted away until she became a disembodied voice, her body
turning to stone. (Ovid, *Metamorphoses* 3.359–398.)   stag: an allusion to
the myth of Actaeon. The huntsman Actaeon, seeking shade and rest in the
forest at noon, inadvertently came upon the goddess Diana and her nymphs
bathing naked in a pool. Incensed at his presence, the goddess sprinkled water
on his face, turning him into a stag. Actaeon fled, pursued by his own hounds,
to which he vainly tried to identify himself, and was torn to pieces. (Ovid,
Metamorphoses 3.138–252.)

L'alma ch' è sol da Dio fatta gentile—
che già d'altrui non po venir tal grazia—
simile al suo fattor stato ritene;
però di perdonar mai non è sazia
a chi col core et col sembiante umile   125
dopo quantunque offese a mercé vene.
Et se contra suo stile ella sostene
d'esser molto pregata, in lui si specchia,
et fal perché 'l peccar più si pavente;
ché non ben si ripente   130
de l'un mal chi de l'altro s'apparecchia.
Poi che Madonna da pietà commossa
degnò mirarme et ricognovve et vide
gir di pari la pena col peccato,
benigna mi redusse al primo stato.   135
Ma nulla à 'l mondo in ch' uom saggio si fide;
ch' ancor poi ripregando i nervi et l'ossa
mi volse in dura selce, et così scossa
voce rimasi de l'antiche some,
chiamando Morte et lei sola per nome.   140

Spirto doglioso errante mi rimembra
per spelunche deserte et pellegrine
piansi molt' anni il mio sfrenato ardire,
et ancor poi trovai di quel mal fine
et ritornai ne le terrene membra,   145
credo per più dolore ivi sentire.
I' segui' tanto avanti il mio desire
ch' un dì, cacciando sì com' io solea,
mi mossi, e quella fera bella et cruda
in una fonte ignuda   150
si stava, quando 'l sol più forte ardea.
Io perché d'altra vista non m'appago
stetti a mirarla, ond' ella ebbe vergogna
et per farne vendetta o per celarse
l'acqua nel viso co le man mi sparse.   155
Vero dirò; forse e' parrà menzogna:
ch' i' senti' trarmi de la propria imago
et in un cervo solitario et vago
di selva in selva ratto mi trasformo,
et ancor de' miei can fuggo lo stormo.   160

Song, I was never the cloud of gold that once descended in a precious rain so that it partly quenched the fire of Jove; but I have certainly been a flame lit by a lovely glance and I have been the bird that rises highest in the air raising her whom in my words I honor; nor for any new shape could I leave the first laurel, for still its sweet shade turns away from my heart any less beautiful pleasure.

---

cloud of gold: beloved by Jupiter, Danae was locked up in a tower by her father and was visited by the god in a rain of gold.   flame: Semele was consumed by lightning when she insisted on seeing her lover Jupiter in his true form. bird: Jupiter, in the shape of an eagle, carried Ganymede off to Olympus.

Canzon, i' non fu' mai quel nuvol d'oro
che poi discese in preziosa pioggia
sì che 'l foco di Giove in parte spense;
ma fui ben fiamma ch' un bel guardo accense,
et fui l'uccel che più per l'aere poggia   165
alzando lei che ne' miei detti onoro;
né per nova figura il primo alloro
seppi lassar, ché pur la sua dolce ombra
ogni men bel piacer del cor mi sgombra.   169

24

If the honored branch that protects one from the anger of heaven when great Jove thunders had not refused me the crown that decorates those who write poetry,

I would be a friend to these goddesses of yours, whom the world so basely abandons; but that injury drives me far away from the inventor of the first olives,

for the sand of Ethiopia does not boil under the hottest sun as much as I burn at losing a thing of my own so dearly loved.

Seek therefore a more tranquil fountain, for mine suffers a dearth of all moisture, except for that which weeping I let fall.

A reply, using the same rhymes, to a sonnet by Andrea Stramazzo da Perugia (Appendix One, p. 603).

honored branch: the laurel.   these goddesses: the Muses.   inventor of the first olives: Minerva, goddess of wisdom, friend of the Muses.

25

Love, from whom my steps have never strayed, used to weep, and I with him at times, to see by the strange and bitter effects that your soul was freed from his knots;

now that God has turned it back to the right path, in my heart lifting both hands to Heaven I thank Him who in His mercy listens kindly to just human prayers.

And if, returning to the life of love, you have found in your way ditches or hills that try to make you abandon your lovely desire,

it was to show how thorny the path is, how mountainous and hard the ascent by which one must rise to true worth.

The recipients of this poem and the next have not been identified.

24

Se l'onorata fronde che prescrive
l'ira del ciel quando 'l gran Giove tona
non m'avesse disdetta la corona
che suole ornar chi poetando scrive,   4

i' era amico a queste vostre dive
le qua' vilmente il secolo abandona;
ma quella ingiuria già lunge mi sprona
da l'inventrice de le prime olive,   8

ché non bolle la polver d'Etiopia
sotto 'l più ardente sol, com' io sfavillo
perdendo tanto amata cosa propia.   11

Cercate dunque fonte più tranquillo,
ché 'l mio d'ogni liquor sostene inopia
salvo di quel che lagrimando stillo.   14

25

Amor piangeva et io con lui tal volta,
dal qual miei passi non fur mai lontani,
mirando per gli effetti acerbi et strani
l'anima vostra de' suoi nodi sciolta;   4

or ch' al dritto camin l'à Dio rivolta,
col cor levando al cielo ambe le mani
ringrazio lui che' giusti preghi umani
benignamente sua mercede ascolta.   8

Et se tornando a l'amorosa vita
per farvi al bel desio volger le spalle
trovaste per la via fossati o poggi,   11

fu per mostrar quanto è spinoso calle
et quanto alpestra et dura la salita
onde al vero valor conven ch' uom poggi.   14

26

More glad than I, was never ship come to land after being battled and conquered by the waves, when its people, showing devotion in their color, kneel on the shore to give thanks;

more glad than I, was never one set free from prison when the cord was already twisted about his neck—now that I see put back in its sheath that sword which made so long war on my lord.

And all you who praise Love in rhyme, to the good weaver of amorous verse give honor, who before had strayed;

for there is more glory in the realm of the elect for one converted spirit, and he is more esteemed, than for ninety and nine others who are just.

27

The successor of Charles, who adorns his brow with the crown of his ancestor, has already taken arms to break the horns of Babylon and of whoever bears her name;

and the vicar of Christ, with the burden of keys and mantle, returns to his nest, so that if some accident does not turn him back he will see Bologna and then noble Rome.

Your gentle and noble lamb beats down the savage wolves, and let it thus befall whoever separates legitimate loves;

console her, therefore, for she still waits, and Rome, who weeps for her bridegroom; and gird on your sword for Jesus now.

The recipient of this poem has not been identified.
successor of Charles: Philip VI of France, the successor of Charles V (and, ultimately, of Charlemagne), declared a Crusade against the Moslems in 1334.   Babylon: Baghdad or Cairo, considered the chief seats of Moslem power.   vicar of Christ: Benedict XII, pope from 1334 to 1342, who was expected to return the seat of the papacy to Rome from Avignon, where it had been transferred in 1310.   lamb. . .wolves: perhaps rival Roman families, perhaps rival Florentine factions.   bridegroom: the pope.

26

Più di me lieta non si vede a terra
nave da l'onde combattuta et vinta,
quando la gente di pietà depinta
su per la riva a ringraziar s'atterra;   4

né lieto più del carcer si diserra
chi 'ntorno al collo ebbe la corda avvinta,
di me veggendo quella spada scinta
che fece al segnor mio sì lunga guerra.   8

Et tutti voi ch' Amor laudate in rima,
al buon testor degli amorosi detti
rendete onor ch' era smarrito in prima;   11

ché più gloria è nel regno degli eletti
d'un spirito converso, et più s'estima,
che di novantanove altri perfetti.   14

27

Il successor di Carlo, che la chioma
co la corona del suo antiquo adorna,
prese à già l'arme per fiaccar le corna
a Babilonia et chi da lei si noma;   4

e 'l vicario de Cristo colla soma
de le chiavi et del manto al nido torna,
sì che s' altro accidente nol distorna
vedrà Bologna et poi la nobil Roma.   8

La mansueta vostra et gentil agna
abatte i fieri lupi, et così vada
chiunque amor legitimo scompagna;   11

consolate lei dunque, ch' ancor bada,
et Roma che del suo sposo si lagna,
et per Jhesù cingete omai la spada.   14

28

O soul awaited in Heaven, blessed and beautiful, who go
clothed with our humanity (not, like others, burdened with it):
that the road may by now be less hard for you (beloved of God,
obedient handmaiden), by which from down here one crosses
over into His kingdom,

behold just now the sweet comfort of a western wind for your
ship, which has already turned away from the blind world to go
to the better port, a wind that will lead it, freed from its former
bonds, through this dark valley where we bewail our own and
others' faults, by a straight course to the true Orient toward
which it is turned.

Perhaps the devout and loving prayers and the holy tears of
mortals have come before the highest Pity; and perhaps they
have never before been so many, or of such quality, that by their
merit eternal Justice at all bent aside from its course.

But that good King who governs Heaven in His grace turns
His eyes to the holy place where He was crucified; wherefore He
breathes into the breast of the new Charles that vengeance
whose delay has harmed us and made Europe sigh for many
years; thus He aids His beloved bride, He whose voice alone
makes Babylon tremble and be afraid.

The recipient of this poem has not been identified. The occasion is the same
Crusade referred to in poem 27.

western wind: Philip VI's proclamation of the Crusade, Paris being to the
west of Rome.

28

O aspettata in Ciel beata et bella
anima che di nostra umanitade
vestita vai (non, come l'altre, carca):
perché ti sian men dure omai le strade
(a Dio diletta, obediente ancella)
onde al suo regno di qua giù si varca,   6
    ecco novellamente a la tua barca,
ch' al cieco mondo à già volte le spalle
per gir al miglior porto,
d'un vento occidental dolce conforto;
lo qual per mezzo questa oscura valle
ove piangiamo il nostro et l'altrui torto
la condurrà de' lacci antichi sciolta
per drittissimo calle
al verace oriente ov' ella è volta.   15

    Forse i devoti et gli amorosi preghi
et le lagrime sante de' mortali
son giunte innanzi a la pietà superna;
et forse non fur mai tante né tali
che per merito lor punto si pieghi
fuor de suo corso la giustizia eterna.   21
    Ma quel benigno Re che 'l ciel governa
al sacro loco ove fu posto in croce
gli occhi per grazia gira,
onde nel petto al novo Carlo spira
la vendetta ch' a noi tardata noce
sì che molt'anni Europa ne sospira;
così soccorre a la sua amata sposa
tal che sol de la voce
fa tremar Babilonia et star pensosa.   30

Whoever dwells between Garonne and the mountains, and between the Rhone and the Rhine and the salt waves, accompanies the Most Christian standards; and all who ever cared for true worth, from the Pyrenees to the farthest horizon, will leave Spain empty along with Aragon;

England, with the islands that Ocean bathes between the Wain and the Columns—as far as any knowledge sounds of sacred Helicon—differing in language and arms and costume, charity spurs all to the high undertaking. Ah! what love, however legitimate or worthy, what sons, what ladies ever were the cause of so just an anger?

There is a part of the world that always lies in ice and frozen snows, all distant from the path of the sun; there, beneath days cloudy and brief, is born a people naturally the enemy of rest, whom dying does not pain.

If these, more devout than in the past, gird on their swords in their Teutonic rage, you can learn how much to value Turks, Arabs, and Chaldeans, with all those who hope in gods on this side of the sea whose waves are blood-colored: a naked, cowardly, and lazy people who never grasp the steel but entrust all their blows to the wind.

Most Christian: title claimed by the kings of France.   those who hope in gods: the Moslems, who were supposed by medieval Christians to be polytheists.   entrust . . . blows to the wind: the Turks were famous as archers.

Chiunque alberga tra Garona e 'l monte
e 'ntra 'l Rodano e 'l Reno et l'onde salse
le 'nsegne cristianissime accompagna;
et a cui mai di vero pregio calse
dal Pireneo a l'ultimo orizonte
con Aragon lassarà vota Ispagna.   36
 Inghilterra con l'isole che bagna
l'Occeano intra 'l Carro et le Colonne,
in fin là dove sona
dottrina del santissimo Elicona,
varie di lingue et d'arme et de le gonne
a l'alta impresa caritate sprona.
Deh qual amor sì licito o sì degno,
qua' figli mai, qua' donne
furon materia a sì giusto disdegno?   45

Una parte del mondo è che si giace
mai sempre in ghiaccio et in gelate nevi,
tutta lontana dal camin del sole;
là sotto i giorni nubilosi et brevi,
nemica naturalmente di pace
nasce una gente a cui il morir non dole.   51
 Questa se più devota che non sòle
col tedesco furor la spada cigne,
Turchi Arabi et Caldei,
con tutti quei che speran nelli Dei
di qua dal mar che fa l'onde sanguigne,
quanto sian da prezzar conoscer dèi:
popolo ignudo paventoso et lento,
che ferro mai non strigne
ma tutt' i colpi suoi commette al vento.   60

Therefore it is time to withdraw our neck from the ancient
yoke and to rend the veil that has been wrapped over our eyes;
let your noble mind, which you hold from Heaven by grace of
the immortal Apollo, and your eloquence now show their power
  both through speech and through praiseworthy writings. For
if reading of Orpheus and Amphion you are not amazed, the
marvel will be even less when Italy with her sons awakes at the
sound of your clear voice, so that she takes up her lance for
Jesus: if this ancient mother looks at the truth, in none of her
quarrels were there ever reasons so lovely and so gay.

  You who, to grow rich with a true treasure, have turned the
ancient and the modern pages, flying up to Heaven even though
in earthly body, you know—from the reign of the son of Mars to
the great Augustus, who with green laurel thrice in triumph
crowned his brow—
  how generous Rome often was with her blood when others
were injured; and now why will she not be, not generous, but
grateful and pious in avenging those cruel wrongs with the
glorious Son of Mary? How then can the enemy hope in human
defenses, if Christ stands with our opposing ranks?

  Orpheus and Amphion: said to move trees and stones, respectively, with
their songs.   son of Mars: Romulus, legendary founder of Rome.

Dunque ora è 'l tempo da ritrare il collo
dal giogo antico, et da squarciare il velo
ch' è stato avolto intorno agli occhi nostri,
et che 'l nobile ingegno che dal cielo
per grazia tien de l'immortale Apollo
et l'eloquentia sua vertù qui mostri   66
    or con la lingua, or co' laudati incostri.
Perché d'Orfeo leggendo et d'Anfione
se non ti meravigli,
assai men fia ch' Italia co' suoi figli
si desti al suon del tuo chiaro sermone
tanto che per Jhesù la lancia pigli:
che s' al ver mira questa antica madre,
in nulla sua tenzione
fur mai cagion sì belle o sì leggiadre.   75

Tu ch' ài per arricchir d'un bel tesauro
volte l'antiche et le moderne carte,
volando al ciel colla terrena soma,
sai da l'imperio del figliuol de Marte
al grande Augusto che di verde lauro
tre volte triunfando ornò la chioma   81
    ne l'altrui ingiurie del suo sangue Roma
spesse fiate quanto fu cortese;
et or perché non fia
cortese no, ma conoscente et pia
a vendicar le dispietate offese
col figliuol glorioso di Maria?
Che dunque la nemica parte spera
ne l'umane difese,
se Cristo sta da la contraria schiera?   90

Think of the reckless daring of Xerxes, who, to tread our
shores, outraged the sea with strange bridges, and you will see
all the Persian women dressed in black for the death of their
husbands, and the sea of Salamis colored red.

And not only that miserable ruin of the unhappy folk of the
East promises victory to you, but also Marathon and the mortal
straits which the Lion with few men defended, and a thousand
others of which you have heard and read. Wherefore it is most
necessary to bend your knees and heart to God, who has
reserved your years for so much good.

Song, you will see Italy and the honored shore that is hidden
from my eyes not by sea, mountain, or river, but only by Love,
who with his noble light makes me desirous where he most
enflames me: nor can nature resist habit. Now go, do not lose
your other companions, for not only under a woman's veil does
Love dwell, for whom we laugh and weep.

Xerxes: Xerxes I of Persia, who invaded Greece via the Hellespoint with a
bridge constructed of ships. He was defeated in a naval battle at Salamis (480
B.C.) and in several land battles.   Marathon: battle (490 B.C.) in which
Darius I (Xerxes' father), invader of Greece, was finally defeated.   mortal
straits: the mountain pass of Thermopylae, defended against Xerxes by Spartan
troops under Leonidas ("the Lion").

Pon mente al temerario ardir di Xerse,
che fece per calcare i nostri liti
di novi ponti oltraggio a la marina,
et vedrai ne la morte de' mariti
tutte vestite a brun le donne perse
et tinto in rosso il mar di Salamina.   96
 Et non pur questa misera ruina
del popolo infelice d'oriente
vittoria t'empromette,
ma Maratona et le mortali strette
che difese il Leon con poca gente,
et altre mille ch' ài ascoltate et lette.
Per che inchinare a Dio molto convene
le ginocchia et la mente
che gli anni tuoi riserva a tanto bene.   105

 Tu vedrai Italia et l'onorata riva,
canzon, ch' agli occhi miei cela et contende
non mar non poggio o fiume
ma solo Amor, che del suo altero lume
più m'invaghisce dove più m'incende,
né natura può star contra 'l costume.
Or movi, non smarrir l'altre compagne,
che non pur sotto bende
alberga Amor, per cui si ride et piagne.   114

29

Green garments, crimson, black, or purple, did never lady wear, nor ever twisted her hair in a blond braid, as beautiful as this one who deprives me of choice and draws me with her from the path of freedom so that I bear no lesser yoke.

And if at times my soul arms itself to complain—for it lacks all counsel when its torment draws it into doubt—the very sight of her calls it back from its unbridled will, for from my heart she erases every delirious undertaking and the sight of her makes every disdain sweet.

For all that I have ever suffered for love and am still to suffer until she who wounded my heart makes him whole again, that rebel against mercy who still makes him yearn, vengeance shall be taken; as long as pride and anger do not close and lock against humility the lovely way that leads to her.

But the hour and the day when I opened my eyes on that lovely black and white which drove me out from the place where Love ran in—they were the new root of this life which pains me, and she in whom our age marvels at itself; and whoever sees her without being awed is made of lead or wood.

A tour de force of Provençal stanza construction. Lines rhyme only from stanza to stanza, but all follow the same scheme; there are internal rhymes in the fourth and sixth lines.

black and white: Laura's eyes.

29

Verdi panni sanguigni oscuri o persi
non vestì donna unquanco
né d'or capelli in bionda treccia attorse
sì bella   come questa che mi spoglia
d'arbitrio et dal camin de libertade
seco mi tira   sì ch' io non sostegno
alcun giogo men grave.   7

Et se pur s'arma talor a dolersi
l'anima a cui vien manco
consiglio ove 'l martir l'adduce in forse,
rappella   lei da la sfrenata voglia
subita vista, ché del cor mi rade
ogni delira   impresa et ogni sdegno
fa 'l veder lei soave.   14

Di quanto per amor giamai soffersi
et aggio a soffrir anco
fin che mi sani 'l cor colei che 'l morse
rubella   di mercé che pur l'envoglia,
vendetta fia; sol che contra umiltade
orgoglio et ira   il bel passo ond' io vegno
non chiuda et non inchiave.   21

Ma l'ora e 'l giorno ch' io le luci apersi
nel bel nero et nel bianco
che mi scacciar di là dove Amor corse
novella   d'esta vita che m'addoglia
furon radice, et quella in cui l'etade
nostra si mira,   la qual piombo o legno
vedendo è chi non pave.   28

No tear, therefore, that I may pour from my eyes for those arrows which in my left side make bloody him who first felt them—no tear turns me from my desire, for the sentence falls on the right place; because of him my soul sighs, and it is just that he wash her wounds.

My thoughts have become alien to me: one driven like me once turned the beloved sword upon herself; nor do I beg her to set me free, for all other paths to Heaven are less straight, and certainly one cannot aspire to the glorious realm in any stronger ship.

Kindly stars that accompanied the fortunate womb when its lovely fruit came down here into the world! for she is a star on earth, and as the laurel its leaf so she preserves the worth of chastity. No lightning ever comes, or unworthy wind, to bend her down!

I know well that to enclose her praises in verse would vanquish whoever put the worthiest hand to writing: what cell of memory is there that can contain all the virtue, all the beauty that one sees who looks in her eyes, sign of all worth, sweet key of my heart?

However much the sun goes round, Love has no dearer pledge, Lady, than you.

---

one driven like me: Dido, who killed herself with Aeneas' sword when he abandoned her.   lightning...unworthy wind: allegorically, passion.

Lagrima dunque che dagli occhi versi—
per quelle che nel manco
lato mi bagna chi primier s'accorse
quadrella—   dal voler mio non mi svoglia,
ché 'n giusta parte la sentenza cade;
per lei sospira   l'alma, et ella è degno
che le sue piaghe lave.   35

Da me son fatti i miei pensier diversi:
tal già qual io mi stanco
l'amata spada in se stessa contorse;
né quella   prego che però mi scioglia,
ché men son dritte al ciel tutt' altre strade
et non s'aspira   al glorioso regno
certo in più salda nave.   42

Benigne stelle che compagne fersi
al fortunato fianco
quando il bel parto giù nel mondo scorse!
ch' è stella   in terra, et come in lauro foglia
conserva verde il pregio d'onestade,
ove non spira   folgore né indegno
vento mai che l'aggrave.   49

So io ben ch' a voler chiuder in versi
suo' laudi fora stanco
chi più degna la mano a scriver porse;
qual cella   è di memoria in cui s'accoglia
quanta vede vertù, quanta beltade
chi gli occhi mira   d'ogni valor segno,
dolce del mio cor chiave?   56

Quanto il sol gira,   Amor più caro pegno,
Donna, di voi non àve.   58

30

A youthful lady under a green laurel
I saw, whiter and colder than snow
not touched by the sun many and many years,
and her speech and her lovely face and her locks
pleased me so that I have her before my eyes
and shall always have wherever I am, on slope or shore.

Then my thoughts will have come to shore
when green leaves are not to be found on a laurel;
when I have a quiet heart and dry eyes
we shall see the fire freeze, and burning snow;
I have not so many hairs in these locks
as I would be willing, in order to see that day, to wait years.

But because time flies and the years flee
and one arrives quickly at death
either with dark or with white locks,
I shall follow the shadow of that sweet laurel
in the most ardent sun or through the snow,
until the last day closes these eyes.

There never have been seen such lovely eyes,
either in our age or in the first years;
they melt me as the sun does the snow:
whence there comes forth a river of tears
that Love leads to the foot of the harsh laurel
that has branches of diamond and golden locks.

30

Giovene donna sotto un verde lauro
vidi più bianca et più fredda che neve
non percossa dal sol molti et molt'anni;
e 'l suo parlare e 'l bel viso et le chiome
mi piacquen sì ch' i' l' ò dinanzi agli occhi
ed avrò sempre ov' io sia in poggio o 'n riva.   6

Allor saranno i miei pensieri a riva
che foglia verde non si trovi in lauro;
quando avrò queto il cor, asciutti gli occhi,
vedrem ghiacciare il foco, arder la neve;
non ò tanti capelli in queste chiome
quanti vorrei quel giorno attender anni.   12

Ma perché vola il tempo et fuggon gli anni
sì ch' a la morte in un punto s'arriva
o colle brune o colle bianche chiome,
seguirò l'ombra di quel dolce lauro
per lo più ardente sole et per la neve,
fin che l'ultimo dì chiuda quest'occhi.   18

Non fur giamai veduti sì begli occhi
o ne la nostra etade o ne' prim' anni
che mi struggon così come 'l sol neve,
onde procede lagrimosa riva
ch' Amor conduce a pie' del duro lauro
ch' à i rami di diamante et d'or le chiome.   24

I fear I shall change my face and my locks
before she with true pity will show me her eyes,
my idol carved in living laurel;
for, if I do not err, today it is seven years
that I go sighing from shore to shore
night and day, in heat and in snow.

Inwardly fire, though outwardly white snow,
alone with these thoughts, with changed locks,
always weeping I shall go along every shore,
to make pity perhaps come into the eyes
of someone who will be born a thousand years from now—
if a well-tended laurel can live so long.

Gold and topaz in the sun above the snow
are vanquished by the golden locks next to those eyes
that lead my years so quickly to shore.

Gold and topaz: an allusion to Psalm 119:12 (Vulgate 118:12): "Ideo dilexi mandata tua super aurum et topazion" (I have loved thy commandments above gold and topaz).

I' temo di cangiar pria volto et chiome
che con vera pietà mi mostri gli occhi
l'idolo mio scolpito in vivo lauro,
ché s' al contar non erro oggi à sett' anni
che sospirando vo di riva in riva
la notte e 'l giorno, al caldo ed a la neve.   30

Dentro pur foco et for candida neve,
sol con questi pensier, con altre chiome,
sempre piangendo andrò per ogni riva,
per far forse pietà venir ne gli occhi
di tal che nascerà dopo mill' anni,
se tanto viver po ben colto lauro.   36

L'auro e i topacii al sol sopra la neve
vincon le bionde chiome presso a gli occhi
che menan gli anni miei sì tosto a riva.   39

31

This noble soul that departs, called before its time to the other life, if up there it is prized as much as it should be, will hold of heaven the most blessed part;

if it dwells between the third light and Mars, the appearance of the sun will be dimmed, since to gaze on this soul's infinite beauty the worthy souls will all be scattered around it;

if it should settle under the fourth nest, each of the three would be less beautiful and it alone would have the fame and the cry;

in the fifth circle it would not dwell; but if it flies higher, I am sure that Jove and every other star will be vanquished.

During an illness of Laura's.
between the third light and Mars: in the sphere of the sun, between Venus and Mars, the fifth.   under the fourth nest: lower than the sun; therefore in the sphere of the moon, of Mercury, or of Venus.   higher: that is, to the sphere of Jupiter, the sixth; of Saturn, the seventh; or of the fixed stars, the eighth.

32

The more I approach that last day that makes all human misery brief, the more I see that Time runs swift and light and that my hope of him is fallacious and empty.

I say to my thoughts: "Not much further now will we go speaking of love, for this hard and heavy earthly burden, like new snow, is melting, and we shall have peace;

"for with it will fall the hope that made us rave so long, and the laughter and the weeping, and the fear and the sorrow:

"we shall see clearly then how often people put themselves forward for uncertain things and how often they sigh in vain."

31

Questa anima gentil che si diparte
anzi tempo chiamata a l'altra vita,
se lassuso è quanto esser de' gradita,
terrà del ciel la più beata parte;   4

s' ella riman fra 'l terzo lume et Marte
fia la vista del sole scolorita,
poi ch' a mirar sua bellezza infinita
l'anime degne intorno a lei fien sparte;   8

se si posasse sotto al quarto nido
ciascuna de le tre saria men bella,
et essa sola avria la fame e 'l grido;   11

nel quinto giro non abitrebbe ella,
ma se vola più alto, assai mi fido
che con Giove sia vinta ogni altra stella.   14

32

Quanto più m'avicino al giorno estremo
che l'umana miseria suol far breve,
più veggio il tempo andar veloce et leve
e 'l mio di lui sperar fallace et scemo.   4

I' dico a' miei pensier: "Non molto andremo
d'amor parlando omai, ché 'l duro et greve
terreno incarco come fresca neve
si va struggendo, onde noi pace avremo;   8

"perché con lui cadrà quella speranza
che ne fe' vaneggiar sì lungamente,
e 'l riso e 'l pianto, et la paura et l'ira: 11

"sì vedrem chiaro poi come sovente
per le cose dubbiose altri s'avanza,
et come spesso indarno si sospira."   14

33

Already the star of love was flaming in the East, and the other
that makes Juno jealous wheeled its rays in the North, bright and
lovely;

the frail old woman, ungirt and barefoot, had already arisen to
spin and had awakened the coals; and that time was piercing
lovers which by custom calls them to lament;

when my hope, already reduced to the quick, reached my heart,
not by the usual way, for sleep kept that closed and pain kept it
wet—

how changed, alas, from what she was before!—and she seemed
to say: "Why does your worth languish? Seeing these eyes is not
yet taken from you."

---

    star of love: the planet Venus as the morning star.   other . . . jealous:
Juno, jealous of Jupiter's love for Callisto, turned her and her son Arcas into
bears, whereupon Jupiter made them constellations, Ursa Major and Ursa
Minor, respectively.

34

Apollo, if the sweet desire is still alive that inflamed you beside
the Thessalian waves, and if you have not forgotten, with the
turning of the years, those beloved blond locks;

against the slow frost and the harsh and cruel time that lasts as
long as your face is hidden, now defend the honored and holy
leaves where you first and then I were limed;

and by the power of the amorous hope that sustained you in
your bitter life, disencumber the air of these impressions.

Thus we shall then together see a marvel—our lady sitting on the
grass and with her arms making a shade for herself.

    Apollo . . . Thessalian waves: for the myth of Apollo and Daphne, see note to
poem 5.

33

Già fiammeggiava l'amorosa stella
per l'oriente, et l'altra che Giunone
suol far gelosa nel settentrione
rotava i raggi suoi lucente et bella;   4

levata era a filar la vecchiarella
discinta et scalza, et desto avea 'l carbone,
et gli amanti pungea quella stagione
che per usanza a lagrimar gli appella;   8

quando mia speme già condutta al verde
giunse nel cor non per l'usata via,
che 'l sonno tenea chiusa e 'l dolor molle—   11

quanto cangiata, oimè, da quel di pria! —
et parea dir: "Perché tuo valor perde?
Veder quest'occhi ancor non ti si tolle."   14

34

Apollo, s' ancor vive il bel desio
che t'infiammava a le tesaliche onde,
et se non ài l'amate chiome bionde,
volgendo gli anni, già poste in oblio,   4

dal pigro gelo et dal tempo aspro et rio
che dura quanto 'l tuo viso s'asconde
difendi or l'onorata et sacra fronde
ove tu prima et poi fu' invescato io,   8

et per vertù de l'amorosa speme
che ti sostenne ne la vita acerba,
di queste impression l'aere disgombra;   11

sì vedrem poi per meraviglia inseme
seder la donna nostra sopra l'erba
et far de la sue braccia a se stessa ombra.   14

35

Alone and filled with care, I go measuring the most deserted fields with steps delaying and slow, and I keep my eyes alert so as to flee from where any human footprint marks the sand.

No other shield do I find to protect me from people's open knowing, for in my bearing, in which all happiness is extinguished, anyone can read from without how I am aflame within.

So that I believe by now that mountains and shores and rivers and woods know the temper of my life, which is hidden from other persons;

but still I cannot seek paths so harsh or so savage that Love does not always come along discoursing with me and I with him.

36

If I thought that by death I would be lightened of this amorous care that weighs me down, with my own hands by now I would have consigned to earth these burdensome members and that weight;

but because I fear that it would be a passage from weeping into weeping and from one war to another, still on this side of the pass that is closed to me I half remain, alas, and half pass over.

It would be time for the pitiless bowstring to have shot the last arrow, already wet and colored with blood;

and I beg Love for it, and that deaf one who left me painted with her colors and does not remember to call me to her.

35

Solo et pensoso i più deserti campi
vo mesurando a passi tardi et lenti,
et gli occhi porto per fuggire intenti
ove vestigio uman la rena stampi.   4

Altro schermo non trovo che mi scampi
dal manifesto accorger de le genti,
perché negli atti d'allegrezza spenti
di fuor si legge com' io dentro avampi.   8

Sì ch' io mi credo omai che monti et piagge
et fiumi et selve sappian di che tempre
sia la mia vita, ch' è celata altrui;   11

ma pur sì aspre vie né sì selvagge
cercar non so ch' Amor non venga sempre
ragionando con meco, et io con lui.   14

36

S' io credesse per morte essere scarco
del pensiero amoroso che m'atterra,
colle mie mani avrei già posto in terra
queste membra noiose et quello incarco;   4

ma perch' io temo che sarebbe un varco
di pianto in pianto et d'una in altra guerra,
di qua dal passo ancor che mi si serra
mezzo rimango, lasso, et mezzo il varco.   8

Tempo ben fora omai d'avere spinto
l'ultimo stral la dispietata corda
ne l'altrui sangue già bagnato et tinto,   11

et io ne prego Amore, et quella sorda
che mi lassò de' suoi color depinto
et di chiamarmi a sé non le ricorda.   14

37

So weak is the thread by which hangs my heavy life that if someone does not aid it, it will soon be at the end of its race; for since the cruel departure I took from my sweet love, there is just one hope that until now has been a cause of life,

saying: "Although you are deprived of the beloved sight, maintain yourself, sad soul. How do you know if you may not return again to a better time and to happier days? or if you may not regain the good you have lost?" This hope sustained me for a time; now it is failing, and I delay in it too much.

Time passes and the hours are so swift to complete their journey that I have not enough time even to think how I run to death; one ray of the sun hardly rises in the East when you will see it reach the other mountains of the opposite horizon by its long and coiling path.

The lives of mortal men are so short, their bodies so heavy and frail, that when I find myself separated by so much from her lovely face, being unable to move myself with the wings of my desire, little is left me of my usual strength, nor do I know how long I can live in this state.

37

Sì è debile il filo a cui s'attene
la gravosa mia vita
che s' altri non l'aita
ella fia tosto di suo corso a riva,
però che dopo l'empia dipartita
che dal dolce mio bene
feci, sol una spene
è stato in fin a qui cagion ch' io viva,   8
   dicendo: "Perché priva
sia de l'amata vista,
mantienti, anima trista;
che sai s' a miglior tempo anco ritorni
et a più lieti giorni,
o se 'l perduto ben mai si racquista?"
Questa speranza mi sostenne un tempo;
or vien mancando, et troppo in lei m'attempo.   16

   Il tempo passa et l'ore son sì pronte
a fornire il viaggio,
ch' assai spazio non aggio
pur a pensar com' io corro a la morte;
a pena spunta in oriente un raggio
di sol, ch' a l'altro monte
de l'adverso orizonte
giunto il vedrai per vie lunghe et distorte.   24
   Le vite son sì corte,
sì gravi i corpi et frali
degli uomini mortali,
che quando io mi ritrovo dal bel viso
cotanto esser diviso,
col desio non possendo mover l'ali,
poco m'avanza del conforto usato,
né so quant' io mi viva in questo stato.   32

Every place makes me sad where I do not see those lovely sweet eyes that carried off the keys of my thoughts, which were sweet as long as it pleased God; and—so that harsh exile may weigh me down even more—if I sleep or walk or sit, I call out for nothing else, and all I have seen since them displeases me.

How many mountains and waters, how much ocean, how many rivers hide from me those two lights, which made my darkness into a clear sky at noon, so that remembering might destroy me the more, and that I might learn from my present cruel and burdensome life how joyous my life was then!

Alas, if by speaking I renew the burning desire that was born the day I left behind the better part of me, and if love can be cured by long forgetfulness, who then forces me back to the bait so that my pain may grow? And why do I not first turn to stone in silence?

Certainly crystal or glass never showed forth a color from within more clearly than my disconsolate soul shows forth through my eyes the cares and the savage sweetness that are in my heart, my eyes that, always eager to weep, seek day and night only for her who will still their desire.

Ogni loco m'atrista ov' io non veggio
quei begli occhi soavi
che portaron le chiavi
de' miei dolci pensier mentre a Dio piacque,
et perché 'l duro esilio più m'aggravi,
s' io dormo o vado o seggio
altro giamai non cheggio,
et ciò ch' i' vidi dopo lor mi spiacque.   40
   Quante montagne et acque,
quanto mar, quanti fiumi
m'ascondon que' duo lumi
che quasi un bel sereno a mezzo 'l die
fer le tenebre mie
a ciò che 'l rimembrar più mi consumi,
et quanto era mia vita allor gioiosa
m'insegni la presente aspra et noiosa.   48

   Lasso, se ragionando si rinfresca
quell'ardente desio
che nacque il giorno ch' io
lassai di me la miglior parte a dietro,
et s' amor se ne va per lungo oblio,
chi mi conduce a l'esca
onde 'l mio dolor cresca,
et perché pria tacendo non m'impetro?   56
   Certo, cristallo o vetro
non mostrò mai di fore
nascosto altro colore
che l'alma sconsolata assai non mostri
più chiari i pensier nostri
et la fera dolcezza ch' è nel core
per gli occhi, che di sempre pianger vaghi
cercan dì et notte pur chi glie n'appaghi.   64

Strange pleasure that in ɲuman minds is often found, to love whatever strange thing brings the thickest crowd of sighs! And I am one of those whom weeping pleases, and it seems that I exert myself that my eyes may always be pregnant with tears, as my heart is with sorrow.

And because speaking of her lovely eyes makes me wish it, and there is nothing that so touches me or makes itself felt so deep within me, I run often and go back within there, that my sorrow may flow more copiously and that both my eyes may be punished with my heart, for they guided me on the road of love.

Those tresses of gold, which ought to make the sun go filled with envy, and that lovely clear gaze where the rays of love are so hot that they kill me before my time, and those skillful words, rare in the world, or unique, which gave themselves to me so courteously,

are taken from me; and I pardon more easily every other offense but the denial of that kind angelic greeting, which used to awaken my heart to its powers with a burning desire; so that I do not think ever to hear anything that will strengthen me except in heaving sighs.

Novo piacer che ne gli umani ingegni
spesse volte si trova,
d'amar qual cosa nova
più folta schiera di sospiri accoglia!
Et io son un di quei che 'l pianger giova,
et par ben ch' io m'ingegni
che di lagrime pregni
sien gli occhi miei, sì come 'l cor di doglia.   72
   Et perché a ciò m'invoglia
ragionar de' begli occhi
né cosa è che mi tocchi
o sentir mi si faccia così a dentro,
corro spesso et rientro
colà donde più largo il duol trabocchi
et sien col cor punite ambe le luci
ch' a la strada d'Amor mi furon duci.   80

   Le treccie d'or che devrien fare il sole
d'invidia molta ir pieno,
e 'l bel guardo sereno
ove i raggi d'Amor sì caldi sono,
che mi fanno anzi tempo venir meno,
et l'accorte parole
rade nel mondo, o sole,
che mi fer già di sé cortese dono   88
   mi son tolte, et perdono
più lieve ogni altra offesa
che l'essermi contesa
quella benigna angelica salute
che 'l mio cor a vertute
destar solea con una voglia accesa,
tal ch' io non penso udir cosa giamai
che mi conforte ad altro ch' a trar guai.   96

And that I may weep still with more delight, her slender hands and her noble arms and her gestures sweetly haughty and her sweet disdain haughtily humble and her lovely youthful breast, a tower of high intellect—these mountainous and wild places hide them from me,

and I do not know if I can hope to see her before I die; for from time to time my hope lifts itself up, but then it cannot maintain itself and falling down again it affirms that it will never see her whom Heaven honors, in whom virtue and courtesy dwell, and where I pray that I may dwell.

Song, if in her sweet place you see our lady, I believe that you believe that she will reach out to you her hand, from which I am so distant; do not touch it, but reverently at her feet tell her that I shall be there as soon as I can, either a disembodied spirit or a man of flesh and bone.

Et per pianger ancor con più diletto,
le man bianche sottili
et le braccia gentili
et gli atti suoi soavemente alteri
e i dolci sdegni alteramente umili
e 'l bel giovenil petto,
torre d'alto intelletto,
mi celan questi luoghi alpestri et feri,   104
    et non so s' io mi speri
vederla anzi ch' io mora;
però ch' ad ora ad ora
s'erge la speme et poi non sa star ferma,
ma ricadendo afferma
di mai non veder lei che 'l ciel onora,
ov' alberga onestate et cortesia,
et dov' io prego che 'l mio albergo sia.   112

Canzon, s' al dolce loco
la donna nostra vedi,
credo ben che tu credi
ch' ella ti porgerà la bella mano
ond' io son sì lontano;
non la toccar, ma reverente ai piedi
le di' ch' io sarò là tosto ch' io possa,
o spirto ignudo od uom di carne et d'ossa.   120

38

Orso, there were never rivers nor lakes, nor sea where every stream empties itself, nor any shadow of wall or hill or branch, nor cloud that covers the sky and showers the world,

nor any other obstacle, however much it hinders human sight, of which I complain as much as of a veil that shades two lovely eyes and seems to say: "Now suffer and weep."

And that downward glance of theirs, which extinguishes all my joy, whether through humility or through pride will be the cause of my dying before my time.

And I complain also of a white hand that has always been alert to do me harm and has made itself an obstacle to my eyes.

Addressed to Orso dell'Anguillara, a prominent Roman nobleman.

39

I so fear the assault of those lovely eyes where Love and my death dwell that I flee them as a boy the rod; and it is a long time since I first leapt to flee.

From now on there is no place so laboriously high that my desire will not seek to mount, in order to avoid one who disperses my every sense and leaves me cold stone as she does.

Therefore, if I have turned back late to see you, in order not to come near her who destroys me, it is a failing perhaps not unworthy of pardon.

I say more: my returning to what one flees and my freeing my heart of so great a fear were no small pledge of my faithfulness toward you.

Addressed to an unidentified person, presumably a resident of Avignon.

38

Orso, e' non furon mai fiumi né stagni
né mare ov' ogni rivo si disgombra,
né di muro o di poggio o di ramo ombra,
né nebbia che 'l ciel copra e 'l mondo bagni,   4

né altro impedimento ond' io mi lagni,
qualunque più l'umana vista ingombra,
quanto d'un vel che due begli occhi adombra
et par che dica: "Or ti consuma et piagni."   8

Et quel lor inchinar ch' ogni mia gioia
spegne o per umiltate o per orgoglio
cagion sarà che 'nanzi tempo i' moia.   11

Et d'una bianca mano anco mi doglio
ch' è stata sempre accorta a farmi noia
et contra gli occhi miei s'è fatta scoglio.   14

39

Io temo sì de' begli occhi l'assalto
ne' quali Amore et la mia morte alberga,
ch' i' fuggo lor come fanciul la verga,
et gran tempo è ch' i' presi il primier salto.   4

Da ora inanzi faticoso od alto
loco non fia dove 'l voler non s'erga
per no scontrar chi miei sensi disperga
lassando, come suol, me freddo smalto.   8

Dunque s' a veder voi tardo mi volsi
per non ravvicinarmi a chi mi strugge,
fallir forse non fu di scusa indegno.   11

Più dico, che 'l tornar a quel ch' uom fugge
e'l cor che di paura tanta sciolsi
fur de la fede mia non leggier pegno.   14

40

If Love or Death does not cut short the new cloth that now I prepare to weave, and if I loose myself from the tenacious birdlime while I join one truth with the other,

I shall perhaps make a work so double between the style of the moderns and ancient speech that (fearfully I dare to say it) you will hear the noise of it even as far as Rome.

But, since I lack, to complete the work, some of the blessed threads that were so plenteous for that beloved father of mine,

why do you keep your hands so closed toward me, contrary to your custom? I beg you to open them, and you will see delightful things result.

Addressed to an unidentified person in Rome.

new cloth: which work of Petrarch's this may be is disputed (suggestions range from the *De remediis utriusque fortunae* to the *Secretum* to the *Rime sparse* themselves).   beloved father of mine: perhaps Livy, perhaps Augustine.

41

When from its own dwelling the tree departs that Phoebus loved in human form, Vulcan pants and sweats at his work in order to renew the harsh arrows for Jove,

who now thunders, now snows, now rains, without respecting Caesar more than Janus; earth weeps, and the sun stays far from us, for he sees his dear friend elsewhere.

Then Saturn and Mars regain boldness, cruel planets, and armed Orion shatters the unfortunate mariners' tillers and shrouds.

Aeolus, angry, makes Neptune and Juno feel, and us, how the lovely face awaited by the angels disappears.

---

its own dwelling: presumably Laura's home was in Avignon.   the tree: see note to poem 5.   harsh arrows: thunderbolts.   Caesar . . . Janus: the months of July and January.   Orion: the constellation traditionally thought to bring storms.   Aeolus . . . Neptune and Juno: god of the winds, god of the sea, and goddess of the air.

40

S' Amore o Morte non dà qualche stroppio
a la tela novella ch' ora ordisco,
et s' io mi svolvo dal tenace visco
mentre che l'un coll'altro vero accoppio,   4

i' farò forse un mio lavor sì doppio
tra lo stil de' moderni e 'l sermon prisco
che (paventosamente a dirlo ardisco)
in fin a Roma n'udirai lo scoppio.   8

Ma però che mi manca a fornir l'opra
alquanto de le fila benedette
ch' avanzaro a quel mio diletto padre,   11

perché tien verso me le man sì strette
contra tua usanza? I' prego che tu l'opra,
et vedrai riuscir cose leggiadre.   14

41

Quando dal proprio sito si rimove
l'arbor ch' amò già Febo in corpo umano,
sospira et suda a l'opera Vulcano
per rinfrescar l'aspre saette a Giove,   4

il qual or tona or nevica et or piove
senza onorar più Cesare che Giano;
la terra piange e 'l sol ci sta lontano
che la sua cara amica ved' altrove.   8

Allor riprende ardir Saturno et Marte,
crudeli stelle, et Orione armato
spezza a' tristi nocchier governi et sarte.   11

Eolo a Nettuno et a Giunon turbato
fa sentire et a noi come si parte
il bel viso dagli angeli aspettato.   14

42

But now that her sweet smile, humble and modest, hides no more its new beauties, the ancient Sicilian smith in vain moves his arms at the forge;

for Jove's arms have been taken out of his hand, though tempered in Aetna to all proof, and his sister seems gradually to be renewed in Apollo's beautiful gaze.

From the western shore there moves a breeze that makes the mariner secure without any exercise of art and awakens the flowers in the grass in every meadow.

Harmful planets flee on every hand, dispersed by her lovely face, for which many tears have already been scattered.

A continuation of the previous poem.

ancient Sicilian smith: Vulcan.   Jove's arms: thunderbolts.   Aetna: the Sicilian volcano, traditionally the location of Vulcan's forge.   his sister: Latona, identified by Macrobius and others as the earth.

43

The son of Latona had already looked down nine times from his high balcony, seeking her who once in vain moved his sighs and now moves those of another;

when, tired with searching, he could not discover where she was dwelling, whether near or far, he showed himself to us like one mad with grief at not finding some much-loved thing.

And thus sadly remaining off by himself, he did not see that face return which shall be praised, if I live, on more than a thousand pages;

and besides, pity had changed her, so that her beautiful eyes were at that time dropping tears: therefore the air retained its earlier state.

---

son of Latona: Apollo.

42

Ma poi che 'l dolce riso umile et piano
più non asconde sue bellezze nove,
le braccia a la fucina indarno move
l'antiquissimo fabbro ciciliano;   4

ch' a Giove tolte son l'arme di mano
temprate in Mongibello a tutte prove,
et sua sorella par che si rinove
nel bel guardo d'Apollo a mano a mano.   8

Del lito occidental si move un fiato
che fa securo il navigar senza arte
et desta i fior tra l'erba in ciascun prato;   11

stelle noiose fuggon d'ogni parte,
disperse dal bel viso inamorato
per cui lagrime molte son già sparte.   14

43

Il figliuol di Latona avea già nove
volte guardato dal balcon sovrano
per quella ch' alcun tempo mosse in vano
i suoi sospiri et or gli altrui commove;   4

poi che cercando stanco non seppe ove
s'albergasse da presso o di lontano,
mostrossi a noi qual uom per doglia insano
che molto amata cosa non ritrove.   8

Et così tristo standosi in disparte,
tornar non vide il viso che laudato
sarà, s' io vivo, in più di mille carte,   11

et pietà lui medesmo avea cangiato
sì che' begli occhi lagrimavan parte:
però l'aere ritenne il primo stato.   14

44

He who had hands so ready to make Thessaly crimson
with civil blood wept for the dead husband of his daughter,
recognized by his well-known features;

and the shepherd who broke Goliath's forehead wept for his
rebellious family and changed his brow over the good Saul, for
which the wild mountain has much cause to grieve.

But you, whom pity never makes pale and who have your
defenses always ready against Love's bow, which he draws in
vain,

you see me torn asunder by a thousand deaths, but nevertheless
no tear has ever fallen from your eyes, but only disdain and
anger.

He who...wept for: Julius Caesar, who defeated his son-in-law and rival
Pompey at the battle of Pharsalia in Thessaly and was said to have wept (according to Lucan, insincerely; according to others, sincerely) when presented
with the head of Pompey, treacherously killed by Ptolemy of Egypt.
shepherd who...wept for: David, who wept over the death of his rebellious
son Absalon (2 Samuel 18:33). When he received word of the death of Saul from
the man who claimed to have killed him, he killed the man in his grief and
cursed Mount Gilboam, where Saul died, so that it became infertile (2 Samuel
1:21).

45

My adversary in whom you are wont to see your eyes, which
Love and Heaven honor, enamors you with beauties not his but
sweet and happy beyond mortal guise.

By his counsel, Lady, you have driven me out of my sweet
dwelling: miserable exile! even though I may not be worthy to
dwell where you alone are.

But if I had been nailed there firmly, a mirror should not have
made you, because you pleased yourself, harsh and proud to my
harm.

Certainly, if you remember Narcissus, this and that course lead
to one goal—although the grass is unworthy of so lovely a
flower.

My adversary: Laura's mirror.   Narcissus: cursed by a lover he had cruel-
ly rejected, Narcissus fell in love with his own image reflected in a forest spring
and wasted away, ultimately transformed into the flower narcissus. (Ovid,
Metamorphoses 3.344–510.)

44

Que' che 'n Tesaglia ebbe le man sì pronte
a farla del civil sangue vermiglia
pianse morto il marito di sua figlia
raffigurato a le fatezze conte;   4

e 'l pastor ch' a Golia ruppe la fronte
pianse la ribellante sua famiglia,
et sopra 'l buon Saul cangiò le ciglia,
ond' assai può dolersi il fiero monte.   8

Ma voi, che mai pietà non discolora
et ch' avete gli schermi sempre accorti
contra l'arco d'Amor che 'ndarno tira,   11

mi vedete straziare a mille morti
né lagrima però discese ancora
da' be' vostr'occhi, ma disdegno et ira.   14

45

Il mio adversario in cui veder solete
gli occhi vostri ch' Amore e 'l Ciel onora
colle non sue bellezze v'innamora
più che 'n guisa mortal soavi et liete.   4

Per consiglio di lui, Donna, m'avete
scacciato del mio dolce albergo fora:
misero esilio! avegna ch' i' non fora
d'abitar degno ove voi sola siete.   8

Ma s' io v'era con saldi chiovi fisso,
non dovea specchio farvi per mio danno
a voi stessa piacendo aspra et superba.   11

Certo, se vi rimembra di Narcisso,
questo et quel corso ad un termino vanno—
ben che di sì bel fior sia indegna l'erba.   14

46

The gold and the pearls, and the red and white flowers that the winter should have made languid and dry, are for me sharp and poisonous thorns that I feel along my breast and my sides.

Therefore my days will be tearful and cut short, for it is rare that a great sorrow grows old, but most I blame those murderous mirrors which you have tired out with your love of yourself.

These imposed silence on my lord, who was praying to you for me; and he became still, seeing your desire ended in yourself.

These were made beside the waters of hell and tempered in the eternal forgetfulness whence the beginning of my death was born.

47

I felt already failing within my heart the spirits that receive life from you; and, since every earthly animal by nature defends itself against death,

I let loose my desire, which now I hold tightly reined in, and I sent it off on the way that is almost lost (because night and day it calls me there, and I against its will lead it elsewhere),

and it led me, late and ashamed, to see your lovely eyes, which I avoid in order not to pain them.

I shall live on a short time now, since one glance of yours has so much power for my life; and then I shall die, unless I obey my desire.

46

L'oro et le perle e i fior vermigli e i bianchi
che 'l verno devria far languidi et secchi
son per me acerbi et velenosi stecchi
ch' io provo per lo petto et per li fianchi.   4

Però i dì miei fien lagrimosi et manchi,
ché gran duol rade volte aven che 'nvecchi;
ma più ne colpo i micidiali specchi
che 'n vagheggiar voi stessa avete stanchi.   8

Questi poser silenzio al signor mio
che per me vi pregava, ond' ei si tacque
veggendo in voi finir vostro desio;   11

questi fuor fabbricati sopra l'acque
d'abisso et tinti ne l'eterno oblio
onde 'l principio de mia morte nacque.   14

47

Io sentia dentr' al cor già venir meno
gli spirti che da voi ricevon vita;
et perché naturalmente s'aita
contra la morte ogni animal terreno,   4

largai 'l desio che i' teng' or molto a freno
et misil per la via quasi smarrita
però che dì e notte indi m'invita
et io contra sua voglia altronde 'l meno,   8

et mi condusse vergognoso et tardo
a riveder gli occhi leggiadri ond' io
per non esser lor grave assai mi guardo.   11

Vivrommi un tempo omai, ch' al viver mio
tanta virtude à sol un vostro sguardo;
et poi morrò, s' io non credo al desio.   14

48

If fire was never put out by fire, nor river ever made dry by rain, but always like is made to grow by like, and sometimes opposite has kindled opposite;

Love, you who govern our thoughts, on whom my one soul in two bodies depends, why in my soul, in unaccustomed guise, do you make desire grow less through desiring much?

Perhaps, as the Nile, falling from on high, with its great noise deafens those who dwell nearby, and as the sun dazzles him who looks on it fixedly,

thus desire, which keeps no proportion with itself, is lost in an object too immense, and through too much spurring flight is slowed.

49

Although I have kept you from lying, as far as I could, and paid you much honor, ungrateful tongue, still you have not brought me honor but shame and anger;

for, the more I need your help to ask for mercy, the colder and colder you stay, and if you say any words they are broken and like those of a man dreaming!

Sad tears, you also every night accompany me, when I wish to be alone, and then you flee when my peace comes!

And you sighs, so ready to give me anguish and sorrow, then you move slow and broken! Only my eyes are not silent about my heart.

48

Se mai foco per foco non si spense
né fiume fu giamai secco per pioggia,
ma sempre l'un per l'altro simil poggia
et spesso l'un contrario l'altro accense, 4

Amor, tu che' pensier nostri dispense,
al qual un'alma in due corpi s'appoggia,
perché fai in lei con disusata foggia
men per molto voler le voglie intense? 8

Forse sì come 'l Nil d'alto caggendo
col gran suono i vicin d'intorno assorda,
e'l sole abbaglia chi ben fiso 'l guarda, 11

così 'l desio che seco non s'accorda
ne lo sfrenato obietto vien perdendo,
et per troppo spronar la fuga è tarda. 14

49

Perch' io t'abbia guardata di menzogna
a mio podere et onorato assai,
ingrata lingua, già però non m'ài
renduto onor, ma fatto ira et vergogna; 4

ché quanto più 'l tuo aiuto mi bisogna
per dimandar mercede, allor ti stai
sempre più fredda, et se parole fai
son imperfette et quasi d'uom che sogna! 8

Lagrime triste, et voi tutte le notti
m'accompagnate ov' io vorrei star solo,
poi fuggite dinanzi a la mia pace! 11

Et voi, sì pronti a darmi angoscia et duolo,
sospiri, allor traete lenti et rotti!
Solo la vista mia del cor non tace. 14

50

At the time when the swift heaven inclines toward the West
and our day flies to people who perhaps await it, beyond, seeing
herself alone in a distant country the tired old woman redoubles
her pilgrim steps and hastens more and more;

and then though alone at the end of her day she is sometimes
consoled by some brief repose where she forgets the labor and
the pain of the way she has passed through. But, alas, whatever
pain the day brings me grows when the eternal light moves to
depart from us.

When the sun turns his flaming wheels to give place to night
and the shadows descend more widely from the highest
mountains, the poor hoer takes up his tools and with words and
mountain tunes lightens his breast of all heaviness;

and then he burdens his table with poor food, similar to those
acorns which all praise and avoid. But let who will be gay from
time to time: for I have never had, I shall not say a happy, but a
restful hour, for all the turning of sky or planet.

50

Ne la stagion che 'l ciel rapido inchina
verso occidente, et che 'l dì nostro vola
a gente che di là forse l'aspetta,
veggendosi in lontan paese sola
la stanca vecchiarella pellegrina
raddoppia i passi et più et più s'affretta;   6
  et poi così soletta
al fin di sua giornata
talora è consolata
d'alcun breve riposo, ov' ella oblia
la noia e 'l mal de la passata via.
Ma, lasso, ogni dolor che 'l dì m'adduce
cresce qualor s'invia
per partirsi da noi l'eterna luce.   14

Come 'l sol volga le 'nfiammate rote
per dar luogo a la notte, onde discende
dagli altissimi monti maggior l'ombra,
l'avaro zappador l'arme riprende
et con parole et con alpestri note
ogni gravezza del suo petto sgombra;   20
  et poi la mensa ingombra
di povere vivande
simili a quelle ghiande
le qua' fuggendo tutto 'l mondo onora.
Ma chi vuol si rallegri ad ora ad ora,
ch' i' pur non ebbi ancor, non dirò lieta,
ma riposata un'ora,
né per volger di ciel né di pianeta.   28

When the shepherd sees the rays of the great planet falling toward the nest where it dwells, and the eastern countryside becoming dark, he rises to his feet and, leaving the grass and the fountains and the beech trees, with his accustomed staff he gently moves his flock;

then, far from people, he enwithes with green branches a hut or a cave; there without cares he stretches himself out and sleeps. Ah cruel Love! but you then most shape me to pursue the voice and the steps and the footprints of a wild creature who destroys me, and you do not seize her, she crouches and flees.

And mariners in some closed valley throw down their limbs, when the sun hides himself, on the hard wood and under the coarse canvas. But I, though he dive into the midst of the wave and leave Spain behind his back and Granada and Morocco and the Columns,

and men and women and the world and animals calm their ills, I put no end to my obstinate trouble: and I grieve that each day adds to my losses, for I am already, still growing in this desire, very near to the tenth year, nor can I guess who will set me free from it.

Quando vede 'l pastor calare i raggi
del gran pianeta al nido ov' egli alberga
e 'mbrunir le contrade d'oriente,
drizzasi in piedi et co l'usata verga,
lassando l'erba et le fontane e i faggi,
move la schiera sua soavemente;   34
    poi lontan da la gente
o casetta o spelunca
di verdi frondi ingiunca,
ivi senza pensier s'adagia et dorme.
Ahi crudo Amor, ma tu allor più m'informe
a seguir d'una fera che mi strugge
la voce e i passi et l'orme,
et lei non stringi che s'appiatta et fugge.   42

E i naviganti in qualche chiusa valle
gettan le membra, poi che 'l sol s'asconde,
sul duro legno et sotto a l'aspre gonne.
Ma io, perché s'attuffi in mezzo l'onde
et lasci Ispagna dietro a le sue spalle
et Granata et Marrocco et le Colonne,   48
    et gli uomini e le donne
e 'l mondo et gli animali
acquetino i lor mali,
fine non pongo al mio ostinato affanno;
et duolmi ch' ogni giorno arroge al danno,
ch' i' son già pur crescendo in questa voglia
ben presso al decim' anno,
né poss' indovinar chi me ne scioglia.   56

And—let me vent myself somewhat in speaking—I see at
evening the oxen returning unharnessed from the fields and the
furrows they have plowed. My sighs, why are they not taken
from me at any time whatsoever? why not my heavy yoke? Why
day and night are my eyes wet?

Miserable me! What was I doing when for the first time I kept
them so fixed on her lovely face, to sculpture it for imagination
in a place whence it would never be moved by any art or force,
until I become the prey of Death, who separates all things? Nor
do I know what to think of her.

Song, if being with me from morning to night has made you of
my party, you will not wish to show yourself everywhere; and
you will be so careless of praise that it will be enough for you to
think from hill to hill how I am reduced by the fire from this
living stone on which I lean.

Et perché un poco nel parlar mi sfogo,
veggio la sera i buoi tornare sciolti
da le campagne et da' solcati colli.
I miei sospiri a me perché non tolti
quando che sia? perché no 'l grave giogo?
perché dì et notte gli occhi miei son molli?   62
    Misero me, che volli
quando primier sì fiso
gli tenni nel bel viso
per iscolpirlo, imaginando, in parte
onde mai né per forza né per arte
mosso sarà fin ch' i' sia dato in preda
a chi tutto diparte!
né so ben anco che di lei mi creda.   70

    Canzon, se l'esser meco
dal matino a la sera
t'à fatto di mia schiera,
tu non vorrai mostrarti in ciascun loco;
et d'altrui loda curerai sì poco
ch' assai ti fia pensar di poggio in poggio
come m'à concio 'l foco
di questa viva petra ov' io m'appoggio.   78

51

Had it come any closer to my eyes, the light that dazzles them from afar, then, just as Thessaly saw her change, I would have changed my every form.

And, since I cannot take on her form any more than I have already (not that it wins me any mercy), my face marked with care, I would be today whatever stone is hardest to cut,

either diamond, or fair marble white for fear perhaps, or a crystal later prized by the greedy and ignorant mob;

and I would be free of my heavy, harsh yoke, because of which I envy that tired old man who with his shoulders makes a shade for Morocco.

Thessaly: see note to poem 5.   old man: the giant Atlas, transformed into a mountain by the head of Medusa, which Perseus showed him on being denied hospitality (Ovid, *Metamorphoses* 4.631–662).

52

Not so much did Diana please her lover when, by a similar chance, he saw her all naked amid the icy waters,

as did the cruel mountain shepherdess please me, set to wash a pretty veil that keeps her lovely blond head from the breeze;

so that she made me, even now when the sky is burning, all tremble with a chill of love.

---

her lover: Actaeon; see note on "stag," poem 23.

51

Poco era ad appressarsi agli occhi miei
la luce che da lunge gli abbarbaglia,
che, come vide lei cangiar Tesaglia,
così cangiato ogni mia forma avrei.   4

Et s' io non posso trasformarmi in lei
più ch' i' mi sia (non ch' a mercé mi vaglia),
di qual petra più rigida s'intaglia
pensoso ne la vista oggi sarei,   8

o di diamante, o d'un bel marmo bianco
per la paura forse, o d'un diaspro
pregiato poi dal vulgo avaro et sciocco;   11

et sarei fuor del grave giogo et aspro
per cui i' ò invidia di quel vecchio stanco
che fa co le sue spalle ombra a Marrocco.   14

52

Non al suo amante più Diana piacque
quando per tal ventura tutta ignuda
la vide in mezzo de le gelide acque,   3

ch' a me la pastorella alpestra et cruda
posta a bagnar un leggiadretto velo
ch' a l'aura il vago et biondo capel chiuda;   6

tal che mi fece, or quand' egli arde 'l cielo,
tutto tremar d'un amoroso gielo.   8

53

Noble spirit, you who govern those members within which dwells pilgrim a valorous, knowing, and wise lord: now that you have gained the honored staff wherewith you correct Rome and her erring citizens and call her back to her ancient path,

I speak to you because I do not see elsewhere a ray of virtue, which is extinguished in the world, nor do I find anyone who is ashamed of doing ill. What Italy expects or yearns for I do not know, for she does not seem to feel her woes, being old, idle, and slow. Will she sleep forever, and will no one ever awaken her? Might I have my hand clutched in her hair!

I do not hope that she will ever move her head from her sluggish sleep for any shouting one can do, she is so heavily oppressed and by such a weight; but not without destiny is our head, Rome, now entrusted to your arms, which can shake her strongly and raise her up.

Put your hand into those venerable locks confidently and into those unkempt tresses, so that this neglectful one may come out of the mud. I, who day and night bewail her torment, place the greater part of my hopes in you: for if the people of Mars are ever to lift up their eyes to their own honor, it seems to me that the grace will befall in your days.

The recipient of this poem may have been the tribune Cola di Rienzo, whose attempt (1347) to reinstate the Roman Republic Petrarch initially supported.

53

Spirto gentil che quelle membra reggi
dentro a le qua' peregrinando alberga
un signor valoroso accorto et saggio:
poi che se' giunto a l'onorata verga
colla qual Roma et suoi erranti correggi
et la richiami al suo antiquo viaggio,   6
    io parlo a te però ch' altrove un raggio
non veggio di vertù, ch' al mondo è spenta,
né trovo chi di mal far si vergogni.
Che s'aspetti non so, né che s'agogni
Italia, che suoi guai non par che senta,
vecchia oziosa et lenta;
dormirà sempre et non fia chi la svegli?
Le man l'avess' io avolto entro' capegli!   14

Non spero che giamai dal pigro sonno
  mova la testa per chiamar ch' uom faccia,
sì gravemente è oppressa et di tal soma;
ma non senza destino a le tue braccia
che scuoter forte et sollevar la ponno
è or commesso il nostro capo Roma.   20
    Pon man in quella venerabil chioma
securamente, et ne le trecce sparte,
sì che la neghittosa esca del fango.
I' che dì et notte del suo strazio piango
di mia speranza ò in te la maggior parte,
ché se 'l popol di Marte
devesse al proprio onore alzar mai gli occhi,
parmi pur ch' a' tuoi dì la grazia tocchi.   28

The ancient walls, which the world still fears and loves and trembles at when it remembers past time and looks back, and the stones where were enclosed the bodies of men who will not be without fame until the universe is dissolved,

and everything which this one ruin carries down, hope through you to repair their every flaw. O great Scipios, O faithful Brutus, how pleasing to you is the news, if it has come to you down there, of how well the office has been placed! How glad I believe Fabricius is, hearing word of it, and he says: "My Rome shall be beautiful again!"

And, if there is any care in Heaven for earthly things, the souls who are citizens up there and have abandoned their bodies to earth beg you for an end to the long civil enmity, because of which the people are not safe, and the path of pilgrimage to their temples is closed,

which were so well tended and now in war have become almost the dens of thieves, and only to the good is the door closed, and among their altars and statues stripped of ornament every cruel enterprise takes place. Ah, how changed these actions! nor do they begin assaults without sounding bells that were placed on high to give thanks to God.

Scipios: the conquerors of Carthage.   Brutus: L. Junius Brutus, founder of the Roman Republic, who led the rebellion against the tyrannical king Tarquin (said to have occurred in 509 B.C.).   Fabricius: C. Fabricius Luscinus, Roman general and consul, victor over Pyrrhus, king of Epirus (third century B.C.).

L'antiche mura ch' ancor teme et ama
et trema 'l mondo quando si rimembra
del tempo andato e 'n dietro si rivolve,
e i sassi dove fur chiuse le membra
di ta' che non saranno senza fama
se l'universo pria non si dissolve,   34
    et tutto quel ch' una ruina involve,
per te spera saldar ogni suo vizio.
O grandi Scipioni, o fedel Bruto,
quanto v'aggrada s' egli è ancor venuto
romor là giù del ben locato offizio!
Come cre' che Fabrizio
si faccia lieto udendo la novella,
et dice: "Roma mia sarà ancor bella!"   42

Et se cosa di qua nel ciel si cura,
l'anime che lassù son cittadine
et ànno i corpi abandonati in terra
del lungo odio civil ti pregan fine
per cui la gente ben non s'assecura,
onde 'l camin a' lor tetti si serra,   48
    che fur già sì devoti, et ora in guerra
quasi spelunca di ladron son fatti,
tal ch' a' buon solamente uscio si chiude,
et tra gli altari et tra le statue ignude
ogni impresa crudel par che se tratti
(deh quanto diversi atti!),
né senza squille s'incomincia assalto
che per Dio ringraziar fur poste in alto.   56

The women in tears, and the defenseless throng of the young, and the exhausted old, who hate themselves and their too long life, and the black friars and the gray and the white, and all the other squadrons of the unfortunate and sick, cry: "O our Lord, help, help!"

and the terrified poor people show you their wounds by thousands and thousands, which would make Hannibal, not to speak of anyone else, pity them. And, if you look well at the House of God, which today is all aflame, if you put out a few sparks the wills that today are so aflame will be calmed: for which your works will be praised in Heaven.

Bears, wolves, lions, eagles, and snakes give frequent trouble to a great marble Column and to themselves do harm; because of them that noble lady weeps who has called you to uproot from her the evil plants that do not know how to flower.

More than a thousand years have passed since those noble souls died who placed her where she was. Ah new people, haughty beyond measure, irreverent to so great a mother! You be her husband, you her father: all help is looked for at your hand, for the greater Father is intent on other works.

Bears...snakes: the various rival families in Rome opposed to the Colonna family.   Column: Stefano Colonna the Elder.

Le donne lagrimose, e 'l vulgo inerme
de la tenera etate, e i vecchi stanchi
ch' ànno sé in odio et la soverchia vita,
e i neri fraticelli, e i bigi, e i bianchi,
coll'altre schiere travagliate e 'nferme,
gridan: "O signor nostro, aita, aita!"   62
    et la povera gente sbigottita
ti scopre le sue piaghe a mille a mille,
ch' Anibale, non ch' altri, farian pio.
Et se ben guardi a la magion di Dio
ch' arde oggi tutta, assai poche faville
spegnendo fien tranquille
le voglie che si mostran sì 'nfiammate,
onde fien l'opre tue nel ciel laudate.   70

    Orsi, lupi, leoni, aquile, et serpi
ad una gran marmorea colonna
fanno noia sovente et a sé danno;
di costor piange quella gentil donna
che t'à chiamato a ciò che di lei sterpi   75
le male piante che fiorir non sanno.
    Passato è già più che 'l millesimo anno
che 'n lei mancar quell'anime leggiadre
che locata l'avean là dov' ell' era.
Ahi nova gente oltra misura altera,
irreverente a tanta et a tal madre!
Tu marito, tu padre:
ogni soccorso di tua man s'attende,
che 'l maggior padre ad altr' opera intende.   84

It rarely happens that injurious Fortune does not fight against high undertakings, for she agrees unwillingly to daring deeds. Now, smoothing the steps by which you have entered, she makes me forgive many other offenses, for at least here she is different from herself;

for, as long as the world can remember, to no mortal man was ever the way so open, as it is to you, to make himself eternal in fame; for you can raise to her feet, if I do not discern falsely, the most noble monarchy in the world. How much glory for you will be the saying: "The others helped her when she was young and strong: this man rescued her from death in her old age!"

On the Tarpeian Mount, Song, you will see a knight whom all Italy honors, who cares more for others than for himself. Say to him: "One who has not yet seen you from close by, except as one falls in love through fame, says that Rome now with her eyes wet with tears keeps crying out to you for mercy from all her seven hills."

Tarpeian Mount: the Capitoline Hill in Rome, where the Tarpeian Rock was located.

Rade volte adiven ch' a l'alte imprese
fortuna ingiuriosa non contrasti,
ch' a gli animosi fatti mal s'accorda.
Ora sgombrando 'l passo onde tu intrasti
famisi perdonar molt' altre offese,
ch' al men qui da se stessa si discorda;   90
    peró che quanto 'l mondo si ricorda
ad uom mortal non fu aperta la via
per farsi, come a te, di fama eterno,
che puoi drizzar, s' i' non falso discerno,
in stato la più nobil monarchia.
Quanta gloria ti fia
dir: "Gli altri l'aitar giovene et forte,
questi in vecchiezza la scampò da morte."   98

Sopra 'l monte Tarpeio, canzon, vedrai
un cavalier ch' Italia tutta onora,
pensoso più d'altrui che di se stesso.
Digli: "Un che non ti vide ancor da presso,
se non come per fama uom s'innamora,
dice che Roma ogniora
con gli occhi di dolor bagnati et molli
ti chier mercé da tutti sette i colli."   106

54

Because in her face she carried the ensign of Love, a foreign beauty moved my vain heart, for every other seemed to me less worthy of honor;

and, as I followed her across the green grass, I heard a loud voice say from afar: "Ah, how many steps you are wasting through the wood!"

Then I drew myself to the shadow of a handsome beech, all full of care, and looking about me I saw my path to be most perilous; and I turned back almost at midday.

55

That fire which I thought had gone out because of the cold season and my age no longer fresh, now renews flames and suffering in my soul.

They were never entirely extinguished, as I see, those embers, but somewhat covered over; and I am afraid that my second error will be the worse. In tears that I scatter by thousands and thousands

my sorrow must flow forth through my eyes from my heart, which has in it the sparks and the tinder, not merely as it was before, but, I fear, growing.

What fire would not have been put out by the floods that my sad eyes are always pouring forth? Love, though I have been tardy in seeing it, wishes me to be untuned between two contraries;

and he puts out snares of such different temper that, when I most hope that my heart can get free of them, then he most enlimes me again with that lovely face.

54

Perch' al viso d'Amor portava insegna,
mosse una pellegrina il mio cor vano,
ch' ogni altra mi parea d'onor men degna;   3

et lei seguendo su per l'erbe verdi,
udi' dir alta voce di lontano:
"Ahi quanti passi per la selva perdi!"   6

Allor mi strinsi a l'ombra d'un bel faggio
tutto pensoso, e rimirando intorno
vidi assai periglioso il mio viaggio;
et tornai in dietro quasi a mezzo 'l giorno.   10

55

Quel foco ch' i' pensai che fosse spento
dal freddo tempo et da l'età men fresca
fiamma et martir ne l'anima rinfresca.   3

Non fur mai tutte spente, a quel ch' i' veggio,
ma ricoperte alquanto le faville,
et temo no 'l secondo error sia peggio.
Per lagrime ch' i' spargo a mille a mille
conven che 'l duol per gli occhi si distille
dal cor, ch' à seco le faville et l'esca,
non pur qual fu, ma pare a me che cresca.   10

Qual foco non avrian già spento et morto
l'onde che gli occhi tristi versan sempre?
Amor, avegna mi sia tardi accorto,
vol che tra duo contrari mi distempre,
et tende lacci in sì diverse tempre
che quand' ò più speranza che 'l cor n'esca,
allor più nel bel viso mi rinvesca.   17

56

If, counting the hours with the blind desire that tortures my heart, I do not deceive myself, now, as I speak, the time is passing that was promised to me and to mercy together.

What shadow is so cruel that it blasts the seed so close to the desired fruit? And within my sheepfold what wild beast roars? Between the grain and my hand what wall is set?

Alas, I do not know; but I do know well that Love brought me into such joyous hope in order to make my life more sorrowful;

and now I remember what I have read: that before the day of his last departure no man is to be called happy.

57

My good fortune is late and slow in coming, my hope uncertain, and my desire mounts and grows, so that both forsaking and waiting are painful to me; and then they are swifter than tigers to depart.

Alas! snow will be warm and black, the sea without waves, and all the fish in the mountains, and the sun will lie down beyond where Euphrates and Tigris have their one source,

before I find in this either peace or truce, or Love or my lady learn another fashion, who have plotted wrongfully against me;

and if I experience any sweetness, it is after so much bitterness that for chagrin the taste is lost. Nothing else ever comes to me from their graces.

56

Se col cieco desir che 'l cor distrugge
contando l'ore no m'inganno io stesso,
ora mentre ch' io parlo il tempo fugge
ch' a me fu insieme et a mercé promesso.   4

Qual ombra è sì crudel che 'l seme adugge
ch' al disiato frutto era sì presso?
et dentro dal mio ovil qual fera rugge?
tra la spiga et la man qual muro è messo?   8

Lasso, nol so, ma sì conosco io bene
che per far più dogliosa la mia vita
Amor m'addusse in sì gioiosa spene;   11

et or di quel ch' i' ò letto mi sovene,
che 'nanzi al dì de l'ultima partita
uom beato chiamar non si convene.   14

57

Mie venture al venir son tarde et pigre,
la speme incerta, e 'l desir monta et cresce,
onde e 'l lassare et l'aspettar m'increscre;
et poi al partir son più levi che tigre.   4

Lasso, le nevi fien tepide et nigre,
e 'l mar senz' onda, et per l'alpe ogni pesce,
et corcherassi il sol là oltre, ond' esce
d'un medesimo fonte Eufrate e Tigre,   8

prima ch' i' trovi in ciò pace né triegua
o Amore o Madonna altr' uso impari,
che m'ànno congiurato a torto incontra;   11

et s' i' ò alcun dolce, è dopo tanti amari
che per disdegno il gusto si dilegua.
Altro mai di lor grazie non m'incontra.   14

58

Rest on one of these, my dear Lord, your cheek which has been tired by weeping; and from now on be more chary of yourself to that cruel one who makes his followers pale.

With the second close off the road on the left to those messengers of his who come that way, and show yourself the same in August as in January, for time grows short for the long way.

And with the third, drink a juice of herbs that will purge your heart of all afflicting cares, sweet at the end though at the beginning sour.

Place me where pleasures are stored up, so that I may not fear the ferryman of Styx—if my request is not presumptuous.

The recipient of this poem has not been identified.
one of these: presumably a pillow.   that cruel one: Love.   the second: perhaps a book of moral reflections.   road on the left: the left side is traditionally that of the irrational, of appetite.   the third: perhaps a cup.   me: the poem, imagined to be speaking.   ferryman of Styx: Charon, who ferries souls in Virgil's underworld. The poem hopes it will be immortal.

59

Although the fault of another takes away from me what drew me first to love, it by no means dissuades me from my firm desire.

Amid the locks of gold Love hid the noose with which he bound me; from those lovely eyes came the freezing ice that passed into my heart
     with the power of a sudden splendor, and the very memory still strips my heart of all other desires.

The sweet sight of that blond hair has since been taken from me, alas; and the motion of two virtuous and lovely lights makes me sad with its flight;
     but, since a good death brings honor, I do not wish Love to loose me from such a knot, for all death or suffering can do.

58

La guancia che fu già piangendo stanca
riposate su l'un, Signor mio caro,
et siate ormai di voi stesso più avaro
a quel crudel che' suoi seguaci imbianca;   4

coll'altro richiudete da man manca
la strada a' messi suoi ch' indi passaro,
mostrandovi un d'agosto et di gennaro,
perch' a la lunga via tempo ne manca;   8

et col terzo bevete un suco d'erba
che purghe ogni pensier che 'l cor afflige,
dolce a la fine et nel principio acerba.   11

Me riponete ove 'l piacer si serba
tal ch' i' non tema del nocchier di Stige—
se la preghiera mia non è superba.   14

59

   Perché quel che mi trasse ad amar prima
altrui colpa mi toglia,
del mio fermo voler già non mi svoglia.   3

Tra le chiome de l'or nascose il laccio
al qual mi strinse Amore,
et da' begli occhi mosse il freddo ghiaccio
che mi passò nel core   7
   con la vertù d'un subito splendore,
che d'ogni altra sua voglia
sol rimembrando ancor l'anima spoglia.   10

Tolta m'è poi di que' biondi capelli,
lasso, la dolce vista,
e 'l volger de' duo lumi onesti et belli
col suo fuggir m'atrista,   14
   ma perché ben morendo onor s'acquista,
per morte né per doglia
non vo' che da tal nodo Amor mi sciolga.   17

60

The noble tree that I have strongly loved for many years, while its lovely branches did not disdain me, made my weak wit flower in its shade and grow in my troubles.

When, I thinking such deceit was absent, it turned from sweet to bitter wood, I turned my thoughts all to one mark, and they now speak always of their sad misfortunes.

What can some lover say, if my youthful rhymes had given him another hope and he loses it because of her?

"Let no poet ever gather from it, nor let Jove favor it, and let it receive the sun's anger so that all its green leaves dry up!"

---

noble tree: the laurel.

61

Blessed be the day and the month and the year and the season and the time and the hour and the instant and the beautiful countryside and the place where I was struck by the two lovely eyes that have bound me;

and blessed be the first sweet trouble I felt on being made one with Love, and the bow and the arrows that pierced me, and the wounds that reach my heart!

Blessed be the many words I have scattered calling the name of my lady, and the sighs and the tears and the desire;

and blessed be all the pages where I gain fame for her, and my thoughts, which are only of her, so that no other has part in them!

60

L' arbor gentil che forte amai molt'anni
(mentre i bei rami non m'ebber a sdegno)
fiorir faceva il mio debile ingegno
a la sua ombra et crescer negli affanni.   4

Poi che, securo me di tali inganni,
fece di dolce sé spietato legno,
i' rivolsi i pensier tutti ad un segno,
che parlan sempre de' lor tristi danni.   8

Che porà dir chi per amor sospira,
s' altra speranza le mie rime nove
gli avesser data et per costei la perde?   11

"Né poeta ne colga mai, né Giove
la privilegi, et al sol venga in ira
tal che si secchi ogni sua foglia verde!"   14

61

Benedetto sia 'l giorno e 'l mese et l'anno
e la stagione e 'l tempo et l'ora e 'l punto
e 'l bel paese e 'l loco ov' io fui giunto
da' duo begli occhi che legato m'ànno;   4

et benedetto il primo dolce affanno
ch' i' ebbi ad esser con Amor congiunto,
et l'arco e le saette ond' i' fui punto,
et le piaghe che 'nfin al cor mi vanno.   8

Benedette le voci tante ch' io
chiamando il nome de mia donna ò sparte,
e i sospiri et le lagrime e 'l desio;   11

et benedette sian tutte le carte
ov' io fama l'acquisto, e 'l pensier mio,
ch' è sol di lei sì ch' altra non v'à parte.   14

62

Father of Heaven, after the lost days, after the nights spent raving with that fierce desire that was lit in my heart when I looked on those gestures so lovely to my hurt,

let it please you at last that with your light I may return to a different life and to more beautiful undertakings, so that, having spread his nets in vain, my harsh adversary may be disarmed.

Now turns, my Lord, the eleventh year that I have been subject to the pitiless yoke that which is always most fierce to the most submissive:

have mercy on my unworthy pain, lead my wandering thoughts back to a better place, remind them that today you were on the Cross.

---

adversary: Satan.

63

Turning your eyes to my strange color, which makes people remember death, pity moved you; wherefore, kindly greeting me, you kept my heart alive.

The frail life that still dwells with me was the open gift of your lovely eyes and your angelic sweet voice; I recognize that the being I have is from them, for they, as one rouses a lazy animal with a rod, so awakened in me my heavy soul.

Lady, you have both keys of my heart in your hand, and of that I am glad, ready to set sail with every wind; for everything from you is to me a sweet honor.

62

Padre del Ciel, dopo i perduti giorni,
dopo le notti vaneggiando spese
con quel fero desio ch' al cor s'accese,
mirando gli atti per mio mal sì adorni,   4

piacciati omai col tuo lume ch' io torni
ad altra vita et a più belle imprese,
sì ch' avendo le reti indarno tese
il mio duro avversario se ne scorni.   8

Or volge, Signor mio, l'undecimo anno
ch' i' fui sommesso al dispietato giogo
che sopra i più soggetti è più feroce: 11

miserere del mio non degno affanno,
reduci i pensier vaghi a miglior luogo,
rammenta lor come oggi fusti in croce.   14

63

Volgendo gli occhi al mio novo colore,
che fa di morte rimembrar la gente,
pietà vi mosse; onde benignamente
salutando teneste in vita il core.   4

La fraile vita ch' ancor meco alberga
fu de' begli occhi vostri aperto dono
et de la voce angelica soave;
da lor conosco l'esser ov' io sono,
che, come suol pigro animal per verga,
così destaro in me l'anima grave.   10
Del mio cor, Donna, l'una et l'altra chiave
avete in mano, et di ciò son contento,
presto di navigare a ciascun vento:
ch' ogni cosa da voi m'è dolce onore.   14

64

If you could, by any angry gestures—by casting your eyes down or bending your head or by being more swift to flee than any other, frowning at my virtuous and worthy prayers—

if you could ever thus or by any other stratagem escape from my breast where Love engrafts many branches from that first laurel, I would say that would be a just reason for your disdain;

for a noble plant clearly does not belong in arid ground, and therefore it is naturally happy to depart from there:

but, since your destiny forbids you to be elsewhere, at least take care not to stay always in a hateful place.

65

Alas, I was little wary at first, the day when Love came to wound me, who step by step has become lord of my life and sits at the summit!

I did not believe that by the power of his file any bit of strength or worthiness would fail in my hardened heart, but so he goes who esteems himself too highly.

From now on any defense is too late, except to test whether Love looks on mortal prayers much or little.

I do not pray—nor can it be—that my heart burn moderately, but that she have her part of the fire.

64

Se voi poteste per turbati segni—
per chinar gli occhi o per piegar la testa,
o per esser più d'altra al fuggir presta,
torcendo 'l viso a' preghi onesti et degni—   4

uscir giamai, o ver per altri ingegni,
del petto ove dal primo lauro innesta
Amor più rami, i' direi ben che questa
fosse giusta cagione a' vostri sdegni;   8

ché gentil pianta in arido terreno
par che si disconvenga, et però lieta
naturalmente quindi si diparte.   11

Ma poi vostro destino a voi pur vieta
l'essere altrove, provedete almeno
di non star sempre in odiosa parte.   14

65

Lasso, che mal accorto fui da prima,
nel giorno ch' a ferir mi venne Amore!
ch' a passo a passo è poi fatto signore
de la mia vita et posto in su la cima.   4

Io non credea per forza di sua lima
che punto di fermezza o di valore
mancasse mai ne l'indurato core,
ma così va chi sopra 'l ver s'estima.   8

Da ora inanzi ogni difesa è tarda,
altra che di provar s' assai o poco
questi preghi mortali Amore sguarda.   11

Non prego già, né puote aver più loco,
che mesuratamente il mio cor arda,
ma che sua parte abbi costei del foco.   14

66

The burdened air and the importunate cloud
compressed from without by the furious winds
must soon convert themselves to rain;
and already almost crystal are the rivers,
and instead of the grass through the valleys
one sees nothing but frost and ice.

And I have in my heart, much colder than ice,
heavy thoughts in such a cloud
as rises sometimes from these valleys,
closed around about against the loving winds
and surrounded by stagnating rivers,
when there falls from the sky the gentlest rain.

In a short time passes every great rain;
and the warmth makes disappear the snows and ice
that make the rivers look so proud;
nor was the sky ever covered by so thick a cloud
that, meeting the fury of the winds,
it did not flee from the hills and the valleys.

But, alas! I am not helped by the flowering of the valleys;
rather I weep in clear weather and in rain,
and in freezing and in warming winds;
for one day my lady will be without her inner ice
and without her outer customary cloud—
when I shall see the sea dry, and the lakes and the rivers.

As long as the sea receives the rivers
and the beasts love shady valleys,
before her eyes will remain the cloud
that makes my eyes give birth to constant rain,
and in her lovely breast the hardened ice
that draws forth from mine such sorrowing winds.

66

L'aere gravato et l'importuna nebbia
compressa intorno da rabbiosi venti
tosto conven che si converta in pioggia;
et già son quasi di cristallo i fiumi,
e 'n vece de l'erbetta per le valli
non se ved' altro che pruine et ghiaccio.   6

Et io nel cor via più freddo che ghiaccio
ò di gravi pensier tal una nebbia
qual si leva talor di queste valli,
serrate incontra a gli amorosi venti
et circundate di stagnanti fiumi,
quando cade dal ciel più lenta pioggia.   12

In picciol tempo passa ogni gran pioggia,
e 'l caldo fa sparir le nevi e 'l ghiaccio
di che vanno superbi in vista i fiumi;
né mai nascose il ciel sì folta nebbia
che sopragiunta dal furor di venti
non fuggisse dai poggi et da le valli.   18

Ma, lasso, a me non val fiorir di valli,
anzi piango al sereno et a la pioggia
et a' gelati et a' soavi venti;
ch' allor fia un dì Madonna senza 'l ghiaccio
dentro, et di for senza l'usata nebbia,
ch' io vedrò secco il mare e' laghi e i fiumi.   24

Mentre ch' al mar descenderanno i fiumi
et le fiere ameranno ombrose valli,
fia dinanzi a' begli occhi quella nebbia
che fa nascer d'i miei continua pioggia
et nel bel petto l'indurato ghiaccio
che tra' del mio sì dolorosi venti.   30

Well may I pardon all the winds
for love of one who between two rivers
closed me in lovely green and sweet ice,
so that I depicted then through a thousand valleys
the shade where I had been; for neither heat nor rain
I feared, nor the sound of shattered cloud.

But never did cloud flee before winds
as on that day, nor river because of rain,
nor ice when the sun opens the valleys.

---

between two rivers: the Sorgue and the Durance.

67

On the left bank of the Tyrrhenian sea, where the waves weep broken by the wind, suddenly I saw that noble branch of which I must write on so many pages.

Love, which boiled within my breast for memory of her blond tresses, pushed me forward, wherefore in a stream that the grass hides I fell, and not like a living person.

Alone, where I was, between the woods and the hills, I felt shame for myself; for so much surely suffices a noble heart, and I wished no other spur.

It pleases me at least to have changed styles, from my eyes to my feet, if through my feet being wet, the others might be dried by a more gracious April.

---

left bank of the Tyrrhenian sea: the western shore of northern Italy.
noble branch: the laurel.

Ben debbo io perdonare a tutt' i venti
per amor d'un che 'n mezzo di duo fiumi
mi chiuse tra 'l bel verde e 'l dolce ghiaccio,
tal ch' i' depinsi poi per mille valli
l'ombra ov' io fui, che né calor né pioggia
né suon curava di spezzata nebbia.   36

Ma non fuggio giamai nebbia per venti
come quel dì, né mai fiumi per pioggia
né ghiaccio quando 'l sole apre le valli.   39

67

Del mar tirreno a la sinistra riva
dove rotte dal vento piangon l'onde,
subito vidi quella altera fronde
di cui conven che 'n tante carte scriva.   4

Amor che dentro a l'anima bolliva
per rimembranza de le treccie bionde
mi spinse, onde in un rio che l'erba asconde
caddi, non già come persona viva.   8

Solo ov' io era tra' boschetti e' colli,
vergogna ebbi di me, ch' al cor gentile
basta ben tanto et altro spron non volli.   11

Piacemi almen d'aver cangiato stile
da gli occhi a' pie', se del lor esser molli
gli altri asciugasse un più cortese aprile.   14

68

The holy sight of your city makes me bewail my evil past, crying: "Get up, wretch! what are you doing?" and shows me the way to mount to Heaven.

But with this thought another jousts, and says to me: "Why do you flee? If you remember, the time is passing now when we should return to see our lady."

I, who hear his argument, then turn to ice within like a man who hears news that suddenly wrings his heart.

The first thought returns, and the second runs away. Which one will win, I do not know; but up to now they have been fighting, and not merely once.

---

your city: Rome. The poem was probably written during Petrarch's visit in 1341.

69

I knew well that natural counsel never prevailed against you, Love; I had experienced so many little snares, so many false promises, had so often felt your fierce claw.

But recently, and I marvel at it (I shall tell it, as one who was involved and took note of it there on the salt waters between the Tuscan shore and Elba and Giglio),

I escaped from your hands, and went on a journey unknown and a foreigner, the winds and heavens and waves driving me;

when behold your ministers (I know not whence) to let me see that one cannot fight against or hide from his destiny.

---

there on the salt waters: while sailing from Marseille to Rome.   Elba and Giglio: islands off the coast of Tuscany.   your ministers: the phrase has not been explained.

68

L'aspetto sacro de la terra vostra
mi fa del mal passato tragger guai;
gridando: "Sta' su, misero, che fai?"
et la via de salir al ciel mi mostra.   4

Ma con questo pensier un altro giostra
et dice a me: "Perché fuggendo vai?
Se ti rimembra, il tempo passa omai
di tornar a veder la donna nostra."   8

I' che 'l suo ragionar intendo, allora
m'agghiaccio dentro in guisa d'uom ch' ascolta
novelle che di subito l'accora;   11

poi torna il primo et questo dà la volta.
Qual vincerà non so, ma 'nfino ad ora
combattuto ànno et non pur una volta.   14

69

Ben sapeva io che natural consiglio,
Amor, contra di te giamai non valse,
tanti lacciuol, tante impromesse false,
tanto provato avea 'l tuo fiero artiglio.   4

Ma novamente, ond' io mi meraviglio
(dirol come persona a cui ne calse
et che 'l notai là sopra a l'acque salse
tra la riva toscana et l'Elba et Giglio),   8

i' fuggia le tue mani et per camino,
agitandom' i venti e 'l ciel et l'onde,
m'andava sconosciuto et pellegrino;   11

quando ecco i tuoi ministri, i' non so donde,
per darmi a diveder ch' al suo destino
mal chi contrasta et mal chi si nasconde.   14

70

Alas, I do not know where to turn the hope that has been by
now betrayed many times! For if there is no one who will listen
to me with pity, why scatter prayers to the heavens so thickly?
But, if it happens that I am not denied the ending of these pitiful
sounds before my death, let it not displease my lord that I beg
him again to let me say freely one day among the grass and
flowers: "It is right and just that I sing and be joyful."

It is just that at some time I sing, since I have sighed for so long a
time that I shall never begin soon enough to make my smiling
equal so many sorrows. And if I could make some sweet saying
of mine give some delight to those holy eyes, oh me blessed
above other lovers! But most when I can say without lying: "A
lady begs me; therefore I wish to speak."

Yearning thoughts, which thus step by step have led me to such
high speech: you see that my lady has a heart of such hard stone
that I cannot by myself pass within it. She does not deign to look
so low as to care about our words; for the heavens do not wish
it, and resisting them I am already weary; therefore, as in my
heart I become hard and bitter: "So in my speech I wish to be
harsh."

"It is right and just . . .": the first line of a *chanso* attributed in many manuscripts to Arnaut Daniel, twelfth-century Provençal poet, and no doubt considered his by Petrarch; it is probably by Guillem de Saint-Gregori.   "A lady
begs me . . .": the first line of a canzone by Guido Cavalcanti, thirteenth-century
Florentine poet.   "So in my speech . . .": the first line of one of Dante's *rime
petrose* (Appendix Two, poem 4).

70

Lasso me, ch' i' non so in qual parte pieghi
la speme ch' è tradita omai più volte!
Che se non è chi con pietà m'ascolte,
perché sparger al ciel sì spessi preghi?
Ma s' egli aven ch' ancor non mi si nieghi
finir anzi 'l mio fine
queste voci meschine,
non gravi al mio signor perch' io il ripreghi
di dir libero un dì tra l'erba e i fiori:
"Drez et rayson es qu' ieu ciant em demori."   10

Ragion è ben ch' alcuna volta io canti
però ch' ò sospirato sì gran tempo
che mai non incomincio assai per tempo
per adequar col riso i dolor tanti.
Et s' io potesse far ch' agli occhi santi   15
porgesse alcun diletto
qualche dolce mio detto,
o me beato sopra gli altri amanti!
Ma più quand' io dirò senza mentire:
"Donna mi priega, per ch' io voglio dire."   20

Vaghi pensier che così passo passo
scorto m'avete a ragionar tant' alto:
vedete che Madonna à 'l cor di smalto
sì forte ch' io per me dentro nol passo.
Ella non degna di mirar sì basso   25
che di nostre parole
curi, ché 'l ciel non vole,
al qual pur contrastando i' son già lasso;
onde come nel cor m'induro e 'naspro,
"Così nel mio parlar voglio esser aspro."   30

What am I saying? or where am I? and who deceives me but my-self and my excessive desire? Nay, if I run through the sky from sphere to sphere, no planet condemns me to weeping. If a mortal veil dulls my sight, what fault is it of the stars or of beautiful things? With me dwells one who night and day troubles me, since she made me go heavy with the pleasure of: "The sweet sight of her and her lovely soft glance."

All things with which the world is beauteous came forth good from the hand of the eternal Workman: but I, who do not dis-cern so far within, am dazzled by the beauty that I see about me, and if I ever return to the true splendor, my eye cannot stay still, it is so weakened by its very own fault, and not by that day when I turned toward her angelic beauty: "In the sweet time of my first age."

"The sweet sight of her . . .": the first line of a canzone by Cino da Pistoia (1270–1336).   "In the sweet time . . .": the first line of Petrarch's canzone, poem 23.

Che parlo, o dove sono, et chi m'inganna
altri ch' io stesso e 'l desiar soverchio?
Già s' i' trascorro il ciel di cerchio in cerchio
nessun pianeta a pianger mi condanna;
se mortal velo il mio veder appanna   35
che colpa è de le stelle
o de le cose belle?
Meco si sta chi dì et notte m'affanna,
poi che del suo piacer mi fe' gir grave
"La dolce vista e 'l bel guardo soave."   40

Tutte le cose di che 'l mondo è adorno
uscir buone de man del mastro eterno,
ma me che così a dentro non discerno
abbaglia il bel che mi si mostra intorno;
et s' al vero splendor giamai ritorno   45
l'occhio non po star fermo,
così l'à fatto infermo
pur la sua propria colpa, et non quel giorno
ch' i' volsi in ver l'angelica beltade
"Nel dolce tempo de la prima etade."   50

71

Because life is short and my wit is afraid of the high undertaking, in neither do I have much confidence; but I hope my pain will be understood there where I desire it to be and where it must be, my pain which in silence I cry out.

Lovely eyes where Love makes his nest, to you I turn my weak style, sluggish in itself, but the great pleasure spurs it; and he who speaks of you receives from the subject a gentle habit, which, with amorous wings lifting him, parts him from every low thought; raised up by them, I come now to say things that I have long carried hidden in my heart.

Not that I do not see how much my praise injures you; but I cannot resist the great desire that is in me since I saw what no thought can equal, let alone speech, mine or others'.

Cause of my sweet bitter state, I know well no other but you understands me. When in your burning rays I become snow, your noble disdain is perhaps offended by my unworthiness. Oh, if that fear did not temper the burning that lights me, happy death! for in their presence I prefer to die rather than live without them.

71

Perché la vita è breve
et l'ingegno paventa a l'alta impresa,
né di lui né di lei molto mi fido;
ma spero che sia intesa
là dov' io bramo et là dove esser deve
la doglia mia, la qual tacendo i' grido.   6
Occhi leggiadri dove Amor fa nido,
a voi rivolgo il mio debile stile
pigro da sé, ma 'l gran piacer lo sprona;
et chi di voi ragiona
tien dal soggetto un abito gentile
che con l'ale amorose
levando, il parte d'ogni pensier vile.
Con queste alzato vengo a dire or cose
ch' ò portate nel cor gran tempo ascose.   15

Non perch' io non m'aveggia
quanto mia laude è 'ngiuriosa a voi,
ma contrastar non posso al gran desio
lo qual è 'n me da poi
ch' i' vidi quel che pensier non pareggia,
non che l'avagli altrui parlar o mio.   21
Principio del mio dolce stato rio,
altri che voi so ben che non m'intende:
quando agli ardenti rai neve divegno,
vostro gentile sdegno
forse ch' allor mia indignitate offende.
O se questa temenza
non temprasse l'arsura che m'incende,
beato venir meno! ché 'n lor presenza
m'è più caro il morir che 'l viver senza.   30

Thus that I am not undone, so frail an object to so powerful a fire, it is not my own worth that rescues me; but fear, a little, which freezes my yearning blood through my veins, makes more solid my heart, that it may flame the longer.

O hills, O valleys, O rivers, O woods, O fields, O witnesses of my heavy life, how many times have you heard me call Death! Ah, dolorous fate! staying destroys me and fleeing does not help me. But if a greater fear did not rein me in, a short and speedy way would bring to an end this bitter and hard suffering; and the fault is hers who does not care.

Sorrow, why do you lead me out of the way to say what I do not wish to say? Suffer me to go where pleasure impels me. For I do not complain of you, eyes serene beyond the mortal course, nor of him who binds me in such a knot.

You see well how many colors Love often paints in my face, and you can think what he does to me within, there where night and day he stands over me with the power he has gathered from you, happy and carefree lights—except that to see yourselves is denied you, but whenever you turn to me you know in another what you are.

Dunque ch' i' non mi sfaccia
sì frale oggetto a sì possente foco,
non è proprio valor che me ne scampi;
ma la paura un poco,
che 'l sangue vago per le vene agghiaccia,
risalda 'l cor perché più tempo avampi.   36
    O poggi, o valli, o fiumi, o selve, o campi,
o testimon de la mia grave vita,
quante volte m'udiste chiamar Morte!
Ahi dolorosa sorte,
lo star mi strugge e 'l fuggir non m'aita!
Ma se maggior paura
non m'affrenasse, via corta et spedita
trarrebbe a fin questa aspra pena et dura,
et la colpa è di tal che non à cura.   45

    Dolor, perché mi meni
fuor di camin a dir quel ch' i' non voglio?
sostien ch' io vada ove 'l piacer mi spigne.
Già di voi non mi doglio,
occhi sopra 'l mortal corso sereni,
né di lui ch' a tal nodo mi distrigne.   51
    Vedete ben quanti color depigne
Amor sovente in mezzo del mio volto,
et potrete pensar qual dentro fammi,
là 've dì et notte stammi
a dosso col poder ch' à in voi raccolto,
luci beate et liete
se non che 'l veder voi stesse v'è tolto,
ma quante volte a me vi rivolgete
conoscete in altrui quel che voi siete.   60

If to you were as well known the divine incredible beauty of which I speak, as it is to whoever looks at it, measured joy your heart would not have; therefore, perhaps your beauty is removed from the natural vigor that opens and turns you.

Happy the soul who sighs for you, heavenly lights for which I thank my life, which is pleasant to me only in this! Alas, why so rarely do you give me what never satiates me? why do you not more often look how Love is destroying me? and why do you immediately deprive me of the good that my soul feels now and again?

I say that now and again, thanks to you, I feel in the midst of my soul a new and strange sweetness, which then takes away every other burden of painful thoughts, so that of a thousand only one is left there.

This little bit of life, no more, profits me, and if this good of mine could last awhile, no state would equal mine. But perhaps others would be made envious, and I proud, by so much honor; so, alas, it is necessary that the limit of laughter be assailed by weeping, and that interrupting those burning thoughts I return to myself and think of myself.

S' a voi fosse sì nota
la divina incredibile bellezza
di ch' io ragiono come a chi la mira,
misurata allegrezza
non avria 'l cor; però forse è remota
dal vigor natural che v'apre et gira.   66
    Felice l'alma che per voi sospira,
lumi del ciel per li quali io ringrazio
la vita che per altro non m'è a grado.
Oimè, perché sì rado
mi date quel dond' io mai non mi sazio?
perché non più sovente
mirate qual Amor di me fa strazio,
et perché mi spogliate immantanente
del ben ch' ad ora ad or l'anima sente?   75

    Dico ch' ad ora ad ora,
vostra mercede, i' sento in mezzo l'alma
una dolcezza inusitata et nova
la qual ogni altra salma
di noiosi pensier disgombra allora,
sì che di mille un sol vi si ritrova.   81
    Quel tanto a me, non più, del viver giova;
et se questo mio ben durasse alquanto,
nullo stato aguagliarse al mio porrebbe.
Ma forse altrui farrebbe
invido et me superbo l'onor tanto;
però, lasso, convensi
che l'estremo del riso assaglia il pianto,
e 'nterrompendo quelli spirti accensi,
a me ritorni et di me stesso pensi.   90

The amorous thought that dwells within in you is revealed to me such that it draws all other joys from my heart; and words and deeds come forth from me then such that I hope to become immortal though the flesh die.

At your appearance anguish and pain flee, and at your departure they return together; but because my enamored memory closes the entrance to them then, they do not come past the external parts. Thus if any good fruit is born from me, from you first comes the seed; in myself I am as it were a dry soil tilled by you, and the praise is yours entirely.

Song, you do not quiet me, rather you inflame me to tell of what steals me away from myself; therefore be sure not to be alone.

L'amoroso pensero
ch' alberga dentro in voi mi si discopre
tal che mi tra' del cor ogni altra gioia;
onde parole et opre
escon di me sì fatte allor ch' i' spero
farmi immortal, perché la carne moia.   96

　　Fugge al vostro apparire angoscia et noia,
et nel vostro partir tornano insieme;
ma perché la memoria innamorata
chiude lor poi l'entrata,
di là non vanno da le parti estreme.
Onde s' alcun bel frutto
nasce di me, da voi vien prima il seme;
io per me son quasi un terreno asciutto
colto da voi, e 'l pregio è vostro in tutto.   105

　　Canzon, tu non m'acqueti, anzi m'infiammi
a dir di quel ch' a me stesso m'invola;
però sia certa de non esser sola.   108

72

My noble Lady, I see in the moving of your eyes a sweet light that shows me the way that leads to Heaven; and through long habit, there within where with Love I sit, almost visibly your heart shines through.

This is the sight that induces me to do well and guides me toward the glorious goal; this alone separates me from the throng. Nor could any human tongue relate what the two divine lights make me feel, both when winter scatters frosts and when, later, the year becomes young again, as it was at the time of my first yearning.

I think: if up there, whence the eternal Mover of the stars deigned to show forth this work on earth, the other works are as beautiful, let the prison open in which I am closed and which locks me from the way to such a life.

Then I turn myself again to my usual war, thanking Nature and the day I was born, which destined me to so much good, and her who to such a hope raised up my heart (for until then I lay heavy and painful to myself, but from then on I have been pleasing even to myself), filling with one high sweet thought that heart of which her lovely eyes have the key.

72

Gentil mia Donna, i' veggio
nel mover de' vostr'occhi un dolce lume
che mi mostra la via ch' al ciel conduce;
et per lungo costume
dentro, là dove sol con Amor seggio,
quasi visibilmente il cor traluce.   6
Questa è la vista ch' a ben far m'induce
et che mi scorge al glorioso fine;
questa sola dal vulgo m'allontana.
Né giamai lingua umana
contar poria quel che le due divine
luci sentir mi fanno
e quando 'l verno sparge le pruine,
et quando poi ringiovenisce l'anno
qual era al tempo del mio primo affanno.   15

Io penso: se là suso,
onde 'l motor eterno de le stelle
degnò mostrar del suo lavoro in terra,
son l'altr'opre sì belle,
aprasi la pregione ov' io son chiuso
et che 'l camino a tal vita mi serra!   21
Poi mi rivolgo a la mia usata guerra,
ringraziando Natura e 'l dì ch' io nacqui
che reservato m'ànno a tanto bene,
et lei ch' a tanta spene
alzò il mio cor (ché 'nsin allor io giacqui
a me noioso et grave,
da quel dì inanzi a me medesmo piacqui),
empiendo d'un pensier alto et soave
quel core ond' ànno i begli occhi la chiave.   30

Nor ever so joyous a state Love or turning Fortune gave to any most their friend in life, that I would not exchange it for one glance of those eyes, from which all my repose comes as every tree comes from its roots.

Lovely angelic sparks that make blessed my life, where the pleasure is lit that sweetly consumes and destroys me: just as every other light disappears and flees where yours shines, so from my heart, when so much sweetness descends into it, every other thing, every thought, goes out, and alone there with you remains Love.

However much sweetness ever was in the hearts of lucky lovers, gathered all in one place, is nothing to what I feel when you at times sweetly amid the lovely black and the white turn to me the light where Love frolics:

and I believe that, from my swaddling clothes and crib, for my imperfection and adverse Fortune Heaven provided this remedy. Your veil does me wrong and your hand, they so often come between my highest delight and your eyes, and so night and day my great desire pours forth to give my breast vent, which takes its form from your varied aspect.

Né mai stato gioioso
Amor o la volubile Fortuna
dieder a chi più fur nel mondo amici,
ch' i' nol cangiassi ad una
rivolta d'occhi ond' ogni mio riposo
vien come ogni arbor vien da sue radici.   36
   Vaghe faville angeliche, beatrici
de la mia vita, ove 'l piacer s'accende
che dolcemente mi consuma et strugge:
come sparisce et fugge
ogni altro lume dove 'l vostro splende,
così de lo mio core,
quando tanta dolcezza in lui discende,
ogni altra cosa, ogni penser va fore
et solo ivi con voi rimanse Amore.   45

   Quanta dolcezza unquanco
fu in cor d'aventurosi amanti, accolta
tutta in un loco, a quel ch' i' sento è nulla,
quando voi alcuna volta
soavemente tra 'l bel nero e 'l bianco
volgete il lume in cui Amor si trastulla;   51
   et credo da le fasce et da la culla
al mio imperfetto, a la fortuna avversa,
questo rimedio provedesse il cielo.
Torto mi face il velo
et la man che sì spesso s'atraversa
fra 'l mio sommo diletto
et gli occhi, onde dì et notte si rinversa
il gran desio per isfogare il petto
che forma tien dal variato aspetto.   60

Because I see, and it sorrows me, that no natural gift of mine is worth anything to me or makes me worthy of so dear a glance, I force myself to be one who may be worthy of the high hope and of the noble fire with which I entirely burn.

If through persevering toil I can become swift to good and slow to ill, disprizer of all the world desires, in a kind judgment that repute could perhaps help me. Certainly the end of my weeping, which my sorrowful heart calls for from nowhere else, will come from the lovely eyes at the end sweetly trembling, ultimate hope of courteous lovers.

Song, one of your sisters has gone before, and I feel the other in the same dwelling making herself ready, wherefore I rule more paper.

Perch' io veggio, et mi spiace,
che natural mia dote a me non vale
né mi fa degno d'un sì caro sguardo,
sforzomi d'esser tale
qual a l'alta speranza si conface
et al foco gentil ond' io tutto ardo.   66
   S' al ben veloce et al contrario tardo,
dispregiator di quanto 'l mondo brama
per solicito studio posso farme,
porrebbe forse aitarme
nel benigno iudicio una tal fama;
certo, il fin de' miei pianti,
che non altronde il cor doglioso chiama,
ven da' begli occhi al fin dolce tremanti,
ultima speme de' cortesi amanti.   75

   Canzon, l'una sorella è poco inanzi
et l'altra sento in quel medesmo albergo
apparecchiarsi, ond' io più carta vergo.   78

73

Since through my destiny that flaming desire forces me to speak which has forced me to sigh always, you, O Love, who arouse me to it, be my guide, and show me the way, and tune my rhymes to my desire;

but not so that my heart is untuned with too much sweetness, as I fear from what I feel where no eye reaches; for speaking inflames me and pricks me on, nor through my wit (whence I fear and tremble), as sometimes occurs, is the great fire of my mind lessened; rather I melt in the sound of the words, as if I were a man of ice in the sun.

At the beginning I thought to find, through speech, for my burning desire some brief repose and some truce. This hope gave me the daring to speak of what I feel; now it abandons me in my need and dissolves.

But still I must follow the high undertaking, continuing my amorous notes, so powerful is the will that carries me away; and Reason is dead, who held the reins, and cannot withstand it. At least let Love show me what to say in such a way that if it ever strikes the ear of my sweet enemy it may make her the friend, not of me, but of pity.

73

Poi che per mio destino
a dir mi sforza quell'accesa voglia
che m'à sforzato a sospirar mai sempre,
Amor, ch' a ciò m'invoglia,
sia la mia scorta e 'nsignimi 'l camino
et col desio le mie rime contempre;   6
    ma non in guisa che lo cor si stempre
di soverchia dolcezza, com' io temo
per quel ch' i' sento ov' occhio altrui non giugne;
ché 'l dir m'infiamma et pugne
né per mi' 'ngegno (ond' io pavento et tremo)
sì come talor sòle
trovo 'l gran foco de la mente scemo,
anzi mi struggo al suon de le parole
pur com' io fusse un uom di ghiaccio al sole.   15

    Nel cominciar credia
trovar parlando al mio ardente desire
qualche breve riposo et qualche triegua;
questa speranza ardire
mi porse a ragionar quel ch' i' sentia,
or m'abbandona al tempo et si dilegua.   21
    Ma pur conven che l'alta impresa segua
continuando l'amorose note,
sì possente è 'l voler che mi trasporta,
et la ragione è morta
che tenea 'l freno et contrastar nol pote.
Mostrimi almen ch' io dica
Amor in guisa che, se mai percote
gli orecchi de la dolce mia nemica,
non mia ma di pietà la faccia amica.   30

I say: if in that age when spirits were so desirous of true honor the industry of certain men wound itself through various countries, passing mountains and seas and seeking out honored things, and plucked of them the loveliest flower;

since God and Nature and Love wished to place completely every virtue in those lovely lights on account of which I live in joy, I need not change countries and pass over this and the other shore: to them I always come back as to the fount of all my health; and when I run desirous to death, only with their sight do I help my state.

As in the force of the winds the tired helmsman at night lifts his head to the two lights that our pole always has, thus in the tempest I endure of love those shining eyes are my constellation and my only comfort.

Alas, but there is too much more that I steal from them now from this side, now from that, as Love informs me, than what comes from them in gracious gift; and the littleness I am makes of them my perpetual norm. Since I first saw them, I have never moved a foot toward doing well without them; thus I have placed them at the summit of me, for my own worth by itself esteems itself false.

Dico: se 'n quella etate
ch' al vero onor fur gli animi sì accesi
l'industria d'alquanti uomini s'avolse
per diversi paesi,
poggi et onde passando et l'onorate
cose cercando, e' l più bel fior ne colse;   36
    poi che Dio et Natura et Amor volse
locar compitamente ogni virtute
in quei be' lumi ond' io gioioso vivo,
questo et quell'altro rivo
non conven ch' i' trapasse et terra mute:
a lor sempre ricorro
come a fontana d'ogni mia salute,
et quando a morte disiando corro,
sol di lor vista al mio stato soccorro.   45

    Come a forza di venti
stanco nocchier di notte alza la testa
a' duo lumi ch' à sempre il nostro polo,
così ne la tempesta
ch' i' sostengo d'amor, gli occhi lucenti
sono il mio segno e 'l mio conforto solo.   51
    Lasso, ma troppo è più quel ch' io ne 'nvolo
or quinci or quindi, come Amor m'informa,
che quel che ven da grazioso dono;
et quel poco ch' i' sono
mi fa di loro una perpetua norma;
poi ch' io li vidi in prima
senza lor a ben far non mossi un'orma,
così gli ò di me posti in su la cima
che 'l mio valor per sé falso s'estima.   60

I could never imagine, let alone tell, the effects that these sweet eyes make in my heart; all the other delights of this life I hold for much less, and all other beauties go behind.

Tranquil peace without any trouble, like that which is eternal in Heaven, moves from their lovely smile. Might I see thus fixedly how Love sweetly governs them, only one day, up close, without any supernal wheel ever turning, nor think of any other nor of myself, and the blinking of my eyes not be frequent!

Alas, I go desiring what cannot be in any way, and I live on my desire out of hope. If only that knot which Love ties around my tongue when the excess of light overpowers my mortal sight were loosened, I would take boldness to speak words at that moment so strange that they would make all who heard them weep. But the deep wounds turn my wounded heart forcefully away; I become pale, and my blood hides itself, I know not where, nor do I remain what I was: and I have become aware that this is the blow with which Love has killed me.

Song, I feel my pen already tired from the long and sweet speech with her, but not my thoughts of speaking with me.

I' non poria giamai
imaginar, non che narrar, gli effetti
che nel mio cor gli occhi soavi fanno;
tutti gli altri diletti
di questa vita ò per minori assai,
et tutte altre bellezze in dietro vanno.   66
    Pace tranquilla senza alcuno affanno,
simile a quella ch' è nel ciel eterna,
move da lor inamorato riso;
così vedess' io fiso
come Amor dolcemente gli governa
sol un giorno da presso
senza volger giamai rota superna,
né pensasse d'altrui né di me stesso,
e 'l batter gli occhi miei non fosse spesso!   75

    Lasso, che disiando
vo quel ch' esser non puote in alcun modo,
et vivo del desir fuor di speranza.
Solamente quel nodo
ch' Amor cerconda a la mia lingua quando
l'umana vista il troppo lume avanza   81
    fosse disciolto, i' prenderei baldanza
di dir parole in quel punto sì nove
che farian lagrimar chi le 'ntendesse.
Ma le ferite impresse
volgon per forza il cor piagato altrove,
ond' io divento smorto
e 'l sangue si nasconde, i' non so dove,
né rimango qual era; et sommi accorto
che questo è 'l colpo di che Amor m'à morto.   90

    Canzone, i' sento già stancar la penna
del lungo et dolce ragionar con lei,
ma non di parlar meco i pensier mei.   93

74

I am already weary of thinking how my thoughts of you are weariless and how I do not yet abandon life to flee so heavy a burden of sighs;

and how, in speaking of your face and hair and lovely eyes that I am always talking about, my tongue and voice have not yet failed, night and day calling your name;

and that my feet are not worn and tired of following your footsteps everywhere, wasting in vain so many steps;

and whence comes the ink, whence the pages that I fill with words of you (if in that I err, it is the fault of Love, not at all a lack of art).

75

The lovely eyes that struck me in such a way that they themselves could heal the wound, but not the power of herbs or of magic art or of any stone distant from our sea,

they have so cut off my path from any other love that only one sweet thought calms my soul; and if my tongue is fain to follow it, the guide, but not my tongue, can be derided.

These are those lovely eyes which make the standards of my lord victorious everywhere, and especially over my side;

these are those lovely eyes that are always in my heart with kindled sparks, wherefore I never tire of speaking of them.

74

Io son già stanco di pensar sì come
i miei pensier in voi stanchi non sono
et come vita ancor non abbandono
per fuggir de' sospir sì gravi some;   4

et come a dir del viso et de le chiome
et de' begli occhi ond' io sempre ragiono
non è mancata omai la lingua e 'l suono,
dì et notte chiamando il vostro nome;   8

et che' pie' miei non son fiaccati et lassi
a seguir l'orme vostre in ogni parte,
perdendo inutilmente tanti passi;   11

et onde vien l'enchiostro, onde le carte
ch' i' vo empiendo di voi (se 'n ciò fallassi,
colpa d'Amor, non già defetto d'arte).   14

75

I begli occhi ond' i' fui percosso in guisa
ch' e' medesmi porian saldar la piaga,
et non già vertù d'erbe o d'arte maga
o di pietra dal mar nostro divisa,   4

m'ànno la via sì d'altro amor precisa
ch' un sol dolce penser l'anima appaga;
et se la lingua di seguirlo è vaga
la scorta po, non ella, esser derisa.   8

Questi son que' begli occhi che l'imprese
del mio signor vittoriose fanno
in ogni parte et più sovra 'l mio fianco;   11

questi son que' begli occhi che mi stanno
sempre nel cor colle faville accese,
perch' io di lor parlando non mi stanco.   14

76

Alluring me with his promises, Love led me back to my former prison and gave the keys to that enemy of mine who still keeps me banished from myself.

I did not become aware of it, alas, until I was in their power, and now, with great distress—who will believe, though I swear it?— I return to freedom sighing;

and like a true suffering prisoner I carry a large part of my chains, and my heart is inscribed in my eyes and on my brow.

When you notice my color, you will say: "If I see and judge aright, this man was not far from death."

77

Even though Polyclitus should for a thousand years compete in looking with all the others who were famous in that art, they would never see the smallest part of the beauty that has conquered my heart.

But certainly my Simon was in Paradise, whence comes this noble lady; there he saw her and portrayed her on paper, to attest down here to her lovely face.

The work is one of those which can be imagined only in Heaven, not here among us, where the body is a veil to the soul;

it was a gracious act, nor could he have done it after he came down to feel heat and cold and his eyes took on mortality.

Polyclitus: Greek sculptor (fifth century B.C.).   Simon: Sienese painter Simone Martini (active 1315–1344), who lived in Avignon during the last years of his life. In addition to the portrait of Laura referred to here (lost), he painted for Petrarch a frontispiece to the works of Virgil (now in Milan).

76

Amor con sue promesse lusingando
mi ricondusse a la prigione antica,
et die' le chiavi a quella mia nemica
ch' ancor me di me stesso tene in bando.   4

Non me n'avidi, lasso, se non quando
fui in lor forza; et or con gran fatica
(chi 'l crederà, perché giurando i' 'l dica?)
in libertà ritorno sospirando;   8

et come vero prigioniero afflitto
de le catene mie gran parte porto
e 'l cor negli occhi et ne la fronte ò scritto.   11

Quando sarai del mio colore accorto
dirai: "S' i' guardo et giudico ben dritto,
questi avea poco andare ad esser morto."   14

77

Per mirar Policleto a prova fiso
con gli altri ch' ebber fama di quell'arte,
mill' anni non vedrian la minor parte
della beltà che m'àve il cor conquiso.   4

Ma certo il mio Simon fu in Paradiso
onde questa gentil donna si parte;
ivi la vide, et la ritrasse in carte
per far fede qua giù del suo bel viso.   8

L'opra fu ben di quelle che nel cielo
si ponno imaginar, non qui tra noi,
ove le membra fanno a l'alma velo;   11

cortesia fe', né la potea far poi
che fu disceso a provar caldo et gielo
et del mortal sentiron gli occhi suoi.   14

78

When Simon received the high idea which, for my sake, put his hand to his stylus, if he had given to his noble work voice and intellect along with form

he would have lightened my breast of many sighs that make what others prize most vile to me. For in appearance she seems humble, and her expression promises peace;

then, when I come to speak to her, she seems to listen most kindly: if she could only reply to my words!

Pygmalion, how glad you should be of your statue, since you received a thousand times what I yearn to have just once!

Pygmalion: the mythological sculptor who carved an ivory statue of a woman so beautiful that he fell in love with it. At his prayer Venus turned the statue into a living woman. (Ovid, *Metamorphoses* 10.243–297.)

79

If the middle and end answer to the beginning of this fourteenth year of sighs, no wind or chill can save me, I feel my burning desire so increase!

Love, with whom I cut no care short, under whose yoke I can never breathe easily, governs me so that I am not half myself, because of my eyes which to my own hurt I so often turn.

Thus I go failing from day to day, so secretly that I alone am aware of it and she who by looking melts my heart;

I have hardly kept my soul with me until now, nor do I know how long its stay with me will be, for death approaches and life flees.

78

Quando giunse a Simon l'alto concetto
ch' a mio nome gli pose in man lo stile,
s' avesse dato a l'opera gentile
colla figura voce ed intelletto,   4

di sospir molti mi sgombrava il petto
che ciò ch' altri à più caro a me fan vile.
Però che 'n vista ella si monstra umile,
promettendomi pace ne l'aspetto,   8

ma poi ch' i' vengo a ragionar con lei,
benignamente assai par che m'ascolte:
se risponder savesse a' detti miei!   11

Pigmaliòn, quanto lodar ti dei
de l'imagine tua, se mille volte
n'avesti quel ch' i' sol una vorrei!   14

79

S' al principio risponde il fine e 'l mezzo
del quartodecimo anno ch' io sospiro,
più non mi po scampar l'aura né 'l rezzo,
sì crescer sento 'l mio ardente desiro.   4

Amor, con cui pensier mai non amezzo,
sotto 'l cui giogo giamai non respiro,
tal mi governa ch' i' non son già mezzo
per gli occhi ch' al mio mal sì spesso giro.   8

Così mancando vo di giorno in giorno
sì chiusamente ch' i' sol me n'accorgo
et quella che guardando il cor mi strugge;   11

a pena infin a qui l'anima scorgo,
né so quanto fia meco il suo soggiorno,
ché la morte s'appressa e 'l viver fugge.   14

80

He who has decided to lead his life
on the deceiving waves and near the rocks,
separated from death by a little ship,
cannot be very far from the end;
therefore he should retire to port
while the tiller can still control the sail.

The soft breeze, to whom I entrusted both sail
and tiller, entering upon this amorous life
and hoping to come to a better port,
carried me to more than a thousand rocks,
and the causes of my sorrowful end
I had not only all around but also within the ship.

Shut up a long time in this blind ship
I wandered without lifting my eyes to the sail
that before my time was carrying me off to my end;
then it pleased Him who gave me life
to call me back far enough from the rocks
that at least from afar I might see the port.

As at night a light in some port
is seen from the deep sea by a boat or ship,
if not obscured by storm or rocks,
thus above the swollen sail
I saw the ensigns of that other life;
and then I sighed toward my end.

80

Chi è fermato di menar sua vita
su per l'onde fallaci et per li scogli,
scevro da morte con un picciol legno,
non po molto lontan esser dal fine;
però sarebbe da ritrarsi in porto
mentre al governo ancor crede la vela.   6

L'aura soave a cui governo et vela
commisi, entrando a l'amorosa vita
et sperando venire a miglior porto,
poi mi condusse in più di mille scogli;
et le cagion del mio doglioso fine
non pur dintorno avea, ma dentro al legno.   12

Chiuso gran tempo in questo cieco legno
errai senza levar occhio a la vela
ch' anzi al mio dì mi trasportava al fine;
poi piacque a lui che mi produsse in vita
chiamarme tanto indietro da li scogli
ch' almen da lunge m'apparisse il porto.   18

Come lume di notte in alcun porto
vide mai d'alto mar nave né legno,
se non gliel tolse o tempestate o scogli,
così di su la gonfiata vela
vid' io le 'nsegne di quell'altra vita;
et allor sospirai verso 'l mio fine.   24

Not because I am yet sure of the end,
for, wishing with the daylight to come to port,
there is still a long journey for so short a life;
and I am afraid, for I see I am in a frail ship
and more than I would wish I see the sail full
with the wind that drove me toward these rocks.

So may I come out alive from these perilous rocks
and my exile reach a good end,
how I yearn to furl the sail
and cast anchor in some port!
Except that I burn like kindled wood,
it is so hard for me to leave my accustomed life.

Lord of my death and of my life:
before I shatter my ship on these rocks
direct to a good port my weary sail.

Non perch' io sia securo ancor del fine,
ché volendo col giorno esser a porto
è gran viaggio in così poca vita;
poi temo, che mi veggio in fraile legno
et più non vorrei piena la vela
del vento che mi pinse in questi scogli.   30

S' io esca vivo de' dubbiosi scogli
et arrive il mio esilio ad un bel fine,
ch' i' sarei vago di voltar la vela
et l'àncore gittar in qualche porto!
Se non ch' i' ardo come acceso legno,
sì m' è duro a lassar l'usata vita.   36

Signor de la mia fine et de la vita:
prima ch' i' fiacchi il legno tra li scogli
drizza a buon porto l'affannata vela.   39

81

I am so weary under the ancient bundle of my sins and bitter habit that I am much afraid I shall fail on the way and fall into the hands of my enemy.

True, a great Friend did come to free me, in His highest and ineffable graciousness; then He flew out of my sight so that I strive in vain to see Him.

But His voice still resounds down here: "O you who labor, here is the way; come to me, if the pass is not blocked by another."

What grace, what love, or what destiny will give me wings like a dove, that I may rest and lift myself up from earth?

---

enemy: the devil.   Friend: Christ.   "O you who labor...": an allusion to Matthew 11:28, "Come unto me, all ye that labour and are heavy laden, and I will give you rest."   "here is the way...": an allusion to John 14:6, "I am the way, the truth, and the life."   dove: an allusion to Psalm 55:6 (Vulgate 54:6), "Who will give me wings as of a dove, that I may fly away and rest?"

82

I have never been weary of loving you, my Lady, nor shall I be while I live; but I have come to the end of hating myself and am weary of my constant weeping,

and I would rather have a blank tombstone than that your name should be accounted to my loss on marble, when my flesh is deprived of my spirit, which now dwell together.

Therefore, if a heart full of faithful love can satisfy you without your torturing it, let it please you to have mercy on it;

and if your disdain seeks to glut itself in any other way, it errs and shall not have what it seeks; for which I greatly thank Love and myself.

81

Io son sì stanco sotto 'l fascio antico
de le mie colpe et de l'usanza ria,
ch' i' temo forte di mancar tra via
et di cader in man del mio nemico.   4

Ben venne a dilivrarmi un grande amico
per somma et ineffabil cortesia;
poi volò fuor de la veduta mia
sì ch' a mirarlo indarno m'affatico.   8

Ma la sua voce ancor qua giù rimbomba:
"O voi che travagliate, ecco 'l camino;
venite a me, se 'l passo altri non serra."   11

Qual grazia, qual amore, o qual destino
mi darà penne in guisa di colomba,
ch' i' mi riposi et levimi da terra?   14

82

Io non fu' d'amar voi lassato unquanco,
Madonna, né sarò mentre ch' io viva;
ma d'odiar me medesmo giunto a riva
et del continuo lagrimar so' stanco,   4

et voglio anzi un sepolcro bello et bianco
che 'l vostro nome a mio danno si scriva
in alcun marmo ove di spirto priva
sia la mia carne, che po star seco anco.   8

Però s' un cor pien d'amorosa fede
può contentarve senza farne strazio,
piacciavi omai di questo aver mercede;   11

se 'n altro modo cerca d'esser sazio
vostro sdegno, erra, et non fia quel che crede;
di che Amor et me stesso assai ringrazio.   14

83

As long as both my temples are not white, which now time vari-
egates little by little, I shall not be fully secure in risking myself
where Love draws and loads his bow.

But I do not fear any longer that he will maim or kill me, or capture me (though he enlime me), or open my heart (though he still
incise its surface with his cruel poisoned darts).

Tears can no longer escape from my eyes; but they know the
way that far, and the passage can hardly be shut to them;

the fierce ray can warm me, but not so that I burn; and the harsh
cruel image can disturb my sleep, but not break it.

84

"Eyes, weep; accompany the heart, which suffers death through
your fault."—"Thus we always do, and we must lament
another's error more than our own."—

"Love through you first had entrance and still comes as if to his
dwelling."—"We opened the way to him because of the hope
that stirred within him who is now dying."—

"The claims are not, as they seem to you, equal, for you still
were most greedy, in that first sight, for your harm and his."—

"Now this is what saddens us more than anything: that perfect
judgments are so rare, and one is blamed for another's fault."

83

Se bianche non son prima ambe le tempie
ch' a poco a poco par che 'l tempo mischi,
securo non sarò ben ch' io m'arrischi
talor ov' Amor l'arco tira et empie.   4

Non temo già che più mi strazi o scempie,
né mi ritenga perch' ancor m'invischi,
né m'apra il cor perché di fuor l'incischi
con sue saette velenose et empie.   8

Lagrime omai dagli occhi uscir non ponno,
ma di gire infin là sanno il viaggio
sì ch' a pena fia mai chi 'l passo chiuda;   11

ben mi po riscaldare il fiero raggio,
non sì ch' i' arda, et può turbarmi il sonno,
ma romper no, l'imagine aspra et cruda.   14

84

"Occhi, piangete, accompagnate il core
che di vostro fallir morte sostene."—
"Così sempre facciamo, et ne convene
lamentar più l'altrui che 'l nostro errore."—   4

"Già prima ebbe per voi l'entrata Amore
là onde ancor come in suo albergo vene."—
"Noi gli aprimmo la via per quella spene
che mosse dentro da colui che more."—   8

"Non son, come a voi par, le ragion pari,
ché pur voi foste ne la prima vista
del vostro et del suo mal cotanto avari."—   11

"Or questo è quel che più ch' altro n'atrista:
che' perfetti giudicii son sì rari,
et d'altrui colpa altrui biasmo s'acquista."   14

85

I have always loved and I still love and I shall day by day love even more that sweet place where weeping I return many times when Love saddens me;

and I am fixed in loving the time and the hour that removed every low care from around me, and above all her whose lovely face makes me in love with doing well, thanks to her example.

But whoever thought to see them all together, to assail my heart now from this side, now from that, these sweet enemies that I so much love?

Love, with what power today you vanquish me! and, except that hope increases with desire, I would fall dead, where I most desire to live.

---

that sweet place: Vaucluse.

86

I shall always hate the window from which Love has by now shot a thousand arrows at me, because none of them has been mortal: for it is good to die when one's life is fortunate,

but my staying longer in my earthly prison is a cause of infinite evils to me, and it pains me the more that they will be immortal along with me, for the soul is never disentangled from the heart.

Miserable soul, who should have been aware by now, through long experience, that there is no one who can turn back time or rein it in!

Many times have I warned her, with such words: "Go away, sad soul, for he who already has behind him his happiest days is not departing early!"

85

Io amai sempre, et amo forte ancora,
et son per amar più di giorno in giorno
quel dolce loco ove piangendo torno
spesse fiate quando Amor m'accora;   4

et son fermo d'amare il tempo et l'ora
ch' ogni vil cura mi levar dintorno,
et più colei lo cui bel viso adorno
di ben far co' suoi esempli m'innamora.   8

Ma chi pensò veder mai tutti insieme
per assalirmi il core, or quindi or quinci,
questi dolci nemici ch' i' tant' amo?   11

Amor, con quanto sforzo oggi mi vinci!
et se non ch' al desio cresce la speme,
i' cadrei morto ove più viver bramo.   14

86

Io avrò sempre in odio la fenestra
onde Amor m'aventò già mille strali
perch' alquanti di lor non fur mortali:
ch' è bel morir mentre la vita è destra,   4

ma 'l sovrastar ne la pregion terrestra
cagion m'è, lasso, d'infiniti mali,
et più mi duol che fien meco immortali
poi che l'alma dal cor non si scapestra.   8

Misera, che devrebbe esser accorta
per lunga esperienza omai che 'l tempo
non è chi 'ndietro volga o chi l'affreni!   11

Più volte l'ò con ta' parole scorta:
"Vattene, trista, che non va per tempo
chi dopo lassa i suoi dì più sereni."   14

87

As soon as he has released the string, a good archer discerns from afar which shot is futile and which he can believe will strike the intended target;

thus you, Lady, felt the shot from your eyes pass straight into my inward parts, wherefore my heart must overflow through the wound with eternal tears;

and I am certain that you said then: "Miserable lover! where does his desire lead him? Here is the arrow by which Love wishes him to die."

Now, since they see how my pain checks me, what my two enemies do in addition is not designed to kill me but to increase my suffering.

88

Since what I hope for is too long in coming and what is left of life is so short, I wish I had been wise earlier, to flee to the rear at more than a gallop;

and I do flee now, even if so weak and lame on one side where desire has twisted me, safe but still in my face bearing scars that I got in the battle of love.

Wherefore I counsel: "You who are in the way, turn back your steps, and you whom Love inflames, do not wait for the fiercest burning,

"for, though I am alive, of a thousand not even one escapes. My enemy was strong, and her I saw wounded in the very heart!"

---

on one side: on the left side, traditionally that of desire and irrationality.

87

Sì tosto come aven che l'arco scocchi,
buon sagittario di lontan discerne
qual colpo è da sprezzare et qual d'averne
fede ch' al destinato segno tocchi;   4

similemente il colpo de' vostr'occhi,
Donna, sentiste a le mie parti interne
dritto passare, onde conven ch' eterne
lagrime per la piaga il cor trabocchi;   8

et certo son che voi diceste allora:
"Misero amante! a che vaghezza il mena?
Ecco lo strale onde Amor vol ch' e' mora."   11

Ora, veggendo come 'l duol m'affrena,
quel che mi fanno i miei nemici ancora
non è per morte ma per più mia pena.   14

88

Poi che mia spene è lunga a venir troppo
et de la vita il trapassar sì corto,
vorreimi a miglior tempo esser accorto
per fuggir dietro più che di galoppo;   4

et fuggo ancor così debile et zoppo
da l'un de' lati ove 'l desio mi à storto,
securo omai; ma pur nel viso porto
segni ch' io presi a l'amoroso intoppo.   8

Ond' io consiglio: "Voi che siete in via,
volgete i passi, et voi ch' Amore avampa,
non v'indugiate su l'estremo ardore,   11

"ché perch' io viva, de mille un no scampa.
Era ben forte la nemica mia,
et lei vid' io ferita in mezzo 'l core."   14

89

Fleeing the prison where Love had kept me for many years to do what he willed with me, it would be long to tell you, Ladies, how much my new liberty was irksome to me.

My heart was saying to me that he could not live one day on his own, and then along the way appeared to me that traitor, in such disguising garments that he would have fooled a wiser man than I.

Wherefore, many times sighing for what I had left, I said: "Alas, the yoke and the chains and the shackles were sweeter than going free!"

Miserable me, for I understood my harm only late, and with how much difficulty today I get free of the error in which I myself wrapped myself!

90

Her golden hair was loosed to the breeze, which turned it in a thousand sweet knots, and the lovely light burned without measure in her eyes, which are now so stingy of it;

and it seemed to me (I know not whether truly or falsely) her face took on the color of pity: I, who had the tinder of love in my breast, what wonder is it if I suddenly caught fire?

Her walk was not that of a mortal thing but of some angelic form, and her words sounded different from a merely human voice:

a celestial spirit, a living sun was what I saw, and if she were not such now, a wound is not healed by the loosening of the bow.

This poem draws on the description of Venus in Virgil's *Aeneid* 1.314–320, 327–328, 402–405, which it echoes in lines 1 and 9–11.

89

Fuggendo la pregione ove Amor m'ebbe
molt'anni a far di me quel ch' a lui parve,
Donne mie, lungo fora ricontarve
quanto la nova libertà m'increbbe.   4

Diceami il cor che per sé non saprebbe
viver un giorno, et poi tra via m'apparve
quel traditore in sì mentite larve
che più saggio di me ingannato avrebbe.   8

Onde più volte sospirando indietro
dissi: "Oimè, il giogo et le catene e i ceppi
eran più dolci che l'andare sciolto!"   11

Misero me, che tardo il mio mal seppi,
et con quanta fatica oggi mi spetro
de l'errore ov' io stesso m'era involto.   14

90

Erano i capei d'oro a l'aura sparsi
che 'n mille dolci nodi gli avolgea,
e 'l vago lume oltra misura ardea
di quei begli occhi, ch' or ne son sì scarsi;   4

e 'l viso di pietosi color farsi
(non so se vero o falso) mi parea:
i' che l'esca amorosa al petto avea,
qual meraviglia se di subito arsi?   8

Non era l'andar suo cosa mortale
ma d'angelica forma, et le parole
sonavan altro che pur voce umana: 11

uno spirto celeste, un vivo sole
fu quel ch' i' vidi, et se non fosse or tale,
piaga per allentar d'arco non sana.   14

91

The beautiful lady whom you so much loved has suddenly departed from us and, I hope, has risen to Heaven, so sweet and gentle were her deeds.

It is time to recover both the keys of your heart, which she possessed while she lived, and to follow her by a straight and unimpeded road: let there be no further earthly weight to hold you down.

Since you are lightened of your greatest burden, you will be able to put down the others easily, rising like a pilgrim who carries little;

you see now how every created thing runs to death, and how light the soul needs to be for the perilous crossing.

The recipient of this poem has not been identified; possibly it was Petrarch's brother Gherardo.

92

Weep, Ladies, and let Love weep with you; weep, Lovers, in every land, since he is dead who was all intent to do you honor while he lived in the world.

For myself, I pray my cruel sorrow that it not prevent my tears and that it be so courteous as to let me sigh as much as is needful to unburden my heart.

Let rhymes weep also, let verses weep, for our loving Messer Cino has recently departed from us.

Let Pistoia weep and her wicked citizens, who have lost so sweet a neighbor; and let Heaven be glad, where he has gone.

On the death of the poet Cino da Pistoia (1270–1336).

91

La bella donna che cotanto amavi
subitamente s'è da noi partita
et, per quel ch' io ne speri, al ciel salita,
sì furon gli atti suoi dolci soavi.   4

Tempo è da ricovrare ambe la chiavi
del tuo cor ch' ella possedeva in vita
et seguir lei per via dritta espedita:
peso terren non sia più che t'aggravi.   8

Poi che se' sgombro de la maggior salma,
l'altre puoi giuso agevolmente porre,
salendo quasi un pellegrino scarco;   11

ben vedi omai sì come a morte corre
ogni cosa creata, et quanto a l'alma
bisogna ir lieve al periglioso varco.   14

92

Piangete, Donne, et con voi pianga Amore,
piangete, amanti, per ciascun paese
poi ch' è morto colui che tutto intese
in farvi, mentre visse al mondo, onore.   4

Io per me prego il mio acerbo dolore
non sian da lui le lagrime contese
et mi sia di sospir tanto cortese
quanto bisogna a disfogare il core.   8

Piangan le rime ancor, piangano i versi,
perché 'l nostro amoroso messer Cino
novellamente s'è da noi partito.   11

Pianga Pistoia e i cittadin perversi
che perduto ànno sì dolce vicino,
et rallegresi il cielo ov' ello è gito.   14

93

Many times had Love already said to me: "Write, write in letters of gold what you have seen, how I change the color of my followers and in one moment make them dead, or alive.

"There was a time when you experienced it in yourself, a well-known example to the chorus of lovers; then another work took you out of my hand, but I caught up with you as you were fleeing,

"and if those lovely eyes in which I showed myself to you, where my sweet fortress was when I broke all the hardness of your heart,

"if they give me back my bow that shatters everything, perhaps you will not always have dry cheeks: for I feed on tears, and you know it."

94

When through my eyes to my deepest heart comes the image that masters me, every other departs, and the powers that the soul distributes leave the members an almost immobile weight;

and from that first miracle is sometimes born the second, that the part driven out, fleeing from itself, comes to a place that takes vengeance and makes exile sweet;

hence in two faces one dead color appears, for the vigor that showed them to be alive is no longer, on either side, where it was initially.

And this I remembered on that day when I saw two lovers be transformed and become in their faces what I often become.

93

Più volte Amor m'avea già detto: "Scrivi,
scrivi quel che vedesti in lettre d'oro,
sì come i miei seguaci discoloro
e 'n un momento gli fo morti et vivi.   4

"Un tempo fu che 'n te stesso 'l sentivi,
volgare esempio a l'amoroso coro;
poi di man mi ti tolse altro lavoro,
ma già ti raggiuns' io mentre fuggivi,   8

"et se' begli occhi ond' io me ti mostrai,
et là dove era il mio dolce ridutto
quando ti ruppi al cor tanta durezza,   11

"mi rendon l'arco ch' ogni cosa spezza,
forse non avrai sempre il viso asciutto:
ch' i' mi pasco di lagrime, et tu 'l sai."   14

94

Quando giugne per gli occhi al cor profondo
l'imagin donna, ogni altra indi si parte,
et le vertù che l'anima comparte
lascian le membra quasi immobil pondo;   4

et del primo miracolo il secondo
nasce talor, che la scacciata parte
da se stessa fuggendo arriva in parte
che fa vendetta e 'l suo esilio giocondo;   8

quinci in duo volti un color morto appare,
perché 'l vigor che vivi gli mostrava
da nessun lato è più là dove stava.   11

Et di questo in quel dì mi ricordava
ch' i' vidi duo amanti trasformare
et far qual io mi soglio in vista fare.   14

95

If I could as well enclose my thoughts in verses as I enclose them in my heart, there is no soul in the world so cruel that I would not make it grieve for pity.

But you, blessed eyes, from whom I received that blow against which no helm or shield availed, you see me entirely, without and within, even though my sorrow does not pour forth in laments.

Since your seeing shines in me as a sunbeam penetrates glass, let my desire suffice, without my speaking.

Alas, Mary and Peter were not harmed by faithfulness, which to me alone is hostile! and I know that besides you no one understands me.

96

I am so vanquished by waiting and by the long war of my sighs, that I hate what I hoped for and my desires and every noose with which my heart is bound.

But that lovely smiling face, which I carry painted in my breast and see wherever I look, forces me, and I am driven back just the same into the first cruel tortures.

I went wrong when first my former path of freedom was cut off and blocked to me, for it is ill to follow what pleases the eyes;

then my soul ran free and unbound to her harm, now she must go at another's behest, though she sinned only once.

95

Così potess' io ben chiudere in versi
i miei pensier come nel cor gli chiudo,
ch' animo al mondo non fu mai sì crudo
ch' i' non facessi per pietà dolersi.   4

Ma voi, occhi beati, ond' io soffersi
quel colpo ove non valse elmo né scudo,
di for et dentro mi vedete ignudo
ben che 'n lamenti il duol non si riversi.   8

Poi che vostro veder in me risplende
come raggio di sol traluce in vetro,
basti dunque il desio senza ch' io dica.   11

Lasso, non a Maria, non nocque a Pietro
la fede ch' a me sol tanto è nemica!
et so ch' altri che voi, nessun m'intende.   14

96

Io son de l'aspettar omai sì vinto
et de la lunga guerra de' sospiri,
ch' i' aggio in odio la speme e i desiri
et ogni laccio onde 'l mio cor è avinto.   4

Ma 'l bel viso leggiadro che depinto
porto nel petto et veggio ove ch' io miri
mi sforza, onde ne' primi empi martiri
pur son contra mia voglia risospinto.   8

Allor errai quando l'antica strada
di libertà mi fu precisa et tolta,
ché mal si segue ciò ch' agli occhi agrada;   11

allor corse al suo mal libera et sciolta,
ora a posta d'altrui conven che vada
l'anima che peccò sol una volta.   14

97

Ah, sweet liberty, how by departing from me you have shown me what my state was when the first arrow made the wound of which I shall never be cured!

My eyes so fell in love with their woes then that the rein of reason no longer avails, for they disdain all mortal works—alas, I so accustomed them at first!

Nor am I permitted to hear anyone who does not speak of my death, and with her name only I fill the air which so sweetly sounds;

Love does not spur me anywhere else, nor do my feet know any other road, nor do my hands know how on paper any other person can be praised.

98

Orso, on your charger can be put a rein that will turn him back from his course, but who can bind your heart so that it cannot get loose, if it desires honor and abhors the contrary?

Do not sigh: no one can take away his worth even though you are prevented from going, for, as public fame makes known, your heart is already there, no other can precede him.

Let it suffice that he will be in the field on the appointed day, under the arms he has from time, love, valor, and birth,

crying: "One with my lord, I burn with a noble desire, but he cannot follow me and suffers and is sick that he is not here."

Addressed to Orso dell'Anguillara, a prominent Roman nobleman, who was apparently prevented (perhaps by an illness) from participating in a tournament.

97

Ahi bella libertà, come tu m'ài,
partendoti da me, mostrato quale
era 'l mio stato quando il primo strale
fece la piaga ond' io non guerrò mai!   4

Gli occhi invaghiro allor sì de' lor guai
che 'l fren de la ragione ivi non vale,
perch' ànno a schifo ogni opera mortale—
lasso, così da prima gli avezzai!   8

Né mi lece ascoltar chi non ragiona
de la mia morte, et solo del suo nome
vo empiendo l'aere che sì dolce sona;   11

Amor in altra parte non mi sprona,
né i pie' sanno altra via, né le man come
lodar si possa in carte altra persona.   14

98

Orso, al vostro destrier si po ben porre
un fren che di suo corso indietro il volga,
ma 'l cor chi legherà che non si sciolga
se brama onore e 'l suo contrario aborre?   4

Non sospirate: a lui non si po torre
suo pregio perch' a voi l'andar si tolga,
ché come fama publica divolga
egli è già là che null'altro il precorre.   8

Basti che si ritrove in mezzo 'l campo
al destinato dì sotto quell'arme
che gli dà il tempo, amor, vertute e 'l sangue,   11

gridando: "D'un gentil desire avampo
col signor mio, che non po seguitarme
et del non esser qui si strugge et langue."   14

99

Since you and I have repeatedly experienced how our hopes turn out to be false, lift your hearts to a happier state, in pursuit of that highest good which never fails.

This mortal life is like a meadow where the serpent lies among the flowers and grass, and if anything we see there pleases our eyes, the result is to enlime our souls more deeply.

You, therefore, if you seek ever to have quiet minds before the last day, follow the few and not the crowd.

Someone could very well say to me: "Brother, you keep showing others the way, where you have often been astray and are now, more than ever."

100

That window where one sun can be seen whenever it pleases her and the other at noon, and that window where the cold air rattles in the short days when Boreas strikes it,

and the stone where, when the days are long, my lady sits thoughtful and converses alone with herself, with however many places her lovely body ever covered with its shadow or marked with a foot,

and the cruel pass where Love struck me, and the new season that year by year renews on that day my ancient wounds,

and the face and the words that are fixed deep in my heart— these make my eyes desire to weep.

---

one sun: Laura. The other is the actual sun. The two windows, facing north and south respectively, are presumably in Laura's house.

99

Poi che voi et io più volte abbiam provato
come 'l nostro sperar torna fallace,
dietro a quel sommo ben che mai non spiace
levate il core a più felice stato.   4

Questa vita terrena è quasi un prato
che 'l serpente tra' fiori et l'erba giace,
et s' alcuna sua vista agli occhi piace
è per lassar più l'animo invescato.   8

Voi dunque, se cercate aver la mente
anzi l'estremo dì queta giamai,
seguite i pochi et non la volgar gente.   11

Ben si può dire a me: "Frate, tu vai
mostrando altrui la via dove sovente
fosti smarrito et or se' più che mai."   14

100

Quella fenestra ove l'un sol si vede
quando a lui piace et l'altro in su la nona,
et quella dove l'aere freddo suona
ne' brevi giorni quando Borrea 'l fiede,   4

e 'l sasso ove a' gran dì pensosa siede
Madonna et sola seco si ragiona,
con quanti luoghi sua bella persona
coprì mai d'ombra o disegnò col piede,   8

e 'l fiero passo ove m'agiunse Amore,
et la nova stagion che d'anno in anno
mi rinfresca in quel dì l'antiche piaghe,   11

e 'l volto et le parole che mi stanno
altamente confitte in mezzo 'l core,
fanno le luci mie di pianger vaghe.   14

101

Alas, I know well that she who pardons no man makes of us her anguished prey, and that the world rapidly abandons us and keeps faith with us but a little while;

I see little reward for much yearning, and already the last day thunders in my heart. But, for all that, Love does not set me free, for he demands the usual tribute from my eyes.

I know how our days, our minutes, and our hours carry off our years, and I am not deceived but beset by forces much greater than magic arts.

Desire and reason have battled for seven and seven years, and the better one will win out, if souls down here can foresee the good.

---

she who pardons no man: Death.

102

Caesar, when the Egyptian traitor made him a present of that honored head, hiding his indubitable joy wept with his eyes, externally, as it is written;

and Hannibal, when he saw Fortune become so cruel to the afflicted empire, laughed among his tearful sad people, to vent his bitter chagrin;

and thus it happens that each soul covers its passion over with the contrary mantle, with a face now clear, now dark.

Therefore if at any time I laugh or sing, I do it because I have no way except this one to hide my anguished weeping.

Caesar: see note on "He who . . . wept for," poem 44.   Hannibal: Carthaginian general, said to have laughed when the senators of Carthage wept at the news of Roman victories in the Second Punic War (202 B.C.).

101

Lasso, ben so che dolorose prede
di noi fa quella ch' a null'uom perdona
et che rapidamente n'abandona
il mondo et picciol tempo ne tien fede;   4

veggio a molto languir poca mercede,
et già l'ultimo dì nel cor mi tuona;
per tutto questo Amor non mi spregiona,
che l'usato tributo agli occhi chiede.   8

So come i dì, come i momenti et l'ore
ne portan gli anni, et non ricevo inganno
ma forze assai maggior che d'arti maghe.   11

La voglia et la ragion combattuto ànno
sette et sette anni, et vincerà il migliore,
s' anime son qua giù del ben presaghe.   14

102

Cesare, poi che 'l traditor d'Egitto
li fece il don de l'onorata testa,
celando l'allegrezza manifesta
pianse per gli occhi fuor, sì come è scritto;   4

et Anibàl, quando a l'imperio afflitto
vide farsi Fortuna sì molesta,
rise fra gente lagrimosa et mesta
per isfogare il suo acerbo despitto;   8

et così aven che l'animo ciascuna
sua passion sotto 'l contrario manto
ricopre co la vista or chiara or bruna.   11

Però s' alcuna volta io rido o canto,
facciol perch' i' non ò se non quest'una
via da celare il mio angoscioso pianto.   14

103

Hannibal was victorious, but he did not know later how to make good use of his victorious fortune; therefore, dear my Lord, take care that the same does not happen to you.

The she-bear, raging for her cubs who found in May a bitter harvest, gnaws herself within and hardens her teeth and claws, to avenge her harms on us.

As long as her recent sorrow burns, therefore, do not put up your honorable sword; rather follow where

your fortune calls, straight along the path that can give you, even after death, for a thousand and a thousand years, honor and fame in the world.

Addressed to Stefano Colonna the Younger, who on May 22, 1333, assaulted by two members of the rival Orsini family, killed them and put their followers to flight.

Hannibal . . . did not know: he failed repeatedly to take advantage of his victories over the Romans in the Second Punic War, most notably after the battle of Cannae (216 B.C.).   she-bear: the Orsini family.

104

The hoped-for virtue that was flowering in you at the age when Love first gave you battle, now produces fruits that are worthy of the flower and make my hope come true.

Therefore my heart tells me I should write on paper something to increase your fame, for nowhere can sculpture be solid enough to give a person life through marble.

Do you believe that Caesar or Marcellus or Paulus or Africanus ever became so famous because of any hammer or anvil?

My Pandolfo, those works are frail in the long run, but our study is the one that makes men immortal through fame.

Addressed to Pandolfo Malatesta, lord of Rimini.

Marcellus or Paulus or Africanus: Roman generals during the Second Punic War; Africanus is P. Cornelius Scipio.   our study: poetry, or letters in general.

103

Vinse Anibàl, et non seppe usar poi
ben la vittoriosa sua ventura;
però, Signor mio caro, aggiate cura
che similmente non avegna a voi.   4

L'orsa, rabbiosa per gli orsacchi suoi
che trovaron di maggio aspra pastura,
rode sé dentro, e i denti et l'unghie endura
per vendicar suoi danni sopra noi.   8

Mentre 'l novo dolor dunque l'accora
non riponete l'onorata spada,
anzi seguite là dove vi chiama   11

vostra fortuna, dritto per la strada
che vi può dar dopo la morte ancora
mille et mille anni al mondo onor et fama.   14

104

L'aspettata vertù che 'n voi fioriva
quando Amor cominciò darvi bataglia
produce or frutto che quel fiore aguaglia
et che mia speme fa venire a riva.   4

Però mi dice il cor ch' io in carte scriva
cosa onde 'l vostro nome in pregio saglia,
che 'n nulla parte sì saldo s'intaglia
per far di marmo una persona viva.   8

Credete voi che Cesare o Marcello
o Paolo od African fossin cotali
per incude giamai né per martello?   11

Pandolfo mio, quest'opere son frali
al lungo andar, ma 'l nostro studio è quello
che fa per fama gli uomini immortali.   14

105

I never wish to sing again as I used to, for I was not understood, wherefore I was scorned, and one can be miserable in a pleasant place.

Always to be sighing helps nothing. Up in the mountains it is already snowing all around; dawn is already close, so I am awake.

A virtuous sweet action is a noble thing, and it pleases me that a lady worthy of love seem high and disdainful, but not proud and stubborn. Love governs his empire without a sword. He who has lost his way, let him turn back; he who has no dwelling, let him sleep on the grass; he who has no gold or loses it, let him quench his thirst from a glass.

I entrusted things to Saint Peter, now no more, no, understand me who can, for I understand myself; an ill tribute is a heavy load to bear.

As much as I can, I disentangle myself and stand free; I hear that Phaeton fell in the Po and died, and already the blackbird has crossed the river.

Ah, come to see it, now I am not willing to; a rock amid the waves is no light matter, nor is the birdlime among the leaves. It pains me much when excessive pride hides many virtues in a beautiful lady. There are some who answer when none calls them; some disappear and flee from those who beg them; some are melted by ice; some day and night wish for death.

The poem is intentionally obscure, full of proverbs, unidentifiable allusions, and ellipses.

Phaeton: see note on "white feathers," poem 23.

105

    Mai non vo' più cantar   com' io soleva,
ch' altri no m'intendeva,   ond' ebbi scorno,
et puossi in bel soggiorno   esser molesto.
    Il sempre sospirar   nulla releva.
Già su per l'alpi neva   d'ogn' intorno;
et è già presso al giorno,   ond' io son desto.   6
    Un atto dolce onesto   è gentil cosa;
et in donna amorosa   ancor m'aggrada
che 'n vista vada   altera et disdegnosa,
non superba et ritrosa.
Amor regge suo imperio senza spada.
Chi smarrita à la strada,   torni indietro;
chi non à albergo, posisi in sul verde;
chi non à l'auro o 'l perde,
spenga la sete sua con un bel vetro.   15

    I' die' in guarda a san Pietro,   or non più, no,
intendami chi po,   ch' i' m'intend' io.
Grave soma è un mal fio   a mantenerlo.
    Quanto posso mi spetro   et sol mi sto.
Fetonte odo che 'n Po   cadde et morio,
et già di là dal rio   passato è 'l merlo.   21
    Deh venite a vederlo,   or i' non voglio,
non è gioco uno scoglio   in mezzo l'onde
e 'ntra le fronde   il visco. Assai mi doglio
quando un soverchio orgoglio
molte vertuti in bella donna asconde.
Alcun è che risponde   a chi nol chiama;
altri chi 'l prega si dilegua et fugge,
altri al ghiaccio si strugge,
altri dì et notte la sua morte brama.   30

The proverb "Love him who loves you" is an ancient fact. I know well what I am saying; now let be; each must learn at his own expense.

A humble lady makes a sweet friend suffer; figs are hard to judge; it seems to me prudent not to begin undertakings that are too difficult,

and in every country there are pleasant dwellings. Infinite hope kills people, and I too have sometimes joined the dance. What little is left to me will please someone, if I wish to give it to him. I rely on Him who rules the world and shelters His followers even in the wood to lead me now with merciful staff among His flocks.

Perhaps not everyone who can read can understand, and he who sets up the net does not always catch, and he who is too subtle breaks his own neck.

When folk await, let not the law be lame. One goes many miles to be at ease; a thing seems a great marvel but then is despised;

hidden beauty is sweetest. Blessed be the key that turned in my heart and let loose my soul and freed it from so heavy a chain and freed my breast of numberless sighs. Where I most sorrowed, another sorrows and by sorrowing makes sweet my sorrow; wherefore I thank Love, for I feel it no more, and it is no less than it was.

Proverbio "Ama chi t'ama"   è fatto antico;
i' so ben quel ch' io dico,   or lass' andare,
ché conven ch' altri impare   a le sue spese.
  Un'umil donna grama   un dolce amico.
Mal si conosce il fico;   a me pur pare
senno a non cominciar   tropp' alte imprese,   36
    et per ogni paese   è bona stanza.
L'infinita speranza   occide altrui,
et anch' io fui   alcuna volta in danza.
Quel poco che m'avanza
fia chi nol schifi s' i' 'l vo' dare a lui.
I' mi fido in colui   che 'l mondo regge
et ch' e' seguaci suoi nel bosco alberga
che con pietosa verga
mi meni a passo omai tra le sue gregge.   45

  Forse ch' ogni uom che legge   non s'intende,
et la rete tal tende   che non piglia;
et chi troppo assottiglia   si scavezza.
  Non sia zoppa la legge   ov' altri attende.
Per bene star si scende   molte miglia.
Tal par gran meraviglia   et poi si sprezza;   51
    una chiusa bellezza   è più soave.
Benedetta la chiave   che s'avvolse
al cor et sciolse   l'alma et scossa l'àve
di catena sì grave
e 'nfiniti sospir del mio sen tolse.
Là dove più mi dolse   altri si dole,
et dolendo adolcisce il mio dolore,
ond' io ringrazio Amore,
che più no 'l sento et è non men che suole.   60

In silence, words skillful and wise are the sound that takes every other care from me, and the dark prison where there is a lovely light;
　violets at night along the shore, wild beasts within the walls, sweet fear and dear custom,
　and from two fountains one river turned in peace to where I desire, and gathered anywhere; love and jealousy have taken away my heart and the stars of that lovely face, which lead me along the smoothest way to my hope at the end of troubles. O my hidden sweetness, and what follows—now peace now war now truce—you never abandon me in this garment.

For my past harms I weep and laugh, for I rely much on what I hear; I enjoy the present and expect better,
　and I go counting the years and I am silent and cry out. I make my nest on a good branch and in such a way that I thank and praise the great refusal
　that has finally vanquished the hardened affect and has engraved in my soul: "I would be heard of and pointed out for it"; and she has erased from it (I am driven so far forward that I shall even say it): "You were not bold enough!" she who has wounded my side and heals it, for whom I write in my heart even more than on paper, who makes me die and live, who at the same time makes me freeze and burn.

---

this garment: the body.

In silenzio parole   accorte et sagge
è 'l suon che mi sottragge   ogni altra cura,
et la pregione oscura   ov' è 'l bel lume;
    le notturne viole   per le piagge,
et le fere selvagge   entr'a le mura,
et la dolce paura,   e 'l bel costume,   66
        et di duo fonti un fiume   in pace vòlto
dov' io bramo, et raccolto   ove che sia;
amor et gelosia   m'ànno il cor tolto,
e i segni del bel vólto
che mi conducon per più piana via
a la speranza mia,   al fin degli affanni.
O riposto mio bene et quel che segue,
or pace or guerra or triegue,
mai non m'abbandonate in questi panni.   75

    De' passati miei danni   piango et rido
perché molto mi fido   in quel ch' i' odo;
del presente mi godo   et meglio aspetto,
    et vo contando gli anni,   et taccio et grido.
E 'n bel ramo m'annido   et in tal modo
ch' i' ne ringrazio et lodo   il gran disdetto   81
        che l'indurato affetto   al fine à vinto,
et ne l'alma depinto: "I' sare' udito
e mostratone a dito,"   et ànne estinto
(tanto innanzi son pinto
ch' i' 'l pur dirò): "Non fostu tant' ardito,"
chi m'à 'l fianco ferito   et chi 'l risalda,
per cui nel cor via più che 'n carta scrivo,
chi mi fa morto et vivo,
chi 'n un punto m'agghiaccia et mi riscalda.   90

106

A new little angel on agile wings came down from Heaven to the fresh shore where I was walking alone by my destiny.

Since she saw me without companion and without guide, a silken snare which she was making she stretched in the grass wherewith the way is green.

Then I was captured, and it did not displease me later, so sweet a light came from her eyes!

107

I do not see where I can escape anymore; those lovely eyes make such long war on me that I fear, alas, the excessive torment will destroy my heart, which never knows a truce.

I wish I could flee, but those love-inspiring rays, which are in my mind night and day, shine so that at the fifteenth year they dazzle me much more than on the first day;

and their likenesses are scattered all around, so that I cannot turn without seeing either that light or a similar one lit from it.

From only one laurel tree such a wood grows green that my adversary, with marvelous art, leads me wherever he wishes, desirous and wandering among the branches.

106

Nova angeletta sovra l'ale accorta
scese dal cielo in su la fresca riva
là 'nd' io passava sol per mio destino.   3

Poi che senza compagna et senza scorta
mi vide, un laccio che di seta ordiva
tese fra l'erba ond' è verde il camino.   6

Allor fui preso, et non mi spiacque poi,
sì dolce lume uscia degli occhi suoi.   8

107

Non veggio ove scampar mi possa omai;
sì lunga guerra i begli occhi mi fanno
ch' i' temo, lasso, no 'l soverchio affanno
distrugga 'l cor che triegua non à mai.   4

Fuggir vorrei, ma gli amorosi rai
che dì et notte ne la mente stanno
risplendon sì ch' al quintodecimo anno
m'abbaglian più che 'l primo giorno assai,   8

et l'imagine lor son sì cosparte
che volver non mi posso ov' io non veggia
o quella o simil indi accesa luce.   11

Solo d'un lauro tal selva verdeggia
che 'l mio avversario con mirabil arte
vago fra i rami ovunque vuol m'adduce.   14

108

Luckier than any other ground, where I once saw Love stop her footsteps, turning toward me those holy lights that make the air clear all around her:

a statue of solid diamond could wear away in time before I could forget her sweet bearing, of which my memory and my heart are so full;

and however many times I shall see you yet, I shall still bend over to look for the print her lovely foot made in that gracious turning.

But if Love is never asleep in a worthy heart, beg my Sennuccio, when you see him, for some little tear or for a sigh.

Addressed to the landscape of Vaucluse, where Petrarch lived intermittently from 1337 until 1353.

Sennuccio: the Florentine poet Sennuccio del Bene (1275?–1349).

109

Alas, whenever Love assails me (which between night and day is more than a thousand times), I return where I saw those sparks burning that make immortal the fire of my heart.

There I become calm, and I have become such that at nones, at vespers, at dawn, and at the evening bell I find them in my thought, so tranquil that I remember and care about nothing else.

The gentle breeze that moves from her bright face with the sound of her wise words, to make sweet fair weather wherever it breathes,

like a spirit of Paradise always in that air seems to comfort me, so that my weary heart breathes easy nowhere else.

---

where I saw: Vaucluse.

108

Aventuroso più d'altro terreno,
ov' Amor vidi già fermar le piante
ver me volgendo quelle luci sante
che fanno intorno a sé l'aere sereno: 4

prima poria per tempo venir meno
un'imagine salda di diamante
che l'atto dolce non mi stia davante
del qual ò la memoria e 'l cor sì pieno;   8

né tante volte ti vedrò giamai
ch' i' non m'inchini a ricercar de l'orme
che 'l bel pie' fece in quel cortese giro.   11

Ma se 'n cor valoroso Amor non dorme,
prega Sennuccio mio, quando 'l vedrai,
di qualche lagrimetta o d'un sospiro.   14

109

Lasso, quante fiate Amor m'assale
(che fra la notte e 'l dì son più di mille)
torno dov' arder vidi le faville
che 'l foco del mio cor fanno immortale.   4

Ivi m'acqueto, et son condotto a tale
ch' a nona a vespro a l'alba et a le squille
le trovo nel pensier tanto tranquille
che di null'altro mi rimembra o cale.   8

L'aura soave che dal chiaro viso
move, col suon de le parole accorte,
per far dolce sereno ovunque spira,   11

quasi un spirto gentil di paradiso
sempre in quell'aere par che mi conforte,
sì che 'l cor lasso altrove non respira.   14

110

Since Love was pursuing me to my accustomed place, I, drawn up like one who expects war and who prepares and closes the passes round about, was armed with my old thoughts.

I turned and saw a shadow on the ground to one side, cast by the sun, and I recognized by it her who, if my judgment does not err, was more worthy of immortal state.

I said within my heart: "Why are you afraid?" but the thought had no sooner come within than the rays that melt me were present;

as with lightning the thunder comes at the same instant, so I was overtaken by those beautiful shining eyes together with a sweet greeting.

---

accustomed place: Vaucluse.

111

The lady on whom my heart always gazes appeared to me where I was sitting alone with lovely thoughts of love, and I to do her honor moved with reverent and pale brow.

As soon as she became aware of my state, she turned to me with hue so changed that it would have disarmed Jove in his greatest fury, and would have killed his wrath.

I trembled, and she, conversing, passed onward, for I could not endure her speech or the sweet sparkling of her eyes.

Now I find myself full of such varied pleasures, thinking back on that greeting, that I feel no pain nor have ever felt any since then.

110

Persequendomi Amor al luogo usato,
ristretto in guisa d'uom ch' aspetta guerra,
che si provede e i passi intorno serra,
de' miei antichi pensier mi stava armato;   4

volsimi et vidi un'ombra che da lato
stampava il sole, et riconobbi in terra
quella che, se 'l giudicio mio non erra,
era più degna d'immortale stato.   8

I' dicea fra mio cor: "Perché paventi?"
ma non fu prima dentro il penser giunto
che i raggi ov' io mi struggo eran presenti;   11

come col balenar tona in un punto,
così fu' io de' begli occhi lucenti
et d'un dolce saluto inseme aggiunto.   14

111

La donna che 'l mio cor nel viso porta,
là dove sol fra bei pensier d'amore
sedea, m'apparve, e io per farle onore
mossi con fronte reverente et smorta.   4

Tosto che del mio stato fussi accorta,
a me si volse in sì novo colore
ch' avrebbe a Giove nel maggior furore
tolto l'arme di mano et l'ira morta.   8

I' mi riscossi, et ella oltra parlando
passò, ché la parola i' non soffersi
né 'l dolce sfavillar de gli occhi suoi.   11

Or mi ritrovo pien di sì diversi
piaceri, in quel saluto ripensando,
che duol non sento né senti' ma' poi.   14

112

Sennuccio, I wish you to know how I am treated and what my life is like: I am burning up and suffering still just as I used to, the breeze turns me about, and I am still just what I was.

Here I saw her all humble and there haughty, now harsh, now gentle, now cruel, now merciful; now clothed in virtue, now in gaiety, now tame, now disdainful and fierce.

Here she sang sweetly and here sat down; here she turned about and here held back her step; here with her lovely eyes she transfixed my heart;

here she said a word, here she smiled, here she frowned. In these thoughts, alas, our lord Love keeps me night and day.

113

Here where I only half am, my Sennuccio (would I were here entirely, and you happy!), I came fleeing the storm and the wind that have so suddenly made the season cruel.

Here I am safe, and I want to tell you why I no longer fear the lightning as I did and why I do not at all find my ardent desire mitigated, not to speak of its being extinguished.

As soon as I reached the palace of Love and saw the birthplace of the sweet and pure breeze that calms the air and banishes the thunder,

Love in my soul, where she rules, rekindled the fire and extinguished fear: what would I do, then, if I looked into her eyes?

---

here: Vaucluse.   storm and the wind: usually interpreted to refer to the corruption of the papal court at Avignon; see the next poem.   birthplace: see note to poem 4.

112

Sennuccio, i' vo' che sapi in qual manera
trattato sono et qual vita è la mia:
ardomi et struggo ancor com' io solia,
l'aura mi volve et son pur quel ch' i' m'era.   4

Qui tutta umile et qui la vidi altera,
or aspra or piana, or dispietata or pia,
or vestirsi onestate or leggiadria,
or mansueta or disdegnosa et fera.   8

Qui cantò dolcemente, et qui s'assise,
qui si rivolse, et qui rattenne il passo,
qui co' begli occhi mi trafisse il core,   11

qui disse una parola, et qui sorrise,
qui cangiò il viso. In questi pensier, lasso,
notte et dì tiemmi il signor nostro Amore.   14

113

Qui dove mezzo son, Sennuccio mio
(così ci foss' io intero et voi contento),
venni fuggendo la tempesta e 'l vento
ch' ànno subito fatto il tempo rio.   4

Qui son securo, et vo' vi dir perch' io
non come soglio il folgorar pavento
et perché mitigato, non che spento,
né mica trovo il mio ardente desio.   8

Tosto che giunto a l'amorosa reggia
vidi onde nacque l'aura dolce et pura
ch' acqueta l'aere et mette i tuoni in bando,   11

Amor ne l'alma ov' ella signoreggia
raccese 'l foco et spense la paura:
che farei dunque gli occhi suoi guardando?   14

114

From wicked Babylon, deserted of all shame, whence all good has flown, the dwelling of sorrow, the mother of errors, I have fled in order to prolong my life.

Here I am alone, and, as Love leads me on, I gather now rhymes and verses, now herbs and flowers, always speaking with him and always thinking of better days; and only this sustains me.

Nor do I care about the mob or about Fortune, nor much about myself or any base thing, nor do I feel within or without much heat;

I ask for only two persons, and I would wish that one had her heart pacified and kindly toward me, the other his foot as whole as it ever was.

Babylon: Avignon. here: in Vaucluse. two persons: the first is Laura; the other may be Cardinal Giovanni Colonna, who suffered from gout.

115

Between two lovers I saw a virtuous and haughty lady, and that lord with her who rules over men and gods; and on one side was the sun, I on the other.

When she saw that she was excluded from the sphere of her more handsome friend, she turned all happy to my eyes, and I may well wish that she never be more fierce toward me.

Suddenly into joy was turned the jealousy that at the first sight of so high an adversary had been born in my heart;

his face, tearful and sad, a little cloud covered over, it so displeased him to be vanquished.

114

De l'empia Babilonia ond' è fuggita
ogni vergogna, ond' ogni bene è fori,
albergo di dolor, madre d'errori,
son fuggito io per allungar la vita.   4

Qui mi sto solo, et come Amor m'invita
or rime et versi, or colgo erbette et fiori,
seco parlando et a tempi migliori
sempre pensando, et questo sol m'aita.   8

Né del vulgo mi cal, né di Fortuna,
né di me molto, né di cosa vile,
né dentro sento né di fuor gran caldo;   11

sol due persone cheggio, et vorrei l'una
col cor ver me pacificato umile,
l'altro col pie', sì come mai fu, saldo.   14

115

In mezzo di duo amanti onesta altera
vidi una donna et quel signor co lei
che fra gli uomini regna et fra li dei;
et da l'un lato il sole, io da l'altro era.   4

Poi che s'accorse chiusa da la spera
de l'amico più bello, a gli occhi miei
tutta lieta si volse, et ben vorrei
che mai non fosse in ver di me più fera.   8

Subito in allegrezza si converse
la gelosia che 'n su la prima vista
per sì alto avversario al cor mi nacque;   11

a lui la faccia lagrimosa et trista
un nuviletto intorno ricoverse,
cotanto l'esser vinto li dispiacque.   14

116

Full of that ineffable sweetness which my eyes drew from her lovely face on that day when I would gladly have closed them so as never to look on any lesser beauties,

I departed from what I most desire; and I have so accustomed my mind to contemplate her alone that it sees nothing else, and whatever is not she, already by ancient habit it hates and scorns.

In a valley closed on all sides, which cools my weary sighs, I arrived alone with Love, full of care, and late;

there I find not ladies but fountains and rocks and the image of that day which my thoughts image forth wherever I may glance.

---

valley: Vaucluse.

117

If the rock that mainly closes this valley, from which its name is derived, had—scornful by nature—its back turned toward Babel and its face toward Rome,

my sighs would have a kinder path to go toward where their hope still lives; now they go scattered, but still each one arrives where I send him, for not one fails;

and over there they are so sweetly welcomed, as I see, that none of them ever comes back, with such delight they stay in those parts.

It is my eyes that are pained; who, as soon as it dawns, in their great desire for the places they are deprived of, give to me weeping, and to my tired feet, labor.

If the rock . . . Rome: if the rock that closes Vaucluse (on the west, in the direction of Avignon) would turn south (toward Rome), the path to Laura would be opened.

116

Pien di quella ineffabile dolcezza
che del bel viso trassen gli occhi miei
nel dì che volentier chiusi gli avrei
per non mirar giamai minor bellezza,   4

lassai quel ch' i' più bramo; et ò sì avezza
la mente a contemplar sola costei
ch' altro non vede, et ciò che non è lei
già per antica usanza odia et disprezza.   8

In una valle chiusa d'ogn' intorno,
ch' è refrigerio de' sospir miei lassi,
giunsi sol con Amor, pensoso et tardo;   11

ivi non donne ma fontane et sassi
et l'imagine trovo di quel giorno
che 'l pensier mio figura ovunque io sguardo.   14

117

Se 'l sasso ond' è più chiusa questa valle
(di che 'l suo proprio nome si deriva)
tenesse vòlto per natura schiva
a Roma il viso et a Babèl le spalle,   4

i miei sospiri più benigno calle
avrian per gire ove lor spene è viva;
or vanno sparsi, et pur ciascuno arriva
là dov' io il mando, ché sol un non falle;   8

et son di là sì dolcemente accolti,
com' io m'accorgo, che nessun mai torna,
con tal diletto in quelle parti stanno.   11

De gli occhi è 'l duol, che tosto che s'aggiorna
per gran desio de' be' luoghi a lor tolti
dànno a me pianto et a' pie' lassi affanno.   14

118

Now remains behind the sixteenth year of my sighs, and I move forward toward the last; yet it seems to me that all this suffering began only recently.

The bitter is sweet to me, and my losses useful, and living heavy; and I pray that my life may outlast my cruel fortune; and I fear that before then Death may close the lovely eyes that make me speak.

Now here I am, alas, and wish I were elsewhere, and wish I wished more, but wish no more, and, by being unable to do more, do all I can;

and new tears for old desires show me to be still what I used to be, nor for a thousand turnings about have I yet moved.

119

A lady much more beautiful than the sun, more bright and of equal age, with famous beauty drew me to her ranks when I was still unripe.

She in my thoughts, my works, and my words, since she is one of the things that are rare in the world, she along a thousand roads always guided me, gaily and proudly.

Only for her I turned back from what I was; after I endured her eyes from close by, for her love I put myself early to difficult undertakings; so that if I reach the port I desire, I hope through her to live a long time, when people will suppose I am dead.

A lady much more beautiful: Glory.

118

Rimansi a dietro il sestodecimo anno
de' miei sospiri, et io trapasso inanzi
verso l'estremo; et parmi che pur dianzi
fosse 'l principio di cotanto affanno. 4

L'amar m'è dolce, et util il mio danno,
e 'l viver grave; et prego che gli avanzi
l'empia fortuna; et temo no chiuda anzi
Morte i begli occhi che parlar mi fanno. 8

Or qui son, lasso, et voglio esser altrove,
et vorrei più volere, et più non voglio,
et per più non poter fo quant' io posso; 11

et d'antichi desir lagrime nove
provan com' io son pur quel ch' i' mi soglio,
né per mille rivolte ancor son mosso. 14

119

Una donna più bella assai che 'l sole
et più lucente et d'altrettanta etade
con famosa beltade
acerbo ancor mi trasse a la sua schiera.
Questa in penseri in opre et in parole,
però ch' è de le cose al mondo rade,
questa per mille strade
sempre inanzi mi fu leggiadra altera. 8
Solo per lei tornai da quel ch' i' era;
poi ch' i' soffersi gli occhi suoi da presso
per suo amor m'er' io messo
a faticosa impresa assai per tempo,
tal che s' i' arrivo al disiato porto
spero per lei gran tempo
viver, quand' altri mi terrà per morto. 15

This my lady led me for many years burning full of youthful longing, as I now understand, only to have of me more
certain proof,

showing me only her shadow or her veil or her garment, but
hiding her face; and I, alas, thinking I saw a great deal, passed
all my young age

happily, and the memory pleases me, now that I see further
into her. I say that just recently, such as I had never before seen
her, she showed herself to me; whence was born ice in my heart,
and it is still there and shall be always until I am in her arms.

But my fear and chill did not prevent me from giving so
much daring to my heart that I threw myself at her feet, to draw
more sweetness from her eyes;

and she, who had taken the veil from my eyes, said to me:
"Friend, now see how beautiful I am, and ask for whatever befits
your years."

"My Lady," I said, "for a long time already I have placed
my love in you, which I now feel so inflamed, wherefore in this
state I cannot wish anything else or unwish anything." Then
with a voice of marvelous temper she replied and with a look
that will make me always fear and hope:

Questa mia donna mi menò molt'anni
pien di vaghezza giovenile ardendo,
sì come ora io comprendo,
sol per aver di me più certa prova,
  mostrandomi pur l'ombra o 'l velo o' panni
talor di sé, ma 'l viso nascondendo;
et io, lasso, credendo
vederne assai, tutta l'età mia nova   23
  passai contento, e 'l rimembrar mi giova
poi ch' alquanto di lei veggi' or più inanzi.
I' dico che pur dianzi
qual io non l'avea vista infin allora
mi si scoverse, onde mi nacque un ghiaccio
nel core, et evvi ancora,
et sarà sempre, fin ch' i' le sia in braccio.   30

  Ma non me 'l tolse la paura o 'l gelo
che pur tanta baldanze al mio cor diedi
ch' i' le mi strinsi a' piedi
per più dolcezza trar de gli occhi suoi;
  et ella, che remosso avea già il velo
dinanzi a' miei, mi disse: "Amico, or vedi
com' io son bella, et chiedi
quanto par si convenga agli anni tuoi."   38
  "Madonna," dissi, "già gran tempo in voi
posi 'l mio amor ch' i' sento or sì infiammato,
ond' a me in questo stato
altro volere o disvoler m'è tolto."
Con voce allor di sì mirabil tempre
rispose, et con un volto
che temer et sperar mi farà sempre: 45

"Rare are those in the world, among so great a throng, who, hearing talk of my worth, have not felt for a short time at least some sparks of love;

"but my adversary, who disturbs all that is good, quickly extinguishes them, wherefore all virtue dies, and another lord reigns who promises a life more tranquil.

"Of your mind, Love, who first opened it, tells me truly things whereby I see that your great desire will make you worthy of an honorable goal; and as you are already one of my rare friends, for a sign you shall see a lady who will make your eyes much more fortunate."

I wished to say "This is impossible," when she said: "Now gaze (and lift your eyes a little to a more hidden place) on a lady who has never shown herself except to a few."

Quickly I inclined my brow ashamed, feeling within a new and greater fire, and she mocked it, saying: "I see well where you stand;

"as the sun with its powerful rays makes every other star quickly disappear, thus the sight of me now appears less beautiful to one vanquished by a greater light. But I do not banish you for all that, for she and I—she first, I later—were brought forth from one seed by one birth."

---

lady who has never shown herself: Virtue.

"Rado fu al mondo fra così gran turba
ch' udendo ragionar del mio valore
non si sentisse al core
per breve tempo almen qualche favilla;
   "ma l' avversaria mia che 'l ben perturba
tosto la spegne, ond' ogni vertù more
et regna altro signore
che promette una vita più tranquilla.   53
   "De la tua mente Amor, che prima aprilla,
mi dice cose veramente ond' io
veggio che 'l gran desio
pur d'onorato fin ti farà degno;
et come già se' de' miei rari amici,
donna vedrai per segno
che farà gli occhi tuoi via più felici."   60

   I' volea dir: "Quest' è impossibil cosa,"
quand' ella: "Or mira (et leva gli occhi un poco
in più riposto loco)
donna ch' a pochi si mostrò giamai."
   Ratto inchinai la fronte vergognosa,
sentendo novo dentro maggior foco,
et ella il prese in gioco,
dicendo: "I' veggio ben dove tu stai;   68
   "sì come 'l sol con suoi possenti rai
fa subito sparire ogni altra stella,
così par or men bella
la vista mia cui maggior luce preme.
Ma io però da' miei non ti diparto
ché questa et me d'un seme,
lei davanti et me poi, produsse un parto."   75

Then was the knot of shame broken that had been tight around my tongue at my first shame, when I became aware of her notice, and I began:

"If what I hear is true, blessed the father and blessed the day that have adorned the world with you and all the time when I have run to see you!

"And if ever I have turned aside from the straight path, it pains me much more than I show, but if I am worthy to hear more about your nature, I burn with the desire." Thoughtful she answered me, and so fixedly held her sweet regard on me, that to my heart she sent her face along with her words:

"As it pleased our eternal Father, each of us was born immortal. Wretches, what does it avail you? It would be better for you that we did not exist.

"Beloved, beautiful, young, and gay we were for a time; now we are at such a pass that she is beating her wings to return to her former hiding place;

"by myself, I am a shade. And now I have told you whatever in so brief a space you can understand." After she had moved thence her feet, saying: "Do not be afraid that I am going away," she gathered a garland of green laurel, which with her own hands she wound round about my temples.

Song, to whoever calls your speech obscure, say: "I do not care, for I hope that soon another messenger will make clear the truth with a clearer voice; I came only to wake men up, if he who commanded me this did not deceive me when I departed from him."

---

garland. . . . laurel: probably a reference to Petrarch's crowning as poet laureate on the Capitol in Rome on Easter Sunday (April 8), 1341.   another messenger: the poem was perhaps written before the fact.

Ruppesi intanto di vergogna il nodo
ch' a la mia lingua era distretto intorno
su nel primiero scorno,
allor quand' io del suo accorger m'accorsi,
   e 'ncominciai: "S' egli è ver quel ch' i' odo,
beato il padre et benedetto il giorno
ch' à di voi il mondo adorno
et tutto 'l tempo ch' a vedervi io corsi!   83
   "Et se mai da la via dritta mi torsi
duolmene forte assai più ch' i' non mostro;
ma se de l'esser vostro
fossi degno udir più, del desir ardo."
Pensosa mi rispose et così fiso
tenne il suo dolce sguardo
ch' al cor mandò co le parole il viso: 90

   "Sì come piacque al nostro eterno padre,
ciascuna di noi due nacque immortale.
Miseri, a voi che vale?
Me' v'era che da noi fosse il defetto.
   "Amate, belle, gioveni, et leggiadre
fummo alcun tempo; et or siam giunte a tale
che costei batte l'ale
per tornar a l'antico suo ricetto;   98
   "i' per me sono un'ombra. Et or t'ò detto
quanto per te sì breve intender puossi."
Poi che i pie' suoi fur mossi,
dicendo: "Non temer ch' i' mi allontani,"
di verde lauro una ghirlanda colse,
la qual co le sue mani
intorno intorno a le mie tempie avolse.   105

   Canzon, chi tua ragion chiamasse oscura,
di': "Non ò cura, perché tosto spero
ch' altro messaggio il vero
farà in più chiara voce manifesto;
i' venni sol per isvegliare altrui,
se chi m'impose questo
non m'ingannò quand' io parti' da lui."   112

120

Those pitying rhymes, in which I saw your wit and your courteous affection, had so much strength in my sight that quickly I put my hand to this pen,

to assure you that I have not yet felt the last bite of her whom with all the world I await, but I did indeed without fear go up to the very entrance of her dwelling;

then I came back, for I saw written over the threshold that the time had not yet come that is prescribed for my life,

although I could not read there the day or the hour. Therefore let your afflicted heart now be calmed, and let it seek a man worthy to be so honored.

Addressed to Antonio da Ferrara, who in 1343 wrote a canzone mourning Petrarch's rumored death.

her whom . . . I await: Death.

121

Now see, Love, how a young woman scorns your rule and cares nothing for my harm, and between two such enemies is so confident.

You are in armor, and she in a mere robe with loose hair is sitting barefoot amid the flowers and the grass, pitiless toward me and proud toward you.

I am a prisoner, but if mercy has kept your bow whole and an arrow or two, take vengeance, Lord, for yourself and for me.

At some time after the copying of Vat. Lat. 3195, the poem that originally occupied this place was expunged and this one substituted for it (see p. 587 for the excluded one).

120

Quelle pietose rime in ch' io m'accorsi
di vostro ingegno e del cortese affetto,
ebben tanto vigor nel mio conspetto
che ratto a questa penna la man porsi,   4

per far voi certo che gli estremi morsi
di quella ch' io con tutto 'l mondo aspetto
mai non senti', ma pur senza sospetto
infin a l'uscio del suo albergo corsi;   8

poi tornai indietro, perch' io vidi scritto
di sopra 'l limitar che 'l tempo ancora
non era giunto al mio viver prescritto,   11

ben ch' io non vi legessi il dì né l'ora.
Dunque s'acqueti omai 'l cor vostro afflitto,
et cerchi uom degno quando sì l'onora.   14

121

Or vedi, Amor, che giovenetta donna
tuo regno sprezza et del mio mal non cura,
et tra duo ta' nemici è sì secura.   3

Tu se' armato, et ella in treccie e 'n gonna
si siede et scalza in mezzo i fiori et l'erba,
ver me spietata e 'ncontr' a te superba.   6

I' son pregion, ma se pietà ancor serba
l'arco tuo saldo et qualcuna saetta,
fa di te et di me, signor, vendetta.   9

122

The heavens have already revolved seventeen years since I first caught fire, and still my fire is not extinguished; when I reflect on my state, I feel in the midst of the flames a chill.

True is the proverb, one's hair will change before one's habits, and human passions are no less intense because of the slackening of sense; the bitter shadow of the heavy veil does that to us.

Ah me, alas! and when will that day be when gazing at the flight of my years I may come out of the fire and out of so long a sorrow?

Will I ever see the day when the sweet air of that lovely face will please these eyes only as much as I wish and as much as is fitting?

---

the heavy veil: the body.

123

That lovely pallor, which covered her sweet smile with a cloud of love, with so much majesty presented itself to my heart that he went to meet it in the midst of my face.

I learned then how they see each other in Paradise; so clearly did that merciful thought open itself, which no one else perceived, but I saw it, for I fix myself nowhere else.

Every angelic expression, every humble gesture that ever appeared in a lady who harbored love, would be scorn beside what I speak of.

She bent to earth her lovely noble glance and in her silence said, as it seemed to me: "Who sends away from me my faithful friend?"

122

Dicesette anni à già rivolto il cielo
poi che 'mprima arsi, et giamai non mi spensi;
quando aven ch' al mio stato ripensi,
sento nel mezzo de le fiamme un gelo.   4

Vero è 'l proverbio ch' altri cangia il pelo
anzi che 'l vezzo, et per lentar i sensi
gli umani affetti non son meno intensi;
ciò ne fa l'ombra ria del grave velo.   8

Oi me, lasso! e quando fia quel giorno
che mirando il fuggir de gli anni miei
esca del foco et di sì lunghe pene?   11

Vedrò mai il dì che pur quant' io vorrei
quell'aria dolce del bel viso adorno
piaccia a quest'occhi, et quanto si convene?   14

123

Quel vago impallidir, che 'l dolce riso
d'un'amorosa nebbia ricoperse,
con tanta maiestade al cor s'offerse
che li si fece incontr' a mezzo 'l viso.   4

Conobbi allor sì come in paradiso
vede l'un l'altro; in tal guisa s'aperse
quel pietoso penser ch' altri non scerse,
ma vidil io, ch' altrove non m'affiso.   8

Ogni angelica vista, ogni atto umile
che giamai in donna ov' amor fosse apparve,
fora uno sdegno a lato a quel ch' io dico.   11

Chinava a terra il bel guardo gentile
et tacendo dicea, come a me parve:
"Chi m'allontana il mio fedele amico?"   14

124

Love, Fortune, and my mind, which avoids what it sees and turns back to the past, afflict me so that I sometimes envy those who are on the other shore.

Love torments my heart, Fortune deprives it of every comfort, and so my foolish mind is troubled and weeps; and thus I must always live struggling in much sorrow.

Nor do I hope that the sweet days will come back, but rather expect that what is left will go from bad to worse; and I have already passed the middle of my course.

Alas, I see all hope fall from my hands, made not of diamond but even of glass, and I see all my thoughts break in half.

the other shore: the next world.

125

If the care that torments me, as it is sharp and dense, so were clothed in a conformable color,
perhaps one burns me and flees who would have part of the heat, and Love would awaken where now he is sleeping;
less solitary would be the prints of my weary feet through fields and across hills, my eyes less wet always: if she were aflame who now stands like ice and leaves not a dram in me that is not fire and flame.

conformable color: appropriate poetic style.

124

Amor, Fortuna, et la mia mente, schiva
di quel che vede et nel passato volta,
m'affliggon sì ch' io porto alcuna volta
invidia a quei che son su l'altra riva.   4

Amor mi strugge 'l cor, Fortuna il priva
d'ogni conforto, onde la mente stolta
s'adira et piange; et così in pena molta
sempre conven che combattendo viva.   8

Né spero i dolci dì tornino indietro,
ma pur di male in peggio quel ch' avanza,
et di mio corso ò già passato 'l mezzo.   11

Lasso, non di diamante ma d'un vetro
veggio di man cadermi ogni speranza
et tutt' i miei pensier romper nel mezzo.   14

125

   Se 'l pensier che mi strugge
com' è pungente et saldo
così vestisse d'un color conforme,
   forse tal m'arde et fugge
ch' avria parte del caldo
et desteriasi Amor là dov' or dorme;   6
   men solitarie l'orme
foran de' miei pie' lassi
per campagne et per colli,
men gli occhi ad ogn'or molli,
ardendo lei che come un ghiaccio stassi
et non lascia in me dramma
che non sia foco et fiamma.   13

Since Love forces me and strips me of all skill, I speak in harsh rhymes naked of sweetness;

but not always does a branch show forth its natural virtue in flower or in leaf.

Let Love and those lovely eyes, where he is sitting in the shade, look on what my heart has shut up in itself. If my sorrow which unburdens itself happens to overflow in weeping or lamenting, the one pains me and the other pains someone else, for I do not polish it.

Sweet graceful rhymes that I used in the first assault of Love, when I had no other arms:

who will ever come who can shatter the stone about my heart, so that at least I can pour myself forth as I used to do?

for it seems to me that I have someone within who always portrays my lady and speaks of her: I am not sufficient to describe her by myself, and I come untuned because of it; alas, so has my sweet comfort fled!

Like a child who can hardly move and untangle his tongue, who is not able to speak but hates to be silent any longer,

thus desire leads me to speak, and I wish my sweet enemy to hear me before I die.

If, perhaps, she takes joy only in her lovely face and flees everything else, do you, green shore, hear it and lend to my sighs so wide a flight that it be always remembered that you were kind to me.

---

green shore: the shore of the river Sorgue, whose source is the fountain of Vaucluse.

Però ch' Amor mi sforza
et di saver mi spoglia,
parlo in rime aspre et di dolcezza ignude;
   ma non sempre a la scorza
ramo né in fior né 'n foglia
mostra di for sua natural vertude.   19
   Miri ciò che 'l cor chiude
Amor et que' begli occhi
ove si siede a l'ombra.
Se 'l dolor che si sgombra
aven che 'n pianto o in lamentar trabocchi,
l'un a me noce, et l'altro
altrui, ch' io non lo scaltro.   26

   Dolci rime leggiadre
che nel primiero assalto
d'Amor usai quand' io non ebbi altr' arme:
   chi verrà mai che squadre
questo mio cor di smalto,
ch' almen com' io solea possa sfogarme?   32
   ch' aver dentro a lui parme
un che Madonna sempre
depinge et de lei parla;
a voler poi ritrarla
per me non basto et par ch' io me ne stempre:
lasso, così m'è scorso
lo mio dolce soccorso.   39

   Come fanciul ch' a pena
volge la lingua et snoda,
che dir non sa ma 'l più tacer gli è noia,
   così 'l desir mi mena
a dire, et vo' che m'oda
la dolce mia nemica anzi ch' io moia.   45
   Se forse ogni sua gioia
nel suo bel viso è solo
et di tutt' altro è schiva,
odil tu, verde riva,
e presta a' miei sospir sì largo volo
che sempre si ridica
come tu m'eri amica.   52

You know well that so beautiful a foot never touched the earth as on that day when you were marked by hers,

wherefore my weary heart comes back with my tormented flanks to share with you their hidden cares.

Would you had hidden away some lovely footprints still among the flowers and grass, that my bitter life might weeping find a place to become calm! but my fearful, yearning soul satisfies itself as best it can.

Wherever I turn my eyes, I find a sweet brightness, thinking: "Here fell the bright light of her eyes."

Whatever grass or flower I gather, I believe that it is rooted in the ground where she was wont

to walk through the meadows beside the river, and sometimes to make herself a seat, fresh, flowering, and green. Thus no part is omitted and to know more exactly would be a loss. Blessed spirit, what are you if you make another become such?

O poor little song, how inelegant you are! I think you know it: stay here in these woods.

Ben sai che sì bel piede
non toccò terra unquanco
come quel dì che già segnata fosti,
   onde 'l cor lasso riede
col tormentoso fianco
a partir teco i lor pensier nascosti.   58
   Così avestu riposti
de' be' vestigi sparsi
ancor tra' fiori et l'erba,
che la mia vita acerba
lagrimando trovasse ove acquetarsi!
ma come po s'appaga
l'alma dubbiosa et vaga.   65

   Ovunque gli occhi volgo
trovo un dolce sereno
pensando: "Qui percosse il vago lume."
   Qualunque erba o fior colgo,
credo che nel terreno
aggia radice ov' ella ebbe in costume   71
     gir fra le piagge e 'l fiume
et talor farsi un seggio
fresco fiorito et verde.
Così nulla sen perde,
et più certezza averne fora il peggio.
Spirto beato, quale
se' quando altrui fai tale?   78

   O poverella mia, come se' rozza!
credo che tel conoschi:
rimanti in questi boschi.   81

126

Clear, fresh, sweet waters, where she who alone seems lady to me rested her lovely body,
   gentle branch where it pleased her (with sighing I remember) to make a column for her lovely side,
      grass and flowers that her rich garment covered along with her angelic breast, sacred bright air where Love opened my heart with her lovely eyes: listen all together to my sorrowful dying words.

   If it is indeed my destiny and Heaven exerts itself that Love close these eyes while they are still weeping,
      let some grace bury my poor body among you and let my soul return naked to this its own dwelling;
         death will be less harsh if I bear this hope to the fearful pass, for my weary spirit could never in a more restful port or a more tranquil grave flee my laboring flesh and my bones.

   There will come a time perhaps when to her accustomed sojourn the lovely, gentle wild one will return
      and, seeking me, turn her desirous and happy eyes toward where she saw me on that blessed day,
         and oh the pity! seeing me already dust amid the stones, Love will inspire her to sigh so sweetly that she will win mercy for me and force Heaven, drying her eyes with her lovely veil.

---

waters: those of the river Sorgue.

126

Chiare fresche et dolci acque
ove le belle membra
pose colei che sola a me par donna,
   gentil ramo ove piacque
(con sospir mi rimembra)
a lei di fare al bel fianco colonna,   6
   erba et fior che la gonna
leggiadra ricoverse
co l'angelico seno,
aere sacro sereno
ove Amor co' begli occhi il cor m'aperse:
date udienzia insieme
a le dolenti mie parole estreme.   13

S' egli è pur mio destino,
e' l cielo in ciò s'adopra,
ch' Amor quest'occhi lagrimando chiuda,
   qualche grazia il meschino
corpo fra voi ricopra,
e torni l'alma al proprio albergo ignuda;   19
   la morte fia men cruda
se questa spene porto
a quel dubbioso passo,
ché lo spirito lasso
non poria mai in più riposato porto
né in più tranquilla fossa
fuggir la carne travagliata et l'ossa.   26

Tempo verrà ancor forse
ch' a l'usato soggiorno
torni la fera bella et mansueta
   et là 'v' ella mi scorse
nel benedetto giorno
volga la vista disiosa et lieta,   32
   cercandomi, et—o pieta—
già terra infra le pietre
vedendo, Amor l'inspiri
in guisa che sospiri
sì dolcemente che mercé m'impetre
et faccia forza al cielo,
asciugandosi gli occhi col bel velo.   39

From the lovely branches was descending (sweet in
memory) a rain of flowers over her bosom,
    and she was sitting humble in such a glory, already covered
with the loving cloud;
    this flower was falling on her skirt, this one on her blond
braids, which were burnished gold and pearls to see that day;
this one was coming to rest on the ground, this one on the water,
this one, with a lovely wandering, turning about seemed to say:
"Here reigns Love."

    How many times did I say to myself then, full of awe: "She
was surely born in Paradise!"
    Her divine bearing and her face and her words and her sweet
smile had so laden me with forgetfulness
    and so divided me from the true image, that I was sighing:
"How did I come here and when?" thinking I was in Heaven, not
there where I was. From then on this grass has pleased me so that
elsewhere I have no peace.

    If you had as many beauties as you have desire, you could
boldly leave the wood and go among people.

    If you had . . . desire: this is addressed to the poem.

Da' be' rami scendea
(dolce ne la memoria)
una pioggia di fior sovra 'l suo grembo,
   et ella si sedea
umile in tanta gloria,
coverta già de l'amoroso nembo;   45
    qual fior cadea sul lembo,
qual su le treccie bionde
ch' oro forbito et perle
eran quel dì a vederle,
qual si posava in terra et qual su l'onde,
qual con un vago errore
girando parea dir: "Qui regna Amore."   52

   Quante volte diss' io
allor, pien di spavento:
"Costei per fermo nacque in paradiso! "
   Così carco d'oblio
il divin portamento
e 'l volto e le parole e 'l dolce riso   58
    m'aveano, et sì diviso
da l'imagine vera,
ch' i' dicea sospirando:
"Qui come venn' io o quando?"
credendo esser in ciel, non là dov' era.
Da indi in qua mi piace
quest'erba sì ch' altrove non ò pace.   65

   Se tu avessi ornamenti quant' ài voglia,
poresti arditamente
uscir del bosco et gir infra la gente.   68

127

Toward where Love spurs me I must turn my sorrowful rhymes, which follow my afflicted mind. Which shall be last, alas, and which first? He who speaks with me about my ills leaves me in doubt, so confusedly he dictates.

But still, however much of the story of my suffering I find written by his very own hand, in the midst of my heart where I so often return, I shall speak out, because sighs take a truce and there is help for sorrow when one speaks. I say that although I gaze intent and fixed on a thousand different things, I see only one lady and her lovely face.

Since my pitiless misfortune has sent me far from my greatest good, misfortune painful, inexorable, and proud, Love maintains me solely with memory: wherefore if I see the world begin to clothe itself in green in youthful guise,

I seem to see at that same unripe age the beautiful young girl who is now a lady; after the sun has mounted on high, making all things warm, it seems to be like the flame of love that masters the deep heart; but when the shorter day laments that the sun turns back step by step, I see her arrived at her fullest days.

127

In quella parte dove Amor mi sprona
conven ch' io volga le dogliose rime
che son seguaci de la mente afflitta:
quai fien ultime, lasso, et qua' fien prime?
Collui che del mio mal meco ragiona
mi lascia in dubbio, sì confuso ditta.   6
    Ma pur quanto la storia trovo scritta
in mezzo 'l cor che sì spesso rincorro
co la sua propria man de' miei martiri
dirò, perché i sospiri
parlando àn triegua et al dolor soccorro.
Dico che perch' io miri
mille cose diverse attento et fiso,
sol una donna veggio e 'l suo bel viso.   14

    Poi che la dispietata mia ventura
m'à dilungato dal maggior mio bene,
noiosa inesorabile et superba,
Amor col rimembrar sol mi mantene:
onde s' io veggio in giovenil figura
incominciarsi il mondo a vestir d'erba,   20
    parmi veder in quella etate acerba
la bella giovenetta ch' ora è donna;
poi che sormonta riscaldando il sole,
parmi qual esser sòle
fiamma d'amor che 'n cor alto s'endonna;
ma quando il dì si dole
di lui che passo passo a dietro torni,
veggio lei giunta a' suoi perfetti giorni.   28

Gazing at leaves on a branch or violets on the ground in the season when the cold becomes less and the better stars gain power, in my eyes I have still the violets and the green with which Love was armed at the beginning of my war so that he still drives me,

and that lovely tender bark which covered then the little members where, today, that noble soul dwells who makes every other pleasure vile to me: so strongly I remember her humble bearing which then was flowering and then grew before her years, sole cause and healing of my woes.

When sometimes I see from afar new snow on the hills struck by the sun, Love controls me as the sun does snow, as I think of that face of more than human beauty, which from afar can make my eyes wet but from close by dazzles them and vanquishes my heart,

where between the white and the gold there is always shown what no mortal eye ever saw, I believe, except my own; and of the hot desire that, when she sighing smiles, inflames me so that my forgetfulness prizes nothing but becomes eternal: nor does summer change it or winter put it out.

In ramo fronde o ver viole in terra
mirando a la stagion che 'l freddo perde
et le stelle miglior acquistan forza,
ne gli occhi ò pur le violette e 'l verde
di ch' era nel principio de mia guerra
Amor armato sì ch' ancor mi sforza,   34
    et quella dolce leggiadretta scorza
che ricopria le pargolette membra
dove oggi alberga l'anima gentile
ch' ogni altro piacer vile
sembiar mi fa: sì forte mi rimembra
del portamento umile
ch' allor fioriva et poi crebbe anzi agli anni,
cagion sola et riposo de' miei affanni.   42

Qualor tenera neve per li colli
dal sol percossa veggio di lontano,
come 'l sol neve mi governa Amore,
pensando nel bel viso più che umano
che po da lunge gli occhi miei far molli
ma da presso gli abbaglia et vince il core,   48
    ove fra 'l bianco et l'aureo colore
sempre si mostra quel che mai non vide
occhio mortal, ch' io creda, altro che 'l mio;
et del caldo desio
che quando sospirando ella sorride
m'infiamma sì che oblio
niente aprezza, ma diventa eterno:
né state il cangia né lo spegne il verno.   56

I never saw after nocturnal rain the wandering stars going
through the clear air and flaming between the dew and the frost,
that I did not have before me her lovely eyes where leans my
weary life, such as I saw them in the shadow of a lovely veil;

and as the sky shone with their beauty that day so I see them
still sparkle, bathed in tears, whence I ever burn. If I see the sun
rise, I sense the approach of the light that enamors me; if setting
at evening, I seem to see her when she departs, leaving all in
darkness behind her.

If my eyes ever saw white with crimson roses in a vase of gold,
just then gathered by virgin hands, they thought they saw the
face of her who excels all other wonders with the three excel-
lences gathered in her:

the blond tresses loosened on her neck, where every milk loses
by comparison, and the cheeks adorned with a sweet fire. If the
breeze but a little moves the white and yellow flowers in the
meadows, the place comes back to mind and the first day when I
saw freed to the air the golden hair from which I so quickly
caught fire.

Non vidi mai dopo notturna pioggia
gir per l'aere sereno stelle erranti
et fiammeggiar fra la rugiada e 'l gielo,
ch' i' non avesse i begli occhi davanti
ove la stanca mia vita s'appoggia,
quali io gli vidi a l'ombra d'un bel velo;   62
     et sì come di lor bellezze il cielo
splendea quel dì, così bagnati ancora
li veggio sfavillare, ond' io sempre ardo.
Se 'l sol levarsi sguardo,
sento il lume apparir che m'innamora;
se tramontarsi al tardo,
parmel veder quando si volge altrove,
lassando tenebroso onde si move.   70

Se mai candide rose con vermiglie
in vasel d'oro vider gli occhi miei
allor allor da vergine man colte,
veder pensaro il viso di colei
ch' avanza tutte l'altre meraviglie
con tre belle eccellenzie in lui raccolte: 76
     le bionde treccie sopra 'l collo sciolte
ov' ogni latte perderia sua prova,
e le guancie ch' adorna un dolce foco.
Ma pur che l'ora un poco
fior bianchi et gialli per le piaggie mova,
torna a la mente il loco
e 'l primo dì ch' i' vidi a l'aura sparsi
i capei d'oro ond' io sì subito arsi.   84

Perhaps I thought I could count the stars one by one and enclose the sea in a little glass when the strange idea came to me to tell in so few pages in how many places the flower of all beauties, remaining in herself, has scattered her light

in order that I may never depart from her; nor shall I, and if at times I flee, in Heaven and earth she has circumscribed my steps, for she is always present to my weary eyes, so that I am all consumed; and thus she stays with me, for I never see another, nor do I wish to, nor in my sighs do I call the name of another.

You know well, Song, that whatever I say is nothing beside the hidden amorous care that night and day I carry in my mind; by its comfort alone I am kept from perishing in so long a war, which would already have killed me, bewailing the absence of my heart; but from the thought of her I gain a stay of death.

Ad una ad una annoverar le stelle
e 'n picciol vetro chiuder tutte l'acque
forse credea, quando in sì poca carta
novo penser di ricontar mi nacque
in quante parti il fior de l'altre belle
stando in se stessa à la sua luce sparta,   90
    a ciò che mai da lei non mi diparta;
né farò io, et se pur talor fuggo,
in cielo e 'n terra m'à racchiuso i passi,
perch' a gli occhi miei lassi
sempre è presente, ond' io tutto mi struggo;
et così meco stassi
ch' altra non veggio mai né veder bramo,
né 'l nome d'altra ne' sospir miei chiamo.   98

Ben sai, canzon, che quant' io parlo è nulla
al celato amoroso mio pensero
che dì et notte ne la mente porto,
solo per cui conforto
in così lunga guerra anco non pero,
che ben m'avria già morto
la lontananza del mio cor piangendo;
ma quinci da la morte indugio prendo.   106

128

My Italy, although speech does not aid those mortal wounds
of which in your lovely body I see so many, I wish at least my
sighs to be such as Tiber and Arno hope for, and Po where I now
sit sorrowful and sad.

Ruler of Heaven, I beg that the mercy that made You come to
earth may now make You turn to Your beloved, holy country.
See, noble Lord, from what trivial causes comes such cruel war:
the hearts that proud fierce Mars makes hard and closed, Father,
do You open and soften and free: cause Your truth (though I am
unworthy) to be heard there through my tongue.

You into whose hands Fortune has given the reins of these
lovely regions for which no pity seems to move you: what are so
many foreign swords doing here? Why is the green earth colored
with barbarian blood?

A vain error cozens you: you see little and think you see
much, for in venal hearts you seek love and loyalty. Whoever
possesses most followers, he is surrounded by most enemies. Oh
deluge gathered in what strange wilderness to overflow our
sweet fields! If this happens to us by our own hands, who can
there be to rescue us?

Addressed to the warring petty lords of Italy. This canzone is Petrarch's most
important political poem, an impassioned plea for peace. It was probably
written during the siege of Parma in 1344-45, during which Petrarch narrowly
escaped capture as he left the city in a convoy.

Tiber and Arno . . . and Po: Petrarch presumably wrote the poem at Sel-
vapiana, near Parma, on the shore of the Po.   foreign swords: it was
common to hire mercenaries from Germany.

128

Italia mia, ben che 'l parlar sia indarno
a le piaghe mortali
che nel bel corpo tuo sì spesse veggio,
piacemi almen che' miei sospir sian quali
spera 'l Tevero et l'Arno,
e 'l Po, dove doglioso et grave or seggio.   6
   Rettor del cielo, io cheggio
che la pietà che ti condusse in terra
ti volga al tuo diletto almo paese:
vedi, Segnor cortese,
di che lievi cagion' che crudel guerra;
e i cor' ch' endura et serra
Marte superbo et fero
apri tu, Padre, e 'ntenerisci et snoda;
ivi fa' che 'l tuo vero,
qual io mi sia, per la mia lingua s'oda.   16

   Voi cui Fortuna à posto in mano il freno
de le belle contrade
(di che nulla pietà par che vi stringa):
che fan qui tante pellegrine spade?
perché 'l verde terreno
del barbarico sangue si depinga?   22
   Vano error vi lusinga,
poco vedete et parvi veder molto,
che 'n cor venale amor cercate o fede;
qual più gente possede
colui é più da' suoi nemici avolto.   27
O diluvio raccolto
di che deserti strani
per inondar i nostri dolci campi!
Se da le proprie mani
questo n'avene, or chi fia che ne scampi?   32

Nature provided well for our safety when she put the shield of
the Alps between us and the Teutonic rage; but our blind desire,
strong against our own good, has contrived to make this healthy
body sick.

Now within the same cage savage beasts and gentle flocks lie
down, so that the better must always groan; and this comes
about through the descendants—to make our sorrow greater—
of that uncivilized people whom, as we read, Marius so
wounded that the memory of the deed has not yet faded, when
thirsty and tired he drank from the river as much blood as
water.

Of Caesar I do not speak, who in every meadow made the
grass scarlet with their veins where he put our steel. Now it
seems, I know not by what malignant stars, that the heavens
hate us: thanks to you, to whom so much was entrusted.

Your divided wills are spoiling the loveliest part of the world.
For what fault, what judgment, or what destiny do you harass
your poor neighbor, and persecute afflicted and scattered
fortunes, and in foreign parts seek men and be glad that they
shed blood and sell their souls for a price? I am speaking to tell
the truth, not from hatred or scorn of anyone.

---

people whom . . . Marius so wounded: the Ambrones and Teutones, whom the
Roman consul Marius defeated at Aquae Sextiae (Aix-en-Provence) in 102
B.C.; 200,000 of them were supposed to have been killed, 90,000 made prisoner.
The river referred to is the Arc.

Ben provide Natura al nostro stato
quando de l'Alpi schermo
pose fra noi et la tedesca rabbia;
ma 'l desir cieco, encontra 'l suo ben fermo,
s'è poi tanto ingegnato
ch' al corpo sano à procurato scabbia.   38
  Or dentro ad una gabbia
fiere selvagge et mansuete gregge
s'annidan sì che sempre il miglior geme;
et è questo del seme
(per più dolor) del popol senza legge,   43
al qual, come si legge,
Mario aperse sì 'l fianco
che memoria de l'opra anco non langue,
quando assetato et stanco
non più bevve del fiume acqua che sangue.   48

  Cesare taccio, che per ogni piaggia
fece l'erbe sanguigne
di lor vene, ove 'l nostro ferro mise.
Or par (non so per che stelle maligne)
che 'l cielo in odio n'aggia,
vostra mercé, cui tanto si commise.   54
  Vostre voglie divise
guastan del mondo la più bella parte.
Qual colpa, qual giudicio, o qual destino
fastidire il vicino
povero, et le fortune afflitte et sparte   59
perseguire, e 'n disparte
cercar gente, et gradire
che sparga 'l sangue et venda l'alma a prezzo?
Io parlo per ver dire,
non per odio d'altrui né per disprezzo.   64

And do you not see, after so many proofs, the Bavarian treachery, which lifting its finger toys with death? Mockery is worse than outright loss, as it seems to me. But your blood is shed more copiously, for another anger whips you on.

From dawn to tierce think about yourselves, and you will see how much he can hold another dear who holds himself so cheap. Noble Latin blood: throw off these harmful burdens, do not make an idol of an empty name; it is on account of our own sins, and not a natural thing, that the slow northerners should conquer us in intellect.

"Is not this the ground that I touched first? Is not this my nest, where I was so sweetly nourished? Is not this my fatherland in which I trust, and my kind and merciful mother, which covers both of my parents?"

By God, let this sometimes move your minds; and with pity look on the tears of the sorrowing people, who only from you (after God) can hope for peace. And, if you merely show some sign of piety, manhood shall take up arms against rage, and the fighting shall be short: for ancient valor is not yet dead in Italic hearts.

---

tierce: the third canonical hour; roughly 9:00 A.M.

Né v'accorgete ancor per tante prove
del bavarico inganno
ch' alzando il dito colla morte scherza?
Peggio è lo strazio, al mio parer, che 'l danno.
Ma 'l vostro sangue piove
più largamente, ch' altr' ira vi sferza.   70
    Da la matina a terza
di voi pensate, et vederete come
tien caro altrui chi tien sé così vile.
Latin sangue gentile:
sgombra da te queste dannose some,   75
non far idolo un nome
vano, senza soggetto;
ché 'l furor de lassù, gente ritrosa,
vincerne d'intelletto
peccato è nostro, et non natural cosa.   80

    "Non è questo 'l terren ch' i' toccai pria?
non è questo il mio nido
ove nudrito fui sì dolcemente?
non è questa la patria in ch' io mi fido,
madre benigna et pia,
che copre l'un et l'altro mio parente?"   86
    Per Dio, questo la mente
talor vi mova, et con pietà guardate
le lagrime del popol doloroso
che sol da voi riposo
dopo Dio spera. Et pur che voi mostriate   91
segno alcun di pietate,
vertù contra furore
prenderà l'arme, et fia 'l combatter corto;
ché l'antico valore
ne l'italici cor non è ancor morto.   96

Lords: see how time flies and how life flees, and how Death is at our backs. You are here now; think of your departure, for the soul must go naked and alone to that perilous path.

As you pass through this valley, let it please you to conquer hatred and anger, winds contrary to a tranquil life; and that time which you now spend in giving others pain, let it be converted to some more worthy action of hand or intellect, to some lovely praise, some virtuous study: thus down here one may be happy and find open the road to Heaven.

Song, I bid you to speak your message courteously, for you must go among a haughty people, and their wills are still full of vicious and old custom, always the enemy of truth. You shall try your fortune among the magnanimous few who love the good; say to them: "Who will protect me? I go crying: Peace, peace, peace!"

---

this valley: this life.

Signor: mirate come 'l tempo vola
et sì come la vita
fugge et la Morte n'è sovra le spalle.
Voi siete or qui; pensate a la partita,
ché l'alma ignuda et sola
conven ch' arrive a quel dubbioso calle.   102
 Al passar questa valle,
piacciavi porre giù l'odio et lo sdegno,
venti contrari a la vita serena;
et quel che 'n altrui pena
tempo si spende, in qualche atto più degno   107
o di mano o d'ingegno,
in qualche bella lode,
in qualche onesto studio si converta:
così qua giù si gode,
et la strada del ciel si trova aperta.   112

 Canzone, io t'ammonisco
che tua ragion cortesemente dica,
perché tra gente altera ir ti convene
et le voglie son piene
già de l'usanza pessima et antica,
del ver sempre nemica.   118
Proverai tua ventura
fra' magnanimi pochi a chi 'l ben piace;
di' lor: "Chi m'assicura?
I' vo gridando: Pace, pace, pace."   122

129

From thought to thought, from mountain to mountain Love guides me; for I find every trodden path to be contrary to a tranquil life.

If there is on some solitary slope a river or spring, or between two peaks a shady valley, there my frightened soul is quieted;

and, as Love leads it on, now it laughs, now weeps, now fears, now is confident: and my face, which follows wherever my soul leads, is clouded and made clear again, and remains but a short time in any one state; and at the sight anyone who had experienced such a life would say: "This man is burning with love and his state is uncertain."

Among high mountains and through harsh woods I find some rest; every inhabited place is a mortal enemy of my eyes.

With every step is born a new thought of my lady, which often turns to pleasure the torment that I bear for her;

and I would hardly wish to change this bitter, sweet life of mine, for I say: "Perhaps Love keeps you for a better time; perhaps, though vile to yourself, you are dear to someone else." And I go over to this thought, sighing: "Now could it be true? But how? but when?"

Where a tall pine or a hillside extends shade, there I sometimes stop, and in the first stone I see I portray her lovely face with my mind.

When I come back to myself, I find my breast wet with pity and then I say: "Alas, where have you come to, from what are you separated?"

But as long as I can hold my yearning mind fixed on the first thought, and look at her and forget myself, I feel Love so close by that my soul is satisfied by its own deception; in so many places and so beautiful I see her, that, if the deception should last, I ask for no more.

129

Di pensier in pensier, di monte in monte
mi guida Amor, ch' ogni segnato calle
provo contrario a la tranquilla vita.
   Se 'n solitaria piaggia rivo o fonte,
se 'nfra duo poggi siede ombrosa valle,
ivi s'acqueta l'alma sbigottita;   6
     et come Amor l'envita
or ride or piange or teme or s'assecura,
e 'l volto, che lei segue ov' ella il mena,
si turba et rasserena
et in un esser picciol tempo dura:
onde a la vista uom di tal vita esperto
diria: "Questo arde et di suo stato è incerto."   13

   Per alti monti et per selve aspre trovo
qualche riposo; ogni abitato loco
è nemico mortal degli occhi miei.
   A ciascun passo nasce un penser novo
de la mia donna, che sovente in gioco
gira 'l tormento ch' i' porto per lei;   19
     et a pena vorrei
cangiar questo mio viver dolce amaro,
ch' i' dico: "Forse anco ti serva Amore
ad un tempo migliore;
forse a te stesso vile, altrui se' caro";
et in questa trapasso sospirando:
"Or porrebbe esser ver? or come? or quando?"   26

   Ove porge ombra un pino alto od un colle
talor m'arresto, et pur nel primo sasso
disegno co la mente il suo bel viso.
   Poi ch' a me torno, trovo il petto molle
de la pietate, et alor dico: "Ahi lasso,
dove se' giunto? et onde se' diviso?"   32
     Ma mentre tener fiso
posso al primo pensier la mente vaga,
et mirar lei et obliar me stesso,
sento Amor sì da presso
che del suo proprio error l'alma s'appaga;
in tante parti et sì bella la veggio
che se l'error durasse, altro non cheggio.   39

I have many times (now who will believe me?) seen her
alive in the clear water and on the green grass and in the trunk of
a beech tree
    and in a white cloud, so beautiful that Leda would have said
that her daughter faded like a star covered by the sun's ray;
    and in whatever wildest place and most deserted shore I
find myself, so much the more beautiful does my thought
shadow her forth. Then, when the truth dispels that sweet
deception, right there in the same place I sit down, cold, a dead
stone on the living rock, like a man who thinks and weeps and
writes.

    Where the shadow of some other mountain does not reach,
toward the highest and freest peak an intense desire is wont to
draw me.
    Thence I begin to measure my losses with my eyes, and then I
weeping unburden my heart of the sorrowful cloud gathered in
it,
    when I see and think how much air separates me from the
lovely face that is always so near to me and so distant. Then to
myself softly: "What do you know, wretch? perhaps off there
someone is sighing now because of your absence." And in this
thought my soul breathes more easily.

    Song, beyond those Alps, where the sky is more clear and
happy, you shall see me again beside a running stream, where
the breeze from a fresh and fragrant laurel can be felt: there is
my heart, and she who steals it from me; here you can see only
my image.

    Leda: mother of Clytemnestra and Helen of Troy, begotten by Zeus in the
form of a swan.   stream: the Sorgue, in Vaucluse.

I' l'ò più volte (or chi fia che mi 'l creda?)
ne l'acqua chiara et sopra l'erba verde
veduto viva, et nel troncon d'un faggio
   e 'n bianca nube, sì fatta che Leda
avria ben detto che sua figlia perde
come stella che 'l sol copre col raggio;   45
   et quanto in più selvaggio
loco mi trovo e 'n più deserto lido,
tanto più bella il mio pensier l'adombra.
Poi quando il vero sgombra
quel dolce error, pur lì medesmo assido
me freddo, pietra morta in pietra viva,
in guisa d'uom che pensi et pianga et scriva.   52

   Ove d'altra montagna ombra non tocchi,
verso 'l maggiore e 'l più espedito giogo
tirar mi suol un desiderio intenso.
   Indi i miei danni a misurar con gli occhi
comincio, e 'ntanto lagrimando sfogo
di dolorosa nebbia il cor condenso,   58
   alor ch' i' miro et penso
quanta aria dal bel viso mi diparte
che sempre m' è sì presso et sì lontano.
Poscia fra me pian piano:
"Che sai tu, lasso? forse in quella parte
or di tua lontananza si sospira."
Et in questo penser l'alma respira.   65

   Canzone, oltra quell'alpe,
là dove il ciel è più sereno et lieto,
mi rivedrai sovr' un ruscel corrente
ove l'aura si sente
d'un fresco et odorifero laureto;
ivi è 'l mio cor et quella che 'l m'invola:
qui veder poi l'imagine mia sola.   72

130

Since the road to mercy is closed to me, on a despairing way I have come far from the eyes where had been placed (I know not by what fate) the guerdon of all my faithfulness.

I feed my heart with sighs, it asks for nothing else, and I live on tears, born to weep; nor do I sorrow for that, for in such a state weeping is sweeter than anyone knows.

And I keep myself to one image, which was not made by Zeuxis or Praxiteles or Phidias, but by a better craftsman and a higher mind.

What Scythia can keep me safe or what Numidia, if, still not glutted by my undeserved exile, Envy can find me even so hidden away?

Zeuxis: Greek painter (fifth century B.C.).   Praxiteles or Phidias: with Polyclitus, the most celebrated sculptors of ancient Greece (fourth and fifth centuries B.C., respectively).   Scythia: the traditional name for northeastern Asia (Siberia, Tartary).   Numidia: the hinterland of northern Africa. Envy: the reference is unknown.

131

I would sing of love in so rare a way that from her cruel side I would draw by force a thousand sighs in a day, and a thousand high desires I would kindle in her frozen mind;

and I would see her lovely face change expression frequently, and her eyes become wet and make more merciful turnings, as one does who repents, when it is too late, of another's suffering and of his own error;

and I would see the scarlet roses moved by the breeze amid the snow, and the ivory uncovered that turns to marble whoever looks on it from close by,

and all for the sake of which I am not a burden to myself in this short life, but rather glory in keeping for a later season.

130

Poi che 'l camin m'è chiuso di mercede,
per desperata via son dilungato
dagli occhi ov' era (i' non so per qual fato)
riposto il guidardon d'ogni mia fede.   4

Pasco 'l cor di sospir, ch' altro non chiede,
e di lagrime vivo, a pianger nato;
né di ciò duolmi, perché in tale stato
è dolce il pianto più ch' altri non crede.   8

Et sol ad una imagine m'attegno
che fe' non Zeusi o Prasitele o Fidia,
ma miglior mastro et di più alto ingegno.   11

Qual Scizia m'assicura o qual Numidia,
s' ancor non sazia del mio esilio indegno
così nascosto mi ritrova Invidia?   14

131

Io canterei d'Amor sì novamente
ch' al duro fianco il dì mille sospiri
trarrei per forza, et mille alti desiri
raccenderei ne la gelata mente;   4

e 'l bel viso vedrei cangiar sovente,
et bagnar gli occhi, et più pietosi giri
far, come suol chi degli altrui martiri
et del suo error quando non val si pente;   8

et le rose vermiglie infra la neve
mover da l'ora, et discovrir l'avorio
che fa di marmo chi da presso 'l guarda,   11

e tutto quel per che nel viver breve
non rincresco a me stesso, anzi mi glorio
d'esser servato a la stagion più tarda.   14

132

If it is not love, what then is it that I feel? But if it is love, before God, what kind of thing is it? If it is good, whence comes this bitter mortal effect? If it is evil, why is each torment so sweet?

If by my own will I burn, whence comes the weeping and lament? If against my will, what does lamenting avail? O living death, O delightful harm, how can you have such power over me if I do not consent to it?

And if I do consent to it, it is wrong of me to complain. Amid such contrary winds I find myself at sea in a frail bark, without a tiller,

so light of wisdom, so laden with error, that I myself do not know what I want; and I shiver in midsummer, burn in winter.

133

Love has set me up like a target for arrows, like snow in the sun, like wax in the fire, like a cloud in the wind; and I am already hoarse, Lady, with calling for mercy, and you do not care.

From your eyes the mortal blow came forth, against which time and place do not avail me; from you alone come forth (and it seems a light matter to you) the sun and the fire and the wind that make me such.

Thoughts of you are arrows, your face a sun, desire a fire; and with all these weapons Love pierces me, dazzles me, and melts me;

and your angelic singing and your words, with your sweet breath against which I cannot defend myself, are the breeze before which my life flees.

132

S' amor non è, che dunque è quel ch' io sento?
ma s' egli è amor, per Dio, che cosa et quale?
se bona, ond' è l'effetto aspro mortale?
se ria, ond' è sì dolce ogni tormento?   4

S' a mia voglia ardo, ond' è 'l pianto e lamento?
s' a mal mio grado, il lamentar che vale?
O viva morte, o dilettoso male,
come puoi tanto in me s' io nol consento?   8

Et s' io 'l consento, a gran torto mi doglio.
Fra sì contrari venti in frale barca
mi trovo in alto mar senza governo,   11

sì lieve di saver, d'error sì carca
ch' i' medesmo non so quel ch' io mi voglio,
e tremo a mezza state, ardendo il verno.   14

133

Amor m'à posto come segno a strale,
come al sol neve, come cera al foco,
et come nebbia al vento; et son già roco,
Donna, mercé chiamando, et voi non cale.   4

Dagli occhi vostri uscio 'l colpo mortale
contra cui non mi val tempo né loco;
da voi sola procede (et parvi un gioco)
il sole e 'l foco e 'l vento ond' io son tale.   8

I pensier son saette, e 'l viso un sole,
e 'l desir foco; e 'nseme con quest'arme
mi punge Amor, m'abbaglia, et mi distrugge;   11

et l'angelico canto et le parole,
col dolce spirto ond' io non posso aitarme,
son l'aura inanzi a cui mia vita fugge.   14

134

Peace I do not find, and I have no wish to make war; and I fear and hope, and burn and am of ice; and I fly above the heavens and lie on the ground; and I grasp nothing and embrace all the world.

One has me in prison who neither opens nor locks, neither keeps me for his own nor unties the bonds; and Love does not kill and does not unchain me, he neither wishes me alive nor frees me from the tangle.

I see without eyes, and I have no tongue and yet cry out; and I wish to perish and I ask for help; and I hate myself and love another.

I feed on pain, weeping I laugh; equally displeasing to me are death and life. In this state am I, Lady, on account of you.

135

Whatever most strange and new thing ever was in whatever wondrous clime, if judged aright it most resembles me: to such a pass have I come, Love. There whence the day comes forth flies a bird that alone, without consort, after voluntary death, is reborn and all renews itself to life.

Thus my desire is unique and thus at the summit of its high thoughts it turns to the sun, and thus it is consumed and thus returns to its former state; it burns and dies and takes again its sinews and lives on, vying with the phoenix.

---

bird that. . . renews: the Arabian phoenix, said to die and be reborn from its funeral pyre every five hundred years.

134

Pace non trovo et non ò da far guerra,
e temo et spero, et ardo et son un ghiaccio,
et volo sopra 'l cielo et giaccio in terra,
et nulla stringo et tutto 'l mondo abbraccio.   4

Tal m'à in pregion che non m'apre né serra,
né per suo mi riten né scioglie il laccio,
et non m'ancide Amore et non mi sferra,
né mi vuol vivo né mi trae d'impaccio.   8

Veggio senza occhi, et non ò lingua et grido,
et bramo di perir et cheggio aita,
et ò in odio me stesso et amo altrui.   11

Pascomi di dolor, piangendo rido,
egualmente mi spiace morte et vita.
In questo stato son, Donna, per vui.   14

135

Qual più diversa et nova
cosa fu mai in qualche stranio clima,
quella, se ben s'estima,
più mi rasembra: a tal son giunto, Amore.
Là onde il dì ven fore
vola un augel che sol, senza consorte,
di volontaria morte
rinasce et tutto a viver si rinova.   8
Così sol si ritrova
lo mio voler, et così in su la cima
de' suoi alti pensieri al sol si volve,
et così si risolve,
et così torna al suo stato di prima;
arde et more et riprende i nervi suoi
et vive poi   con la fenice a prova.   15

There is a stone out there on the Indian Sea so bold that by nature it draws iron to itself and steals it from the wood, so that ships founder. This prove I among the waves of bitter weeping, for that lovely rock has with its hard pride brought my life to where it must founder.

Thus a stone has robbed my soul (stealing my heart which once was a hard thing and held me, who now am divided and scattered), a stone more greedy to draw flesh than iron. Oh my cruel chance, being in the flesh I see myself drawn to shore by a living sweet magnet!

In the farthest west there is a wild creature more quiet and gentle than anything else, but weeping and sorrow and death she carries within her eyes; most wary must be whatever sight turns toward her: as long as it does not meet her eyes it can see all the rest safely.

But I, incautious, miserable, run always to my own hurt, and I know well how much I have suffered from it and expect to still; but my greedy desire, which is blind and deaf, transports me so, that her lovely holy face and desirous eyes will cause my death to come by this angelic innocent wild creature.

---

stone . . . draws iron: the fabulous account of the magnet is from the elder Pliny's *Natural History*.   wild creature: the fabulous catablepa, whose glance kills (also in Pliny).

Una petra è sì ardita
là per l'indico mar, che da natura
tragge a sé il ferro e 'l fura
dal legno, in guisa che' navigi affonde.
Questo prov' io fra l'onde
d'amaro pianto che quel bello scoglio
à col suo duro argoglio
condutta ove affondar conven mia vita.   23
    Così l'alm' à sfornita
(furando 'l cor che fu già cosa dura
et me tenne un, ch' or son diviso et sparso)
un sasso a trar più scarso
carne che ferro. O cruda mia ventura!
che 'n carne essendo veggio trarmi a riva
ad una viva   dolce calamita.   30

    Ne l'estremo occidente
una fera è soave et queta tanto
che nulla più, ma pianto
et doglia et morte dentro agli occhi porta;
molto convene accorta
esser qual vista mai ver lei si giri:
pur che gli occhi non miri,
l'altro puossi veder securamente.   38
    Ma io incauto dolente
corro sempre al mio male, et so ben quanto
n'ò sofferto et n'aspetto; ma l'engordo
voler ch' è cieco et sordo
sì mi trasporta che 'l bel viso santo
et gli occhi vaghi fien cagion ch' io pera
di questa fera   angelica innocente.   45

There wells forth in the south, taking its name from the sun, a fountain that by nature always boils at night and is cold by day; and by so much it grows cold as the sun mounts or grows more near. Thus it happens to me that I am a fount and dwelling of tears:

when the lovely light that is my sun departs, and sad and alone are my eyes and the night is dark to them, then I burn; but if the gold and the rays appear of that living sun, within and without I feel myself altogether change and turn to ice, so cold I become!

Epirus has another spring, of which it is written that though cold it rekindles every extinguished torch and puts out any that is aflame. My soul, not yet harmed by any fire of love, approaching but a little that cold one for whom I ever sigh,

caught fire entirely, and such suffering was never seen by sun or star, for it would have moved a heart of marble to pity; and, after setting it on fire, frozen and lovely virtue put it out again. Thus often she has relit and extinguished my heart: I know it who feel it, and often I am angered by it.

---

fountain that . . . is cold: according to Pliny and other ancients, this fountain is in Africa.   Epirus has another spring: Pliny and others relate this wonder of the fountain at the shrine of Zeus in Dordona.

Surge nel mezzo giorno
una fontana, e tien nome dal sole,
che per natura sòle
bollir le notti e 'n sul giorno esser fredda;
et tanto si raffredda
quanto 'l sol monta et quanto è più da presso.
così aven a me stesso
che son fonte di lagrime et soggiorno: 53
    quando 'l bel lume adorno
ch' è 'l mio sol s'allontana, et triste et sole
son le mie luci et notte oscura è loro,
ardo allor; ma se l'oro
e i rai veggio apparir del vivo sole,
tutto dentro et di for sento cangiarme
et ghiaccio farme,   così freddo torno.   60

Un'altra fonte à Epiro
di cui si scrive ch' essendo fredda ella
ogni spenta facella
accende, et spegne qual trovasse accesa.
L'anima mia, ch' offesa
ancor non era d'amoroso foco,
appressandosi un poco
a quella fredda ch' io sempre sospiro,   68
    arse tutta, et martiro
simil giamai né sol vide né stella,
ch' un cor di marmo a pietà mosso avrebbe;
poi che 'nfiammata l'ebbe,
rispensela vertù gelata et bella.
Così più volte à 'l cor racceso et spento,
i 'l so che 'l sento   et spesso me n'adiro.   75

Out beyond all our shores, in the famous islands of Fortune, there are two springs: whoever from the one drinks, dies laughing, and whoever from the other, escapes. A similar chance stamps my life, for I could die laughing for the great pleasure that I take, if cries of sorrow did not temper it.

Love, who guide me still even to shades hidden and dark to fame, we shall not speak of this spring, which we see always full but with largest vein when the sun is united with Taurus; thus my eyes weep at all times, but most at the season when I saw my lady.

If anyone should wish to know, Song, what I am doing, you can say: "Beside a great stone in a closed valley, whence Sorgue comes forth, he is; nor is there anyone to see him save Love, who never leaves him even for a step, and the image of one who destroys him: he, for his part, flees all other persons."

---

two springs: Pomponius Mela, Latin geographer (first century A.D.), locates them in the Canary Islands.   this spring: the fountain of Vaucluse.
Taurus: by the Julian calendar, the sun enters Taurus around April 14.

Fuor tutt' i nostri lidi
ne l'isole famose di Fortuna,
due fonti à; chi de l'una
bee mor ridendo, et chi de l'altra, scampa.
Simil fortuna stampa
mia vita, ché morir poria ridendo
del gran piacer ch' io prendo,
se nol temprassen dolorosi stridi.   83
    Amor ch' ancor mi guidi
pur a l'ombra di fama occulta et bruna,
tacerem questa fonte ch' ogni or piena
ma con più larga vena
veggiam quando col Tauro il sol s'aduna:
così gli occhi miei piangon d'ogni tempo
ma più nel tempo   che Madonna vidi.   90

    Chi spiasse, canzone,
quel ch' i' fo, tu poi dir: "Sotto un gran sasso
in una chiusa valle ond' esce Sorga
si sta; né chi lo scorga
v'è se no Amor, che mai nol lascia un passo,
et l'imagine d'una che lo strugge,
ch' e' per sé fugge   tutt' altre persone."

136

May fire from Heaven rain down on your tresses, wicked one, since doing ill pleases you so, who after eating acorns and drinking from the river have become great and rich by making others poor,

nest of treachery, where is hatched whatever evil is spread through the world today, slave of wine, bed, and food, in whom intemperance shows its utmost power!

Through your chambers young girls and old men go frisking, and Beelzebub in the midst with the bellows and fire and mirrors.

And you were not brought up amid pillows in the shade, but naked to the wind and barefoot among the thorns; now you live in such a way—may the stink of it reach God!

Addressed to the papal court at Avignon.
tresses: the papal court is personified as the whore of Babylon (Apocalypse 17).   acorns and . . . the river: traditionally, the food and drink of the Golden Age, here characterizing the poverty of the primitive Church.

137

Greedy Babylon has so filled the sack with God's anger, with perverse and wicked vices, that it is bursting; and she has made not Jove and Pallas her gods but Venus and Bacchus.

Waiting for justice I struggle and grow weary; but still I see a new sultan for her, who will make one seat (not as soon as I wish) and that will be in Baghdad.

Her idols shall be scattered on the ground and her proud towers, enemies of Heaven; and her tower-keepers shall be burned from the outside as from within.

Beautiful souls, the friends of virtue, shall hold the world, and then we shall see the age become golden and full of the ancient worthiness.

Babylon: the papal court at Avignon.   Jove and Pallas . . . Venus and Bacchus: gods of justice, wisdom, love, and wine, respectively.   I see a new Sultan: equating the papal court with Moslems, who were supposed to be idol worshippers, Petrarch hopes that the papal palace in Avignon will be destroyed and the seat of idolatry unified in Baghdad (properly, the seat of the caliph).

136

Fiamma dal Ciel su le tue treccie piova,
malvagia che dal fiume et da le ghiande
per l'altrui impoverir se' ricca et grande,
poi che di mal oprar tanto ti giova,   4

nido di tradimenti in cui si cova
quanto mal per lo mondo oggi si spande,
de vin serva, di letti, et di vivande,
in cui lussuria fa l'ultima prova!   8

Per le camere tue fanciulle et vecchi
vanno trescando, et Belzebùb in mezzo
co' mantici et col foco et co li specchi.   11

Già non fostu nudrita in piume al rezzo,
ma nuda al vento et scalza fra gli stecchi;
or vivi sì ch' a Dio ne venga il lezzo.   14

137

L'avara Babilonia à colmo il sacco
d'ira di Dio, e di vizii empi et rei,
tanto che scoppia, ed à fatti suoi dei
non Giove et Palla, ma Venere et Bacco.   4

Aspettando ragion mi struggo et fiacco;
ma pur novo soldan veggio per lei,
lo qual farà (non già quand' io vorrei)
sol una sede, et quella fia in Baldacco.   8

Gl'idoli suoi sarranno in terra sparsi
et le torre superbe al ciel nemiche,
e i suoi torrer di for come dentro arsi.   11

Anime belle et di virtute amiche
terranno il mondo, et poi vedrem lui farsi
aureo tutto et pien de l'opre antiche.   14

138

Fountain of sorrow, dwelling of wrath, school of errors, and temple of heresy, once Rome, now false wicked Babylon, for whom there is so much weeping and sighing:

O foundry of deceits, cruel prison where good dies and evil is created and nourished, a hell for the living: it will be a great miracle if Christ does not finally show his anger against you.

Founded in chaste and humble poverty, against your founders you lift your horns, you shameless whore! And where have you placed your hopes?

In your adulterers, in your ill-gotten riches that are so great? Constantine will not come back now. But since Hell shelters him, may it carry you off, too!

Addressed to the papal court at Avignon.

Constantine: emperor of Rome (A.D. 306–337), he legalized Christianity. In the Middle Ages he was thought to have assigned to the popes temporal sovereignty in the West in the so-called *Donation of Constantine,* demonstrated by Lorenzo Valla in the fifteenth century to be a forgery. The last two lines of the poem have never received satisfactory explanation, and the translation is a guess.

139

The more desirously I spread my wings toward you, O sweet flock of friends, the more does Fortune with birdlime entangle my flight and make me go astray.

My heart, which against his will I send about, is always with you in that open valley where the land most embosoms our sea; the other day I departed weeping from him.

I to the left, he took the straight road; I drawn by force, he led by Love; he to Jerusalem, and I to Egypt.

But patience is a comfort in sorrow; for through long usage established between us, our being together is rare and short.

Addressed to friends left behind in Italy, perhaps near Venice or Naples.

to the left: to the west, toward Provence.   Jerusalem: the Promised Land, happiness.   Egypt: the land of slavery, where Babylon (Avignon) is located.

138

Fontana di dolore, albergo d'ira,
scola d'errori et templo d'eresia,
già Roma or Babilonia falsa et ria,
per cui tanto si piange et si sospira,   4

o fucina d'inganni, o pregion dira
ove 'l ben more e 'l mal si nutre et cria,
di vivi inferno: un gran miracol fia
se Cristo teco alfine non s'adira.   8

Fondata in casta et umil povertate,
contra' tuoi fondatori alzi le corna,
putta sfacciata! Et dove ài posto spene?   11

Negli adulteri tuoi, ne le mal nate
ricchezze tante? or Constantin non torna.
Ma tolga il mondo tristo che 'l sostene!   14

139

Quanto più disiose l'ali spando
verso di voi, o dolce schiera amica,
tanto fortuna con più visco intrica
il mio volare et gir mi face errando.   4

Il cor che mal suo grado a torno mando
è con voi sempre in quella valle aprica
ove 'l mar nostro più la terra implica;
l'altr' ier da lui partimmi lagrimando.   8

I' da man manca, e' tenne il camin dritto;
i' tratto a forza, et e' d'Amore scorto,
egli in Jerusalèm, et io in Egitto.   11

Ma sofferenza è nel dolor conforto;
ché per lungo uso già fra noi prescritto
il nostro esser insieme è raro et corto.   14

140

Love, who lives and reigns in my thought and keeps his principal seat in my heart, sometimes comes forth all in armor into my forehead, there camps, and there sets up his banner.

She who teaches us to love and to be patient, and wishes my great desire, my kindled hope, to be reined in by reason, shame, and reverence, at our boldness is angry within herself.

Wherefore Love flees terrified to my heart, abandoning his every enterprise, and weeps and trembles; there he hides and no more appears outside.

What can I do, when my lord is afraid, except stay with him until the last hour? For he makes a good end who dies loving well.

141

As sometimes in the summertime the simple butterfly, seeking the light, will in its desire fly into someone's eyes, whereby it dies and the other is pained:

so always I run to my fated sun, her eyes whence such sweetness comes to me, for Love cares nothing for the rein of reason, and discernment is vanquished by desire.

And I see well how much they shun me, and I know truly that I shall die of it, for my strength cannot hold out against the suffering;

but so sweetly does Love dazzle me that I bewail another's pain and not my own harm, and my soul, blind, consents to her own death.

140

Amor, che nel penser mio vive et regna
e 'l suo seggio maggior nel mio cor tene,
talor armato ne la fronte vene;
ivi si loca et ivi pon sua insegna.   4

Quella ch' amare et sofferir ne 'nsegna
e vol che 'l gran desio, l'accesa spene
ragion, vergogna, et reverenza affrene,
di nostro ardir fra se stessa si sdegna.   8

Onde Amor paventoso fugge al core,
lasciando ogni sua impresa, et piange et trema;
ivi s'asconde et non appar più fore.   11

Che poss' io far, temendo il mio signore,
se non star seco infin a l'ora estrema?
ché bel fin fa chi ben amando more.   14

141

Come talora al caldo tempo sòle
semplicetta farfalla al lume avezza
volar negli occhi altrui per sua vaghezza,
onde aven ch' ella more, altri si dole: 4

così sempre io corro al fatal mio sole
de gli occhi onde mi ven tanta dolcezza,
che 'l fren de la ragion Amor non prezza,
e chi discerne è vinto da chi vole.   8

E veggio ben quant' elli a schivo m'ànno
e so ch' i' ne morrò veracemente,
ché mia vertù non po contra l'affanno;   11

ma sì m'abbaglia Amor soavemente
ch' i' piango l'altrui noia et no 'l mio danno,
et cieca al suo morir l'alma consente.   14

142

To the sweet shade of those beautiful leaves
I ran, fleeing a pitiless light
that was burning down upon me from the third heaven;
and already the snow was disappearing from the hills
thanks to the loving breeze that renews the season,
and through the meadows the grass bloomed and the branches.

The world never saw such graceful branches
nor did the wind ever move such green leaves
as showed themselves to me in that first season;
so that, fearing the burning light,
I chose for my refuge no shade of hills
but that of the tree most favored in Heaven.

A laurel defended me then from the heavens;
wherefore often, desirous of its lovely branches,
since then I have gone through woods and across hills:
nor have I ever again found trunk or leaves
so honored by the supernal light
that they did not change their quality according to the season.

Therefore, more and more firm from season to season,
following where I heard myself called from Heaven
and guided by a mild and clear light,
I have come back always devoted to the first branches,
both when on earth are scattered their leaves
and when the sun turns green the hills.

---

beautiful leaves: the leaves of the laurel.

142

A la dolce ombra de le belle frondi
corsi fuggendo un dispietato lume
che 'n fin qua giù m'ardea dal terzo cielo;
et disgombrava già di neve i poggi
l'aura amorosa che rinova il tempo,
et fiorian per le piagge l'erbe e i rami.   6

Non vide il mondo sì leggiadri rami
né mosse il vento mai sì verdi frondi
come a me si mostrar quel primo tempo,
tal che temendo de l'ardente lume
non volsi al mio refugio ombra di poggi,
ma de la pianta più gradita in cielo.   12

Un lauro mi difese allor dal cielo,
onde più volte, vago de' bei rami,
da po' son gito per selve et per poggi;
né giamai ritrovai tronco né frondi
tanto onorate dal superno lume
che non mutasser qualitate a tempo.   18

Però più fermo ogni or di tempo in tempo,
seguendo ove chiamar m'udia dal cielo
e scorto d'un soave et chiaro lume,
tornai sempre devoto ai primi rami
et quando a terra son sparte le frondi
et quando il sol fa verdeggiare i poggi.   24

Woods, rocks, fields, rivers, and hills—
all that is made—are vanquished and changed by time;
wherefore I ask pardon of these leaves
if, the heavens turning many years,
I have made ready to flee the enlimed branches
as soon as I began to see the light.

So pleasing to me at first was that sweet light
that joyfully I traversed great hills
in order to approach the beloved branches.
Now the shortness of life and the place and the season
show me another pathway to go to Heaven
and bear fruit, not merely flowers and leaves.

Another love, other leaves, and another light,
another climbing to Heaven by other hills
I seek (for it is indeed time), and other branches.

---

the season: probably Lent.   other branches: those of the cross (see poem 62).

143

When I hear you speak so sweetly, as Love himself inspires his
followers, my kindled desire sends forth sparks that ought to set
on fire even the souls of the dead;

I find my beautiful lady, then, present wherever she was once
sweet or kind to me, with that bearing by which she makes me—
not to the sound of any bell but sighs—often wake up.

Her locks loosed to the breeze, I see her turning back; and so she
comes beautiful into my heart, being the one who has its key.

But my excessive delight, which is an obstacle to my tongue,
does not have the daring to show forth what she is like enthroned within.

The recipient of this poem was presumably a love poet.

Selve, sassi, campagne, fiumi, et poggi,
quanto è creato, vince et cangia il tempo;
ond' io cheggio perdono a queste frondi
se rivolgendo poi molt'anni il cielo
fuggir disposi gl'invescati rami
tosto ch' i' 'ncominciai di veder lume.   30

Tanto mi piacque prima il dolce lume
ch' i' passai con diletto assai gran poggi
per poter appressar gli amati rami;
ora la vita breve e 'l loco e 'l tempo
mostranmi altro sentier di gire al cielo
et di far frutto, non pur fior et frondi.   36

Altr'amor, altre frondi, et altro lume,
altro salir al ciel per altri poggi
cerco (che n'è ben tempo), et altri rami.   39

143

Quando io v'odo parlar sì dolcemente
com' Amor proprio a' suoi seguaci instilla,
l'acceso mio desir tutto sfavilla
tal ch' enfiammar devria l'anime spente;   4

trovo la bella donna allor presente
ovunque mi fu mai dolce o tranquilla,
ne l'abito ch' al suon non d'altra squilla
ma di sospir mi fa destar sovente.   8

Le chiome a l'aura sparse et lei conversa
indietro veggio, et così bella riede
nel cor come colei che tien la chiave;   11

ma 'l soverchio piacer, che s'atraversa
a la mia lingua, qual dentro ella siede
di mostrarla in palese ardir non àve.   14

144

I never saw the sun rise so fair when the sky is most free of mist, nor after a rain the heavenly arc diversify itself through the air with so many colors,

as, on the day when I took on my burden of love, I saw her face flaming transform itself, which—and I am sparing of words—no mortal thing can equal.

I saw Love moving her lovely eyes so gently that every other sight from then on began to seem dark to me,

Sennuccio, I saw him and the bow he was drawing, so that afterward my life was no longer free of care and still yearns to see him again.

145

Place me where the sun kills the flowers and the grass, or where the ice and the snow overcome him; place me where his chariot is temperate and light, or where those dwell who yield him to us or those who take him away;

place me in lowly or proud fortune, in sweet clear air or dark and heavy; place me in the night, in day long or short, in ripe maturity or early youth;

place me in Heaven or on earth or in the abyss, on a high mountain, in a deep and swampy valley; make me a free spirit or one fixed in his members;

place me in obscurity or in illustrious fame: still I shall be what I have been, shall live as I have lived, continuing my trilustral sighing.

The poem is an amplification of lines 17–24 of Horace's "Integer vitae" (*Odes* 1.22).

trilustral: fifteen-year; a lustrum is a period of five years.

144

Né così bello il sol giamai levarsi
quando 'l ciel fosse più de nebbia scarco,
né dopo pioggia vidi 'l celeste arco
per l'aere in color tanti variarsi,   4

in quanti fiammeggiando trasformarsi
nel dì ch' io presi l'amoroso incarco
quel viso al quale (et son nel mio dir parco)
nulla cosa mortal pote aguagliarsi.   8

I' vidi Amor che' begli occhi volgea
soave sì ch' ogni altra vista oscura
da indi in qua m'incominciò apparere,   11

Sennuccio, i' 'l vidi et l'arco che tendea,
tal che mia vita poi non fu secura
et è sì vaga ancor del rivedere.   14

145

Ponmi ove 'l sole occide i fiori et l'erba,
o dove vince lui il ghiaccio et la neve;
ponmi ov' è il carro suo temprato et leve,
et ov' è chi cel rende o chi cel serba;   4

ponmi in umil fortuna od in superba,
al dolce aere sereno, al fosco et greve;
ponmi a la notte, al dì lungo ed al breve,
a la matura etate od a l'acerba;   8

ponmi in cielo od in terra od in abisso,
in alto poggio, in valle ima et palustre,
libero spirto od a' suoi membri affisso;   11

ponmi con fama oscura o con illustre:
sarò qual fui, vivrò com' io son visso,
continuando il mio sospir trilustre.   14

146

O noble spirit beauteous and warm with burning virtue, for whom I line so many pages, O sole unblemished dwelling place of chastity, tower founded secure on deep worth,

O flame, O roses scattered on a sweet drift of living snow, in which I mirror and polish myself, O pleasure for which I lift my wings toward your lovely face, which shines brighter than all the sun warms:

with your name, if my rhymes were understood so far away, I would fill Thule and Bactria, the Don and the Nile, Atlas, Olympus, and Calpe.

Since I cannot bear it to all four parts of the world, the lovely country shall hear it that the Apennines divide and the sea and the Alps surround.

Thule: name of an island traditionally supposed to be the most northerly of all lands.   Bactria: a region of Persia, a province in the empire of Alexander the Great.   Atlas: a mountain in Morocco.   Calpe: Gibraltar. lovely country: Italy.

147

When my desire, which turns and rules me with two burning spurs and a hard bit, transgresses from time to time our usual law, in order to make my spirits partly contented,

he finds one who on my brow reads the fears and boldness of my deepest heart; and he sees Love, who corrects his enterprise, lightning in her piercing angry eyes.

Therefore, like one who fears the blow of angry Jove, he draws back, for great fear reins in great desire;

but cooling fires and trembling hopes in my soul, which is transparent as glass, sometimes make clear again her sweet countenance.

---

blow of angry Jove: the thunderbolt.

146

O d'ardente vertute ornata et calda
alma gentil cui tante carte vergo,
o sol già d'onestate intero albergo,
torre in alto valor fondata et salda, 4

o fiamma, o rose sparse in dolce falda
di viva neve in ch' io mi specchio et tergo,
o piacer onde l'ali al bel viso ergo
che luce sovra quanti il sol ne scalda: 8

del vostro nome se mie rime intese
fossin sì lunghe, avrei pien Tyle et Battro,
la Tana e 'l Nilo, Atlante Olimpo et Calpe. 11

Poi che portar nol posso in tutte et quattro
parti del mondo, udrallo il bel paese
ch'Appennin parte e 'l mar circonda et l'Alpe. 14

147

Quando 'l voler, che con due sproni ardenti
et con un duro fren mi mena et regge,
trapassa ad or ad or l'usata legge
per far in parte i miei spirti contenti, 4

trova chi le paure et gli ardimenti
del cor profondo ne la fronte legge;
et vede Amor, che sue imprese corregge,
folgorar ne' turbati occhi pungenti. 8

Onde come colui che 'l colpo teme
di Giove irato, si ritragge indietro,
ché gran temenza gran desire affrena; 11

ma freddo foco et paventosa speme
de l'alma che traluce come un vetro
talor sua dolce vista rasserena. 14

148

Not Tesino, Po, Varo, Arno, Adige, or Tiber, Euphrates, Tigris,
Nile, Hermus, Indus or Ganges, Don, Danube, Alpheus,
Garonne, the sea-breaker Timavus, Rhone, Ebro, Rhine, Seine,
Elbe, Loire, or Hebrus—

not ivy, fir, pine, beech, or juniper—could lessen the fire that
wearies my sad heart as much as a lovely stream that from time
to time weeps along with me, and the slender tree that in my
rhymes I beautify and celebrate.

I find this a help amid the assaults of Love, where I must live out
in armor my life that goes by with such great leaps.

Then let this lovely laurel grow on the fresh bank; and he who
planted it, let him—in its sweet shade, to the sound of the
waters—write high and happy thoughts!

On planting a laurel on the banks of the Sorgue in Vaucluse.
Tesino . . . Hebrus: the first six rivers are in Italy; the next six are in Africa,
Asia Minor, and Asia; the rest are in Europe.   stream: the Sorgue.

149

From time to time her angelic form and her sweet smile become less harsh toward me, and the sky of her face and happy
eyes less dark.

What are these sighs doing with me now, that used to be born of
sorrow and showed forth my anguished, desperate life? If I happen to turn my face toward her in order to calm my heart, I seem
to see Love defending my cause and helping me.

But still I do not find this war coming to an end, nor any state
of my heart tranquil: for the more hope makes me confident, the
more my desire burns.

148

Non Tesin, Po, Varo, Arno, Adige et Tebro,
Eufrate, Tigre, Nilo, Ermo, Indo et Gange,
Tana, Istro, Alfeo, Garona, e 'l mar che frange,
Rodano, Ibero, Ren, Sena, Albia, Era, Ebro—   4

non edra, abete, pin, faggio o genebro—
poria 'l foco allentar che 'l cor tristo ange
quant' un bel rio ch' ad ogni or meco piange
co l'arboscel che 'n rime orno et celebro.   8

Questo un soccorso trovo fra gli assalti
d'Amore, ove conven ch' armato viva
la vita che trapassa a sì gran salti.   11

Così cresca il bel lauro in fresca riva,
et chi 'l piantò pensier leggiadri et alti
ne la dolce ombra al suon de l'acque scriva!   14

149

Di tempo in tempo mi si fa men dura
l'angelica figura e 'l dolce riso,
et l'aria del bel viso
e de gli occhi leggiadri meno oscura.   4

Che fanno meco omai questi sospiri
che nascean di dolore
et mostravan di fore
la mia angosciosa et desperata vita?
S' aven che 'l volto in quella parte giri
per acquetare il core,
parmi vedere Amore
mantener mia ragione et darmi aita.   12
Né però trovo ancor guerra finita
né tranquillo ogni stato del cor mio,
ché più m'arde 'l desio
quanto più la speranza m'assicura.   16

150

"What are you doing, soul? what do you think? shall we ever have peace? shall we ever have a truce? or shall we have eternal war?"—"What will happen to us I do not know, but from what I can see, our suffering does not please her lovely eyes."—

"What does that help, if with those eyes in summer she turns us to ice, to fire in winter?"—"Not she, but he who controls them."—"What is that to us, if she sees it and is silent?"—

"Sometimes her tongue is silent but her heart cries out with a loud voice, and though her face is dry and gay she is weeping where no one can see though he gaze at her."—

"For all that, my mind is not satisfied, and the sorrow breaks out that gathers and stagnates in it; for the unfortunate do not believe in great hopes."

---

he who controls them: the god of love.

151

Never did weary pilot flee to port from the black tempestuous wave of the sea, as I flee from my dark and turbid care to where my great desire spurs and inclines me;

nor did any divine light ever vanquish mortal sight, as does mine that high ray from the lovely sweet mild white and black where Love gilds and sharpens his arrows.

Not at all blind I see him, but bearing a quiver, naked except where shame veils him; a boy with wings, not depicted but alive.

There he shows me what he hides from many: for bit by bit within her lovely eyes I read whatever I say of Love and whatever I write.

---

white and black: Laura's eyes

150

"Che fai, alma? che pensi? avrem mai pace?
avrem mai tregua? od avrem guerra eterna?"—
"Che fia di noi non so, ma in quel ch' io scerna
a' suoi begli occhi il mal nostro non piace."—   4

"Che pro, se con quelli occhi ella ne face
di state un ghiaccio, un foco quando inverna?"—
"Ella non, ma colui che gli governa."—
"Questo ch' è a noi, s' ella sel vede et tace?"—   8

"Talor tace la lingua e 'l cor si lagna
ad alta voce, e 'n vista asciutta et lieta
piange dove mirando altri nol vede."—   11

"Per tutto ciò la mente non s'acqueta,
rompendo il duol che 'n lei s'accoglie et stagna,
ch' a gran speranza uom misero non crede."   14

151

Non d'atra et tempestosa onda marina
fuggio in porto giamai stanco nocchiero,
com' io dal fosco et torbido pensero
fuggo ove 'l gran desio mi sprona e 'nchina;   4

né mortal vista mai luce divina
vinse, come la mia quel raggio altero
del bel dolce soave bianco et nero
in che in suoi strali Amor dora et affina.   8

Cieco non già, ma faretrato il veggo,
nudo se non quanto vergogna il vela,
garzon con ali, non pinto ma vivo.   11

Indi mi mostra quel ch' a molti cela,
ch' a parte a parte entro a' begli occhi leggo
quant' io parlo d'Amore et quant' io scrivo.   14

152

This humble wild creature, this tiger's or she-bear's heart that comes in human appearance and in the shape of an angel, so wheels me about in laughter and tears between fear and hope, that she makes uncertain my every state.

If she does not soon either accept me or else free me from the bit and bridle, but still, as she is wont, keeps me between the two, by that sweet poison I feel going from my heart through my veins, Love, my life is over.

My fragile and weary strength cannot any longer bear so many changes; for in the same moment it burns, freezes, blushes, and turns pale.

It hopes by fleeing to put an end to its suffering, as one who fails from hour to hour; for he is indeed powerless who is unable to die.

153

Go, hot sighs, to her cold heart, break the ice that fights against pity; and if mortal prayers are heard in Heaven, let death or mercy end my torment.

Go forth, sweet thoughts, speaking of what her sweet gaze cannot reach; if her cruelty or my star still strikes against us, we shall be out of hope and out of error.

You can well say, not perhaps fully, that our state is as unquiet and dark as hers is peaceful and bright.

Go confident now, for Love comes with you; and cruel fortune may well end, if I know the weather by the signs of my sun.

152

Questa umil fera, un cor di tigre o d'orsa
che 'n vista umana o 'n forma d'angel vene,
in riso e 'n pianto, fra paura et spene
mi rota sì ch' ogni mio stato inforsa.   4

Se 'n breve non m'accoglie o non mi smorsa,
ma pur come suol far tra due mi tene,
per quel ch' io sento al cor gir fra le vene
dolce veneno, Amor, mia vita è corsa.   8

Non po più la vertù fragile et stanca
tante varietati omai soffrire,
che 'n un punto arde, agghiaccia, arrossa, e 'mbianca.   11

Fuggendo spera i suoi dolor finire
come colei che d'ora in ora manca,
ché ben po nulla chi non po morire.   14

153

Ite, caldi sospiri, al freddo core,
rompete il ghiaccio che pietà contende;
et se prego mortale al ciel s'intende
morte o mercé sia fine al mio dolore.   4

Ite, dolci penser, parlando fore
di quello ove 'l bel guardo non s'estende;
se pur sua asprezza o mia stella n'offende,
sarem fuor di speranza et fuor d'errore.   8

Dir se po ben per voi, non forse a pieno,
che 'l nostro stato è inquieto et fosco,
sì come 'l suo pacifico et sereno.   11

Gite securi omai, ch' Amor ven vosco;
et ria fortuna po ben venir meno,
s' ai segni del mio sol l'aere conosco.   14

154

The stars and the heavens and the elements vied with all their arts and put every ultimate care into that living light, where Nature is mirrored and the sun, which finds its equal nowhere else.

The work is so high, so lovely and new, that a mortal glance cannot look at it fixedly, Love in her beautiful eyes so seems to rain down sweetness and grace without measure.

The air struck by their rays burns with chastity and becomes such that it far surpasses our speech and thought;

no low desire is felt there, but desire of honor, of virtue. Now when was base desire ever extinguished by highest beauty?

155

Jove and Caesar were never so moved, the former to thunder, the latter to wound, that pity would not have put out their anger and shaken them from their accustomed weapon:

my lady was weeping, and my lord wished me to be there to see her and to hear her laments, in order to fill me with sorrow and desire, to probe my marrow and bones.

That sweet weeping Love drew, nay sculpted, and those gentle words he wrote, on a diamond in the midst of my heart,

where with strong and ingenious keys he still often returns to draw forth from it precious tears and long and heavy sighs.

154

Le stelle, il cielo, et gli elementi a prova
tutte lor arti et ogni estrema cura
poser nel vivo lume in cui Natura
si specchia e 'l sol, ch' altrove par non trova.   4

L'opra è sì altera, sì leggiadra et nova,
che mortal guardo in lei non s'assecura,
tanta negli occhi bei for di misura
par ch' Amore et dolcezza et grazia piova.   8

L'aere percosso da' lor dolci rai
s'infiamma d'onestate, et tal diventa
che 'l dir nostro e 'l penser vince d'assai;   11

basso desir non è ch' ivi si senta,
ma d'onor, di vertute. Or quando mai
fu per somma beltà vil voglia spenta?   14

155

Non fur ma' Giove et Cesare sì mossi
(a folminar colui, questo a ferire)
che pietà non avesse spente l'ire
e lor de l'usate arme ambeduo scossi: 4

piangea Madonna, e 'l mio signor ch' i' fossi
volse a vederla et suoi lamenti a udire,
per colmarmi di doglia et di desire
et ricercarmi le medolle et gli ossi.   8

Quel dolce pianto mi depinse Amore,
anzi scolpio, et que' detti soavi
mi scrisse entro un diamante in mezzo 'l core,   11

ove con salde ed ingegnose chiavi
ancor torna sovente a trarne fore
lagrime rare et sospir lunghi et gravi.   14

156

I saw on earth angelic qualities and heavenly beauties unique in the world, so that the memory pleases and pains me, for whatever I look on seems dreams, shadows, and smoke.

And I saw those two beautiful lights weeping that have a thousand times made the sun envious; and I heard amid sighs words that would make mountains move and rivers stand still.

Love, wisdom, worth, piety, and sorrow made, weeping, a sweeter music than any other to be heard in the world;

and the heavens were so intent upon the harmony that no leaf on any branch was seen to move, so much sweetness filled the air and the wind.

157

That always cruel and honored day so sent to my heart its lively image that no wit or style can ever describe it; but often I return to it with memory.

Her gestures adorned with all noble pity, and her sweet bitter lamenting that I heard, made me in doubt if she were a mortal woman or a goddess, for she made the sky clear all around.

Her head was fine gold, her face warm snow, ebony her eyebrows, and her eyes two stars whence Love never bent his bow in vain;

pearls and crimson roses, where gathered sorrow formed ardent beautiful words, her sighs flame, her tears crystal.

156

I' vidi in terra angelici costumi
et celesti bellezze al mondo sole,
tal che di rimembrar mi giova et dole
ché quant' io miro par sogni, ombre, et fumi.   4

Et vidi lagrimar que' duo bei lumi
ch' àn fatto mille volte invidia al sole,
et udi' sospirando dir parole
che farian gire i monti et stare i fiumi.   8

Amor, senno, valor, pietate, et doglia
facean piangendo un più dolce concento
d'ogni altro che nel mondo udir si soglia;   11

ed era il cielo a l'armonia sì intento
che non se vedea in ramo mover foglia,
tanta dolcezza avea pien l'aere e 'l vento.   14

157

Quel sempre acerbo et onorato giorno
mandò sì al cor l'imagine sua viva
che 'ngegno o stil non fia mai che 'l descriva;
ma spesso a lui co la memoria torno.   4

L'atto d'ogni gentil pietate adorno
e 'l dolce amaro lamentar ch' i' udiva
facean dubbiar se mortal donna o diva
fosse che 'l ciel rasserenava intorno.   8

La testa or fino, et calda neve il volto,
ebeno i cigli, et gli occhi eran due stelle
onde Amor l'arco non tendeva in fallo;   11

perle et rose vermiglie ove l'accolto
dolor formava ardenti voci et belle,
fiamma i sospir, le lagrime cristallo.   14

158

Wherever I rest or turn my weary eyes to quiet the yearning that impels them, I find one who portrays a beautiful lady there, to make my desires spring always green.

She seems with graceful sorrow to breathe deep pity that wrings a noble heart; beyond sight, my ears seem to hear her speak aloud her eloquent words and holy sighs.

Love and the truth were with me to say that those beauties I saw were unique in the world, never seen before under the stars;

nor were such devoted and sweet words ever heard before, nor did the sun ever see such lovely tears come forth from such beautiful eyes.

---

one who portrays: the imagination.

159

In what part of Heaven, in what Idea was the pattern from which Nature copied that lovely face, in which she has shown down here all that she is capable of doing up there?

What nymph in a fountain, in the woods what goddess ever loosed to the breeze locks of such fine gold? When did a heart gather within itself so many virtues? although the sum of them is guilty of my death.

He looks in vain for divine beauty who never saw her eyes, how sweetly she turns them;

he does not know how Love heals and how he kills, who does not know how sweetly she sighs and how sweetly she speaks and sweetly laughs.

See notes to poems 90 and 145.

158

Ove ch' i' posi gli occhi lassi o giri
per quetar la vaghezza che gli spinge,
trovo chi bella donna ivi depinge,
per far sempre mai verdi i miei desiri.   4

Con leggiadro dolor par ch' ella spiri
alta pietà che gentil core stringe;
oltra la vista, agli orecchi orna e 'nfinge
sue voci vive et suoi santi sospiri.   8

Amor e 'l ver fur meco a dir che quelle
ch' i' vidi eran bellezze al mondo sole,
mai non vedute più sotto le stelle;   11

né sì pietose et sì dolci parole
s'udiron mai, né lagrime sì belle
di sì belli occhi uscir mai vide 'l sole.   14

159

In qual parte del Ciel, in quale Idea
era l'esempio onde Natura tolse
quel bel viso leggiadro in ch' ella volse
mostrar qua già quanto lassù potea?   4

Qual ninfa in fonti, in selve mai qual dea
chiome d'oro sì fino a l'aura sciolse?
quando un cor tante in sé vertuti accolse?
ben che la somma è di mia morte rea.   8

Per divina bellezza indarno mira
chi gli occhi de costei giamai non vide,
come soavemente ella gli gira;   11

non sa come Amor sana et come ancide,
chi non sa come dolce ella sospira
et come dolce parla et dolce ride.   14

160

Love and I, as full of wonder as anyone who ever saw some incredible thing, gaze on her when she speaks or laughs, who resembles herself and no other.

From the lovely clear sky of her tranquil brow my two faithful stars so sparkle that there is no other light to inflame and guide whoever wishes to love nobly.

What a miracle it is, when on the grass she sits like a flower! or when she presses her white breast against a green tree-trunk!

What sweetness it is in the spring to see her walking alone with her thoughts, weaving a garland for her polished curling gold!

161

O scattered steps, O yearning, ready thoughts, O tenacious memory, O savage ardor, O powerful desire, O feeble heart, O my eyes, not eyes but fountains—

O leaves, the honor of famous brows, O sole ensign of the twin deservings, O laborious life, O sweet error, which make me go seeking across shores and mountains—

O lovely face where Love has put both the spurs and the rein with which he rakes and turns me as he pleases, and no kicking avails—

O noble loving souls, if there are any in the world, and you, naked shades and dust: ah, stay to see what my suffering is!

---

leaves: laurel leaves.

160

Amor et io, sì pien di meraviglia
come chi mai cosa incredibil vide,
miriam costei quand' ella parla o ride
che sol se stessa et nulla altra simiglia.   4

Dal bel seren de le tranquille ciglia
sfavillan sì le mie due stelle fide
ch' altro lume non è ch' infiammi et guide
chi d'amar altamente si consiglia.   8

Qual miracolo è quel, quando tra l'erba
quasi un fior siede, o ver quand' ella preme
col suo candido seno un verde cespo!   11

Qual dolcezza è ne la stagione acerba
vederla ir sola coi pensier suoi inseme,
tessendo un cerchio a l'oro terso et crespo!   14

161

O passi sparsi, o pensier vaghi et pronti,
o tenace memoria, o fero ardore,
o possente desire, o debil core,
oi occhi miei (occhi non già, ma fonti);   4

o fronde, onor de le famose fronti,
o sola insegna al gemino valore;
o faticosa vita, o dolce errore,
che mi fate ir cercando piagge et monti;   8

o bel viso, ove Amor inseme pose
gli sproni e 'l fren ond' el mi punge et volve
come a lui piace, e calcitrar non vale;   11

o anime gentili et amorose,
s' alcuna à 'l mondo, et voi, nude ombre et polve:
deh, ristate a veder quale è 'l mio male!   14

162

Happy and fortunate flowers and well-born grass, whereon my lady is wont to walk in thought, shore that listen to her sweet words and keep some print of her lovely foot,

slender trees and green unripe leaves, delicate pale violets, shady woods where strikes the sun who makes you with her rays tall and proud,

O lovely countryside, O pure river that bathe her lovely face and bright eyes and take your nature from that living light:

how much do I envy you her virtuous and dear gestures! By now there cannot be among you even one stone that is not learning to burn with my flame.

Addressed to the landscape of Vaucluse; the river is the Sorgue.

163

Love, you who see openly my every thought and the harsh steps where you alone guide me, reach your eyes to the depths of my heart, which appears to you but is hidden from all others.

You know what I have suffered in following you; and still day by day you climb from mountain to mountain, and pay no attention to me who am so weary, and the path is too steep for me.

I do see from afar the sweet light toward which you spur and turn me through these hard ways; but I do not have wings, as you do, to be able to fly.

You leave my desires content as long as I am consumed with a high love and it does not displease her that I sigh for her.

162

Lieti fiori et felici, et ben nate erbe
che Madonna pensando premer sòle,
piaggia ch' ascolti sue dolci parole
et del bel piede alcun vestigio serbe,   4

schietti arboscelli et verdi frondi acerbe,
amorosette et pallide viole,
ombrose selve ove percote il sole
che vi fa co' suoi raggi alte et superbe,   8

o soave contrada, o puro fiume
che bagni il suo bel viso et gli occhi chiari
et prendi qualità dal vivo lume: 11

quanto v'invidio gli atti onesti et cari!
Non fia in voi scoglio omai che per costume
d'arder co la mia fiamma non impari.   14

163

Amor, che vedi ogni pensero aperto
e i duri passi onde tu sol mi scorgi,
nel fondo del mio cor gli occhi tuoi porgi
a te palese, a tutt' altri coverto.   4

Sai quel che per seguirte ò già sofferto,
et tu pur via di poggio in poggio sorgi
di giorno in giorno, et di me non t'accorgi,
che son sì stanco e 'l sentier m'è troppo erto.   8

Ben veggio io di lontano il dolce lume
ove per aspre vie mi sproni et giri,
ma non ò come tu da volar piume.   11

Assai contenti lasci i miei desiri
pur che ben desiando i' mi consume
né le dispiaccia che per lei sospiri.   14

164

Now that the heavens and the earth and the wind are silent, and sleep reins in the beasts and the birds, Night drives her starry car about, and in its bed the sea lies without a wave,

I am awake, I think, I burn, I weep; and she who destroys me is always before me, to my sweet pain: war is my state, full of sorrow and suffering, and only thinking of her do I have any peace.

Thus from one clear living fountain alone spring the sweet and the bitter on which I feed; one hand alone heals me and pierces me.

And that my suffering may not reach an end, a thousand times a day I die and a thousand am born, so distant am I from health.

165

As her white foot through the green grass virtuously moves its sweet steps, a power that all around her opens and renews the flowers seems to issue from her tender soles.

Love, who enlimes only generous hearts nor deigns to try his power elsewhere, makes to rain from her lovely eyes a delight so warm that I care for no other good nor desire other bait.

And with her walk and her gentle glance her most sweet words accord, and her mild, humble, slow gestures.

From those four sparks, and not those alone, is born the great fire on which I live and burn, for I have become a nocturnal bird in the sun.

164

Or che 'l ciel et la terra e 'l vento tace
et le fere e gli augelli il sonno affrena,
notte il carro stellato in giro mena
et nel suo letto il mar senz' onda giace,   4

vegghio, penso, ardo, piango; et chi mi sface
sempre m'è inanzi per mia dolce pena:
guerra è 'l mio stato, d'ira e di duol piena,
et sol di lei pensando ò qualche pace.   8

Così sol d'una chiara fonte viva
move 'l dolce et l'amaro ond' io mi pasco,
una man sola mi risana et punge;   11

et perché 'l mio martir non giunga a riva,
mille volte il dì moro et mille nasco,
tanto da la salute mia son lunge.   14

165

Come 'l candido pie' per l'erba fresca
i dolci passi onestamente move,
vertù che 'ntorno i fiori apra et rinove
de le tenere piante sue par ch' esca.   4

Amor, che solo i cor leggiadri invesca
né degna di provar sua forza altrove,
da' begli occhi un piacer sì caldo piove
ch' i' non curo altro ben né bramo altr'esca.   8

Et co l'andar et col soave sguardo
s'accordan le dolcissime parole
et l'atto mansueto umile et tardo.   11

Di tai quattro faville, et non già sole,
nasce 'l gran foco di ch' io vivo et ardo,
che son fatto un augel notturno al sole.   14

166

If I had stayed in the cave where Apollo became a prophet, Florence would perhaps have her poet today, not only Verona and Mantua and Arunca;

but, since my ground produces no more reeds from the water of that rock, I must follow another planet and with my hooked sickle reap thistles and thorns from my field.

The olive tree is dry, and the waters have turned elsewhere that flow down from Parnassus and at one time made it flourish.

Thus misfortune or my fault deprives me of all good fruit, if eternal Jove does not rain His grace down upon me.

---

cave: the shrine of Apollo at Delphi, on Mount Parnassus, traditionally the earliest of his oracles.   Florence: Dante is excluded probably because he wrote in Italian rather than Latin.   Verona and Mantua and Arunca: birthplaces of Catullus, Virgil, and Juvenal, respectively.   planet: probably Saturn.   olive tree: sacred to Minerva, goddess of wisdom. Parnassus: mountain sacred to Apollo and the Muses.

167

When Love bends her lovely eyes to the ground and with his own hands gathers together her wandering breath into a sigh and then looses it in a clear, soft, angelic, divine voice,

I feel my heart sweetly stolen away and my thoughts and desires so change within me that I say: "Now comes the final plundering of me, if Heaven reserves me for so virtuous a death."

But the sound that binds my senses with its sweetness, reins in my soul, though ready to depart, with the great desire for the blessedness of listening;

so I live on, and thus she both threads and unwinds the spool of my appointed life, this only heavenly siren among us.

---

heavenly siren: according to the myth of Er (Plato, *Republic*, book 10; known to Petrarch through Cicero and Macrobius), the heavenly spheres are attached to the spindle of Necessity, and each is governed by a siren whose singing constitutes the harmony of the spheres; the three Fates govern the spindle and sing with the sirens.

166

S' i' fussi stato fermo a la spelunca
là dove Apollo diventò profeta,
Fiorenza avria forse oggi il suo poeta,
non pur Verona et Mantoa et Arunca;   4

ma perché 'l mio terren più non s'ingiunca
de l'umor di quel sasso, altro pianeta
conven ch' i' segua et del mio campo mieta
lappole et stecchi co la falce adunca.   8

L'oliva è secca, et è rivolta altrove
l'acqua che di Parnaso si deriva,
per cui in alcun tempo ella fioriva.   11

Così sventura o ver colpa mi priva
d'ogni buon frutto, se l'eterno Giove
de la sua grazia sopra me non piove.   14

167

Quando Amor i belli occhi a terra inchina,
e i vaghi spirti in un sospiro accoglie
co le sue mani, et poi in voce gli scioglie
chiara, soave, angelica, divina,   4

sento far del mio cor dolce rapina
et sì dentro cangiar penseri et voglie
ch' i' dico: "Or fien di me l'ultime spoglie:
se 'l ciel sì onesta morte mi destina."   8

Ma 'l suon che di dolcezza i sensi lega
col gran desir d'udendo esser beata
l'anima al dipartir presta raffrena;   11

così mi vivo, et così avolge et spiega
lo stame de la vita che m'è data
questa sola fra noi del ciel sirena.   14

168

Love sends me that sweet thought which is an old confidant between us and comforts me and says that I was never so close as I am now to what I yearn and hope for.

I, who have found his words sometimes false and sometimes true, do not know whether to believe him, and I live between the two: neither yes nor no sounds whole in my heart.

In the meanwhile time passes, and in the mirror I see myself nearing the season that is contrary to his promise and to my hope.

Now come what will: I am not the only one who is growing old, and my desire does not vary at all with age; but I do fear that what remains of life may be short.

169

Full of a yearning thought that makes me stray away from all others and go alone in the world, from time to time I steal myself away from myself, still seeking only her whom I should flee;

and I see her pass so sweet and cruel that my soul trembles to rise in flight, such a crowd of armed sighs she leads, this lovely enemy of Love and me.

If I do not err, I do perceive a gleam of pity on her cloudy, proud brow, which partly clears my sorrowing heart:

then I collect my soul, and, when I have decided to discover my ills to her, I have so much to say to her that I dare not begin.

168

Amor mi manda quel dolce pensero
che secretario antico è fra noi due,
et mi conforta et dice che non fue
mai come or presto a quel ch' io bramo et spero.   4

Io, che talor menzogna et talor vero
ò ritrovato le parole sue,
non so s' il creda, et vivomi intra due:
né sì né no nel cor mi sona intero.   8

In questa passa 'l tempo, et ne lo specchio
mi veggio andar ver la stagion contraria
a sua impromessa et a la mia speranza.   11

Or sia che po: già sol io non invecchio,
già per etate il mio desir non varia,
ben temo il viver breve che n'avanza.   14

169

Pien d'un vago penser che me desvia
da tutti gli altri et fammi al mondo ir solo,
ad or ad ora a me stesso m'involo,
pur lei cercando che fuggir devria;   4

et veggiola passar sì dolce et ria
che l'alma trema per levarsi a volo,
tal d'armati sospir conduce stuolo
questa bella d'Amor nemica et mia.   8

Ben, si i' non erro, di pietate un raggio
scorgo fra 'l nubiloso altero ciglio,
che 'n parte rasserena il cor doglioso;   11

allor raccolgo l'alma, et poi ch' i' aggio
di scovrirle il mio mal preso consiglio,
tanto gli ò a dir che 'ncominciar non oso.   14

170

Many times from her kind expression I have learned boldness, with my faithful guides, to assail with virtuous skillful words my enemy so humble and mild of bearing.

But her eyes then make my thought vain, for Love, who alone can do so, has placed in her hands all my fortune, all my destiny, my good, my ill, my life, and my death.

Wherefore I have never been able to form a word that was understood by any but myself, Love has made me so trembling and weak!

And I see well how burning Love binds one's tongue, steals away one's breath: he who can say how he burns is in but a little fire.

---

my faithful guides: my eyes.

171

Love has brought me within the reach of lovely, cruel arms that unjustly kill me, and if I complain he redoubles my torment; thus it is still better that I die loving and be silent, as I am wont;

for she could burn the Rhine with her eyes and break his every ridge of ice when he is most frozen, and her pride is so equal to her beauties that it seems to displease her that she pleases.

With my own wit I can take away none of the lovely diamond with which her heart is so hard; the rest of her is a piece of marble that moves and breathes;

nor will she ever, for all her disdain, and for all her dark looks, take away from me my hopes and my sweet sighs.

170

Più volte già dal bel sembiante umano
ò preso ardir co le mie fide scorte
d'assalir con parole oneste accorte
la mia nemica in atto umile et piano.   4

Fanno poi gli occhi suoi mio penser vano
per ch' ogni mia fortuna, ogni mia sorte,
mio ben, mio male, et mia vita et mia morte
quei che solo il po far l'à posto in mano.   8

Ond' io non pote' mai formar parola
ch' altro che da me stesso fosse intesa,
così m'à fatto Amor tremante et fioco.   11

Et veggi' or ben che caritate accesa
lega la lingua altrui, gli spirti invola:
chi po dir com' egli arde è 'n picciol foco.   14

171

Giunto m'à Amor fra belle et crude braccia
che m'ancidono a torto, et s' io mi doglio
doppia 'l martir; onde pur com' io soglio
il meglio è ch' io mi mora amando et taccia;   4

ché poria questa il Ren qualor più agghiaccia
arder con gli occhi, et rompre ogni aspro scoglio,
et à sì egual a le bellezze orgoglio
che di piacer altrui par che le spiaccia.   8

Nulla posso levar io per mi' 'ngegno
del bel diamante ond' ell' à il cor sì duro,
l'altro è d' un marmo che si mova et spiri;   11

ned ella a me, per tutto 'l suo disdegno
torrà giamai, né per sembiante oscuro,
le mie speranze e i mei dolci sospiri.   14

172

O Envy the enemy of virtue, you who gladly fight against good beginnings, by what path did you so silently enter that lovely breast, and with what art do you change it?

You have plucked up by the roots my salvation: you made her think me too fortunate a lover, she who for a while accepted my humble and chaste prayers and now seems to hate and refuse them.

But though with bitter, cruel gesture she weep at my luck and laugh at my weeping, she cannot change even one of my thoughts;

though she kill me a thousand times a day, I shall still love her and hope in her; for if she terrifies me, Love gives me confidence.

173

Gazing at the clear sun of her lovely eyes, where there is one who often makes mine red and wet, my weary soul leaves my heart for its earthly paradise;

then, finding it so full of sweetness and bitterness, it sees that whatever is woven in the world is cobwebs, and it complains to Love, whose spurs are so hot, whose bit is so hard.

Between these two extremes so contrary and mixed, now with frozen desires, now with kindled, it stays thus half miserable and half happy;

but few happy thoughts and many sad ones: mostly it repents of its bold enterprise, such fruit is born from such a root.

One . . . wet: the god of love.

172

O Invidia nimica di vertute,
ch' a' bei principii volentier contrasti,
per qual sentier così tacita intrasti
in quel bel petto, et con qual arti il mute?   4

Da radice n'ài svelta mia salute:
troppo felice amante mi mostrasti
a quella che' miei preghi umili et casti
gradì alcun tempo, or par ch' odi' et refute.   8

Né però che con atti acerbi et rei
del mio ben pianga e del mio pianger rida
poria cangiar sol un de' pensier mei,   11

non perché mille volte il dì m'ancida
fia ch' io non l'ami et ch' i' non speri in lei;
ché s' ella mi spaventa, Amor m'affida.   14

173

Mirando 'l sol de' begli occhi sereno
ov' è chi spesso i miei depinge et bagna,
dal cor l'anima stanca si scompagna
per gir nel paradiso suo terreno;   4

poi trovandol di dolce et d'amar pieno,
quant' al mondo si tesse opra d'aragna
vede, onde seco et con Amor si lagna,
ch' à sì caldi gli spron, sì duro 'l freno.   8

Per questi estremi duo contrari et misti,
or con voglie gelate, or con accese,
stassi così fra misera et felice;   11

ma pochi lieti et molti penser tristi,
e 'l più si pente de l'ardite imprese,
tal frutto nasce di cotal radice.   14

174

A cruel star was the one I was born under (if the heavens have as much power over us as some believe) and a cruel cradle where I lay new born, and cruel ground where I later set my feet,

and a cruel lady who with her eyes, and with the bow whom I pleased only as a target, made the wound about which, Love, I have not been silent to you, for with those same weapons you can heal it.

But you are pleased by my pain; not she, for it is not harsh enough, and the blow is from an arrow, not a spear.

Still it consoles me that it is better to languish for her than enjoy another, and you swear it to me by your golden arrow, and I believe you.

175

When I remember the time and the place where I lost myself, and the dear knot with which Love with his own hand bound me (he so made bitterness seem sweet and weeping, pleasure),

I am all sulphur and tinder, and my heart is a fire lit by those gentle words which I always hear, so aflame within that I joy in my flames and I live on that, and for aught else I care little.

That sun which shines only to my eyes with her lovely beams warms me at evening just as she did early today;

and from afar she so ignites and kindles me, that the memory, still fresh and whole, points out to me that knot and the place and the time.

174

Fera stella (se 'l cielo à forza in noi
quant' alcun crede) fu sotto ch' io nacqui,
et fera cuna dove nato giacqui,
et fera terra ov 'e' pie' mossi poi,   4

et fera donna che con gli occhi suoi
et con l'arco a cui sol per segno piacqui
fe' la piaga onde, Amor, teco non tacqui,
ché con quell'arme risaldar la poi.   8

Ma tu prendi a diletto i dolor miei;
ella non già, perché non son più duri,
e 'l colpo è di saetta et non di spiedo.   11

Pur mi consola che languir per lei
meglio è che gioir d'altra, et tu mel giuri
per l'orato tuo strale, et io tel credo.   14

175

Quando mi vene inanzi il tempo e 'l loco
ov' i' perdei me stesso, e 'l caro nodo
ond' Amor di sua man m'avinse in modo
che l'amar mi fe' dolce e 'l pianger gioco,   4

solfo et esca son tutto, e 'l cor un foco
da quei soavi spirti i quai sempre odo
acceso dentro sì ch' ardendo godo,
et di ciò vivo et d'altro mi cal poco.   8

Quel sol che solo agli occhi mei resplende
coi vaghi raggi ancor indi mi scalda
a vespro tal qual era oggi per tempo;   11

et così di lontan m'alluma e 'ncende
che la memoria ad ogni or fresca et salda
pur quel nodo mi mostra e 'l loco e 'l tempo.   14

176

Through the midst of the inhospitable savage woods, where even armed men go at great risk, I go without fear, nor can anything terrify me except the sun that has Love's living rays.

And I go singing (oh my unwise thoughts!) of her whom the heavens could not make far from me, for she is before my eyes and with her I seem to see ladies and damsels, but they are firs and beeches.

I seem to hear her, when I hear the branches and the breeze and the leaves, and birds lamenting, and the waters fleeing with a murmur across the green grass.

Rarely has the silence, the solitary chill of a shady wood pleased me so much; except that I lose too much of my sun.

---

woods: the forest of Ardennes, through which Petrarch traveled during the war between the counts of Brabant and Flanders, in 1333.

177

Love has shown me a thousand slopes in one day and a thousand rivers through the famous Ardennes, for he gives wings to the feet and hearts of his followers to make them fly up to the third heaven.

It is sweet to me to have been there alone, unarmed where armed Mars strikes without warning, as if I had been a ship at sea without tiller or mast, full of heavy and secret thoughts.

Still, coming to the end of the dark day, remembering from where I come and with what wings, I am afraid because of my too great daring;

but the lovely country and the delightful river with serene welcome reassure my heart, already turned toward where his light dwells.

---

third heaven: sphere of the planet Venus.   lovely country and the delight-ful river: Provence (possibly the region of Lyons) and the Rhone.

176

Per mezz' i boschi inospiti et selvaggi
onde vanno a gran rischio uomini et arme,
vo securo io, ché non po spaventarme
altri che 'l sol ch' à d'Amor vivo i raggi.   4

E vo cantando (o penser miei non saggi!)
lei che 'l ciel non poria lontana farme,
ch' i' l'ò negli occhi, et veder seco parme
donne et donzelle, et sono abeti et faggi.   8

Parmi d'udirla, udendo i rami et l'ore
et le frondi, et gli augei lagnarsi, et l'acque
mormorando fuggir per l'erba verde.   11

Raro un silenzio, un solitario orrore
d'ombrosa selva mai tanto mi piacque,
se non che dal mio sol troppo si perde.   14

177

Mille piagge in un giorno et mille rivi
mostrato m'à per la famosa Ardenna
Amor, ch' a' suoi le piante e i cori impenna
per fargli al terzo ciel volando ir vivi.   4

Dolce m'è sol, senz' arme esser stato ivi
dove armato fier Marte et non acenna,
quasi senza governo et senza antenna
legno in mar, pien di penser gravi et schivi.   8

Pur giunto al fin de la giornata oscura,
rimembrando ond' io vegno et con quai piume,
sento di troppo ardir nascer paura;   11

ma 'l bel paese e 'l dilettoso fiume
con serena accoglienza rassecura
il cor già vòlto ov' abita il suo lume.   14

178

Love at the same time spurs me and reins me in, reassures and terrifies me, burns and freezes me, is kind and disdainful to me, calls me to him and drives me away, now keeps me in hope and now in sorrow,

now high now low he leads my weary heart; wherefore my wandering desire loses the trace and seems displeased by its dearest pleasure, full of such strange error is my mind!

A friendly thought shows my mind the crossing—not of water poured out through the eyes—by which it may go quickly where it hopes to be happy;

then, as if a greater force turned it back from there, it must follow another path and against its will consent to its slow death and mine.

---

crossing: the way to virtue, where weeping would be unnecessary.
another path: that of love.

179

Geri, when from time to time my sweet enemy who is so proud becomes angry with me, one comfort is given me that I may not perish, through whose virtue alone my soul is able to breathe:

wherever she angrily turns her eyes, who hopes to deprive my life of light, I show her mine full of such true humility that she necessarily draws back all her anger.

And if that were not so, I would not go to see her otherwise than to see the face of Medusa, which made people become marble.

You therefore do the same; for I see all other help cut off, and flight avails nothing against the wings that our lord uses.

A reply, using the same rhymes, to a sonnet by Geri Gianfigliazzi, a Florentine friend (Appendix One, p. 609).

178

Amor mi sprona in un tempo et affrena,
assecura et spaventa, arde et agghiaccia,
gradisce et sdegna, a sé mi chiama et scaccia,
or mi tene in speranza et or in pena,   4

or alto or basso il meo cor lasso mena;
onde 'l vago desir perde la traccia
e 'l suo sommo piacer par che li spiaccia,
d'error sì novo la mia mente è piena.   8

Un amico penser le mostra il vado
(non d'acqua che per gli occhi si resolva)
da gir tosto ove spera esser contenta;   11

poi quasi maggior forza indi la svolva,
conven ch' altra via segua et mal suo grado
a la sua lunga et mia morte consenta.   14

179

Geri, quando talor meco s'adira
la mia dolce nemica ch' è sì altera,
un conforto m'è dato ch' i' non pera,
solo per cui vertù l'alma respira: 4

ovunque ella sdegnando li occhi gira,
che di luce privar mia vita spera,
le mostro i miei pien d'umiltà sì vera
ch' a forza ogni suo sdegno indietro tira.   8

E ciò non fusse, andrei non altramente
a veder lei che 'l volto di Medusa,
che facea marmo diventar la gente.   11

Così dunque fa' tu; ch' i' veggio esclusa
ogni altra aita, e 'l fuggir val niente
dinanzi a l'ali che 'l signor nostro usa.   14

180

Po, you may well carry along with your powerful and rapid waves; but my spirit that is hidden there within is not hampered by your or anyone's force;

for, without tacking alternately to port and starboard, straight into the breeze toward the golden leaves, beating his wings which further his desire, he overcomes the current and the wind and the sail and the oars.

King of rivers, proud and haughty, who meet the sun when he brings us the day and in the west leave behind a more lovely light:

you carry on your horn what is mortal of me; the other part, covered with the feathers of love, returns flying to his sweet dwelling.

Written while sailing eastward down the river Po.
golden leaves: Laura's hair.   King of rivers: a traditional epithet for the Po.   light: Laura.   horn: according to classical mythology, river gods were horned.   the other part: the immortal part, the spirit.

181

Love set out amid the grass a gay net of gold and pearls, under a branch of the evergreen tree that I so love, although it has more sad than happy shadows.

The bait was that seed he sows and harvests, sweet and bitter, which I fear and desire; the birdcall was never so soft and quiet since the day when Adam opened his eyes;

and the bright light that makes the sun disappear was lightening all around, and the rope was wrapped around the hand that surpasses ivory and snow.

Thus I fell into the net; and I have been captured here by her sweet bearing, and her angelic words, and pleasure and desire and hope.

---

gold and pearls: Laura's hair, braided with pearls.   evergreen tree: the laurel.

180

Po, ben puo' tu portartene la scorza
di me con tue possenti et rapide onde,
ma lo spirto ch' iv' entro si nasconde
non cura né di tua né d'altrui forza;   4

lo qual, senz' alternar poggia con orza,
dritto per l'aure, al suo desir seconde
battendo l'ali, verso l'aurea fronde
l'acqua e 'l vento e la vela e i remi sforza.   8

Re degli altri, superbo altero fiume
che 'ncontri 'l sol quando e' ne mena 'l giorno
e 'n ponente abandoni un più bel lume: 11

tu te ne vai col mio mortal sul corno;
l'altro, coverto d'amorose piume,
torna volando al suo dolce soggiorno.   14

181

Amor fra l'erbe una leggiadra rete
d'oro e di perle tese sott' un ramo
dell'arbor sempre verde ch' i' tant' amo,
ben che n'abbia ombre più triste che liete.   4

L'esca fu 'l seme ch' egli sparge et miete
dolce et acerbo, ch' i' pavento et bramo;
le note non fur mai, dal dì ch' Adamo
aperse gli occhi, sì soavi et quete;   8

e 'l chiaro lume che sparir fa 'l sole
folgorava dintorno, e 'l fune avolto
era a la man ch' avorio et neve avanza.   11

Così caddi a la rete, et qui m'àn colto
gli atti vaghi et l'angeliche parole
e 'l piacer e 'l desire et la speranza.   14

182

Love inflames my heart with ardent zeal and makes it shrink with icy fear; and he makes my mind uncertain which is greater, the hope or the fear, the flame or the frost.

I tremble under the hottest sky, burn under the coldest, always full of desire and fear at a lady's hiding the wisdom of a living man within her trim garment or under a little veil.

Of these pains, my very own is the first, to burn day and night; and how great the sweet illness is no thought can grasp, not to mention verses or rhyme;

the other pain I suffer less, for my flame is such that all men are equal before her, and he who thinks to fly as high as her light, he spreads his wings in vain.

183

If that sweet glance of hers and those soft skillful little words kill me, and if Love makes her so strong over me when she merely speaks or when she smiles,

alas, what will happen if perhaps, through some fault of mine or some unhappy chance, she should exclude pity from her eyes and defy me to death, whereas now she defends me?

Therefore if I tremble and go with a freezing heart whenever I see her expression change, this fear is born of long experience:

a woman is a changeable thing by nature, and I know well that a state of love lasts little time in the heart of a woman.

182

Amor che 'ncende il cor d'ardente zelo
di gelata paura il ten costretto;
et qual sia più fa dubbio a l'intelletto
la speranza o 'l temor, la fiamma o 'l gelo.   4

Trem' al più caldo, ard' al più freddo cielo,
sempre pien di desire et di sospetto
pur come donna in un vestire schietto
celi un uom vivo, o sotto un picciol velo.   8

Di queste pene è mia propia la prima,
arder dì et notte; et quanto è 'l dolce male
né 'n penser cape, non che 'n versi o 'n rima;   11

l'altra non già, che 'l mio bel foco è tale
ch' ogni uom pareggia, et del suo lume in cima
chi volar pensa indarno spiega l'ale.   14

183

Se 'l dolce sguardo di costei m'ancide
et le soavi parolette accorte,
et s' Amor sopra me la fa sì forte
sol quando parla o ver quando sorride,   4

lasso, che fia se forse ella divide—
o per mia colpa o per malvagia sorte—
gli occhi suoi da mercé, sì che di morte
là dove or m'assicura allor mi sfide?   8

Però s' i' tremo et vo col cor gelato
qualor veggio cangiata sua figura,
questo temer d'antiche prove è nato: 11

femina è cosa mobile per natura,
ond' io so ben ch' un amoroso stato
in cor di donna picciol tempo dura.   14

184

Love, Nature, and that sweet humble soul, where every high virtue dwells and reigns, have combined against me: Love is contriving to make me die outright, and in that he follows his usual style;

Nature holds that soul with so delicate a tie that she can sustain no force; she is so shy that she does not deign to dwell any longer in wearisome, low life.

Thus the breath moment by moment is failing in those lovely dear virtuous limbs that have been a mirror of true gracefulness,

and if Pity does not rein Death in, alas, I see well in what state are these vain hopes on which I have been wont to live.

185

With the gilded feathers around her noble white neck this phoenix forms without art so dear a necklace that it sweetens every heart and consumes mine;

she forms a natural diadem that lights the air around, and the silent flint of Love draws from it a subtle liquid fire that burns me in the coldest frost.

A scarlet dress with cerulean border sprinkled with roses veils her lovely shoulders: a new garment and unique beauty.

Fame puts her away and hides her in the fragrant rich bosom of the Arabian mountains, but she flies haughty through our own skies.

---

gilded feathers: Laura's hair.   scarlet . . . cerulean: the traditional colors, along with gold, of the phoenix's plumage.

184

Amor, Natura et la bella alma umile
ov' ogn' alta vertute alberga et regna
contra me son giurati: Amor s'ingegna
ch' i' mora a fatto e 'n ciò segue suo stile;   4

Natura ten costei d'un sì gentile
laccio che nullo sforzo è che sostegna;
ella è sì schiva ch' abitar non degna
più ne la vita faticosa et vile.   8

Così lo spirto d'or in or ven meno
a quelle belle care membra oneste
che specchio eran di vera leggiadria;   11

et s' a Morte Pietà non stringe 'l freno,
lasso, ben veggio in che stato son queste
vane speranze ond' io viver solia.   14

185

Questa fenice de l'aurata piuma
al suo bel collo candido gentile
forma senz' arte un sì caro monile
ch' ogni cor addolcisce e 'l mio consuma;   4

forma un diadema natural ch' alluma
l'aere dintorno, et 'l tacito focile
d'Amor tragge indi un liquido sottile
foco che m'arde a la più algente bruma.   8

Purpurea vesta d'un ceruleo lembo
sparso di rose i belli omeri vela,
novo abito et bellezza unica et sola!   11

Fama ne l'odorato et ricco grembo
d'arabi monti lei ripone et cela,
che per lo nostro ciel sì altera vola.   14

186

If Virgil and Homer had seen that sun which I see with my eyes, they would have exerted all their powers to give her fame and would have mixed together the two styles:

for which Aeneas would be angry; and Achilles, Ulysses, and the other demigods, and he who ruled the world so well for fifty-six years, and he whom Aegisthus killed, would all be sad.

That ancient flower of virtue and arms, what a similar star he had with this new flower of chastity and beauty!

Ennius sang of him an inelegant song, I of her; and ah! may my wit not displease her, may she not despise my praises!

---

he who ruled: the emperor Augustus.   he whom Aegisthus killed: Agamemnon, king of Argos.   ancient flower: Cornelius Scipio Africanus, conqueror of Carthage.   Ennis: Roman poet (239–169? B.C.), a friend of Scipio and author of a long poem on the Punic Wars.

187

When Alexander came to the famous tomb of the fierce Achilles, he sighing said: "O fortunate one, who found so clear a trumpet, one who wrote such high things of you!"

But this pure and white dove, whose equal I think never lived in the world, she resounds very little in my frail style. Thus each one's destiny is fixed;

for she is worthy of Homer and Orpheus and of the shepherd whom Mantua still honors, worthy to have them always singing only of her,

but a deformed star and her fate, cruel only in this, have entrusted her to one who adores her lovely name but perhaps mars her praise when he speaks.

When Alexander came: Petrarch derived this incident from Cicero's *Pro Archia.* Alexander is Alexander the Great.   trumpet: Homer. shepherd: Virgil, as author of the *Eclogues.*

186

Se Virgilio et Omero avessin visto
quel sole il qual vegg' io con gli occhi miei,
tutte lor forze in dar fama a costei
avrian posto et l'un stil coll'altro misto;   4

di che sarebbe Enea turbato, et tristo
Achille, Ulisse et gli altri semidei,
et quel che resse anni cinquantasei
sì bene il mondo, et quel ch' ancise Egisto.   8

Quel fiore antico di vertuti et d'arme,
come sembiante stella ebbe con questo
novo fior d'onestate et di bellezze!   11

Ennio di quel cantò ruvido carme,
di quest'altro io, et o, pur non molesto
gli sia il mio ingegno e 'l mio lodar non sprezze!   14

187

Giunto Alessandro a la famosa tomba
del fero Achille, sospirando disse:
"O fortunato che sì chiara tromba
trovasti et chi di te sì alto scrisse!"   4

Ma questa pura et candida colomba
a cui non so s' al mondo mai par visse
nel mio stil frale assai poco rimbomba.
Così son le sue sorti a ciascun fisse;   8

ché d'Omero dignissima e d'Orfeo
o del pastor ch' ancor Mantova onora,
ch' andassen sempre lei sola cantando,   11

stella difforme et fato sol qui reo
commise a tal che 'l suo bel nome adora
ma forse scema sue lode parlando.   14

188

Life-giving sun, you first loved that branch which is all I love; now, unique in her sweet dwelling, she flourishes, without an equal since Adam first saw his and our lovely bane.

Let us stay to gaze at her, I beg and call on you, O sun, and you still run away and shadow the hillsides all around and carry off the day, and fleeing you take from me what I most desire.

The shadow that falls from that low hill where my gentle fire is sparkling, where the great laurel was a little sapling,

growing as I speak, takes from my eyes the sweet sight of the blessed place where my heart dwells with his lady.

---

that branch: the laurel.   that low hill: see note to poem 4.

189

My ship laden with forgetfulness passes through a harsh sea, at midnight, in winter, between Scylla and Charybdis, and at the tiller sits my lord, rather my enemy;

each oar is manned by a ready, cruel thought that seems to scorn the tempest and the end; a wet, changeless wind of sighs, hopes, and desires breaks the sail;

a rain of weeping, a mist of disdain wet and loosen the already weary ropes, made of error twisted up with ignorance.

My two usual sweet stars are hidden; dead among the waves are reason and skill; so that I begin to despair of the port.

188

Almo sol, quella fronde ch' io sola amo
tu prima amasti, or sola al bel soggiorno
verdeggia et senza par poi che l'adorno
suo male et nostro vide in prima Adamo.   4

Stiamo a mirarla, i' ti pur prego et chiamo,
o sole; et tu pur fuggi et fai dintorno
ombrare i poggi et te ne porti il giorno,
et fuggendo mi tòi quel ch' i' più bramo.   8

L'ombra che cade da quell'umil colle
ove favilla il mio soave foco,
ove 'l gran lauro fu picciola verga,   11

crescendo mentr' io parlo, agli occhi tolle
la dolce vista del beato loco
ove 'l mio cor con la sua donna alberga.   14

189

Passa la nave mia colma d'oblio
per aspro mare a mezza notte il verno
enfra Scilla et Caribdi, et al governo
siede 'l signore anzi 'l nimico mio;   4

à ciascun remo un penser pronto et rio
che la tempesta e 'l fin par ch' abbi a scherno;
la vela rompe un vento umido eterno
di sospir, di speranze et di desio;   8

pioggia di lagrimar, nebbia di sdegni
bagna et rallenta le già stanche sarte
che son d'error con ignoranzia attorto.   11

Celansi i duo mei dolci usati segni,
morta fra l'onde è la ragion et l'arte
tal ch' i' 'ncomincio a desperar del porto.   14

190

A white doe on the green grass appeared to me, with two golden horns, between two rivers, in the shade of a laurel, when the sun was rising in the unripe season.

Her look was so sweet and proud that to follow her I left every task, like the miser who as he seeks treasure sweetens his trouble with delight.

"Let no one touch me," she bore written with diamonds and topazes around her lovely neck. "It has pleased my Caesar to make me free."

And the sun had already turned at midday; my eyes were tired by looking but not sated, when I fell into the water, and she disappeared.

---

doe: traditionally sacred to Diana.   two golden horns: corresponding to Laura's braids.   two rivers: the Sorgue and the Durance.   "Let no one touch me . . .": according to Solinus (third century A.D.) three hundred years after Caesar's death white stags were found with collars inscribed "Noli me tangere, Caesaris sum" (Do not touch me, I am Caesar's).   diamonds and topazes: emblems of steadfastness and chastity, respectively.   my Caesar: probably God.

191

As it is eternal life to see God, nor can one desire more, nor is it right to desire more, so, Lady, seeing you makes me happy in this short and frail life of mine.

Nor have I ever seen you as beautiful as you are at this hour, if my eye tells my heart the truth, oh sweet hour that makes blessed my thoughts, that surpasses every high hope, every desire!

And if its fleeing were not so swift I would ask no more, for if some live only on odors, and the fame of it is believed,

and some on water or on fire, satisfying their taste and touch with things that lack all sweetness, why should I not live on the life-giving sight of you?

Some live only on odors . . . fire: natural history from Pliny and Solinus.

190

Una candida cerva sopra l'erba
verde m'apparve con duo corna d'oro,
fra due riviere all'ombra d'un alloro,
levando 'l sole a la stagione acerba.   4

Era sua vista sì dolce superba
ch' i' lasciai per seguirla ogni lavoro,
come l'avaro che 'n cercar tesoro
con diletto l'affanno disacerba.   8

"Nessun mi tocchi," al bel collo d'intorno
scritto avea di diamanti et di topazi.
"Libera farmi al mio Cesare parve."   11

Et era 'l sol già vòlto al mezzo giorno,
gli occhi miei stanchi di mirar, non sazi,
quand' io caddi ne l'acqua et ella sparve.   14

191

Sì come eterna vita è veder Dio
né più si brama né brama più lice,
così me, Donna, il voi veder felice
fa in questo breve et fraile viver mio.   4

Né voi stessa com' or bella vid' io
giamai, se vero al cor l'occhio ridice,
dolce del mio penser ora beatrice
che vince ogni alta speme, ogni desio!   8

Et se non fusse il suo fuggir sì ratto,
più non demanderei; ché s' alcun vive
sol d'odore et tal fama fede acquista,   11

alcun d'acqua o di foco, e 'l gusto e 'l tatto
acquetan cose d'ogni dolzor prive,
i' perché non de la vostra alma vista?   14

192

Let us stay, Love, to see our glory, things high and wonderful beyond Nature. Look well how much sweetness rains down on her, see this light that shows Heaven on earth!

See how much skill has gilded and impearled and incarnadined that noble body never seen elsewhere, which sweetly moves feet and eyes through the shady cloister of these lovely hills!

The young green grass and the flowers of a thousand colors scattered under that ancient black oak beg that her lovely foot touch or press them;

and the sky takes fire with shining sparks all around and visibly rejoices to be made clear by eyes so lovely.

193

I nourish my mind with a food so noble that I do not envy Jove his ambrosia and nectar; for when I merely gaze, oblivion rains into my heart of all other sweetness, and I drink Lethe to the bottom.

When I hear things said and write them down in my heart, so that I will always find them to sigh about, rapt by Love's hand I know not where, from one countenance I drink in a double sweetness;

for that voice, pleasing even in Heaven, utters words so gracious and dear, that he could not conceive it who has not heard it.

Then all together in less than a span appears all that Art, Wit, and Nature and Heaven can do in this life.

192

Stiamo, Amor, a veder la gloria nostra,
cose sopra Natura altere et nove.
Vedi ben quanta in lei dolcezza piove,
vedi lume che 'l Cielo in terra mostra;   4

vedi quant'arte dora e 'mperla e 'nostra
l'abito eletto et mai non visto altrove,
che dolcemente i piedi et gli occhi move
per questa di bei colli ombrosa chiostra!   8

L'erbetta verde e i fior di color mille
sparsi sotto quell'elce antiqua et negra
pregan pur che 'l bel pe' li prema o tocchi,   11

e 'l ciel di vaghe et lucide faville
s'accende intorno e 'n vista si rallegra
d'esser fatto seren da sì belli occhi.   14

193

Pasco la mente d'un sì nobil cibo
ch' ambrosia et nettar non invidio a Giove,
ché sol mirando, oblio ne l'alma piove
d'ogni altro dolce, et Lete al fondo bibo.   4

Talor ch' odo dir cose e 'n cor describo
per che da sospirar sempre ritrove,
ratto per man d'Amor (né so ben dove)
doppia dolcezza in un volto delibo;   8

ché quella voce infin al ciel gradita
suona in parole sì leggiadre et care
che pensar nol poria chi non l'à udita.   11

Allor inseme in men d'un palmo appare
visibilmente quanto in questa vita
Arte, Ingegno, et Natura e 'l Ciel po fare.   14

194

The gentle breeze that makes the hills clear again, awakening the flowers through this shady wood, I recognize by its soft breath on whose account I must rise in labor and in fame.

To find again a place where my weary heart can lean, I flee from my sweet native Tuscan air; to lighten my turbid dark thought I seek my sun and hope to see it today;

in whom I find such and so many sweetnesses that Love forcibly leads me back to her; then he dazzles me so that my fleeing is slow.

To escape, I would need wings, not armor; but the heavens give me death in this light, for when I am afar I am tormented, and when I am close by I burn.

---

   breeze: the Italian, *L'aura,* is a pun on Laura's name. Petrarch makes this pun frequently.   hills: the region around Avignon.

195

From day to day my face and hair are changing, but not for that do I give up the sweetly baited hook or unhand the green enlimed branches of the tree that regards neither sun nor frost.

The sea will be without water and the sky without stars when I no longer fear and desire her lovely shadow and no longer hate and love the deep wound of love that I hide so ill.

I do not hope ever to have rest from my labors, until I am disboned and dismuscled and disfleshed or my enemy feels pity for me.

Every impossible thing will happen before another than she or Death heals the wound that Love made in my heart with her lovely eyes.

---

   the tree that regards . . . nor frost: the evergreen laurel.   enemy: Laura.

194

L'aura gentil che rasserena i poggi,
destando i fior per questo ombroso bosco,
al soave suo spirto riconosco
per cui conven che 'n pena e 'n fama poggi.   4

Per ritrovar ove 'l cor lasso appoggi,
fuggo dal mi' natio dolce aere tosco;
per far lume al penser torbido et fosco
cerco 'l mio sole et spero vederlo oggi;   8

nel qual provo dolcezze tante et tali
ch' Amor per forza a lui mi riconduce,
poi sì m'abbaglia che 'l fuggir m'è tardo.   11

I' chiedrei a scampar non arme, anzi ali,
ma perir mi dà 'l ciel per questa luce,
ché da lunge mi struggo et da presso ardo.   14

195

Di dì in dì vo cangiando il viso e 'l pelo,
né però smorso i dolci inescati ami
né sbranco i verdi et invescati rami
de l'arbor che né sol cura né gelo.   4

Senz' acqua il mare et senza stelle il cielo
fia innanzi ch' io non sempre tema et brami
la sua bell'ombra, et ch' i' non odi' et ami
l'alta piaga amorosa che mal celo.   8

Non spero del mio affanno aver mai posa
infin ch' i' mi disosso et snervo et spolpo,
o la nemica mia pietà n'avesse.   11

Esser po in prima ogni impossibil cosa
ch' altri che Morte od ella sani 'l colpo
ch' Amor co' suoi belli occhi al cor m'impresse.   14

196

The calm breeze that comes murmuring through the green leaves to strike my brow makes me remember when Love gave me the first deep sweet wounds

and makes me see the lovely face that she hides from me, which jealousy or anger keeps hidden from me; and her golden locks now twisted with pearls and gems, then loosened and more blond than polished gold,

which she let loose so sweetly and gathered again with such a charming manner that as I think back on it my mind still trembles.

Time wound them afterward into tighter knots and bound my heart with so strong a cord that only Death will be able to untie it.

197

The heavenly breeze that breathes in that green laurel, where Love smote Apollo in the side and on my neck placed a sweet yoke so that I restore my liberty only late,

has the power over me that Medusa had over the old Moorish giant, when she turned him to flint; nor can I shake loose that lovely knot by which the sun is surpassed, not to say amber or gold:

I mean the blond locks and the curling snare that so softly bind tight my soul, which I arm with humility and nothing else.

Her very shadow turns my heart to ice and tinges my face with white fear, but her eyes have the power to turn it to marble.

---

gold: the Italian, *l'auro*, is a pun on *lauro* (laurel).

196

L'aura serena che fra verdi fronde
mormorando a ferir nel volto viemme
fammi risovenir quand' Amor diemme
le prime piaghe sì dolci profonde,   4

e 'l bel viso veder ch' altri m'asconde,
che sdegno o gelosia celato tiemme,
et le chiome, or avolte in perle e 'n gemme,
allora sciolte et sovra or terso bionde,   8

le quali ella spargea sì dolcemente
et raccogliea con sì leggiadri modi
che ripensando ancor trema la mente.   11

Torsele il tempo poi in più saldi nodi
et strinse 'l cor d'un laccio sì possente
che Morte sola fia ch' indi lo snodi.   14

197

L'aura celeste che 'n quel verde lauro
spira ov' Amor ferì nel fianco Apollo
et a me pose un dolce giogo al collo,
tal che mia libertà tardi restauro,   4

po quello in me che nel gran vecchio mauro
Medusa quando in selce transformollo;
né posso dal bel nodo omai dar crollo
là 've il sol perde, non pur l'ambra o l'auro,   8

dico le chiome bionde e 'l crespo laccio
che sì soavemente lega et stringe
l'alma, che d'umiltate et non d'altro armo.   11

L'ombra sua sola fa 'l mio cor un ghiaccio
et di bianca paura il viso tinge,
ma gli occhi ànno vertù di farne un marmo.   14

198

The soft breeze spreads and waves in the sun the gold that Love spins and weaves with his own hands; there with her lovely eyes and with those very locks he binds my weary heart and winnows my light spirits.

I have no marrow in my bones or blood in my tissue that I do not feel trembling if I even approach where she is, who often weighs and balances in a frail scale my death and life together,

when I see those lights burn from which I take fire and those knots shine which have bound me, now on the right shoulder, now on the left.

I cannot tell it, for I cannot comprehend it, my intellect is overcome by two such lights and oppressed and wearied by so much sweetness!

knots: Laura's braids.

199

O beautiful hand that grasps my heart and encloses in a little space all my life, hand where Nature and Heaven have put all their art and all their care to do themselves honor,

neat soft fingers, the color of five oriental pearls, and only bitter and cruel to wound me: to make me rich, Love now opportunely consents that you be naked.

White, light, and dear glove, that covered clear ivory and fresh roses: who ever saw in the world such sweet spoils?

Would I had again as much of that lovely veil! Oh the inconstancy of human life! Even this is a theft, and one is coming who will deprive me of it.

198

L'aura soave al sole spiega et vibra
l'auro ch' Amor di sua man fila et tesse;
là da' belli occhi et de le chiome stesse
lega 'l cor lasso e i lievi spirti cribra.   4

Non ò medolla in osso o sangue in fibra
ch' i' non senta tremar pur ch' i' m'apresse
dove è chi morte et vita inseme, spesse
volte, in frale bilancia appende et libra,   8

vedendo ardere i lumi ond' io m'accendo,
et folgorare i nodi ond' io son preso
or su l'omero destro et or sul manco.   11

I' nol posso ridir, ché nol comprendo,
da ta' due luci è l'intelletto offeso
et di tanta dolcezza oppresso et stanco.   14

199

O bella man che mi destringi 'l core
e 'n poco spazio la mia vita chiudi,
man ov' ogni arte et tutti loro studi
poser Natura e 'l Ciel per farsi onore,   4

di cinque perle oriental colore,
et sol ne le mie piaghe acerbi et crudi,
diti schietti soavi: a tempo ignudi
consente or voi per arricchirme Amore.   8

Candido leggiadretto et caro guanto
che copria netto avorio et fresche rose:
chi vide al mondo mai sì dolci spoglie?

Così avess' io del bel velo altrettanto!
O inconstanzia de l'umane cose,
pur questo è furto, et vien chi me ne spoglie.   14

200

Not only that one naked hand, which clothes itself again to my heavy sorrow, but the other, and those two arms, are alert and swift to press my timid, humble heart.

Love stretches a thousand snares, and none in vain, among those beautiful new virtuous forms that so adorn her high heavenly vesture that no human style or wit can add to it:

her clear eyes and starry brows, her lovely angelic mouth, full of pearls and roses and sweet words

that make one tremble with wonder, and her forehead, and her hair, which when seen at noon in summer vanquish the sun.

201

My luck and Love had so blessed me with a lovely golden, silken embroidery, that I had almost reached the high point of my happiness thinking to myself: "Who has worn this!"

Nor does that day, which made me rich and poor at the same time, ever come to mind without my being moved with anger and sorrow, full of shame and amorous scorn

that I did not hold my noble spoils more tightly when it was needful, and was not more constant against the force of a mere angel,

or, fleeing, did not add wings to my feet and take vengeance at least on that hand which draws from my eyes so many tears.

---

embroidery: the glove referred to in poem 199.

200

Non pur quell'una bella ignuda mano
che con grave mio danno si riveste,
ma l'altra et le duo braccia accorte et preste
son a stringere il cor timido et piano.   4

Lacci Amor mille, et nesun tende invano
fra quelle vaghe nove forme oneste
ch' adornan sì l'alto abito celeste
ch' agiunger nol po stil né 'ngegno umano: 8

li occhi sereni et le stellanti ciglia,
la bella bocca angelica di perle
piena et di rose, et di dolci parole   11

che fanno altrui tremar di meraviglia,
et la fronte, et le chiome ch' a vederle
di state a mezzo dì vincono il sole.   14

201

Mia ventura et Amor m'avean sì adorno
d'un bello aurato et serico trapunto,
ch' al sommo del mio ben quasi era aggiunto
pensando meco: "A chi fu quest' intorno!"   4

Né mi riede a la mente mai quel giorno
che mi fe' ricco et povero in un punto
ch' i' non sia d'ira et di dolor compunto,
pien di vergogna et d'amoroso scorno   8

che la mia nobil preda non più stretta
tenni al bisogno et non fui più costante
contra lo sforzo sol d'un'angioletta,   11

o, fuggendo, ale non giunsi a le piante
per far almen di quella man vendetta
che de li occhi mi trae lagrime tante.   14

202

From beautiful, clear, shining, living ice comes the flame that kindles and melts me, and it so dries and drains my veins and heart that invisibly I perish.

Death, his arm already raised to strike, as the angry heavens thunder or as a lion roars, goes pursuing my life which flees from him; and I, full of fear, tremble and am silent.

Pity mixed with Love could still, to save me, interpose itself, a double column, between my weary soul and the mortal blow;

but I do not believe it will, nor do I see it on the face of that sweet enemy and lady of mine; for that I do not blame her, but my fortune.

203

Alas, I burn and I am not believed; rather all believe me except for her, who is above all others and whom alone I wish to believe me; she does not seem to believe it, but still she sees it.

Infinite beauty and little faith, do you not see my heart in my eyes? If it were not for my star, I should surely find mercy at the very fountain of pity.

This ardor of mine, which matters so little to you, and your praises in my well-known rhymes, could perhaps yet inflame thousands;

for in my thought I see, O my sweet fire, a tongue cold in death and two lovely eyes closed, which after us will remain full of embers.

202

D'un bel chiaro polito et vivo ghiaccio
move la fiamma che m'incende et strugge,
et sì le vene e 'l cor m'asciuga et sugge
che 'nvisibilemente i' mi disfaccio.   4

Morte, già per ferire alzato 'l braccio,
come irato ciel tona o leon rugge
va perseguendo mia vita che fugge,
et io pien di paura tremo et taccio.   8

Ben poria ancor pietà con amor mista
per sostegno di me, doppia colonna,
porsi fra l'alma stanca e 'l mortal colpo;   11

ma io nol credo, né 'l conosco in vista
di quella dolce mia nemica et donna;
né di ciò lei ma mia ventura incolpo.   14

203

Lasso, ch' i' ardo et altri non mel crede,
sì crede ogni uom se non sola colei
ch' è sovr' ogni altra et ch' i' sola vorrei:
ella non par che 'l creda, et sì sel vede.   4

Infinita bellezza et poca fede:
non vedete voi 'l cor nelli occhi mei?
Se non fusse mia stella, i' pur devrei
al fonte di pietà trovar mercede.   8

Quest' arder mio di che vi cal sì poco
e i vostri onori in mie rime diffusi
ne porian infiammar fors' ancor mille,   11

ch' i' veggio nel penser, dolce mio foco,
fredda una lingua et duo belli occhi chiusi
rimaner dopo noi pien di faville.   14

204

Soul, who see so many different things, and hear and read and speak and write and think, my wandering eyes, and you among the other senses who guide to my heart her high holy words:

for how much would you ever wish to have come either later or earlier to the road that we follow so ill, if you were not to find there those lovely bright lights or the prints of her beautiful feet?

Now with so clear a light and such signs, we must not lose our way in that brief journey which can make us worthy of an eternal dwelling;

push on toward Heaven, O my tired heart, through the clouds of her sweet disdain following her virtuous steps and divine light.

205

Sweet angers, sweet disdains and sweet returns to peace, sweet harm, sweet suffering and sweet weight of it, sweet speech and sweetly understood, now a soothing breeze, now full of sweet flame!

Soul, do not complain, but be patient and still, and temper the sweet bitterness that has harmed us with the sweet honor that you have in loving her to whom I said: "You alone please me."

Perhaps once someone will say, sighing, colored with sweet envy: "This man endured much in his time for a most noble love."

Another: "O Fortune the enemy of my eyes! Why did I not see her? Why did she not come later or else I earlier?"

204

Anima che diverse cose tante
vedi, odi et leggi, et parli et scrivi et pensi:
occhi miei vaghi, et tu fra li altri sensi
che scorgi al cor l'alte parole sante: 4

per quanto non vorreste o poscia od ante
esser giunti al camin che sì mal tiensi,
per non trovarvi i duo bei lumi accensi
né l'orme impresse de l'amate piante? 8

Or con sì chiara luce et con tai segni
errar non dèsi in quel breve viaggio
che ne po far d'eterno albergo degni; 11

sforzati al cielo, o mio stanco coraggio,
per la nebbia entro de' suoi dolci sdegni
seguendo i passi onesti e 'l divo raggio. 14

205

Dolci ire, dolci sdegni et dolci paci,
dolce mal, dolce affanno et dolce peso,
dolce parlare et dolcemente inteso,
or di dolce òra, or pien di dolci faci! 4

Alma, non ti lagnar ma soffra et taci,
et tempra il dolce amaro che n'à offeso
col dolce onor che d'amar quella ài preso
a cui io dissi: "Tu sola mi piaci." 8

Forse ancor fia chi sospirando dica,
tinto di dolce invidia: "Assai sostenne
per bellissimo amor quest' al suo tempo." 11

Altri: "O Fortuna agli occhi miei nemica!
perché non la vid' io? perché non venne
ella più tardi, o ver io più per tempo?" 14

206

If I ever said it, let her hate me by whose love I live, without which I would die; if I said it, let my days be few and miserable, and my soul the minion of some low power; if I said it, let every star be armed against me and at my side be fear and jealousy and my enemy more cruel toward me always and more beautiful!

If I said it, let Love use all his golden arrows on me and the leaden ones on her; if I said it, let Heaven and earth, men and gods be against me, and she ever more pitiless; if I said it, let her who with her blind torch sends me straight to death still stay as she is wont and let her never show herself kinder or more merciful to me either in act or speech!

If I ever said it, let me find this short and harsh road full of what I least desire; if I said it, let the fierce ardor that makes me go astray grow equally with the fierce ice in her; if I said it, let my eyes never see the sun clear nor his sister, nor lady nor damsel, but only a terrible whirlwind such as Pharaoh saw when he pursued the Jews!

If I said it, let pity be dead for me and courtesy, with as many sighs as I ever breathed; if I said it, let her speech become harsh, which was so gentle the day when I gave myself up as vanquished; if I said it, let me be hateful to her whom I would be willing, alone, closed in a dark cell from the day when I left the breast until my soul is uprooted from me, to adore—and perhaps I would do it!

Like poem 29, a tour de force of Provençal stanza construction (the stanzas rhyme in pairs), intentionally obscure.

golden arrows . . . leaden ones: in Ovid's account of Apollo and Daphne, Cupid's golden arrows instill love, his leaden ones aversion. See note to poem 5. her blind torch: his hidden yearning for her.   his sister: the moon. Pharaoh . . . Jews: when the Red Sea closed over Pharaoh's army (Exodus 14:23–28); the whirlwind was suggested by Exodus 15:10.

206

S' i' 'l dissi mai, ch' i' vegna in odio a quella
del cui amor vivo et senza 'l qual morrei;
s' i' 'l dissi, che' miei dì sian pochi et rei
et di vil signoria l'anima ancella;
s' i' 'l dissi, contra me s'arme ogni stella,
et dal mio lato sia
paura et gelosia,
et la nemica mia
più feroce ver me sempre et più bella!   9

S' i' 'l dissi, Amor l'aurate sue quadrella
spenda in me tutte, et l'impiombate in lei;
s' i' 'l dissi, cielo et terra, uomini et Dei
mi sian contrari, et essa ogni or più fella;
s' i' 'l dissi, chi con sua cieca facella
dritto a morte m'invia
pur come suol si stia,
né mai più dolce o pia
ver me si mostri in atto od in favella!   18

S' i' 'l dissi mai, di quel ch' i' men vorrei
piena trovi quest'aspra et breve via;
s' i' 'l dissi, il fero ardor che mi desvia
cresca in me quanto il fier ghiaccio in costei;
s' i' 'l dissi, unqua non veggian li occhi mei
sol chiaro o sua sorella,
né donna né donzella,
ma terribil procella
qual Faraone in perseguir li Ebrei!   27

S' i' 'l dissi, coi sospir quant' io mai fei
sia pietà per me morta et cortesia;
s' i' 'l dissi, il dir s'innaspri che s'udia
sì dolce allor che vinto mi rendei;
s' i' 'l dissi, io spiaccia a quella ch' i' torrei
sol chiuso in fosca cella,
dal dì che la mamella
lasciai fin che si svella
da me l'alma, adorar—forse e 'l farei!   36

But if I did not say it, may she who in my young age opened my heart to hope still steer this weary little bark of mine with the tiller of her native mercifulness; nor let her change but be still as she was wont when I could do no more (when I lost myself, nor should I lose more): he does ill who so soon forgets such faithfulness.

I never said it, nor could I say it for gold or for cities or for castles; let the truth conquer, therefore, and remain in the saddle, and let falsehood fall vanquished to earth! Love, you know all that is in me: if she inquires about us, tell her what you must about me; I would say that he who has to languish is three or four or six times more blessed if he dies first.

For Rachel I have served and not for Leah, nor could I live with another; and I would endure, if Heaven called us, going off with her on the chariot of Elijah.

Rachel . . . Leah: Jacob served Laban for seven years in order to marry his daughter Rachel; on the wedding night Laban substituted Rachel's older sister Leah, and Jacob agreed to serve another seven years for Rachel (Genesis 29:13–30). Petrarch's line presumably explains the occasion of the poem: he has been accused of saying that Laura is a screen for his love of another woman.
Elijah: the prophet, who was carried off to Heaven in a fiery chariot (2 Kings 2:11).

Ma s' io nol dissi, chi sì dolce apria
meo cor a speme ne l'età novella
regg' ancor questa stanca navicella
col governo di sua pietà natia;
né diventi altra, ma pur qual solia
quando più non potei
(che me stesso perdei
né più perder devrei):
mal fa chi tanta fé sì tosto oblia.   45

I' nol dissi giamai, né dir poria
per oro o per cittadi o per castella;
vinca 'l ver dunque e si rimanga in sella,
e vinta a terra caggia la bugia!
Tu sai in me il tutto, Amor: s' ella ne spia
dinne quel che dir dei;
i' beato direi
tre volte e quattro e sei
chi devendo languir si morì pria.   54

Per Rachel ò servito e non per Lia,
né con altra saprei
viver; e sosterrei,
quando 'l ciel ne rappella,
girmen con ella in sul carro de Elia.   59

207

I believed that by now I could live as I have lived these past years, without new studies and without new stratagems; now that from my lady I do not obtain the usual help, you see, Love, where you have led me in teaching me such an art.

I do not know whether to be incensed that at my age you make me become a thief of her lovely light, without which I would be living in so much suffering. Would I had learned in my first years the style that I must now take on, for in youthful failings there is less shame.

Her gentle eyes, from which I am wont to take life, were of their high, divine beauty so generous to me at the beginning that I lived like a man who is helped, not by his own wealth, but by hidden aid from outside; and I harmed neither them nor others.

Now, although it pains me, I become annoying and importunate; for a wretch who is starving sometimes commits actions which, in a better state, he would have blamed in someone else. If envy has closed to me the hand of pity, let my amorous hunger and my powerlessness excuse me.

For I have sought more than a thousand ways to find out if any mortal thing could keep me alive one day without them. My soul, since it finds rest nowhere else, still runs to those angelic sparks, and I, who am of wax, return to the fire;

and I consider where what I desire is least guarded, and as a bird on the branch is soonest taken where he is least afraid, so from her lovely face I steal now one, now another glance, and by them I am both nourished and set on fire.

207

Ben mi credea passar mio tempo omai
come passato avea quest'anni a dietro,
senz' altro studio et senza novi ingegni;
or poi che da Madonna i' non impetro
l'usata aita, a che condutto m'ài
tu 'l vedi, Amor, che tal arte m'insegni.   6
   Non so s' i' me ne sdegni,
che 'n questa età mi fai divenir ladro
del bel lume leggiadro
senza 'l qual non vivrei in tanti affanni.
Così avess' io i primi anni
preso lo stil ch' or prender mi bisogna,
che 'n giovenil fallir è men vergogna.   13

   Li occhi soavi ond' io soglio aver vita
de le divine lor alte bellezze
furmi in sul cominciar tanto cortesi,
che 'n guisa d'uom cui non proprie ricchezze
ma celato di for soccorso aita
vissimi, che né lor né altri offesi.   19
   Or, ben ch' a me ne pesi,
divento ingiurioso et importuno;
ché 'l poverel digiuno
ven ad atto talor che 'n miglior stato
avria in altrui biasmato.
Se le man di pietà invidia m'à chiuse,
fame amorosa e 'l non poter mi scuse.   26

   Ch' i' ò cercate già vie più di mille
per provar senza lor se mortal cosa
mi potesse tener in vita un giorno.
L'anima, poi ch' altrove non à posa,
corre pur a l'angeliche faville,
et io che son di cera al foco torno;   32
   et pongo mente intorno
ove si fa men guardia a quel ch' i' bramo,
et come augel in ramo
ove men teme, ivi più tosto è colto,
così dal suo bel volto
l'involo or uno et or un altro sguardo,
et di ciò insieme mi nutrico et ardo.   39

I feed on my death and live in flames: strange food and a wondrous salamander! But it is no miracle, it is willed by such a one. I lay in his sorrowing flock like a happy lamb for a time; now at the end Love and Fortune treat me as they do the rest:

thus spring has roses and violets, winter has snow and ice. Therefore if I seek here and there some nourishment for my short life, if she wishes to call it theft, so rich a lady ought to allow someone to live on what is hers if she does not miss it.

Who does not know on what I live and have always lived since the day when first I saw those lovely eyes that made me change my life and my ways? Who can know all the complexions of men, though he search through the earth and sea on all shores? Behold, one man lives by odors there along the great river,

I here with fire and light soothe my frail and starving spirits. Love (I wish to tell you), it does not befit a lord to be so stingy. You have your arrows and bow; let me die at your hand, not from this yearning: a good death honors one's whole life.

A hidden flame is hottest, and if it grows it can no longer be hidden in any way. Love, I know, I feel it at your hands. You saw it well when I so silently burned; now my own cries pain me, now I go a nuisance to near and far.

O world, O vain thoughts! O my strong destiny, where do you carry me? Oh from how lovely a light was that tenacious hope born in my heart, with which she binds and oppresses it, she who with your power leads me to death! The fault is yours, mine the loss and the suffering.

---

salamander: said to inhabit fire.   one man lives . . . river: a race said by Pliny to live beside the Ganges.

Di mia morte mi pasco et vivo in fiamme,
stranio cibo et mirabil salamandra!
ma miracol non è, da tal si vole.
Felice agnello a la penosa mandra
mi giacqui un tempo; or a l'estremo famme
et Fortuna et Amor pur come sòle: 45
    così rose et viole
à primavera, e 'l verno à neve et ghiaccio.
Però s' i' mi procaccio
quinci et quindi alimenti al viver curto,
se vol dir che sia furto,
sì ricca donna deve esser contenta
s' altri vive del suo, ch' ella nol senta.   52

Chi nol sa di ch' io vivo, et vissi sempre
dal dì che 'n prima que' belli occhi vidi
che mi fecer cangiar vita et costume?
Per cercar terra et mar da tutt' i lidi
chi po saver tutte l'umane tempre?
L'un vive, ecco, d'odor là sul gran fiume,   58
    io qui di foco et lume
queto i frali et famelici mei spirti.
Amor (et vo' ben dirti),
disconvensi a signor l'esser sì parco.
Tu ài li strali et l'arco,
fa di tua man, non pur bramand', io mora;
ch' un bel morir tutta la vita onora.   65

Chiusa fiamma è più ardente, et se pur cresce,
in alcun modo più non po celarsi.
Amor, i' 'l so, che 'l provo a le tue mani.
Vedesti ben quando sì tacito arsi,
or de' miei gridi a me medesmo incresce,
che vo noiando et prossimi et lontani.   75
    O mondo, o penser vani!
O mia forte ventura, a che m'adduce?
O di che vaga luce
al cor mi nacque la tenace speme
onde l'annoda et preme
quella che con tua forza al fin mi mena!
La colpa è vostra et mio 'l danno et la pena.   78

Thus from loving well I gain torments, and I ask to be pardoned for another's crime; rather for my own, for I should have turned my eyes away from the excessive light, closed my ears to the siren song; and still I do not repent that my heart is overflowing with sweet poison.

I am waiting for him to loose the last arrow who shot the first: and, if I judge aright, it will be a kind of pity to kill quickly, since he is not disposed to make of me anything but what he usually does; he dies well who escapes from sorrow.

My song, I shall stand firm on the field, for it is dishonor to die fleeing; and I reproach myself for all my laments, so sweet are my fate, my weeping, my sighs, and my death! Servant of Love who read these lines, there is no good in the world that is equal to my ills.

Così di ben amar porto tormento,
et del peccato altrui cheggio perdono—
anzi del mio, che devea torcer li occhi
dal troppo lume, et di sirene al suono
chiuder li orecchi, et ancor non men pento
che di dolce veleno il cor trabocchi.   84
Aspett' io pur che scocchi
l'ultimo colpo chi mi diede 'l primo;
et fia, s' i' dritto estimo,
un modo di pietate occider tosto,
non essendo ei disposto
a far altro di me che quel che soglia:
ché ben muor chi morendo esce di doglia.   91

Canzon mia, fermo in campo
starò, ch' elli è disnor morir fuggendo;
et me stesso reprendo
di tai lamenti, sì dolce è mia sorte,
pianto, sospiri et morte.
Servo d'Amor che queste rime leggi:
ben non à 'l mondo che 'l mio mal pareggi.   98

208

Swift river, from your Alpine spring gnawing a way for yourself
(whence you take your name), who night and day come desirous
down with me to where Love leads me and only Nature leads
you:

go on before; neither weariness nor sleep reins in your course;
and, before you give the sea his due, look closely where the grass
is greener and the air more clear.

There is that living, sweet sun of ours, who adorns and
beflowers your left bank; perhaps (oh what do I hope for!) my
slowness pains her.

Kiss her foot or her lovely white hand; tell her (let your kiss be
heard as words): "The spirit is ready, but the flesh is weary."

Addressed to the river Rhone.
gnawing . . . name: the Italian is a pun on *rodendo* (gnawing) and *Rodano*
(Rhone).   your left bank: Avignon is on the eastern bank of the
Rhone.   "The spirit is ready . . .": an allusion to Matthew 26:41, "Spiritus
quidem promptus est, caro autem infirma" (The spirit is ready, but the flesh is
weak).

209

The sweet hills where I left myself, when I departed from the
place I can never depart from, are before me as I go, and still
behind me is that sweet burden Love has entrusted to me.

Within myself I am often amazed at myself, for I still go and yet
have not moved from the sweet yoke that I have shaken off in
vain many times, but the farther I go from it the closer I come.

As a hart struck by an arrow, with the poisoned steel within its
side, flees and feels more pain the faster it runs,

so I, with that arrow in my left side which destroys me and at the
same time delights me, am tormented by sorrow and weary
myself with fleeing.

---

sweet hills: those of Vaucluse.   arrow in my left side: see note to poem 29.

208

Rapido fiume, che d'alpestra vena
rodendo intorno (onde 'l tuo nome prendi)
notte et dì meco disioso scendi
ov' Amor me, te sol Natura mena: 4

vattene innanzi, il tuo corso non frena
né stanchezza né sonno; et pria che rendi
suo dritto al mar, fiso u' si mostri attendi
l'erba più verde et l'aria più serena.   8

Ivi è quel nostro vivo et dolce sole
ch' adorna e 'nfiora la tua riva manca;
forse (o che spero!) el mio tardar le dole.   11

Basciale 'l piede o la man bella et bianca;
dille (e 'l basciar sie 'n vece di parole):
"Lo spirto è pronto, ma la carne è stanca."   14

209

I dolci colli ov' io lasciai me stesso,
partendo onde partir giamai non posso,
mi vanno innanzi, et emmi ogni or a dosso
quel caro peso ch' Amor m'à commesso.   4

Meco di me mi meraviglio spesso
ch' i' pur vo sempre, et non son ancor mosso
dal bel giogo più volte indarno scosso,
ma com' più me n'allungo et più m'appresso.   8

Et qual cervo ferito di saetta
col ferro avelenato dentr' al fianco
fugge et più duolsi quanto più s'affretta,   11

tal io, con quello stral dal lato manco
che mi consuma et parte mi diletta,
di duol mi struggo et di fuggir mi stanco.   14

210

Not from the Spanish Ebro to the Indian Hydaspes, not though you seek each slope by the sea, not from the Red shore to the Caspian wave, neither in Heaven nor on earth, is there more than one phoenix.

What crow on the right or raven on the left may sing my fate? or what weird Sister enspool it? for I alone find pity deaf as an asp, wretch, where I hope to be happy!

For I do not wish to speak of her; whoever sees her, she fills all his heart with sweetness and love: so much she has with her, and so much she offers to others!

And to make the sweetness that I feel bitter and cruel, either she pretends or she does not care or she does not see how these temples are blossoming white before their time.

Ebro: see note to poem 148.   Hydaspes: a tributary of the Indus. crow on the right or raven on the left: according to Cicero, favorable omens; Petrarch expects only unfavorable omens.   what weird Sister enspool it: the three Fates spin, wind on a spool, and cut the thread of a person's life; in other words, Petrarch expects to die soon.

211

Desire spurs me, Love guides and escorts me, Pleasure draws me, Habit carries me away; Hope entices and encourages me and reaches out his right hand to my weary heart,

and my wretched heart grasps it and does not see how blind and treacherous this guide of ours is; the senses govern and reason is dead; and one yearning desire is born after another.

Virtue, honor, beauty, gentle bearing, sweet words brought us to the lovely branches, that my heart may be sweetly enlimed.

One thousand three hundred twenty-seven, exactly at the first hour of the sixth day of April, I entered the labyrinth, nor do I see where I may get out of it.

See note to poem 3.

210

Non da l'ispano Ibero a l'indo Idaspe
ricercando del mar ogni pendice,
né dal lito vermiglio a l'onde caspe,
né 'n ciel né 'n terra è più d'una fenice.   4

Qual destro corvo o qual manca cornice
canti 'l mio fato, o qual Parca l'innaspe?
ché sol trovo pietà sorda com' aspe,
misero, onde sperava esser felice.   8

Ch' i' non vo' dir di lei, ma chi la scorge,
tutto 'l cor di dolcezza et d'amor gl'empie,
tanto n'à seco et tant' altrui ne porge.   11

Et per far mie dolcezze amare et empie,
o s'infinge o non cura o non s'accorge
del fiorir queste inanzi tempo tempie.   14

211

Voglia mi sprona, Amor mi guida et scorge,
Piacer mi tira, Usanza mi trasporta;
Speranza mi lusinga et riconforta
et la man destra al cor già stanco porge,   4

e 'l misero la prende et non s'accorge
di nostra cieca et disleale scorta;
regnano i sensi et la ragion è morta;
de l'un vago desio l'altro risorge.   8

Vertute, onor, bellezza, atto gentile,
dolci parole ai be' rami n'àn giunto
ove soavemente il cor s'invesca.   11

Mille trecento ventisette, a punto
su l'ora prima, il dì sesto d'aprile,
nel laberinto intrai, né veggio ond' esca.   14

212

Blessed in sleep and satisfied to languish, to embrace shadows, and to pursue the summer breeze, I swim through a sea that has no floor or shore, I plow the waves and found my house on sand and write on the wind;

and I gaze yearning at the sun so that he has already put out with his brightness my power of sight; and I pursue a wandering, fleeing doe with a lame, sick, slow ox.

Blind and weary to everything except my harm, which I trembling seek day and night, I call only Love and my Lady and Death;

thus for twenty years—heavy, long labor—I have gained only tears and sighs and sorrow: under such a star I took the bait and the hook!

213

Graces that generous Heaven allots to few, virtues rare beyond the custom of men, beneath blond hair the wisdom of gray age, and in a humble lady high divine beauty,

singular, strange charm and singing that is felt in the soul, a heavenly walk and a lovely ardent spirit that breaks all that is hard and makes every height bow down,

and those lovely eyes that turn hearts to stone, powerful enough to brighten the abyss and night and to take souls from their bodies and give them to others,

with speech full of sweet high insights, and sighs sweetly broken—by these magicians was I transformed.

212

Beato in sogno et di languir contento,
d'abbracciar l'ombre et seguir l'aura estiva,
nuoto per mar che non à fondo o riva;
solco onde, e 'n rena fondo, et scrivo in vento;   4

e 'l sol vagheggio si ch' elli à già spento
col suo splendor la mia vertù visiva;
et una cerva errante et fugitiva
caccio con un bue zoppo e 'nfermo et lento.   8

Cieco et stanco ad ogni altro ch' al mio danno,
il qual dì et notte palpitando cerco,
sol Amor et Madonna et Morte chiamo.   11

Così venti anni, grave et lungo affanno,
pur lagrime et sospiri et dolor merco:
in tale stella presi l'esca et l'amo!   14

213

Grazie ch' a pochi il Ciel largo destina,
rara vertù non già d'umana gente,
sotto biondi capei canuta mente
e 'n umil donna alta beltà divina,   4

leggiadria singulare et pellegrina
e 'l cantar che ne l'anima si sente,
l'andar celeste e 'l vago spirto ardente
ch' ogni dur rompe et ogni altezza inchina,   8

et que' belli occhi che i cor fanno smalti,
possenti a rischiarar abisso et notti
et torre l'alme a' corpi et darle altrui,   11

col dir pien d'intelletti dolci et alti,
coi sospiri soavemente rotti:
da questi magi transformato fui.   14

214

Three days before, a soul had been created in a place
where it might put its care in things high and new
and despise what the many prize.
She, still uncertain of her fated course,
alone, thoughtful, young, and free,
in springtime entered a lovely wood.

A tender flower had been born in that wood
the day before, with its root in a place
that could not be approached by a soul still free;
for there were snares there of form so new
and such pleasure hastened one's course
that to lose liberty was there a prize.

Dear, sweet, high, laborious prize,
which quickly turned me to the green wood,
accustomed to making us stray in the midst of our course!
And I have later sought through the world from place to place
if verses or precious stones or juice of strange herbs
could one day make my mind free.

But now, alas, I see that my flesh shall be free
from that knot for which it is most greatly prized,
before medicines old or new
can heal the wounds I received in that wood
thick with thorns; on account of them it is my lot
to come out lame, and I entered with so swift a course!

Full of snares and thorns is the course
that I must complete, where a light, free
foot would be in need, one whole in every place.
But you, Lord, who have all pity's praise,
reach me your right hand in this wood:
let your sun vanquish this my strange shadow.

Three days before: the soul had been born into a body fit for high enterprise
and had completed the first three of the six ages of man—infancy, childhood,
adolescence (traditionally said to end at twenty-one), maturity, growing old, old
age.   flower: no doubt a rose, referring to Laura.   knot: the one joining
the body to the soul.   lame: because wounded in the left foot; see note to
poem 88.   my wandering consort: my erring soul, the bride of the body.

214

Anzi tre dì creata era alma in parte
da por sua cura in cose altere et nove
et dispregiar di quel ch' a' molti è 'n pregio;
quest' ancor dubbia del fatal suo corso,
sola pensando pargoletta et sciolta,
intrò di primavera in un bel bosco.   6

Era un tenero fior nato in quel bosco
il giorno avanti, et la radice in parte
ch' appressar nol poteva anima sciolta;
ché v'eran di lacciuo' forme sì nove,
et tal piacer precipitava al corso,
che perder libertate ivi era in pregio.   12

Caro, dolce, alto et faticoso pregio
che ratto mi volgesti al verde bosco,
usato di sviarne a mezzo 'l corso!
Et ò cerco poi 'l mondo a parte a parte
se versi o petre o suco d'erbe nove
mi rendesser un dì la mente sciolta.   18

Ma, lasso, or veggio che la carne sciolta
fia di quel nodo ond' è 'l suo maggior pregio
prima che medicine antiche o nove
saldin le piaghe ch' i' presi in quel bosco
folto di spine, ond' i' ò ben tal parte
che zoppo n'esco, e 'ntravi a sì gran corso!   24

Pien di lacci et di stecchi un duro corso
aggio a fornire, ove leggera et sciolta
pianta avrebbe uopo et sana d'ogni parte.
Ma tu, Signor, ch' ài di pietate il pregio,
porgimi la man destra in questo bosco,
vinca 'l tuo sol le mie tenebre nove.   30

Guard my state from those new beauties
which, breaking off my life's course,
have made me a dweller in the shady wood:
Make again, if it can be, unbound and free
my wandering consort; and let yours be the praise
if I find her again with You in a better place.

Now behold in part my strange doubts:
if any worth is alive in me or all run out,
if my soul is free or captive in the wood.

if I find her again with You: if my resurrected flesh is reunited with my soul and saved at the Last Judgment.   captive in the wood: see note on "amorous wood," poem 22.

215

In noble blood a humble and quiet life, with a high intellect a pure heart, the fruit of age in the flower of youth, and with thoughtful aspect a happy soul,

have all been gathered together in this lady by her planet— rather by the King of the stars—and the true honor, the deserved praises, and the great worth that would weary any divine poet.

Love has joined himself with chastity in her, with natural beauty gracious habit, and gestures that speak in silence,

and I know not what in her eyes, which in an instant can make bright the night, darken the day, embitter honey, and sweeten wormwood.

Guarda 'l mio stato a le vaghezze nove
che 'nterrompendo di mia vita il corso
m'àn fatto abitador d'ombroso bosco;
rendimi, s' esser po, libera et sciolta
l'errante mia consorte, et fia tuo 'l pregio
s' ancor teco la trovo in miglior parte.   36

Or ecco in parte le question mie nove:
s' alcun pregio in me vive o 'n tutto è corso,
o l'alma sciolta o ritenuta al bosco.   39

215

In nobil sangue vita umile et queta,
et in alto intelletto un puro core,
frutto senile in sul giovenil fiore,
e 'n aspetto pensoso anima lieta   4

raccolto à 'n questa donna il suo pianeta—
anzi 'l Re de le stelle— e 'l vero onore,
le degne lode e 'l gran pregio e 'l valore
ch' è da stancar ogni divin poeta.   8

Amor s'è in lei con onestate aggiunto,
con beltà naturale, abito adorno
et un atto che parla con silenzio,   11

et non so che nelli occhi che 'n un punto
po far chiara la notte, oscuro il giorno,
e 'l mel amaro, et addolcir l'assenzio.   14

216

All day I weep; and then at night, when miserable mortals take rest, I find that I am in tears and that my pains are doubled; thus I spend my time weeping.

With sad moisture I am consuming my eyes and with sorrow my heart; and I am the most wretched of animals, so that the arrows of Love keep me ever banished from peace.

Alas! for from one sun to the next, and from one night to the next, I have already run through most of this death which is called life!

I grieve more for the fault of another than for my ills; for living pity and the help I have relied on see me burn in the fire and do not aid me.

217

Once I wished to make myself heard with so just a lament and in such fervent rhymes that I would make a fire of pity felt in the hard heart that is frozen in midsummer,

and, with the wind of my hot words, break the cruel cloud that cools and veils it, or else make her hateful to others, who hides her lovely eyes with which she melts me.

Now I no longer seek hatred for her nor pity for myself, since I do not wish the former and the latter is beyond me; such was my star and such my cruel fate!

But I sing her divine beauty, that when I have departed from this flesh the world may know that my death is sweet.

216

Tutto 'l dì piango; et poi la notte, quando
prendon riposo i miseri mortali,
trovomi in pianto et raddopiarsi i mali;
così spendo 'l mio tempo lagrimando.   4

In tristo umor vo li occhi consumando
e 'l cor in doglia; et son fra li animali
l'ultimo, sì che li amorosi strali
mi tengon ad ogni or di pace in bando.   8

Lasso, che pur da l'un a l'altro sole
et da l'una ombra a l'altra ò già 'l più corso
di questa morte che si chiama vita!   11

Più l'altrui fallo che 'l mi' mal mi dole,
ché pietà viva e 'l mio fido soccorso
vedem' arder nel foco et non m'aita.   14

217

Già desiai con sì giusta querela
e 'n sì fervide rime farmi udire
ch' un foco di pietà fessi sentire
al duro cor ch' a mezza state gela,   4

et l'empia nube che 'l rafredda et vela
rompesse a l'aura del mi' ardente dire,
o fessi quell'altrui in odio venire
che' belli (onde mi strugge) occhi mi cela.   8

Or non odio per lei, per me pietate
cerco; ché quel non vo', questo non posso,
tal fu mia stella et tal mia cruda sorte.   11

Ma canto la divina sua beltate
che quand' i' sia di questa carne scosso
sappia 'l mondo che dolce è la mia morte.   14

218

However many graceful, lovely ladies she finds herself with, she who has no equal in the world, with her lovely face she makes of the others what the day makes of the lesser stars.

Love seems to speak at my ear, saying: "As long as she is seen on earth, life will be good; afterward we shall see it darkened, see virtues die and my realm with them.

"As if Nature were to take away the sun and the moon from the heavens, the winds from the air, from the earth grass and leaves, from man intellect and words,

"from the sea the fish and the waves: so dark and darker will things be and deserted, if Death closes and hides her eyes."

219

The new singing and the weeping of the birds at daybreak make the valleys echo, and the murmuring of the liquid crystals down in shining, fresh and rapid streams.

She whose face is snow, whose hair is gold, in whose love was never any deceit or failing, awakens me with the sound of her amorous dance, combing the white fleece of her aged husband.

Thus I awake to salute the dawn and the sun which is with her, and even more that other sun by which I was dazzled in my first years and am still.

I have seen them some days rise together, and in an instant, in a moment, seen him make the stars, her make him disappear.

---

new singing: the birds have begun to sing again in the spring.   She whose face is snow: Aurora, goddess of the dawn, wife of ancient Tithonus.

218

Tra quantunque leggiadre donne et belle
giunga costei ch' al mondo non à pare,
col suo bel viso suol dell'altre fare
quel che fa 'l dì de le minori stelle.   4

Amor par ch' a l'orecchie mi favelle,
dicendo: "Quanto questa in terra appare
fia 'l viver bello; et poi 'l vedrem turbare,
perir vertuti e 'l mio regno con elle.   8

"Come Natura al ciel la luna e 'l sole,
a l'aere i venti, a la terra erbe et fronde,
a l'uomo et l'intelletto et le parole,   11

"et al mar ritollesse i pesci et l'onde:
tanto et più fien le cose oscure et sole
se Morte li occhi suoi chiude et asconde."   14

219

Il cantar novo e 'l pianger delli augelli
in sul dì fanno retentir le valli,
e 'l mormorar de' liquidi cristalli
giù per lucidi freschi rivi et snelli.   4

Quella ch' à neve il volto, oro i capelli,
nel cui amor non fur mai inganni né falli,
destami al suon delli amorosi balli,
pettinando al suo vecchio i bianchi velli.   8

Così mi sveglio a salutar l'aurora
e 'l sol ch' è seco, et più l'altro ond' io fui
ne' primi anni abagliato et son ancora.   11

I' gli ò veduti alcun giorno ambedui
levarsi inseme, e 'n un punto e 'n un'ora
quel far le stelle et questo sparir lui.   14

220

Where and from what mine did Love take the gold to make two blond tresses? From what bush did he pluck the rose and in what meadow the fresh and tender frost, to give them pulse and breath?

Where the pearls with which he breaks and reins in sweet words, chaste and strange? Where the beauties, so many and so divine, of that forehead brighter than the heavens?

From what angels and from what sphere did he send that heavenly singing which so melts me that by now little remains to melt?

From what sun was born the high kindly light of those lovely eyes from which I receive war and peace, that burn my heart in ice and fire?

221

What destiny of mine, what compulsion, or what deception brings me unarmed back to the field where I am always conquered? and if I escape from it, I shall marvel; if I die, the loss is mine.

Not loss at all, but gain: so sweet in my heart are the sparks and the bright lightning that dazzle and torment it, and in which I take fire and am already burning for the twentieth year.

I hear the messengers of Death when I see her lovely eyes appear and lighten from afar; then, if it happens that drawing near she turns them toward me,

Love with so much sweetness both wounds me and anoints my wound that I cannot recapture it in thought, let alone tell it: for neither my wit nor my tongue can equal the truth.

---

the twentieth year: the poem thus dates itself 1347. See note to poem 266.

220

Onde tolse Amor l'oro et di qual vena
per far due treccie bionde? e 'n quali spine
colse le rose, e 'n qual piaggia le brine
tenere e fresche, et die' lor polso et lena?   4

onde le perle in ch' ei frange et affrena
dolci parole oneste et pellegrine?
onde tante bellezze et sì divine
di quella fronte più che 'l ciel serena?   8

Da quali angeli mosse et di qual spera
quel celeste cantar che mi disface
sì che n'avanza omai da disfar poco?   11

Di qual sol nacque l'alma luce altera
di que' belli occhi ond' io ò guerra et pace,
che mi cuocono il cor in ghiaccio e 'n foco?   14

221

Qual mio destin, qual forza o qual inganno
mi riconduce disarmato al campo,
là 've sempre son vinto? et s' io ne scampo,
meraviglia n'avrò; s' i' moro, il danno.   4

Danno non già, ma pro, sì dolci stanno
nel mio cor le faville e 'l chiaro lampo
che l'abbaglia et lo strugge e 'n ch' io m'avampo,
et son già ardendo nel vigesimo anno.   8

Sento i messi di Morte ove apparire
veggio i belli occhi e folgorar da lunge;
poi s' aven ch' appressando a me li gire,   11

Amor con tal dolcezza m'unge et punge
ch' i' nol so ripensar, non che ridire,
ché né 'ngegno né lingua al vero agiunge.   14

222

"Happy and yet sad, in company and yet alone, Ladies who go talking by the way, where is my life, my death? Why is she not with you as she is wont to be?"

"We are happy in thinking of that sun; we are sad because we lack her company, which envious jealousy takes from us, grieving at another's good as if at its own harm."

"Who can put a rein on lovers or give them laws?" "No one can do so to the soul; to the body, anger and rigor can. This is now proved in her, at other times in us;

"but often the heart can be read from the brow, thus we saw her high beauty darkened and her eyes all bedewed with tears."

223

When the sun bathes in the sea his gilded chariot and darkens our air and my mind, with the heavens and with the stars and with the moon I begin an anguished, bitter night;

then, alas, to one who does not listen I tell all my troubles one by one, and I quarrel with the world and with my blind fortune, with Love, with my lady, and with myself.

Sleep is banished and there is no rest, but sighs and laments till dawn, and tears that the soul sends forth to the eyes.

Then the dawn comes and lights up the dark air, but not me; the sun that burns and delights my heart, only that one can sweeten my suffering.

222

"Liete et pensose, accompagnate et sole,
Donne che ragionando ite per via:
ove è la vita, ove la morte mia?
perché non è con voi com' ella sòle?"　　　　　4

"Liete siam per memoria di quel sole,
dogliose per sua dolce compagnia
la qual ne toglie invidia et gelosia
che d'altrui ben quasi suo mal si dole."　　　　8

"Chi pon freno a li amanti o dà lor legge?"
"Nessun a l'alma; al corpo, ira et asprezza;
questo or in lei, talor si prova in noi.　　　　11

"Ma spesso ne la fronte il cor si legge,
sì vedemmo oscurar l'alta bellezza
et tutti rugiadosi li occhi suoi."　　　　　14

223

Quando 'l sol bagna in mar l'aurato carro
et l'aere nostro et la mia mente imbruna,
col cielo et co le stelle et co la luna
un'angosciosa et dura notte innarro:　　　　4

poi, lasso, a tal che non m'ascolta narro
tutte le mie fatiche ad una ad una,
et col mondo et con mia cieca fortuna,
con Amor, con Madonna et meco garro.　　　　8

Il sonno è 'n bando et del riposo è nulla,
ma sospiri et lamenti infin a l'alba
e lagrime che l'alma a li occhi invia.　　　　11

Vien poi l'aurora et l'aura fosca inalba,
me no; ma 'l sol che 'l cor m'arde et trastulla,
quel po solo adolcir la doglia mia.　　　　14

224

If faithfulness in love, an unfeigning heart, a sweet yearning, a courteous desire—if chaste desires kindled in a noble fire, a long wandering in a blind labyrinth—

if to have all my thoughts written on my brow, or barely understood in broken words, or cut off by fear or shame—if a pallor like the violet's, tinted with love—

if to love another more than oneself—if to be always sighing and weeping, feeding on sorrow and anger and trouble—

if to burn from afar and freeze close by—if these are the causes that I untune myself with love, yours will be the blame, Lady, mine the loss.

225

Twelve ladies virtuously languid—rather twelve stars—and in the midst a sun I saw, gay and alone in a little bark such that I know not if its like ever plowed the waves;

I do not believe its like carried Jason to the fleece with which everyone wishes to be dressed today, nor the shepherd on whose account Troy still grieves, of which two so much noise is made in the world.

Then I saw them in a triumphal chariot, and my Laurel with her holy, retiring manner sitting to the side and sweetly singing:

not human things or a mortal vision. Happy Automedon, happy Tiphys, who steered such charming folk!

Jason: Jason sailed with other heroes in the *Argo*—the first ship—to Colchis, on the eastern shore of the Black Sea, to capture the Golden Fleece.   shepherd: Paris. He was a shepherd on Mount Ida when he judged the beauty of Venus, Minerva, and Juno, giving Venus the prize in exchange for the love of Helen, whom he carried off in his ship to Troy.   Automedon: Achilles' charioteer.   Tiphys: the helmsman of the *Argo*.

224

S' una fede amorosa, un cor non finto,
un languir dolce, un desiar cortese,
s' oneste voglie in gentil foco accese,
un lungo error in cieco laberinto,   4

se ne la fronte ogni penser depinto,
od in voci interrotte a pena intese
or da paura or da vergogna offese,
s' un pallor di viola et d'amor tinto,   8

s' aver altrui più caro che se stesso,
se sospirare et lagrimar mai sempre
pascendosi di duol d'ira et d'affanno,   11

s' arder da lunge et agghiacciar da presso,
son le cagion ch' amando i' mi distempre:
vostro, Donna, 'l peccato et mio fia 'l danno.   14

225

Dodici donne onestamente lasse,
anzi dodici stelle, e 'n mezzo un sole
vidi in una barchetta allegre et sole
qual non so s' altra mai onde solcasse;   4

simil non credo che Jasòn portasse
al vello onde oggi ogni uom vestir si vole,
né 'l pastor di ch' ancor Troia si dole,
de' qua' duo tal romor al mondo fasse.   8

Poi le vidi in un carro triunfale,
Laurea mia con suoi santi atti schifi
sedersi in parte et cantar dolcemente: 11

non cose umane o vision mortale.
Felice Autumedòn, felice Tifi
che conduceste sì leggiadra gente!   14

226

No sparrow was ever so alone on any roof as I am, nor any beast in any wood, for I do not see her lovely face, and I know no other sun, nor do these eyes have any other object.

To weep always is my highest delight, laughing is pain, food is gall and poison, night is labor, and a clear sky is dark to me, and my bed is a harsh battlefield.

Sleep is truly, as they say, akin to death, and relieves the heart of the sweet care that keeps it in life.

Sole in the world, rich, happy country, green flowering banks, shady meadows: you possess and I yearn for my treasure.

No sparrow . . . so alone: an allusion to Psalm 102:7 (Vulgate 101:8), "Vigilavi, et factus sum sicut passer solitarius in tecto" (I have watched, and have become as a sparrow alone on the housetop).   happy country: the region around Vaucluse, near the Sorgue.

227

Breezes that surround those curling blond locks and move in them and are moved by them softly, and scatter that sweet gold and then gather it again and recurl it in lovely knots:

you are in those eyes whence the wasps of love so sting me that even from here I feel it and weep and staggering seek my treasure, like an animal that shies and stumbles;

for now I seem to find her and now I become aware that I am far from her, now I am consoled, now dejected, now I see what I wish, now what is true.

Happy air, stay with that sweet living ray. And you, running, clear stream, why can I not exchange paths with you?

---

stream: presumably the Sorgue; apparently Petrarch is in Vaucluse, Laura in Avignon.

226

Passer mai solitario in alcun tetto
non fu quant' io, né fera in alcun bosco,
ch' i' non veggio 'l bel viso et non conosco
altro sol, né quest'occhi ànn' altro obietto.   4

Lagrimar sempre è 'l mio sommo diletto,
il rider doglia, il cibo assenzio et tosco,
la notte affanno e 'l ciel seren m'è fosco,
et duro campo di battaglia il letto.   8

Il sonno è veramente, qual uom dice,
parente de la morte e 'l cor sottragge
a quel dolce penser che 'n vita il tene.   11

Solo al mondo paese almo felice,
verdi rive fiorite, ombrose piagge:
voi possedete et io piango il mio bene.   14

227

Aura che quelle chiome bionde et crespe
cercondi et movi et se' mossa da loro
soavemente, et spargi quel dolce oro
et poi 'l raccogli e 'n bei nodi il rincrespe: 4

tu stai nelli occhi ond' amorose vespe
mi pungon sì che 'n fin qua il sento et ploro,
et vacillando cerco il mio tesoro
come animal che spesso adombre e 'ncespe;   8

ch' or mel par ritrovar et or m'accorgo
ch' i' ne son lunge, or mi sollievo or caggio,
ch' or quel ch' i' bramo or quel ch' è vero scorgo.   11

Aer felice, col bel vivo raggio
rimanti; et tu, corrente et chiaro gorgo:
ché non poss' io cangiar teco viaggio?   14

228

With his right hand Love opened my left side and planted there in the midst of my heart a laurel so green that it would surpass and weary any emerald.

My pen, a plow, with my laboring sighs, and the raining down from my eyes of a sweet liquid have so beautified it, that its fragrance has reached Heaven, so that I do not know if any leaves have ever equaled it.

Fame, honor, and virtue and charm, chaste beauty in celestial habit, are the roots of the noble plant.

Such do I find it in my breast, wherever I may be, a happy burden, and with chaste prayers I adore it and bow to it as to a holy thing.

229

I sang, now I weep, and I take no less sweetness from weeping than I took from singing, for my senses, still in love with heights, are intent on the cause, not its outward effects.

Thence I bring away equally mildness and harshness, cruel gestures and humble and courteous; nor do any weights weigh me down, nor does any point of disdain shatter my armor.

Let them keep toward me their accustomed style, Love, my lady, the world, and my fortune; I think I shall never be anything but happy.

Whether I live or die or languish, there is no nobler state than mine under the moon, so sweet is the root of the bitter!

228

Amor co la man destra il lato manco
m'aperse, et piantovvi entro in mezzo 'l core
un lauro verde sì che di colore
ogni smeraldo avria ben vinto et stanco.   4

Vomer di penna con sospir del fianco
e 'l piover giù dalli occhi un dolce umore
l'adornar sì ch' al ciel n'andò l'odore,
qual non so già se d'altre frondi unquanco.   8

Fama, onor, et vertute et leggiadria,
casta bellezza in abito celeste
son le radici de la nobil pianta.   11

Tal la mi trovo al petto ove ch' i' sia,
felice incarco! et con preghiere oneste
l'adoro e 'nchino come cosa santa.   14

229

Cantai, or piango; et non men di dolcezza
del pianger prendo che del canto presi,
ch' a la cagion, non a l'effetto intesi
son i miei sensi vaghi pur d'altezza.   4

Indi et mansuetudine et durezza
et atti feri et umili et cortesi
porto egualmente; né me gravan pesi,
né l'arme mie punta di sdegni spezza.   8

Tengan dunque ver me l'usato stile
Amor, Madonna, il mondo et mia fortuna,
ch' i' non penso esser mai se non felice;   11

viva o mora o languisca, un più gentile
stato del mio non è sotto la luna,
sì dolce è del mio amaro la radice.   14

230

I wept, now I sing; for that living sun does not hide from my eyes her heavenly light, in which virtuous Love clearly reveals his sweet power and his holy ways;

thus he is wont to draw from me such a river of tears to shorten the thread of my life, that wings and feathers could not rescue me, let alone bridge or ford or oars or sail.

So deep and from so full a source was my weeping and so distant the shore, that I could hardly reach it even in thought.

Pity sends me not laurel or a palm but the tranquil olive, and clears the weather, and dries my tears, and wishes me still to live.

---

palm: emblem of victory.   olive: emblem of peace.

231

I was living contented with my fate, without tears and without any envy; for if other lovers have more favorable fortune, a thousand of their pleasures are not worth one of my torments.

Now those lovely eyes, for which I shall never repent my sorrows and would not wish them less even by one, are covered by so heavy and dark a cloud that it has almost extinguished the sun of my life.

O Nature, merciful and cruel mother, whence do you have such power and such contrary wills, to make and unmake things so charming?

From one living Fountain all powers are received; but how do You consent, O highest Father, that another despoil us of your dear gift?

---

cloud: sickness.   another: Death.

230

I' piansi, or canto; ché 'l celeste lume
quel vivo sole alli occhi miei non cela,
nel qual onesto Amor chiaro revela
sua dolce forza et suo santo costume;   4

onde e' suol trar di lagrime tal fiume,
per accorciar del mio viver la tela,
che non pur ponte o guado o remi o vela
ma scampar non potienmi ale né piume.   8

Sì profondo era et di sì larga vena
il pianger mio, et sì lunge la riva,
ch' i' v'aggiungeva col penser a pena.   11

Non lauro o palma, ma tranquilla oliva
pietà mi manda, et 'l tempo rasserena,
e 'l pianto asciuga et vuol ancor ch' i' viva.   14

231

I' mi vivea di mia sorte contento
senza lagrime et senza invidia alcuna,
ché s' altro amante à più destra fortuna,
mille piacer non vaglion un tormento.   4

Or quei belli occhi, ond' io mai non mi pento
de le mie pene et men non ne voglio una,
tal nebbia copre sì gravosa et bruna
che 'l sol de la mia vita à quasi spento.   8

O Natura, pietosa et fera madre:
onde tal possa et sì contrarie voglie
di far cose et disfar tanto leggiadre?   11

D'un vivo fonte ogni poder s'accoglie;
ma tu come 'l consenti, o sommo Padre,
che del tuo caro dono altri ne spoglie?   14

232

Anger vanquished the victorious Alexander and made him in part lesser than Philip. What does it help him that only Pyrgoteles and Lysippus engraved and only Apelles painted him?

Anger carried off Tydeus in such a rage that, dying, he gnawed Menalippus. Anger had made Sulla not merely blear-eyed, but entirely blind; in the end it killed him.

Valentinianus knows that anger leads to this punishment; and he knows it who died of it, Ajax, powerful over many and then over himself.

Anger is a brief madness; for one who does not rein it in, it becomes a long madness that often carries its owner to shame and sometimes to death.

---

anger . . . Alexander: a traditional allusion (found in Cicero and Justinus) to the dangers of anger; in a drunken rage Alexander the Great murdered a close friend.   Philip: Philip of Macedon, Alexander's father.   Pyrgoteles . . . Apelles: according to Pliny, Alexander decreed that only Pyrgoteles was to portray him in marble, only Lysippus in bronze, only Apelles in paint.   Tydeus: in Statius' *Thebaid*, one of the seven against Thebes. He killed Menalippus but received his death wound from him; he ordered Menalippus' head brought to him and gnawed on it.   Sulla: Roman patrician leader and dictator, said to have died of anger.   Valentinianus: Roman emperor in the west (A.D. 364–375), supposed to have died of apoplexy in a fit of rage.   Ajax: he went mad with disappointment and killed himself after the Greeks awarded the armor of the dead Achilles to Ulysses.

232

Vincitore Alessandro l'ira vinse
et fe 'l minore in parte che Filippo:
ché li val se Pirgotile et Lisippo
l'intagliar solo et Apelle il depinse?   4

L'ira Tideo a tal rabbia sospinse
che morendo ei si rose Menalippo;
l'ira cieco del tutto, non pur lippo,
fatto avea Silla, a l'ultimo l'estinse.   8

Sa 'l Valentinian ch' a simil pena
ira conduce; et sa 'l quei che ne more,
Ajace, in molti et poi in se stesso forte.   11

Ira è breve furore; et chi nol frena,
è furor lungo che 'l suo possessore
spesso a vergogna et talor mena a morte.   14

233

What good fortune was mine, that from one of the two loveliest eyes that ever were, when I saw them disturbed and darkened by pain, there came a power that made my own sick and dark!

I having returned to relieve the hunger of seeing her whom alone in the world I care for, Heaven and Love were less cruel to me than ever, if I put together all the other graces they have bestowed on me.

For from my lady's right eye—rather her right sun—to my right eye came the illness that delights me and does not pain me;

and, just as if it had intellect and wings, it passed into me like a star flying through the heavens; and Nature and Pity held their course.

233

Qual ventura mi fu quando da l'uno
de' duo i più belli occhi che mai furo,
mirandol di dolor turbato et scuro,
mosse vertù che fe' 'l mio infermo et bruno!   4

Send' io tornato a solver il digiuno
di veder lei che sola al mondo curo,
fummi il ciel et Amor men che mai duro,
se tutte altre mie grazie inseme aduno;   8

ché dal destr' occhio—anzi dal destro sole—
de la mia donna al mio destr' occhio venne
il mal che mi diletta et non mi dole;   11

et pur com' intelletto avesse et penne,
passò quasi una stella che 'n ciel vole;
et Natura et Pietate il corso tenne.   14

234

O little room that used to be a port from my fierce daily storms, now you are a fountain of nocturnal tears, which in the daytime I keep hidden for shame!

O little bed that used to be a rest and comfort among so many labors, with what sorrowful urns does Love bathe you, with those ivory hands cruel only toward me, and so unjustly!

Nor do I flee only my hiding place and my rest, but even more myself and my thoughts that used to raise me in flight as I followed them;

and I seek (whoever thought it?) the mob, inimical and hateful to me, as a refuge: so afraid am I of being alone.

235

Alas, Love carries me off where I do not wish to go, and I see well that we are crossing beyond what is permitted; thus I am much more troublesome than I am wont to her who is enthroned monarch in my heart.

Nor did ever a wise helmsman keep from the rocks a ship laden with precious merchandise, as I always keep my weak bark from the blows of her harsh pride,

but a tearful rain and fierce winds of infinite sighs have driven it, for in my sea now there is horrible night and winter

where it carries annoyance to others and nothing but pain and torment to itself, already vanquished by the waves, bereft of sails and tiller.

234

O cameretta che già fosti un porto
a le gravi tempeste mie diurne:
fonte se' or di lagrime notturne
che 'l dì celate per vergogna porto.   4

O letticciuol che requie eri et conforto
in tanti affanni: di che dogliose urne
ti bagna Amor con quelle mani eburne,
solo ver me crudeli a sì gran torto!   8

Né pur il mio secreto e 'l mio riposo
fuggo, ma più me stesso e 'l mio pensero
che seguendol talor levommi a volo;   11

e 'l vulgo a me nemico et odioso
(chi 'l pensò mai?) per mio refugio chero,
tal paura ò di ritrovarmi solo.   14

235

Lasso, Amor mi trasporta ov' ir non voglio,
et ben m'accorgo che 'l dever si varca;
onde a chi nel mio cor siede monarca
sono importuno assai più ch' i' non soglio.   4

Né mai saggio nocchier guardò da scoglio
nave di merci preziose carca,
quant' io sempre la debile mia barca
da le percosse del suo duro orgoglio,   8

ma lagrimosa pioggia et fieri venti
d'infiniti sospiri or l'ànno spinta,
ch' è nel mio mare orribil notte et verno   11

ov' altrui noie, a sé doglie et tormenti
porta et non altro già, da l'onde vinta,
disarmata di vele et di governo.   14

236

Love, I transgress and I see my transgression, but I act like a man who burns with a fire in his breast; for the pain still grows, and my reason fails and is almost overcome by my sufferings.

I used to rein in my hot desire so as not to darken her clear face; I can no longer do it: you have taken the reins from my hand, and my despairing soul has acquired boldness.

Therefore, if my soul hazards herself beyond her usual style, you are doing it—who so inflame and spur her that she attempts every difficult way toward her salvation—

and even more those heavenly, rare gifts which my lady has. Now at least make her perceive it, and make her pardon herself for my transgressions.

237

The sea has not so many creatures among its waves,
nor up there beyond the circle of the moon
were so many stars ever seen by any night,
nor do so many birds dwell in the woods,
nor did any field ever have so much grass, or any meadow,
as I have cares in my heart every evening.

From day to day I hope now for the last evening,
which will separate in me the living earth from the waves
and let me sleep in some meadow:
for so many troubles no man under the moon
ever suffered as I do, the woods know it
that I go searching through alone day and night.

---

separate . . . from the waves: probably a reference to Augustine's allegorical interpretation of Genesis 1, according to which the separation of the dry land from the sea is taken to mean conversion or the passage to the next life (*Confessions* 13.17–18); here, "the living earth" is Petrarch's soul, "the waves" his flesh, or principle of mutability.

236

Amor, io fallo et veggio il mio fallire,
ma fo sì com' uom ch' arde e 'l foco à 'n seno;
ché 'l duol pur cresce, et la ragion ven meno,
et è già quasi vinta dal martire.   4

Solea frenare il mio caldo desire
per non turbare il bel viso sereno;
non posso più, di man m'ài tolto il freno,
et l'alma desperando à preso ardire.   8

Però s' oltra suo stile ella s' aventa,
tu 'l fai, che sì l'accendi et sì la sproni
ch' ogni aspra via per sua salute tenta;   11

et più 'l fanno i celesti et rari doni
ch' à in sé Madonna; or fa' almen ch' ella il senta
et le mie colpe a se stessa perdoni.   14

237

Non à tanti animali il mar fra l'onde,
né lassù sopra 'l cerchio de la luna
vide mai tante stelle alcuna notte,
né tanti augelli albergan per li boschi,
né tant' erbe ebbe mai campo né piaggia
quant' à 'l mio cor pensier ciascuna sera.   6

Di dì in dì spero omai l'ultima sera
che scevri in me dal vivo terren l'onde
et mi lasci dormire in qualche piaggia;
ché tanti affanni uom mai sotto la luna
non sofferse quant' io, sannolsi i boschi
che sol vo ricercando giorno et notte.   12

I have never had a tranquil night,
but have gone sighing morning and evening
since Love made me a citizen of the woods.
Before I rest, the sea will be without waves,
and the sun will receive his light from the moon,
and the flowers of April will die in every meadow.

I go consuming myself from meadow to meadow
full of cares all day; then I weep at night;
nor have I any steadfastness except as does the moon.
As soon as I see the darkening of evening,
sighs from my breast and from my eyes waves
come forth to wet the grass and blow down the woods.

Cities are hateful to me, friendly the woods
to my cares, which through this high meadow
I go venting with the murmuring of the waves
through the sweet silence of the night:
so that all day I await the evening,
for the sun to depart and make way for the moon.

Ah, would that with the lover of the moon
I had fallen asleep in some green wood,
and that she who before vespers gives me evening
with the moon and with Love to that shore
might come alone to stay there one night,
and that the day might stay, and the sun, forever under the
    waves!

Beside harsh waves in the light of the moon,
O song born at night amid the woods:
you shall see a rich shore tomorrow evening.

---

lover of the moon: Endymion, whom Diana fell in love with; she visited him
nightly as he slept on Mount Latmos.

I' non ebbi giamai tranquilla notte,
ma sospirando andai matino et sera,
poi ch' Amor femmi un cittadin de' boschi;
ben fia, prima ch' i' posi, il mar senz' onde,
et la sua luce avrà 'l sol da la luna,
e i fior d'april morranno in ogni piaggia,   18

Consumendo mi vo di piaggia in piaggia
el dì pensoso, poi piango la notte;
né stato ò mai se non quanto la luna.
Ratto come imbrunir veggio la sera
sospir del petto et de li occhi escono onde
da bagnar l'erbe et da crollare i boschi.   24

Le città son nemiche, amici i boschi
a' miei pensier che per quest'alta piaggia
sfogando vo col mormorar de l'onde
per lo dolce silenzio de la notte,
tal ch' io aspetto tutto 'l dì la sera
che 'l sol si parta et dia luogo a la luna.   30

Deh, or foss' io col vago de la luna
adormentato in qua' che verdi boschi,
et questa ch' anzi vespro a me fa sera
con essa et con Amor in quella piaggia
sola venisse a starsi ivi una notte,
e 'l dì si stesse e 'l sol sempre ne l'onde!   36

Sovra dure onde al lume de la luna,
canzon nata di notte in mezzo i boschi,
ricca piaggia vedrai deman da sera.   39

238

A regal nature, an angelic intellect, a bright soul, ready sight, lynxlike eye, swift foresight, a thought high and truly worthy of that breast!

A goodly number of ladies having been chosen to adorn the high festive day, his sound discernment quickly saw among so many lovely faces the most perfect.

With his hand he commanded the others, greater in age or fortune, to remove to one side, and graciously he received her to himself.

With kindly expression he kissed her eyes and brow, so that each lady was made glad; me his sweet strange act filled with envy.

On the occasion of the visit to Avignon of a prominent ruler, perhaps Charles of Luxemburg (later the emperor Charles IV, with whom Petrarch corresponded), who visited the papal court in 1346.

239

At the time near dawn when so sweetly the breeze
in the springtime is wont to move the flowers
and the little birds begin their verses,
so sweetly I feel my thoughts within my soul
stirred by him who has them all in his power,
that I must return to my notes.

Could I but tune in such sweet notes
my sighs that they would sweeten the breeze,
bringing her to account who overpowers me!
But winter will be the season of flowers
before love flowers in that noble soul
that never cared for rhymes or verses.

238

Real natura, angelico intelletto,
chiara alma, pronta vista, occhio cerviero,
providenzia veloce, alto pensero
et veramente degno di quel petto!   4

Sendo di donne un bel numero eletto
per adornar il dì festo et altero,
subito scorse il buon giudicio intero
fra tanti et sì bei volti il più perfetto.   8

L'altre, maggior di tempo o di fortuna,
trarsi in disparte comandò con mano
et caramente accolse a sé quell'una;   11

li occhi et la fronte con sembiante umano
basciolle sì che rallegrò ciascuna;
me empiè d'invidia l'atto dolce et strano.   14

239

Là ver l'aurora, che sì dolce l'aura
al tempo novo suol movere i fiori
et li augelletti incominciar lor versi,
sì dolcemente i pensier dentro a l'alma
mover mi sento a chi li à tutti in forza
che ritornar convenmi a le mie note.   6

Temprar potess' io in sì soavi note
i miei sospiri ch' addolcissen Laura,
facendo a lei ragion ch' a me fa forza!
Ma pria fia 'l verno la stagion de' fiori
ch' amor fiorisca in quella nobil alma
che non curò giamai rime né versi.   12

How many tears, alas, and how many verses
have I already scattered in my time! And in how many notes
have I attempted to humble that soul!
She stands there, a harsh mountain to the sweet breeze
that can move the leaves and flowers
but can do nothing if opposed by a greater power.

Love is wont to vanquish men and gods with his power,
as one reads in prose and in verses,
and I experienced it at the first budding of the flowers;
now not my lord nor his notes
nor my weeping nor my prayers can cause Laura
to free either from life or from torment this soul.

For the last need, O wretched soul,
mobilize all your wit, all your power,
while we still have the breath of life.
There is nothing in the world that cannot be done by verses;
they know how to enchant asps with their notes,
not to speak of adorning the frost with new flowers.

Now the meadows are laughing with new grass and flowers:
it cannot be that her angelic soul
will be deaf to the sound of the amorous notes;
if our cruel fortune has greater power,
weeping and singing our verses
we shall go with a lame ox hunting the breeze.

In a net I catch the breeze and on ice flowers,
and in verses I woo a deaf and rigid soul
who esteems neither the power of Love nor his notes.

Quante lagrime, lasso, et quanti versi
ò già sparti al mio tempo, e 'n quante note
ò riprovato umiliar quell'alma!
Ella si sta pur com' aspr' alpe a l'aura
dolce, la qual ben move frondi et fiori
ma nulla po se 'ncontr' a maggior forza.   18

Omini et dei solea vincer per forza
Amor, come si legge in prose e 'n versi,
et io 'l provai in sul primo aprir de' fiori;
ora né 'l mio signor, né le sue note,
né 'l pianger mio, né i preghi pon far Laura
trarre o di vita o di martir quest'alma.   28

A l'ultimo bisogno, o misera alma,
accampa ogni tuo ingegno, ogni tua forza,
mentre fra noi di vita alberga l'aura.
Nulla al mondo è che non possano i versi:
et li aspidi incantar sanno in lor note,
non che 'l gelo adornar di novi fiori.   30

Ridon or per le piagge erbette et fiori:
esser non po che quella angelica alma
non senta il suon de l'amorose note;
se nostra ria fortuna è di più forza,
lagrimando et cantando i nostri versi
et col bue zoppo andrem cacciando l'aura.   36

In rete accolgo l'aura e 'n ghiaccio i fiori,
e 'n versi tento sorda et rigida alma
che né forza d'Amor prezza né note.   39

240

I have begged Love, and I beg him again, to persuade you to pardon me—O my sweet suffering, my bitter delight—if with complete faithfulness I bend aside from my straight path.

I cannot deny, Lady, nor do I deny, that Reason, who reins in every good soul, in me is overcome by Desire, who leads sometimes in a direction where I am forced to follow him.

You, with that heart that the heavens make bright with so clear an intellect, with such high virtue—as much as ever rained down from a benign star—

ought to say, mercifully and without scorn: "What else can this man do? my face consumes him. Why is he so desirous, and why am I so beautiful?"

241

That high lord before whom one cannot hide or flee or make any defense had kindled my mind to sweet pleasure with a burning arrow of love;

and, although the first blow was bitter and mortal in itself, to advance his undertaking he took a dart of pity; and from both sides he pierces and assails my heart.

One wound burns and pours forth smoke and flame; the other, tears, which sorrow distills through my eyes on account of your suffering state.

Nor in spite of those two fountains does any spark decrease of the fire that inflames me; rather my pity increases my desire.

240

I' ò pregato Amor, e 'l ne riprego,
che mi scusi appo voi, dolce mia pena,
amaro mio diletto, se con piena
fede dal dritto mio sentier mi piego.   4

I' nol posso negar, Donna, et nol nego,
che la ragion ch' ogni bona alma affrena
non sia dal voler vinta, ond' ei mi mena
talor in parte ov' io per forza il sego.   8

Voi con quel cor che di sì chiaro ingegno,
di sì alta vertute il cielo alluma
quanto mai piovve da benigna stella,   11

devete dir pietosa et senza sdegno:
"Che po questi altro? il mio volto il consuma.
Ei perché ingordo, et io perché sì bella?"   14

241

L'alto signor dinanzi a cui non vale
nasconder né fuggir né difesa,
di bel piacer m'avea la mente accesa
con un ardente et amoroso strale;   4

et, ben che 'l primo colpo aspro et mortale
fossi da sé, per avanzar sua impresa
una saetta di pietate à presa
et quinci et quindi il cor punge et assale.   8

L'una piaga arde et versa foco et fiamma,
lagrime l'altra, che 'l dolor distilla
per li occhi mei del vostro stato rio;   11

né, per duo fonti, sol una favilla
rallenta de l'incendio che m'infiamma,
anzi per la pietà cresce 'l desio.   14

242

"Gaze on that hill, O my tired, yearning heart: there yesterday
we left her who for a while cared somewhat for us, and was
sorry for us, and now wishes to draw forth from our eyes a lake.

"Go you back there, to the only place where I am glad to be; try
if perhaps it is not time to lessen our grief, which until now
has been growing, O sharer and foreteller of my suffering."

Now you have forgotten yourself and talk to your heart as if he
were still with you, wretch full of vain and foolish thoughts!

For when you went away, parting from your high desire, your
heart stayed with her and hid within her lovely eyes.

---

hill: see note to poem 4.

243

Fresh, shady, flowering green hill, where, sometimes thoughtful,
sometimes singing, she sits and gives testimony here of the
spirits in Heaven, she who dims the fame of all the world:

my heart, who wished to leave me for her—and he acted most
wisely, and even more so if he never comes back—now goes
counting where the grass is signed by that lovely foot and is wet
from these eyes.

He draws close to her, and at every step he says: "Ah, would
that wretch were here even for a little, for he is already tired of
weeping and of living."

She smiles at that, and the portions are not equal: I am a stone
without my heart, but you are a paradise, O holy, lucky, sweet
place!

242

"Mira quel colle, o stanco mio cor vago:
ivi lasciammo ier lei ch' alcun tempo ebbe
qualche cura di noi et le n'encrebbe,
or vorria trar de li occhi nostri un lago.   4

"Torna tu in là, ch' io d'esser sol m'appago;
tenta se forse ancor tempo sarebbe
da scemar nostro duol che 'nfin qui crebbe,
o del mio mal participe et presago."   8

Or tu ch' ài posto te stesso in oblio
et parli al cor pur come e' fusse or teco,
miser et pien di pensier vani et sciocchi!   11

ch' al dipartir dal tuo sommo desio
tu te n'andasti, e' si rimase seco
et si nascose dentro a' suoi belli occhi.   14

243

Fresco ombroso fiorito et verde colle
ov' or pensando et or cantando siede,
et fa qui de' celesti spiriti fede
quella ch' a tutto 'l mondo fama tolle: 4

il mio cor che per lei lasciar mi volle—
et fe' gran senno, et più se mai non riede—
va or contando ove da quel bel piede
segnata è l'erba et da quest'occhi è molle.   8

Seco si stringe et dice a ciascun passo:
"Deh, fusse or qui quel miser pur un poco,
ch' è già di pianger et di viver lasso!"   11

Ella sel ride, et non è pari il gioco:
tu paradiso, i' senza cor un sasso,
o sacro, aventuroso et dolce loco!   14

244

My ills oppress me, and I am terrified by the worst, toward which I see so broad and smooth a way that I have entered this madness and with hard cares rave to you;

I do not know whether to ask God for war or peace, for the loss is heavy and the shame is cruel. But why languish any longer? It will be with us as is already ordained at the highest throne.

Although I am not worthy of that great honor which you do me, for Love deceives you, who oft makes a healthy eye see crooked,

still my counsel is to lift your soul to that heavenly kingdom and to spur your heart, for the road is long and the time is short.

A reply, using the same rhymes, to a sonnet by Giovanni Dondi dell'Orologio (Appendix One, p. 605).

245

Two roses, fresh and gathered in paradise the other day, when the first day of May was born, a lovely gift, equally divided by a lover old and wise between two younger ones,

with words and a smile sweet enough to teach a wild man love, made a sparkling, amorous ray change the faces of both.

"The sun does not see an equal pair of lovers," he said, smiling and sighing together; and, embracing both, he looked around.

Thus he divided the roses and his words; and my weary heart still is glad and fearful. Oh happy eloquence! Oh glad day!

244

Il mal mi preme et mi spaventa il peggio,
al qual veggio sì larga et piana via
ch' i' son intrato in simil frenesia,
et con duro penser teco vaneggio;   4

né so se guerra o pace a Dio mi cheggio,
ché 'l danno è grave et la vergogna è ria.
Ma perché più languir? di noi pur fia
quel ch' ordinato è già nel sommo seggio.   8

Ben ch' i' non sia di quel grand' onor degno
che tu mi fai, ché te n'inganna Amore
che spesso occhio ben san fa veder torto,   11

pur d'alzar l'alma a quel celeste regno
è il mio consiglio et di spronare il core,
perché 'l camin è lungo e 'l tempo è corto.   14

245

Due rose fresche et colte in paradiso
l'altr'ier, nascendo il dì primo di maggio,
bel dono et d'un amante antiquo et saggio
tra duo minori egualmente diviso,   4

con sì dolce parlar et con un riso
da far innamorare un uom selvaggio,
di sfavillante et amoroso raggio
et l'un' et l'altro fe' cangiare il viso.   8

"Non vede un simil par d'amanti il sole,"
dicea ridendo et sospirando insieme,
et stringendo ambedue volgeasi a torno.   11

Così partia le rose et le parole,
onde 'l cor lasso ancor s'allegra et teme:
o felice eloquenzia! o lieto giorno!   14

246

The breeze that softly sighing moves the green laurel and her golden hair, with sights new and charming makes souls wander from their bodies.

White rose born among hard thorns, when will anyone find her like on earth? Glory of our age! O living Jove, send, I pray, my end before hers!

so that I may not see that great public loss, and the world left without its sun, nor my own eyes, which have no other light;

nor my soul, which does not wish to think of anything else, nor my ears, which cannot hear anything else, left without her chaste sweet words.

---

golden: with a pun both on *lauro* (laurel) and *l'aura* (breeze).

247

It will perhaps seem to someone that, in my praise of her whom I adore on earth, my style errs in making her noble beyond all others, holy, wise, charming, chaste, and beautiful.

I believe the opposite, and I am afraid that she is offended by my too humble words, since she is worthy of much higher and finer ones: and who does not believe me, let him come to see her.

Then he will say: "What this man aspires to would exhaust Athens, Arpinum, Mantua, and Smyrna, and the one and the other lyre.

"Mortal tongue cannot reach her divine state; Love drives and draws his tongue, not by choice but by destiny."

Athens, Arpinum, Mantua: birthplaces of Demosthenes, Cicero, and Virgil, respectively.   Smyrna: one of the cities claiming to be the birthplace of Homer.   the one and the other lyre: Greek and Latin lyric poetry.

246

L'aura che 'l verde lauro et l'aureo crine
soavemente sospirando move
fa con sue viste leggiadrette et nove
l'anime da' lor corpi pellegrine.   4

Candida rosa nata in dure spine,
quando fia chi sua pari al mondo trove?
Gloria di nostra etate! O vivo Giove,
manda, prego, il mio in prima che 'l suo fine!   8

sì ch' io non veggia il gran publico danno
e 'l mondo remaner senza 'l suo sole
né li occhi miei, che luce altra non ànno;   11

né l'alma, che pensar d'altro non vole,
né l'orecchie, ch' udir altro non sanno,
senza l'oneste sue dolci parole.   14

247

Parrà forse ad alcun che 'n lodar quella
ch' i' adoro in terra, errante sia 'l mio stile
faccendo lei sovr' ogni altra gentile,
santa, saggia, leggiadra, onesta et bella.   4

A me par il contrario, et temo ch' ella
non abbia a schifo il mio dir troppo umile,
degna d'assai più alto et più sottile;
et chi nol crede venga egli a vedella,   8

sì dirà ben: "Quello ove questi aspira
è cosa da stancare Atene, Arpino,
Mantova et Smirna, et l'una et l'altra lira.   11

"Lingua mortale al suo stato divino
giunger non pote; Amor la spinge et tira
non per elezion ma per destino."   14

248

Whoever wishes to see all that Nature and Heaven can do among us, let him come gaze on her, for she alone is a sun, not merely for my eyes, but for the blind world, which does not care for virtue;

and let him come soon, for Death steals first the best and leaves the wicked: awaited in the kingdom of the blessed, this beautiful mortal thing passes and does not endure.

He will see, if he comes in time, every virtue, every beauty, every regal habit, joined together in one body with marvelous tempering;

then he will say that my rhymes are mute, my wit overcome by the excess of light. But if he delays too long he shall have reason to weep forever.

249

What fear is mine when I remember that day when I left my lady sad and thoughtful, and my heart with her! and yet there is nothing I more gladly think of or more often.

I see her again standing humbly among lovely ladies, like a rose among the lesser flowers, neither gay nor sorrowing, like one who is afraid but feels no other ill.

She had put off her usual ornaments, the pearls and garlands and gay clothing, and laughter and song and her sweet kind speech.

Thus I left my life fearing; now sad auguries and dreams and black thoughts assail me, please God they may be false!

248

Chi vuol veder quantunque po Natura
e 'l Ciel tra noi, venga a mirar costei
ch' è sola un sol, non pur a li occhi mei
ma al mondo cieco che vertù non cura;   4

et venga tosto, perché Morte fura
prima i migliori et lascia star i rei:
questa aspettata al regno delli dei
cosa bella mortal passa et non dura.   8

Vedrà, s' arriva a tempo, ogni vertute,
ogni bellezza, ogni real costume
giunti in un corpo con mirabil tempre;   11

allor dirà che mie rime son mute,
l'ingegno offeso dal soverchio lume.
Ma se più tarda, avrà da pianger sempre.   14

249

Qual paura ò quando mi torna a mente
quel giorno ch' i' lasciai grave et pensosa
Madonna e 'l mio cor seco! et non è cosa
che sì volentier pensi et sì sovente.   4

I' la riveggio starsi umilemente
tra belle donne, a guisa d'una rosa
tra minor fior, né lieta né dogliosa,
come chi teme et altro mal non sente.   8

Deposta avea l'usata leggiadria,
le perle et le ghirlande et i panni allegri,
e 'l riso e 'l canto e 'l parlar dolce umano.   11

Così in dubbio lasciai la vita mia;
or tristi auguri, et sogni et penser negri
mi dànno assalto, et piaccia a Dio che 'nvano!   14

250

Though afar, my lady was wont to console me in sleep with the sweet angelic sight of her, but now she terrifies me and makes me sorrowful, nor have I any defense against either sorrow or fear;

for often I seem to see in her face true pity mixed with heavy pain, and to hear things that persuade my heart to disarm itself of joy and hope.

"Do you not remember that last evening," she says, "when, leaving your eyes moist, I departed forced by time?

"I could not nor did I wish to tell you then; now I tell you as something tested and true: do not hope ever to see me on earth."

251

Oh wretched, horrible vision! Is it then true that before her time her kindly light is extinguished, that has made my life contented in both sorrow and good hopes?

But how is it that so great a noise does not sound through other messengers, and that I hear it from herself? Now let God and Nature not permit it, let my sad opinion be false!

I must still hope for the sweet sight of her lovely face, which keeps me alive and gives honor to our world.

If to rise to the eternal mansions she has indeed left her lovely dwelling, I pray that my last day may not be tardy.

250

Solea lontana in sonno consolarme
con quella dolce angelica sua vista
Madonna, or mi spaventa et mi contrista,
né di duol né di tema posso aitarme;   4

ché spesso nel suo volto veder parme
vera pietà con grave dolor mista,
et udir cose onde 'l cor fede acquista
che di gioia et di speme si disarme.   8

"Non ti soven di quella ultima sera,"
dice ella, "ch' i' lasciai li occhi tuoi molli
et sforzata dal tempo me n'andai?   11

"I' non tel potei dir allor, né volli;
or tel dico per cosa esperta et vera:
non sperar di vedermi in terra mai."   14

251

O misera et orribil visione!
E' dunque ver che 'nnanzi tempo spenta
sia l'alma luce che suol far contenta
mia vita in pene et in speranze bone?   4

Ma come è che sì gran romor non sone
per altri messi et per lei stessa il senta?
Or già Dio et Natura nol consenta,
et falsa sia mia trista opinione!   8

A me pur giova di sperare ancora
la dolce vista del bel viso adorno
che me mantene e 'l secol nostro onora.   11

Se per salir a l'eterno soggiorno
uscita è pur del bell'albergo fora,
prego non tardi il mio ultimo giorno.   14

252

Fearing for my state I now weep, now sing, and hope and fear, and in sighs and rhymes vent my burden. Love files away at my afflicted heart with all his might.

Now will it ever be that her lovely holy face will give back to these eyes their first light (alas, I do not know what to think of myself), or will it condemn them to eternal weeping?

Will Heaven, to take what is due it, not care what happens to those on earth, whose sun her eyes are, for they see nothing else?

In such fear and in such perpetual war I live that I am no longer what I was before, like one who on a perilous road is afraid and loses his way.

253

O sweet glances, O eloquent little words, will the day ever come when I shall see you again and hear you? O blond locks with which Love binds my heart and thus captured leads it to death!

O lovely face given to me for my harsh fate, which I always weep for and never enjoy! O close deceptions and loving fraud, to give me a pleasure that only brings me pain!

And if sometimes from those lovely gentle eyes, where my life and my thoughts dwell, there comes to me perhaps some chaste sweetness,

quickly, in order to drive me away and to disperse any good I possess, Fortune, who is always so swift to harm me, makes suddenly appear horses or ships for me to travel on.

252

In dubbio di mio stato, or piango or canto,
et temo et spero, et in sospiri e 'n rime
sfogo il mio incarco. Amor tutte sue lime
usa sopra 'l mio core afflitto tanto.   4

Or fia giamai che quel bel viso santo
renda a quest'occhi le lor luci prime
(lasso, non so che di me stesso estime)
o li condanni a sempiterno pianto,   8

et per prendere il Ciel debito a lui,
non curi che si sia di loro in terra
di ch' egli è 'l sole et non veggiono altrui?   11

In tal paura e 'n sì perpetua guerra
vivo ch' i' non son più quel che già fui,
qual chi per via dubbiosa teme et erra.   14

253

O dolci sguardi, o parolette accorte,
or fia mai il dì ch' i' vi riveggia et oda?
O chiome bionde, di che 'l cor m'annoda
Amor et così preso il mena a morte!   4

O bel viso, a me dato in dura sorte
di ch' io sempre pur pianga et mai non goda!
O chiuso inganno et amorosa froda,
darmi un piacer che sol pena m'apporte!   8

Et se talor da' belli occhi soavi,
ove mia vita e 'l mio pensero alberga,
forse mi ven qualche dolcezza onesta,   11

subito, a ciò ch' ogni mio ben disperga
et m'allontane, or fa cavalli or navi
Fortuna, ch' al mio mal sempre è sì presta.   14

254

I still listen, and I hear no news of my sweet and beloved enemy, nor do I know what to think or say to myself, fear and hope so pierce my heart.

To be so beautiful has harmed some in the past; this one is more beautiful than any other and more chaste: perhaps God wishes to take such a friend of virtue away from earth and make her a star in Heaven,

rather a sun. And if this is so, my life, my short reposes, and my long troubles have come to an end. O harsh parting,

why have you put me so far from my misfortunes? My brief tale is already told and my time filled up in the middle of my years.

255

To wish for evening, to hate the dawn, that is the habit of untroubled happy lovers; for me evening redoubles woes and weeping. Morning for me is a happier hour,

when sometimes in the same moment both suns open as it were two Orients, so similar in beauty and light that the very heavens fall in love with earth,

as they did when the first boughs were green that have their roots in my heart, because of which I must always love another more than myself.

Thus two contrary hours have their will of me, and it is natural that I desire the one that calms me, fear and hate the one that brings me suffering.

254

I' pur ascolto, et non odo novella
de la dolce et amata mia nemica,
né so ch' i' me ne pensi o ch' i' mi dica,
sì 'l cor tema e speranza mi puntella.   4

Nocque ad alcuna già l'esser sì bella,
questa più d'altra è bella et più pudica:
forse vuol Dio tal di vertute amica
torre a la terra e 'n ciel farne una stella,   8

anzi un sole. Et se questo è, la mia vita,
i miei corti riposi e i lunghi affanni
son giunti al fine. O dura dipartita,   11

perché lontan m'ài fatto da' miei danni?
La mia favola breve è già compita,
et fornito il mio tempo a mezzo gli anni.   14

255

La sera desiare, odiar l'aurora
soglion questi tranquilli et lieti amanti;
a me doppia la sera et doglia et pianti.
La mattina è per me più felice ora,   4

ché spesso in un momento apron allora
l'un sole et l'altro, quasi duo levanti
di beltate et di lume sì sembianti
ch' anco il ciel de la terra s'innamora,   8

come già fece allor che' primi rami
verdeggiar che nel cor radice m'ànno,
per cui sempre altrui più che me stesso ami.   11

Così di me due contrarie ore fanno,
et chi m'acqueta è ben ragion ch' i' brami,
et tema et odi' chi m'adduce affanno.   14

256

Could I but take vengeance on her who gazing and speaking destroys me and then, to increase my pain, hides herself and flees, taking from me her eyes so sweet and cruel!

Thus little by little she consumes and saps my afflicted, tired spirits, and like a fierce lion she roars over my heart at night, when I ought to rest.

My soul, which Death drives from its dwelling, leaves me, and loosed from that knot goes off still to her who menaces it.

I marvel if at some time, while my soul speaks to her and weeps and then embraces her, her sleep is not broken, if she is listening.

257

On the lovely face that I sigh and yearn for, my desirous, intense eyes were fixed, when Love—as if to say "What are you thinking?"—held out to me that honored hand which is my second love.

My heart, caught (like a fish on the hook or like a young bird on a limed branch) where he finds a living example of virtue, did not turn his busied senses toward the truth;

but my sight, deprived of its object, almost dreaming, made a way for itself, without which its good is imperfect.

My soul, between both of my glories, felt in herself I know not what heavenly new delight and strange sweetness.

256

Far potess' io vendetta di colei
che guardando et parlando mi distrugge
et, per più doglia, poi s'asconde et fugge,
celando li occhi a me sì dolci et rei!   4

Così li affitti et stanchi spirti mei
a poco a poco consumando sugge,
e 'n sul cor quasi fiero leon rugge
la notte, allor quand' io posar devrei.   8

L'alma, cui morte del suo albergo caccia,
da me si parte; et di tal nodo sciolta
vassene pur a lei che la minaccia.   11

Meravigliomi ben s' alcuna volta,
mentre le parla et piange et poi l'abbraccia,
non rompe il sonno suo, s' ella l'ascolta.   14

257

In quel bel viso ch' i' sospiro et bramo
fermi eran li occhi desiosi e 'ntensi,
quando Amor porse—quasi a dir: "Che pensi?"—
quella onorata man che second' amo.   4

Il cor, preso ivi come pesce a l'amo
onde a ben far per vivo esempio viensi,
al ver non volse li occupati sensi,
o come novo augello al visco in ramo;   8

ma la vista, privata del suo obietto,
quasi sognando si facea far via
senza la qual è 'l suo bene imperfetto.   11

L'alma, tra l'una et l'altra gloria mia,
qual celeste non so novo diletto
et qual strania dolcezza si sentia.   14

258

Lively sparks came from those two lovely lights so sweetly lightening toward me, and from a wise heart, sighing, came such gentle floods of eloquence

that the very memory seems to consume me, when I look back at that day and think how my spirits swooned at the change in her harsh custom.

My soul, nourished always in sorrow and pain (how great is the power of an established habit!), was so weak against the double pleasure

that at the mere taste of the unaccustomed good, trembling now with fear, now with hope, it was often on the point of abandoning me.

259

I have always sought a solitary life—the riverbanks know it and the meadows and the woods—so as to avoid these deaf and blear-eyed minds that have lost the path to Heaven;

and if my wishes in this were fulfilled, beyond the sweet air of the Tuscan regions, Sorgue would have me still among its lovely shady hills, for it helps me to weep and to sing.

But my fortune, always my enemy, drives me back to the place where I am angered to see my treasure in the mud;

it has this once become a friend to this hand by which I write, and perhaps not unjustly: Love saw it, my lady and I know it.

---

place: probably Avignon.

258

Vive faville uscian de' duo bei lumi
ver me sì dolcemente folgorando,
et parte d'un cor saggio, sospirando,
d'alta eloquenzia sì soavi fiumi,   4

che pur il rimembrar par mi consumi,
qualor a quel dì torno, ripensando
come venieno i miei spirti mancando
al variar de' suoi duri costumi.   8

L'alma nudrita sempre in doglia e 'n pene
(quanto è 'l poder d'una prescritta usanza!)
contra 'l doppio piacer sì 'nferma fue   11

ch' al gusto sol del disusato bene,
tremando or di paura or di speranza,
d'abandonarme fu spesso entra due.   14

259

Cercato ò sempre solitaria vita—
le rive il sanno et le campagne e i boschi—
per fuggir questi ingegni sordi et loschi
che la strada del Cielo ànno smarrita;   4

et se mia voglia in ciò fusse compita,
fuor del dolce aere de' paesi toschi
ancor m'avria tra' suoi bei colli foschi
Sorga, ch' a pianger et cantar m'aita.   8

Ma mia fortuna, a me sempre nemica,
mi risospigne al loco ov' io mi sdegno
veder nel fango il bel tesoro mio;   11

a la man ond' io scrivo è fatta amica
a questa volta, et non è forse indegno:
Amor sel vide, et sa 'l Madonna et io.   14

260

Under such a star I saw two lovely eyes, all full of virtue and sweetness, that beside those charming nests of Love my weary heart scorns all other sights.

She who is most praised in any age, on any foreign shores, cannot equal her: not she who with her beauty brought labors to Greece and to Troy the last shrieks,

not the lovely Roman who with the steel opened her chaste and angry breast, not Polyxena, Hypsiphyle, or Argia.

This excellence of hers is a great glory, if I do not err, of Nature's; to me most high delight, but one that comes slowly and swiftly goes away.

---

she who...shrieks: Helen of Troy.   lovely Roman: Lucretia, a Roman matron raped by the tyrant Tarquinius. She killed herself after telling her husband and his friends of the deed; the incident led to the expulsion of the king and the establishment of the Roman republic.   Polyxena, Hypsiphyle, or Argia: daughter of Priam of Troy, beloved by Achilles; daughter of Thoas, king of Lemnos, seduced by Jason during the voyage of the *Argo*; daughter of Adrastus of Argos, wife of Oedipus' son Polynices.

261

Whatever lady hopes to have glorious fame for wisdom, virtue, courtesy, let her look fixedly into the eyes of that enemy of mine, whom the world calls my lady.

There she may learn how honor is won, how God is loved, how chastity is joined with gaiety, and what is the straight way to go to Heaven, which awaits and desires her,

there the speech that no style can equal, and the lovely silences, and those dear manners which human wit cannot set forth on any page.

She cannot learn there the infinite beauty that dazzles us, for that sweet light is acquired by luck and not by art.

260

In tale stella duo belli occhi vidi,
tutti pien d'onestate et di dolcezza,
che presso a quei d'Amor leggiadri nidi
il mio cor lasso ogni altra vista sprezza.   4

Non si pareggi a lei qual più s'aprezza
in qual ch' etade, in quai che strani lidi:
non chi recò con sua vaga bellezza
in Grecia affanni, in Troia ultimi stridi,   8

no la bella romana che col ferro
apre il suo casto et disdegnoso petto,
non Polissena, Isifile et Argia.   11

Questa eccellenzia è gloria, s' i' non erro,
grande a Natura; a me sommo diletto,
ma che ven tardo et subito va via.   14

261

Qual donna attende a gloriosa fama
di senno, di valor, di cortesia
miri fiso nelli occhi a quella mia
nemica che mia donna il mondo chiama.   4

Come s'acquista onor, come Dio s'ama,
come è giunta onestà con leggiadria
ivi s'impara, et qual è dritta via
di gir al Ciel, che lei aspetta et brama,   8

ivi 'l parlar che nullo stile aguaglia,
e 'l bel tacere, et quei cari costumi
che 'ngegno uman non po spiegar in carte.   11

L'infinita bellezza ch' altrui abbaglia
non vi s'impara, ché quei dolci lumi
s'acquistan per ventura et non per arte.   14

262

"Life is most dear, it seems to me, and after that, true virtue in a beautiful woman." "You reverse the order! There never were, mother, things lovely or dear without virtue,

"and whoever lets herself be deprived of honor is no longer a lady and no longer alive; and if she appears the same to sight, her life is much more harsh and cruel than death, and more bitter with sorrow.

"Nor did I ever marvel at Lucretia, except that she needed the steel to die and that her sorrow alone did not suffice."

Let all philosophers of all times come and speak about this: all their ways will be low, and her alone we shall see mount up in flight!

A dialogue between Laura(?) and her mother.
Lucretia: see note on "lovely Roman," poem 260.

263

Victorious triumphal tree, the honor of emperors and of poets, how many days you have made sorrowful and glad for me in this my brief mortal life!

True Lady, concerned for naught but honor, which above all others you harvest, you do not fear the birdlime or the snares or nets of Love, nor does any deception avail against your wisdom!

Nobility of blood and the other things prized among us—pearls and rubies and gold—like a vile burden, you equally despise;

your high beauty, which has no equal in the world, is painful to you except insofar as it seems to adorn and set off your lovely treasure of chastity.

After this poem, Vat. Lat. 3195 has seven blank pages.
tree: the laurel.

262

"Cara la vita, et dopo lei mi pare
vera onestà che 'n bella donna sia."
"L'ordine volgi; e' non fur, madre mia,
senza onestà mai cose belle o care,   4

"et qual si lascia di suo onor privare
né donna è più, né viva; et se qual pria
appare in vista, è tal vita aspra et ria
via più che morte et di più pene amare.   8

"Nè di Lucrezia mi meravigliai,
se non come a morir le bisognasse
ferro et non le bastasse il dolor solo."   11

Vengan quanti filosofi fur mai
a dir di ciò, tutte lor vie fien basse,
et quest'una vedremo alzarsi a volo!   14

263

Arbor vittoriosa triunfale,
onor d'imperadori et di poeti:
quanti m'ài fatto dì dogliosi et lieti
in questa breve mia vita mortale!   4

Vera Donna, et a cui di nulla cale
se non d'onor che sovr' ogni altra mieti,
né d'Amor visco temi o lacci o reti,
né 'nganno altrui contra 'l tuo senno vale: 8

gentilezza di sangue et l'altre care
cose tra noi, perle et robini et oro,
quasi vil soma egualmente dispregi;   11

l'alta beltà ch' al mondo non à pare
noia t'è se non quanto il bel tesoro
di castità par ch' ella adorni et fregi.   14

264

I go thinking and in thought pity for myself assails me, so strong that it often leads me to a weeping different from my accustomed one: for, seeing every day the end coming near, a thousand times I have asked God for those wings with which our intellect raises itself from this mortal prison to Heaven.

But until now no prayer or sigh or weeping of mine has helped me; and that is just, for he who, able to stand, has fallen along the way deserves to lie on the ground against his will. Those merciful arms in which I trust I see still open; but fear grasps my heart at the examples of others, and I tremble for my state; another spurs me and I am perhaps at the end.

One thought speaks to my mind and says: "What are you yearning for still? whence do you expect help? Wretch, do you not understand with how much dishonor for you time is passing? Decide wisely, decide, and from your heart pluck up every root of the pleasure that can never make one happy and does not let one breathe.

"If you have already long been tired and disgusted by that false fleeting sweetness which the treacherous world gives, why do you place your hopes in it any longer? for it lacks any peace or stability. As long as your body is alive, you have in your own keeping the rein of your thoughts. Ah, grasp it now while you can, for delay is perilous, as you know, and to begin now will not be early.

---

merciful arms: the outstretched arms of the crucified Christ.

264

I' vo pensando, et nel penser m'assale
una pietà sì forte di me stesso
che mi conduce spesso
ad altro lagrimar ch' i' non soleva:
ché vedendo ogni giorno il fin più presso,
mille fiate ò chieste a Dio quell'ale
co le quai del mortale
carcer nostr'intelletto al Ciel si leva.   8
    Ma infin a qui niente mi releva
prego o sospiro o lagrimar ch' io faccia;
et così per ragion conven che sia,
ché chi possendo star cadde tra via
degno è che mal suo grado a terra giaccia.   13
Quelle pietose braccia
in ch' io mi fido veggio aperte ancora,
ma temenza m'accora
per gli altrui esempli, et del mio stato tremo,
ch' altri mi sprona et son forse a l'estremo.   18

    L'un penser parla co la mente, et dice:
"Che pur agogni? onde soccorso attendi?
Misera, non intendi
con quanto tuo disnore il tempo passa?
Prendi partito accortamente, prendi,
et del cor tuo divelli ogni radice
del piacer che felice
nol po mai fare et respirar nol lassa.   26
    "Se già è gran tempo fastidita et lassa
se' di quel falso dolce fuggitivo
che 'l mondo traditor può dare altrui,
a che ripon' più la speranza in lui?
ché d'ogni pace et di fermezza è privo.   31
Mentre che 'l corpo è vivo,
ài tu 'l freno in bailia de' penser tuoi.
Deh stringilo or che poi,
ché dubbioso è 'l tardar, come tu sai,
e 'l cominciar non fia per tempo omai.   36

"You know very well how much sweetness your eyes have taken from the sight of her who I wish were still to be born so we might have peace. You remember well, and you must remember, her image, when it ran to your heart, where perhaps a flame from any other torch could not have entered.

"She set it afire, and if the deceiving flame has lasted many years, awaiting a day that, luckily for our salvation, will never come, now raise yourself to a more blessed hope by gazing at the heavens that revolve about you, immortal and adorned; for if down here your desire, so happy in its ills, is satisfied by a glance, a talk, a song, what will that pleasure be, if this is so great?"

On the other side a sweet sharp thought, enthroned within my soul in difficult and delightful weight, oppresses my heart with desire and feeds it with hope; for the sake of kindly glorious fame, it does not feel when I freeze or when I flame, or if I am pale or thin; and if I kill it, it is reborn stronger than before.

This thought has been growing with me day by day since I slept in swaddling clothes, and I fear that one tomb will enclose us both; for when my soul is naked of my members, this desire will not be able to come with it. But if the Latins and the Greeks talk of me after my death, that is a wind; therefore, since I fear to be always gathering what one hour will scatter, I wish to embrace the truth, to abandon shadows.

"Già sai tu ben quanta dolcezza porse
agli occhi tuoi la vista di colei,
la qual anco vorrei
ch' a nascer fosse, per più nostra pace.
Ben ti ricordi et ricordar ten dei
de l'imagine sua, quand' ella corse
al cor, là dove forse
non potea fiamma intrar per altrui face.   44
    "Ella l'accese, et se l'ardor fallace
durò molt'anni in aspettando un giorno
che per nostra salute unqua non vene,
or ti solleva a più beata spene
mirando 'l ciel che ti si volve intorno   49
immortal et adorno;
ché dove del mal suo qua giù sì lieta
vostra vaghezza acqueta
un mover d'occhi, un ragionar, un canto,
quanto fia quel piacer, se questo è tanto?"   54

    Da l'altra parte un pensier dolce et agro,
con faticosa e dilettevol salma
sedendosi entro l'alma,
preme 'l cor di desio, di speme il pasce;
che sol per fama gloriosa et alma
non sente quand' io agghiaccio o quand' io flagro,
s' i' son pallido o magro;
et s' io l'occido più forte rinasce.   62
    Questo d'allor ch' i' m'addormiva in fasce
venuto è di dì in dì crescendo meco,
et temo ch' un sepolcro ambeduo chiuda;
poi che fia l'alma de le membra ignuda
non po questo desio più venir seco.   67
Ma se 'l latino e 'l greco
parlan di me dopo la morte, è un vento;
ond' io, perché pavento
adunar sempre quel ch' un'ora sgombre,
vorre' 'l ver abbracciar, lassando l'ombre.   72

But that other desire of which I am full seems to overshadow all
others born beside it, and time flies while I write of another,
not caring about myself; and the light of those lovely eyes,
which gently melts me with its clear heat, holds me in with a rein
against which no wit or force avails me.

What does it profit me therefore to oil my little bark, since it is
held among the rocks by two such knots? You who entirely free
me from all the other knots which in different ways bind the
world, my Lord, why do you not finally take from my brow this
shame? For like a dreamer I seem to have Death before my eyes,
and I wish to defend myself but have no weapons.

I see what I am doing, and I am not deceived by an imperfect
knowledge of the truth; rather Love forces me, who never lets
anyone who too much believes him follow the path of honor;
and from time to time I feel in my heart a noble disdain, harsh
and severe, which brings all my hidden thoughts to my brow,
where others can see them.

For the more one desires honor, the more one is forbidden to
love a mortal thing with the faith that belongs to God alone.
And this with a loud voice calls back my reason, which wanders
after my senses; but although it hears and thinks to come back,
its bad habit drives it further and depicts for my eyes her who
was born to make me die, since she pleased me and herself too
much.

Ma quell'altro voler di ch' i' son pieno
quanti press' a lui nascon par ch' adugge,
et parte il tempo fugge
che scrivendo d'altrui di me non calme;
e 'l lume de' begli occhi che mi strugge
soavemente al suo caldo sereno
mi ritien con un freno
contra cui nullo ingegno o forza valme.   80
    Che giova dunque perché tutta spalme
la mia barchetta, poi che 'nfra li scogli
è ritenuta ancor da ta' duo nodi?
Tu che dagli altri che 'n diversi modi
legano 'l mondo in tutto mi disciogli,   85
Signor mio, ché non togli
omai dal volto mio questa vergogna?
Ché 'n guisa d'uom che sogna
aver la morte inanzi gli occhi parme,
et vorrei far difesa et non ò l'arme.   90

    Quel ch' i' fo veggio, et non m'inganna il vero
mal conosciuto, anzi mi sforza Amore
che la strada d'onore
mai nol lassa seguir chi troppo il crede;
et sento ad ora ad or venirmi al core
un leggiadro disdegno aspro et severo
ch' ogni occulto pensero
tira in mezzo la fronte, ov' altri 'l vede.   98
    Ché mortal cosa amar con tanta fede
quanto a Dio sol per debito convensi
più si disdice a chi più pregio brama.
Et questo ad alta voce anco richiama
la ragione sviata dietro ai sensi;   103
ma perch' ell' oda et pensi
tornare, il mal costume oltre la spigne
et agli occhi depigne
quella che sol per farmi morir nacque,
perch' a me troppo et a se stessa piacque.   108

Nor do I know what space was ordained for me by the
heavens when I came newly down to earth to suffer the bitter
war that I have managed to combine against myself; nor,
because of my bodily veil, can I foresee the day that closes life;
but I see my hair changing and every desire within.

Now that I believe I am near or not very far from the time of
my departure, like one whom losing has made wary and wise, I
go thinking back where I left the journey to the right, which
reaches a good port: and on one side I am pierced by shame and
sorrow, which turn me back; on the other I am not freed from a
pleasure so strong in me by habit that it dares to bargain with
Death.

Song, here I am, and my heart is much colder with fear than
frozen snow, since I feel myself perishing beyond all doubt, for
still deliberating I have wound on the spool a great part now of
my short thread; nor was weight ever so heavy as what I now
sustain in this state, for with Death at my side I seek new counsel
for my life, and I see the better but I lay hold on the worse.

Né so che spazio mi si desse il cielo
quando novellamente io venni in terra
a soffir l'aspra guerra
che 'ncontra me medesmo seppi ordire,
né posso il giorno che la vita serra
antiveder per lo corporeo velo;
ma variarsi il pelo
veggio, et dentro cangiarsi ogni desire.   116
   Or ch' i' mi credo al tempo del partire
esser vicino o non molto da lunge,
come chi 'l perder face accorto et saggio
vo ripensando ov' io lassai 'l viaggio
da la man destra ch' a buon porto aggiunge: 121
et da l'un lato punge
vergogna et duol che 'ndietro mi rivolve,
dall'altro non m'assolve
un piacer per usanza in me sì forte
ch' a patteggiar n'ardisce co la Morte.   126

   Canzon, qui sono ed ò 'l cor via più freddo
de la paura che gelata neve,
sentendomi perir senz' alcun dubbio,
ché pur deliberando ò vòlto al subbio
gran parte omai de la mia tela breve;   131
né mai peso fu greve
quanto quel ch' i' sostengo in tale stato
che co la Morte a lato
cerco del viver mio novo consiglio,
et veggio 'l meglio et al peggior m'appiglio.   136

265

A harsh heart and wild cruel desire in a sweet, humble, angelic form, if this rigor she has taken up continues long, will have spoils of me that bring little honor;

for when the flowers, grass, and leaves are born or die, when it is bright day and when it is dark night, I weep at all times. From fate, from my lady, and from Love I have much to grieve me.

I live only on hope, remembering that I have seen a little water, by always trying, finally wear away marble and solid rock:

there is no heart so hard that by weeping, praying, loving, it may not sometime be moved, no will so cold that it cannot be warmed.

266

My dear Lord, every thought draws me devotedly to see you whom I always see, but my fortune (what can it do to me that is worse?) keeps me reined in and wheels me and turns me about.

And then the sweet desire that Love inspires in me leads me to death so gradually that I am not aware of it, and while I call out in vain for my two lights, wherever I am there is sighing day and night.

Devotion to my lord, love of my lady are the chains where with much labor I am bound, and I myself took them on!

A green Laurel, a noble Column, the latter for fifteen, the former for eighteen years, I have carried in my breast and have never put from me.

Addressed to Cardinal Giovanni Colonna, Petrarch's friend and patron. Sennuccio del Bene wrote a sonnet in reply (Appendix One, p. 607).

Column: a pun on the name Colonna.   fifteen: Petrarch fell in love with Laura in 1327; he met Giovanni Colonna in 1330. The poem thus dates itself 1345. See note to poem 221.

265

Aspro core et selvaggio et cruda voglia
in dolce umile angelica figura,
se l'impreso rigor gran tempo dura,
avran di me poco onorata spoglia;   4

ché quando nasce et mor fior erba et foglia,
quando è 'l dì chiaro et quando è notte oscura,
piango ad ogni or. Ben ò di mia ventura,
di Madonna, et d'Amore onde mi doglia.   8

Vivo sol di speranza, rimembrando
che poco umor già per continua prova
consumar vidi marmi et pietre salde: 11

non è sì duro cor che lagrimando,
pregando, amando talor non si smova,
né sì freddo voler che non si scalde.   14

266

Signor mio caro, ogni pensier mi tira
devoto a veder voi cui sempre veggio;
la mia fortuna (or che mi po far peggio?)
mi tene a freno et mi travolve et gira;   4

poi quel dolce desio ch' Amor mi spira
menami a morte ch' i' non me n'aveggio;
et mentre i miei duo lumi indarno cheggio,
dovunque io son dì et notte si sospira.   8

Carità di signore, amor di donna
son le catene ove con molti affanni
legato son, perch' io stesso mi strinsi;   11

un lauro verde, una gentil colonna
quindeci l'una et l'altro diciotto anni
portato ò in seno, et giamai non mi scinsi.   14

267

Alas the lovely face, alas the gentle glance, alas the proud, care-free bearing! Alas the speech that made every harsh or savage mind humble and every base man valiant!

And alas the sweet smile whence came forth the dart from which now I expect death, no other good! Regal soul, worthy of empire if you had not come down among us so late:

for you I must burn, in you breathe, for I have been only yours; and if I am deprived of you, it pains me more than any other misfortune;

with hope you filled me and with desire, when I left still alive that highest pleasure, but the wind carried off the words.

According to Petrarch's note in his copy of the works of Virgil, Laura died in Avignon on April 6, 1348, and he received word of her death on May 19 of that year. See note to poem 3.

268

What shall I do? What do you counsel me, Love? It is surely time to die, and I have delayed more than I would wish.

My lady is dead and has my heart with her, and if I wish to follow it I must break off these cruel years,

for I never hope to see her on this side, and waiting is pain-ful to me, since by her departure my every joy is turned to weep-ing, every sweetness of my life is taken away.

Love, you feel how great is the bitter heavy loss, and there-fore I complain to you; and I know that you are pained by my grief—

or rather ours, for we have wrecked our ship on the same rock and in the same instant the sun is darkened for us both.

267

Oimè il bel viso, oimè il soave sguardo,
oimè il leggiadro portamento altero!
Oimè il parlar ch' ogni aspro ingegno et fero
facevi umile ed ogni uom vil, gagliardo!   4

Et oimè il dolce riso onde uscio 'l dardo
di che morte, altro bene omai non spero!
Alma real dignissima d'impero
se non fossi fra noi scesa sì tardo: 8

per voi conven ch' io arda e 'n voi respiro,
ch' i' pur fui vostro; et se di voi son privo
via men d'ogni sventura altra mi dole;   11

di speranza m'empieste et di desire
quand' io parti' dal sommo piacer vivo,
ma 'l vento ne portava le parole.   14

268

   Che debb' io far? che mi consigli, Amore?
Tempo è ben di morire,
ed ò tardato più ch' i' non vorrei.
   Madonna è morta et à seco il mio core,
et volendol seguire,
interromper conven quest'anni rei,
     perché mai veder lei   6
di qua non spero, e l'aspettar m'è noia
poscia ch' ogni mia gioia
per lo suo dipartire in pianto è volta,
ogni dolcezza de mia vita è tolta.   11

   Amore, tu 'l senti, ond' io teco mi doglio,
quant' è 'l danno aspro et grave;
et so che del mio mal ti pesa et dole,
   anzi del nostro, perch' ad uno scoglio
avem rotto la nave,
et in un punto n'è scurato il sole.   17

What skill could ever match in words my sorrowful state?
Ah bereaved, ungrateful world! you have great reason to weep
with me, for with her you have lost all the good that was in you.

Your glory is fallen, and you do not see it; nor were you
worthy, while she lived down here, to know her
  or to be touched by her holy feet, for a thing so beautiful
ought to adorn Heaven with its presence.
  But I, alas, who without her love neither mortal life nor
myself, I weep, call out for her. This is left to me of all that hope,
and this alone maintains me here.

Alas, her beautiful face has become clay, which was wont
to give testimony among us of Heaven and the happiness up
there!
  Her invisible form is in Paradise, set free from the veil that
here shadowed the flower of her years,
    to be clothed with it again another time, and never to lose
it, when so much the more kindly and beautiful we shall see her
become as eternal beauty is higher than mortal.

More beautiful than ever and more queenly she comes to
my mind, as to a place where she knows the sight of her is most
pleasing;
  this is one column of my life; the other is her bright name,
which sounds so sweetly in my heart.

    Qual ingegno a parole
poria aguagliare il mio doglioso stato?
Ahi orbo mondo, ingrato,
gran cagion ài di dover pianger meco,
che quel bel ch' era in te perduto ài seco.   22

    Caduta è la tua gloria, et tu nol vedi,
né degno eri, mentr' ella
visse qua giù, di aver sua conoscenza
    né d'esser tocco da' suoi santi piedi,
perché cosa sì bella
devea 'l Ciel adornar di sua presenza.   28
    Ma io, lasso, che senza
lei né la vita mortal né me stesso amo,
piangendo la richiamo:
questo m'avanza di cotanta spene,
et questo solo ancor qui mi mantene.   33

    Oimè, terra è fatto il suo bel viso
che solea far del Cielo
et del ben di lassù fede fra noi!
    L'invisibil sua forma è in Paradiso,
disciolta di quel velo
che qui fece ombra al fior degli anni suoi,   39
    per rivestirsen poi
un'altra volta et mai più non spogliarsi,
quando alma et bella farsi
tanto più la vedrem quanto più vale
sempiterna bellezza che mortale.   44

    Più che mai bella et più leggiadra donna
tornami inanzi come
là dove più gradir sua vista sente;
    questa è del viver mio l'una colonna,
l'altra è 'l suo chiaro nome,
che sona nel mio cor sì dolcemente.   50

But, remembering that my hope is dead, which was alive while she was in flower, Love knows what I become, and, I hope, she sees it who is now so close to the truth.

Ladies, you who wondered at her beauty and her angelic life and her bearing so heavenly on earth:
grieve for me, and let pity for me vanquish you, not for her, who has risen to such peace and has left me in sad war,
so that, if the way to follow her is long closed to me, only what Love says to me holds me back from cutting the knot. But he speaks within, thus:

"Rein in the great sorrow that transports you; for excessive desire will lose the Heaven where your heart aspires,
where she is alive who seems dead, and she smiles to herself at her beautiful remains and sighs only for you;
"and she begs you not to extinguish her fame, which sounds in many places still by your tongue, but rather to make bright your voice with her name, if her eyes were ever sweet or dear to you."

Flee the clear sky and greenery, do not approach where there is laughter and singing, my song, no, but where there is weeping; it is not fitting for you to be among cheerful people, disconsolate widow in black garments.

Ma tornandomi a mente
che pur morta è la mia speranza viva
allor ch' ella fioriva,
sa ben Amor qual io divento, et (spero)
vede 'l colei ch' è or sì presso al vero.   55

Donne, voi che miraste sua beltate
et l'angelica vita
con quel celeste portamento in terra:
    di me vi doglia, et vincavi pietate;
non di lei, ch' è salita
a tanta pace, et m'à lassato in guerra   61
    tal che s' altri mi serra
lungo tempo il cammin da seguitarla,
quel ch' Amor meco parla
sol mi riten ch' io non recida il nodo.
Ma e' ragiona dentro in cotal modo: 66

    "Pon freno al gran dolor che ti trasporta,
ché per soverchie voglie
si perde 'l Cielo ove 'l tuo core aspira,
    "dove è viva colei ch' altrui par morta
et di sue belle spoglie
seco sorride et sol di te sospira,   72
    "et sua fama, che spira
in molte parti ancor per la tua lingua,
prega che non estingua,
anzi la voce al suo nome rischiari,
se gli occhi suoi ti fur dolci né cari."   77

    Fuggi 'l sereno e 'l verde,
non t'appressare ove sia riso o canto,
canzon mia, no, ma pianto;
non fa per te di star fra gente allegra,
vedova sconsolata in veste negra.   82

269

Broken are the high Column and the green Laurel that gave shade to my weary cares; I have lost what I do not hope to find again, from Boreas to Auster or from the Indian to the Moorish Sea.

You have taken from me, O Death, my double treasure that made me live glad and walk proudly; neither land nor empire can restore it, nor orient gem, nor the power of gold.

But, since this is the intent of destiny, what can I do except have my soul sad, my eyes always wet, and my face bent down?

Oh our life that is so beautiful to see, how easily it loses in one morning what has been acquired with great difficulty over many years!

---

broken . . . Column: Cardinal Giovanni Colonna died on July 3, 1348. from Boreas to Auster: from north to south.   Moorish Sea: the Mediterranean at Morocco.

270

Love, if you wish me to return to the old yoke, as you seem to show, in order to subdue me you will have to pass another test, marvelous and new. Find my beloved treasure in the earth where it is hidden from me, for which I go so poor, and the wise chaste heart where my life used to dwell;

and, if it is true that your power is as great in Heaven and in the Abyss as it is said to be (for here among us I believe every noble person feels your worth and power), take back from Death what she has taken from us, and set up your standard again in that beautiful face.

269

Rotta è l'alta colonna e 'l verde lauro
che facean ombra al mio stanco pensero;
perduto ò quel che ritrovar non spero
dal borea a l'austro o dal mar indo al mauro.   4

Tolto m'ài, Morte, il mio doppio tesauro
che mi fea viver lieto et gire altero,
et ristorar nol po terra né impero,
né gemma oriental né forza d'auro.   8

Ma se consentimento è di destino,
che posso io più se no aver l'alma trista,
umidi gli occhi sempre, e 'l viso chino?   11

O nostra vita ch' è sì bella in vista,
com' perde agevolmente in un matino
quel che 'n molti anni a gran pena s'acquista.   14

270

   Amor, se vuo' ch' i' torni al giogo antico,
come par che tu mostri, un'altra prova
meravigliosa et nova
per domar me conventi vincer pria.
Il mio amato tesoro in terra trova,
che m' è nascosto, ond' io son sì mendico,
e 'l cor saggio pudico
ove suol albergar la vita mia;   8
   et s' egli è ver che tua potenzia sia
nel Ciel sì grande come si ragiona
et ne l'abisso (perché qui fra noi
quel che tu val' et puoi
credo che 'l sente ogni gentil persona),
ritogli a Morte quel ch' ella n'à tolto
et ripon le tue insegne nel bel volto.   15

Put back in her lovely eyes the living light that was my guide and the gentle flame that still, alas! inflames me though it is extinguished—oh, what did it do when still burning? Never was hart or doe seen to seek spring or river with so much desire as I seek the sweet manner whence I have already received much that is bitter; and I expect more,

if I well understand myself and my yearning, which makes me rave from merely thinking, and go where the road fails, and with my weary mind follow something that I never hope to reach. Now I do not deign to come at your summons, for you have no power outside of your own kingdom.

Make me feel that gentle breeze without as I feel it still within; it had power, singing, to quiet scorn and anger, to make clear the tempestuous mind and lighten it of all dark, base clouds, and it lifted my style up above itself to heights that now it cannot reach.

Make my hope equal to my desire; and, since the soul is stronger in its rights, give back to my eyes and ears their proper object, without which their operation is imperfect and my life is death. In vain now you exert your force on me, when the earth covers my first love.

Riponi entro 'l bel viso il vivo lume
ch' era mia scorta, et la soave fiamma
ch' ancor, lasso, m'infiamma
essendo spenta. Or che fea dunque ardendo?
E' non si vide mai cervo né damma
con tal desio cercar fonte né fiume
qual io il dolce costume
onde ò già molto amaro; et più n'attendo,   23
    se ben me stesso et mia vaghezza intendo,
che mi fa vaneggiar sol del pensero
et gire in parte ove la strada manca,
et co la mente stanca
cosa seguir che mai giugner non spero.
Or al tuo richiamar venir non degno,
che segnoria non ài fuor del tuo regno.   30

Fammi sentir de quell'aura gentile
di for, sì come dentro ancor si sente,
la qual era possente,
cantando, d'acquetar li sdegni et l'ire,
di serenar la tempestosa mente
et sgombrar d'ogni nebbia oscura et vile,
ed alzava il mio stile
sovra di sé dove or non poria gire.   38
    Aguaglia la speranza col desire,
et poi che l'alma è in sua ragion più forte,
rendi agli occhi, agli orecchi il proprio oggetto
senza qual imperfetto
è lor oprare e 'l mio vivere è morte.
Indarno or sovra me tua forza adopre
mentre 'l mio primo amor terra ricopre.   45

Make me see again the lovely glance that was sunlight on the ice that used to weigh me down: let me find you at that pass where my heart passed over, never to return; take your golden arrows and take your bow, and let her speak to me as she was wont, with the sound of those words in which I learned what love is.

Move that tongue where were ever set the hooks that caught me and the bait that I ever desire, and hide your snares among her curling blond hair, for my desire is enlimed nowhere else; with your own hand spread her locks to the wind, there bind me, and you can content me.

No one shall ever set me free from that golden snare, artfully neglected and thick with ringlets, nor from the burning spirit of her sight, sweetly cruel, which day and night kept my amorous desire more green than any laurel or myrtle when the wood clothes or divests itself of leaves and the meadow of grass.

But, since Death has been so proud as to shatter the knot from which I feared to escape, and since you cannot find one to tie a second knot, however you wander through the world, what does it profit, Love, to keep trying your stratagems? The season is past, you have lost the arms at which I trembled: what can you do to me now?

Fa' ch' io riveggia il bel guardo ch' un sole
fu sopra 'l ghiaccio ond' io solea gir carco;
fa' ch' i' ti trovi al varco
onde senza tornar passò 'l mio core;
prendi i dorati strali et prendi l'arco,
et facciamisi udir sì come sole
col suon de le parole
ne le quali io imparai che cosa è amore.   53

   Movi la lingua ov' erano a tutt'ore
disposti gli ami ov' io fui preso et l'esca
ch' i' bramo sempre; e i tuoi lacci nascondi
fra i capei crespi et biondi,
ché 'l mio volere altrove non s'invesca;
spargi co le tue man le chiome al vento,
ivi mi lega, et puo' mi far contento.   60

   Dal laccio d'or non sia mai chi me scioglia
negletto ad arte, e 'nnanellato et irto,
né de l'ardente spirto
de la sua vista dolcemente acerba,
la qual dì et notte più che lauro o mirto
tenea in me verde l'amorosa voglia
quando si veste et spoglia
di fronde il bosco et la campagna d'erba.   68

   Ma poi che Morte è stata sì superba
che spezzò il nodo ond' io temea scampare,
né trovar poi quantunque gira il mondo
di che ordischi 'l secondo,
che giova, Amor, tuoi ingegni ritentare?
Passata è la stagion, perduto ài l'arme
di ch' io tremava: ormai che puoi tu farme?   75

Your weapons were those eyes from which came forth arrows lit with invisible fire, and they feared reason but little, for no human defense avails against Heaven; pensiveness and silence, laughter and gaiety, virtuous habit and courteous speech, and words that if understood would make a base soul noble,

the angelic, humble, mild appearance that was praised so much now on this side, now on that, and her sitting and her standing, which often left one in doubt which to praise more— with these arms you vanquished every hard heart; now you are disarmed and I am safe.

Those souls that the heavens incline to your rule you bind now in one manner, now in another; but me you have been able to bind only in one knot, for the heavens ordained no more. That one is broken and in liberty I do not rejoice but I weep and cry: "Ah, noble pilgrim, what divine judgment bound me first and loosed you first?

"God, who so soon took you away from the world, showed us so much high virtue only to inflame our desire." Certainly now I do not fear any new wounds from your hand, Love: in vain you bend your bow, your shots go wild; its power fell with the closing of her lovely eyes.

Death has freed me, Love, from all your laws; she who was my lady has gone to Heaven, leaving my life sorrowful and free.

L'arme tue furon gli occhi onde l'accese
saette uscivan d'invisibil foco,
et ragion temean poco
ché 'ncontra 'l Ciel non val difesa umana,
il pensar e 'l tacer, il riso e 'l gioco,
l'abito onesto e 'l ragionar cortese,
le parole che 'ntese
avrian fatto gentil d'alma villana,   83
　　l'angelica sembianza umile et piana
ch' or quinci or quindi udia tanto lodarsi,
e 'l sedere et lo star che spesso altrui
poser in dubbio a cui
devesse il pregio di più laude darsi:
con quest'armi vincevi ogni cor duro;
or se' tu disarmato, i' son securo.   90

　　Gli animi ch' al tuo regno il cielo inchina
leghi ora in uno et ora in altro modo,
ma me sol ad un nodo
legar potei, ché 'l ciel di più non volse.
Quell'uno è rotto e 'n libertà non godo
ma piango et grido: "Ahi, nobil pellegrina,
qual sentenzia divina
me legò innanzi et te prima disciolse?   98
　　"Dio, che sì tosto al mondo ti ritolse,
ne mostrò tanta et sì alta virtute
solo per infiammar nostro desio."
Certo omai non tem' io,
Amor, de la tua man nove ferute;
indarno tendi l'arco, a voito scocchi:
sua virtù cadde al chiuder de' begli occhi.   105

　　Morte m'à sciolto, Amor, d'ogni tua legge;
quella che fu mia donna al Ciel è gita,
lasciando trista et libera mia vita.   108

271

That burning knot in which I was hour by hour caught for twenty-one whole years, Death has untied; I had never experienced such sorrow, nor do I now believe that one can die of grief.

Love, not wishing to lose me yet, had set another snare among the grass and kindled another fire with new tinder, so that only with great difficulty could I have escaped from it.

And if it had not been for much experience of my first labors, I would have been captured and all the more burned for being drier wood.

Death has freed me another time, and has broken the knot and has put out and scattered the fire: Death, against whom no power or wit avails.

272

Life flees and does not stop an hour, and Death comes after by great stages; and present and past things make war on me, and future things also,

and remembering and expecting both weigh down my heart now on this side, now on that, so that in truth, except that I take pity on myself, I would already be beyond these thoughts.

If my sad heart ever experienced any sweetness, it comes before me; and then on the other hand I see the winds turbulent for my voyaging,

I see storm in the port, and my helmsman wearied now, and the masts and lines broken, and the beautiful stars extinguished that I used to gaze at.

271

L'ardente nodo ov' io fui, d'ora in ora
contando, anni ventuno interi preso
Morte disciolse, né giamai tal peso
provai, né credo ch' uom di dolor mora.   4

Non volendomi Amor perdere ancora,
ebbe un altro lacciuol fra l'erba teso
et di nova esca un altro foco acceso,
tal ch' a gran pena indi scampato fora.   8

Et se non fosse esperienzia molta
de' primi affanni, i' sarei preso et arso
tanto più quanto son men verde legno.   11

Morte m'à liberato un'altra volta
et rotto 'l nodo, e 'l foco à spento et sparso,
contra la qual non val forza né 'ngegno.   14

272

La vita fugge et non s'arresta un'ora,
et la Morte vien dietro a gran giornate;
et le cose presenti et le passate
mi dànno guerra et le future ancora,   4

e 'l rimembrare et l'aspettar m'accora
or quinci or quindi; sì che 'n veritate,
se non ch' i' ò di me stesso pietate,
i' sarei già di questi pensier fora.   8

Tornami avanti s' alcun dolce mai
ebbe 'l cor tristo; et poi da l'altra parte
veggio al mio navigar turbati i venti,   11

veggio fortuna in porto, et stanco omai
il mio nocchier, et rotte arbore et sarte,
e i lumi bei che mirar soglio spenti.   14

273

What are you doing? What are you thinking? Why do you still look back to a time that can never return anymore? My comfortless soul, why do you still add fuel to the fire where you are burning?

The gentle words and the sweet glances that you have described and depicted one by one, have been taken from the earth; and it is, you well know, unseasonable and too late to seek them here.

Ah, do not renew what kills us; do not follow any longer a deceptive yearning thought, but a firm and certain one that may guide us to a good end.

Let us seek Heaven, if nothing pleases us here; for we ill saw that beauty if living and dead it was to rob us of peace.

274

Give me peace, O my cruel thoughts! Is it not enough that Love, Fortune, and Death besiege me around and at the very gates, without having to find other enemies within?

And you, my heart, are you still what you used to be? Disloyal only to me, you keep sheltering fierce spies and you have become an ally of my enemies, who are so alert and swift.

In you Love sets out his secret messages, in you Fortune sets out her every pomp, and Death the memory of that blow

which must break what is left of me, in you my wandering thoughts arm themselves with error: therefore I blame you alone for my every ill.

273

Che fai? che pensi? ché pur dietro guardi
nel tempo che tornar non pote omai?
Anima sconsolata, ché pur vai
giugnendo legno al foco ove tu ardi?   4

Le soavi parole e i dolci sguardi
ch' ad un ad un descritti et depinti ài
son levati de terra, et è, ben sai,
qui ricercarli intempestivo et tardi.   8

Deh, non rinovellar quel che n'ancide,
non seguir più penser vago fallace
ma saldo et certo ch' a buon fin ne guide;   11

cerchiamo 'l Ciel se qui nulla ne piace,
ché mal per noi quella beltà si vide
se viva et morta ne devea tor pace.   14

274

Datemi pace, o duri miei pensieri!
non basta ben ch' Amor, Fortuna et Morte
mi fanno guerra intorno e 'n su le porte,
senza trovarmi dentro altri guerreri?   4

Et tu, mio cor, ancor se' pur qual eri?
disleal a me sol, che fere scorte
vai ricettando et se' fatto consorte
de' miei nemici sì pronti et leggieri.   8

In te i secreti suoi messaggi Amore,
in te spiega Fortuna ogni sua pompa,
et Morte la memoria di quel colpo   11

che l'avanzo di me conven che rompa,
in te i vaghi pensier s'arman d'errore:
per che d'ogni mio mal te solo incolpo.   14

275

My eyes, darkened is our sun, rather it has risen to Heaven and there shines, there we shall see it again, there it awaits us and perhaps is pained by our delay.

My ears, the angelic words are sounding in a place where there is someone who understands better. My feet, your province does not extend to where she is who used to make you work.

Therefore why do you fight against me? I was not the reason that you can no longer see her, hear her, and find her on earth.

Blame Death; rather, praise Him who binds and looses, and in an instant opens and closes up, and after weeping can make one glad.

276

Since the bright angelic sight of her has with its sudden departure left my soul in great sorrow and in dark horror, I seek to lighten my pain by speaking.

Certainly it is a just grief that leads me to lament (she who is its cause knows it, and Love knows it), for my heart had no other remedy against the ills of which life is full;

this remedy, your hand, Death, has taken from me. And you, happy earth, who cover and guard and have with you that lovely human face,

where do you leave me, unconsoled and blinded, since the sweet loving mild light of my eyes is no longer with me?

275

Occhi miei, oscurato è 'l nostro sole,
anzi è salito al Cielo et ivi splende,
ivi il vedremo, ancora ivi n'attende
et di nostro tardar forse li dole.   4

Orecchie mie, l'angeliche parole
sonano in parte ove è chi meglio intende.
Pie' miei, vostra ragion là non si stende
ov' è colei ch' esercitar vi sole.   8

Dunque perché mi date questa guerra?
Già di perder a voi cagion non fui
vederla, udirla et ritrovarla in terra.   11

Morte biasmate; anzi laudate Lui
che lega et scioglie, e 'n un punto apre et serra,
et dopo 'l pianto sa far lieto altrui.   14

276

Poi che la vista angelica serena
per subita partenza in gran dolore
lasciato à l'alma e 'n tenebroso orrore,
cerco parlando d'allentar mia pena.   4

Giusto duol certo a lamentar mi mena
(sassel chi n'è cagione, et sallo Amore),
ch' altro rimedio non avea 'l mio core
contra i fastidi onde la vita è piena;   8

questo un, Morte, m'à tolto la tua mano.
Et tu che copri et guardi et ài or teco,
felice terra! quel bel viso umano: 11

me dove lasci sconsolato et cieco,
poscia che 'l dolce et amoroso et piano
lume degli occhi miei non è più meco?   14

277

If Love does not bring new counsel, I shall have to change my life, so much fear and sorrow press upon my sad soul; for desire lives though hope is dead,

and my life is terrified and unconsoled altogether, night and day it weeps, weary, without a tiller in a stormy sea and on a perilous way without a trusty guide.

An imagined guide is leading it, for the true one is in the earth; rather she is in Heaven, whence she shines through even more brightly to my heart,

not to my eyes, for a sorrowful veil robs them of the light they desire and makes my hair change so early.

278

In her most beautiful, most flourishing age, when Love is wont to have most power over us, leaving her earthly vesture to earth, my vital breeze has departed from me

and, alive and beautiful and naked, has risen to Heaven; from there she rules me, from there she forces me. Ah, why does my last day not divest me of my mortal part, that day which is the first of the next life,

so that, as my thoughts go after her, so, light, unburdened, and glad my soul may follow her, and I may flee this trouble?

All the delay is merely to my loss, to make me a heavier burden to myself. Oh what a beautiful death that would have been, three years ago today!

---

three years ago today: if Petrarch had died the same day as Laura.

277

S' Amor novo consiglio non n'apporta,
per forza converrà che 'l viver cange,
tanta paura et duol l'alma trista ange;
ché 'l desir vive e la speranza è morta,   4

onde si sbigottisce et si sconforta
mia vita in tutto, et notte et giorno piange
stanca, senza governo in mar che frange,
e 'n dubbia via senza fidata scorta.   8

Imaginata guida la conduce,
ché la vera è sotterra; anzi è nel Cielo,
onde più che mai chiara al cor traluce,   11

agli occhi no, ch' un doloroso velo
contende lor la disiata luce
et me fa sì per tempo cangiar pelo.   14

278

Ne l'età sua più bella et più fiorita,
quando aver suol Amor in noi più forza,
lasciando in terra la terrena scorza
è l'aura mia vital da me partita   4

et viva et bella et nuda al Ciel salita;
indi mi signoreggia, indi mi sforza.
Deh, perché me del mio mortal non scorza
l'ultimo dì, ch' è primo a l'altra vita,   8

che, come i miei pensier dietro a lei vanno,
così leve espedita et lieta l'alma
la segua, et io sia fuor di tanto affanno?   11

Ciò che s'indugia è proprio per mio danno,
per far me stesso a me più grave salma.
O che bel morir era, oggi è terzo anno!   14

279

If I hear birds lamenting, or green leaves moving softly in the summer breeze, or the faint murmuring of shining waves from a flowering and fresh bank

where I am sitting in thoughts of love and writing, I see her whom Heaven showed us and the earth hides from us, I see and hear and understand her, for, still alive, from far away she replies to my sighs.

"Ah, why do you consume yourself so before the time?" she says, pityingly. "Why do you still pour forth a sorrowful river from your sad eyes?

"Do not weep for me, for my days became eternal by dying, and, when I seemed to close my eyes, I opened them on the internal light."

280

I have never been anywhere where I could see so clearly what I wish to see, not since I no longer see it, or where I felt so much freedom or filled the heavens with such amorous cries;

nor have I ever seen a valley with so many hidden, trusty places for sighing; nor do I believe that Love ever had, in Cyprus or on any other shore, such sweet nests.

The waters speak of love and the breeze and the branches and the little birds and the fish and the flowers and the grass, all together begging me always to love.

But you, born in a happy hour, who call me from Heaven: by the memory of your untimely death you beg me to scorn the world and its sweet hooks.

On Vaucluse.

279

Se lamentar augelli, o verdi fronde
mover soavemente a l'aura estiva,
o roco mormorar di lucide onde
s'ode d'una fiorita et fresca riva   4

là 'v' io seggia d'amor pensoso et scriva,
lei che 'l Ciel ne mostrò, terra n'asconde
veggio et odo et intendo, ch' ancor viva
di sì lontano a' sospir miei risponde.   8

"Deh, perché inanzi 'l tempo ti consume?"
mi dice con pietate. "A che pur versi
degli occhi tristi un doloroso fiume?   11

"Di me non pianger tu, ch' e' miei dì fersi,
morendo, eterni; et ne l'interno lume,
quando mostrai de chiuder, gli occhi apersi."   14

280

Mai non fui in parte ove sì chiar vedessi
quel che veder vorrei poi ch' io nol vidi,
né dove in tanta libertà mi stessi,
né 'mpiessi il ciel de sì amorosi stridi;   4

né giamai vidi valle aver sì spessi
luoghi da sospirar riposti et fidi,
né credo già ch' Amore in Cipro avessi
o in altra riva sì soavi nidi.   8

L'acque parlan d'amore, et l'òra e i rami,
et gli augelletti e i pesci e i fiori et l'erba,
tutti inseme pregando ch' i' sempre ami.   11

Ma tu, ben nata, che dal Ciel mi chiami,
per la memoria di tua morte acerba
preghi ch' i' sprezzi 'l mondo e i suoi dolci ami.   14

281

How many times, fleeing others and, if it is possible, myself, do I seek my sweet hiding place, bathing with my eyes the grass and my breast, breaking with my sighs the air all around!

How many times alone, full of fear, have I gone into shadowy dark places, seeking in my thought the high delight that Death has taken, so that I often call for Death!

Now in the form of a nymph or other goddess who comes forth from the deepest bed of Sorgue and sits on the bank,

now I have seen her treading the fresh grass like a living woman, showing by her face that she is sorry for me.

---
hiding place: Vaucluse.

282

Happy soul who often come back to console my sorrowing nights with your eyes, which Death has not put out but has made beautiful beyond mortal custom:

how I rejoice that you consent to make glad my sad days with the sight of you! Thus I begin to find your beauties present in their usual surroundings.

Where I went singing of you many years, now, as you see, I go weeping for you—no, not weeping for you but for my loss.

I find but one repose in so much anguish, that when you return I know you, by your walk, by your voice, by your face, by your dress.

---
usual surroundings: Vaucluse.

281

Quante fiate al mio dolce ricetto
fuggendo altrui et, s' esser po, me stesso
vo con gli occhi bagnando l'erba e 'l petto,
rompendo co' sospir l' aere da presso!   4

Quante fiate sol, pien di sospetto,
per luoghi ombrosi et foschi mi son messo,
cercando col penser l'alto diletto
che Morte à tolto, ond' io la chiamo spesso!   8

Or in forma di ninfa o d'altra diva
che del più chiaro fondo di Sorga esca
et pongasi a sedere in su la riva,   11

or l'ò veduto su per l'erba fresca
calcare i fior com' una donna viva,
mostrando in vista che di me le 'ncresca.   14

282

Alma felice che sovente torni
a consolar le mie notti dolenti
con gli occhi tuoi, che morte non à spenti
ma sovra 'l mortal modo fatti adorni :   4

quanto gradisco ch' e' miei tristi giorni
a rallegrar de tua vista consenti!
così comincio a ritrovar presenti
le tue bellezze a' suoi usati soggiorni.   8

Là 've cantando andai di te molt'anni
or, come vedi, vo di te piangendo—
di te piangendo no, ma de' miei danni.   11

Sol un riposo trovo in molti affanni,
che quando torni te conosco e 'ntendo
a l'andar, a la voce, al volto, a' panni.   14

283

You have discolored, Death, the most beautiful face that was ever seen and extinguished the most beautiful eyes; you have loosed the spirit most on fire with ardent virtues from the most charming and most beautiful bodily knot.

In one instant you have taken from me all my wealth; you have imposed silence on the gentlest accents that were ever heard, and filled me with laments: whatever I see and whatever I hear is painful to me.

My lady does indeed come back to console so much sorrow, for pity leads her back, nor do I find any other help in this life:

and if I could tell how she speaks and how she shines, I would inflame with love not only a man's but a tiger's or a bear's heart.

284

So short is the time and the thought so swift which give my lady back to me though she is dead, that the remedy is close by for my great sorrow; as long as I see her, nothing pains me.

Love, who has bound me and keeps me in torment, trembles when he sees her at the gate of the soul, where she still slays me, so alert, so sweet to see, and so gentle of voice.

She comes like a lady to her dwelling, proud, with her clear brow driving out of my dark, heavy heart the sad thoughts;

my soul, who cannot bear so much light, sighs and says: "Oh, blessed the hours of the day when you opened this path with your eyes!"

283

Discolorato ài, Morte, il più bel volto
che mai si vide, e i più begli occhi spenti;
spirto più acceso di vertuti ardenti
del più leggiadro et più bel nodo ài sciolto.   4

In un momento ogni mio ben m'ài tolto,
post' ài silenzio a' più soavi accenti
che mai s'udiro, et me pien di lamenti:
quant' io veggio m'è noia et quant' io ascolto.   8

Ben torna a consolar tanto dolore
Madonna, ove pietà la riconduce,
né trovo in questa vita altro soccorso;   11

et se come ella parla et come luce
ridir potessi, accenderei d'amore
non dirò d'uom, un cor di tigre o d'orso.   14

284

Sì breve è 'l tempo e 'l penser sì veloce
che mi rendon Madonna così morta,
ch' al gran dolor la medicina è corta:
pur mentr' io veggio lei, nulla mi noce.   4

Amor, che m'à legato et tienmi in croce,
trema quando la vede in su la porta
de l'alma, ove m'ancide ancor sì scorta,
si dolce in vista, et sì soave in voce.   8

Come donna in suo albergo altera vene,
scacciando de l'oscuro et grave core
co la fronte serena i pensier tristi;   11

l'alma, che tanta luce non sostene,
sospira et dice: "O benedette l'ore
del dì che questa via con li occhi apristi!"   14

285

Never did a pitying mother to her dear son or a loving wife to her beloved husband give with so many sighs, with such anxiety, such faithful counsel in a perilous time,

as she gives to me, who, seeing from her eternal home my heavy exile, often returns to me with her usual affection and with her brow adorned with double pity,

now that of a mother, now that of a lover. Now she fears, now she burns with virtuous fire; and in her speech she shows me what in this journey I must avoid or pursue,

telling over the events of our life, begging me not to delay in lifting up my soul. And only while she speaks do I have peace—or at least a truce.

286

If I could portray the gentle breath of the sighs that I hear from her who here was my lady (now she is in Heaven but seems to be here and to live and feel and walk and love and breathe),

oh what hot desires would I move by speaking! so assiduous and kind she returns where I am, fearing lest I become weary along the way or turn back or to the left.

She teaches me to go straight up, and I, who understand her chaste allurements and her just prayers with their sweet, low, pitying murmur,

I must rule and bend myself according to her because of the sweetness I take from her words, which would have the power to make a stone weep.

285

Né mai pietosa madre al caro figlio
né donna accesa al suo sposo diletto
die' con tanti sospir, con tal sospetto
in dubbio stato sì fedel consiglio,   4

come a me quella che 'l mio grave esiglio
mirando dal suo eterno alto ricetto
spesso a me torna co l'usato affetto,
et di doppia pietate ornata il ciglio,   8

or di madre, or d'amante. Or teme or arde
d'onesto foco, et nel parlar mi mostra
quel che 'n questo viaggio fugga o segua,   11

contando i casi de la vita nostra,
pregando ch' a levar l'alma non tarde.
Et sol quant' ella parla ò pace, o tregua.   14

286

Se quell'aura soave de' sospiri
ch' i' odo di colei che qui fu mia
donna (or è in Cielo et ancor par qui sia
et viva et senta et vada et ami et spiri)   4

ritrar potessi, or che caldi desiri
movrei parlando, sì gelosa et pia
torna ov' io son, temendo non fra via
mi stanchi o 'ndietro o da man manca giri.   8

Ir dritto alto m'insegna, et io, che 'ntendo
le sue caste lusinghe e i giusti preghi
col dolce mormorar pietoso et basso,   11

secondo lei conven mi regga et pieghi,
per la dolcezza che del suo dir prendo,
ch' avria vertù di far piangere un sasso.   14

287

My Sennuccio, though you have left me alone and sorrowing, still I take comfort that from the body, where you were a prisoner and dead, you have risen high in flight.

Now you see both the one and the other pole and the wandering stars and their winding journey, and you see how short our seeing is; therefore I temper my grief with your joy.

But I beg you to salute all in the third sphere: Guittone and messer Cino and Dante, our Franceschino, and all that band.

To my lady you can well say in how much weeping I live and have become a beast of the woods, remembering her beautiful face and her holy works.

On the death of Petrarch's friend Sennuccio del Bene, a Florentine poet, who died in November 1349.

third sphere: that of the planet Venus, imagined as the dwelling of the souls of love poets: Guittone d'Arezzo, Cino da Pistoia, Dante, Franceschino degli Albizi.

288

I have filled all this air with sighs, gazing from the harsh hills at the sweet plain where she was born, who, having my heart in her hand when budding and when bearing fruit,

has gone to Heaven and has made me such with her sudden parting that my weary eyes, seeking her from afar and in vain, leave no place near them dry.

There is no shrub or stone in these mountains, no branch or green leaf on these slopes, no flower in these valleys, or blade of grass,

no trickle of water comes from these springs, nor do these woods have beasts so savage that they do not know how bitter my sorrow is.

---

hills: those of Vaucluse.   plain: see note to poem 4.

287

Sennuccio mio, benché doglioso et solo
m'abbi lasciato, i' pur mi riconforto,
perché del corpo ov' eri preso et morto
alteramente se' levato a volo.   4

Or vedi inseme l' un et l' altro polo,
le stelle vaghe et lor viaggio torto,
et vedi il veder nostro quanto è corto;
onde col tuo gioir tempro 'l mio duolo.   8

Ma ben ti prego che 'n la terza spera
Guitton saluti, et messer Cino, et Dante,
Franceschin nostro et tutta quella schiera.   11

A la mia donna puoi ben dire in quante
lagrime io vivo et son fatt' una fera,
membrando il suo bel viso et l'opre sante.   14

288

I' ò pien di sospir quest'aere tutto,
d'aspri colli mirando il dolce piano
ove nacque colei ch' avendo in mano
meo cor in sul fiorire e 'n sul far frutto   4

è gita al Cielo, ed àmmi a tal condutto
col subito partir che di lontano
gli occhi miei stanchi lei cercando invano
presso di sé non lassan loco asciutto.   8

Non è sterpo né sasso in questi monti,
non ramo o fronda verde in queste piagge,
non fiore in queste valli o foglia d'erba,   11

stilla d'acqua non ven di queste fonti,
né fiere àn questi boschi sì selvagge,
che non sappian quanto è mia pena acerba.   14

289

The glorious flame that enlivened me, beautiful beyond the beautiful, to whom Heaven was so kind and so courteous here, too early for me has returned to her own country and to her star, which is worthy of her.

Now I begin to awaken, and I see it was for the best that she resisted my desire and tempered those burning youthful lusts with a face both sweet and angry.

I thank her for it and her high counsel, who with her mild face and her gentle angers made me think of my salvation as I burned.

Oh charming arts and worthy effects of them! One of us worked with words, the other with glances: I, glory in her; she, virtue in me.

290

How the world goes! now I am pleased and delighted by what most displeased me, now I see and feel that in order to have salvation I had torment, and brief war for eternal peace.

Oh hope, oh desire, always deceptive and for lovers more so by a hundred times! Oh how much worse it would have been if she had contented me, who is now enthroned in Heaven and lies in earth!

But blind Love and my deaf mind led me so astray that by their lively force I had to go where Death was;

blessed be she who turned my course toward a better shore and, alluring my wicked ardent will, reined it in that I might not perish!

289

L'alma mia fiamma oltra le belle bella,
ch' ebbe qui 'l Ciel sì amico et sì cortese,
anzi tempo per me nel suo paese
è ritornata et a la par sua stella.   4

Or comincio a svegliarmi, et veggio ch' ella
per lo migliore al mio desir contese
et quelle voglie giovenili accese
temprò con una vista dolce et fella.   8

Lei ne ringrazio e 'l suo alto consiglio
che col bel viso e co' soavi sdegni
fecemi ardendo pensar mia salute.   11

O leggiadre arti et lor effetti degni:
l'un co la lingua oprar, l'altra col ciglio,
io gloria in lei, et ella in me virtute!   14

290

Come va 'l mondo! or mi diletta et piace
quel che più mi dispiacque, or veggio et sento
che per aver salute ebbi tormento,
et breve guerra per eterna pace.   4

O speranza, o desir sempre fallace,
et degli amanti più ben per un cento!
O quant' era il peggior farmi contento
quella ch' or siede in Cielo e 'n terra giace!   8

Ma 'l cieco Amor et la mia sorda mente
mi traviavan sì ch' andar per viva
forza mi convenia dove Morte era: 11

benedetta colei ch' a miglior riva
volse il mio corso e l'empia voglia ardente
lusingando affrenò perch' io non pera!   14

291

When I see the dawn coming down from the sky with rosy brow and golden hair, Love assails me, and I turn pale and say, sighing: "There Laura is now.

"O happy Tithonus, you well know the hour when you will recover your dear treasure, but what must I do about the sweet laurel? for if I wish to see it, I must die.

"Your partings are not so hard, for at least at night she comes back, not repelled by your white locks;

"my nights are made sad and my days dark by her who carried off my thoughts and left me nothing of herself but her name."

---

dawn: the goddess Aurora, married to the aged Tithonus.   "There Laura is now": *Laura ora* (Laura now) is a pun on *l'aurora* (the dawn).

292

Those eyes of which I spoke so warmly, and the arms and the hands and the feet and the face that had so estranged me from myself and isolated me from other people,

the curling locks of pure shining gold, and the lightning of the angelic smile that used to make a paradise on earth, all are a bit of dust that feels nothing.

And I still live, at which I am sorrowful and angry, left without the light I loved so, in a great tempest and a dismasted ship.

Now here let there be an end to my song of love; dry is the vein of my accustomed wit, and my lyre is turned to weeping.

291

Quand' io veggio dal ciel scender l'Aurora
co la fronte di rose et co' crin d'oro,
Amor m'assale ond' io mi discoloro
et dico sospirando: "Ivi è Laura ora.   4

"O felice Titòn, tu sai ben l'ora
da ricovrare il tuo caro tesoro;
ma io che debbo far del dolce alloro?
ché se 'l vo' riveder, conven ch' io mora.   8

"I vostri dipartir non son sì duri,
ch' almen di notte suol tornar colei
che non à schifo le tue bianche chiome;   11

"le mie notti fa triste e i giorni oscuri
quella che n'à portato i penser miei,
né di sé m'à lasciato altro che 'l nome."   14

292

Gli occhi di ch' io parlai sì caldamente,
et le braccia et le mani e i piedi e 'l viso
che m'avean sì da me stesso diviso
et fatto singular da l'altra gente,   4

le crespe chiome d'or puro lucente
e 'l lampeggiar de l'angelico riso
che solean fare in terra un paradiso,
poca polvere son che nulla sente.   8

Et io pur vivo, onde mi doglio et sdegno,
rimaso senza 'l lume ch' amai tanto
in gran fortuna e 'n disarmato legno.   11

Or sia qui fine al mio amoroso canto;
secca è la vena de l'usato ingegno,
et la cetera mia rivolta in pianto.   14

293

If I had thought that the sound of my sighs in rhyme would be so pleasing, from the time of my first sighs I would have made them in number more frequent, in style more rare.

Now that she is dead who made me speak, who stood there at the summit of my thought, I cannot—and I no longer have so sweet a file—make harsh, dark rhymes into sweet, bright ones.

And certainly all my effort in that time was only to give vent to my sorrowing heart in some fashion, not to gain fame.

I sought to weep, not to get honor from my weeping; now I am willing to please, but that high one calls me, silent and weary, after her.

294

Beautiful and lively she used to stay in my heart like a high lady in a humble, low place; now I have become, with her passing, not merely mortal, but dead, and she is a goddess.

My soul, despoiled and deprived of all its wealth, and Love, naked and broken of his light, ought to break a stone with pity; but there is no one to tell or write their sorrow,

for they weep within, where every ear is deaf except mine, who am burdened by so much pain that nothing is left to me but sighing.

Truly, we are dust and shadow; truly, desire is blind and greedy; truly, hope deceives.

293

S' io avesse pensato che sì care
fossin le voci de' sospir miei in rima,
fatte l'avrei dal sospirar mio prima
in numero più spesse, in stil più rare.   4

Morta colei che mi facea parlare
et che si stava de' pensier miei in cima,
non posso, et non ò più sì dolce lima,
rime aspre et fosche far soavi et chiare.   8

Et certo ogni mio studio in quel tempo era
pur di sfogare il doloroso core
in qualche modo, non d'acquistar fama.   11

Pianger cercai, non già del pianto onore;
or vorrei ben piacer, ma quella altera
tacito stanco dopo sé mi chiama.   14

294

Soleasi nel mio cor star bella et viva
com' alta donna in loco umile et basso;
or son fatto io, per l'ultimo suo passo,
non pur mortal, ma morto, et ella è diva.   4

L'alma d'ogni suo ben spogliata et priva,
Amor de la sua luce ignudo et casso,
devrian de la pietà romper un sasso;
ma non è chi lor duol riconti o scriva,   8

ché piangon dentro, ov' ogni orecchia è sorda
se non la mia, cui tanta doglia ingombra
ch' altro che sospirar nulla m'avanza.   11

Veramente siam noi polvere et ombra,
veramente la voglia cieca e 'ngorda,
veramente fallace è la speranza.   14

295

My thoughts used to converse together gently about their object: "She will soon feel pity and be sorry for the delay; perhaps she now speaks of us, or hopes, or fears."

Since the last day and the final hour have despoiled this present life of her, she sees, hears, and feels our state from Heaven: no other hope of her remains.

Oh noble miracle! Oh happy soul! Oh high, rare, unexampled beauty, which soon returned whence it came!

There for her good works she has a crown and palm, who made so bright and famous in the world her virtue and my madness.

296

I used to accuse myself and now I excuse, rather I praise myself and hold myself much more dear for the worthy prison, for the sweet bitter blow that I have kept hidden for so many years.

Envious Fates, you so soon broke the spindle that was spinning a soft, bright thread around my bonds, and that rare golden arrow for which death was pleasing beyond our custom!

For there was never a soul so in love with gaiety in its days, with liberty, with life, that it would not change its natural tendency

and choose rather always to groan for her than to sing for anyone else, and to die content with such a wound, and to live in such a bond.

295

Soleano i miei penser soavemente
di lor oggetto ragionare inseme:
"Pietà s'appressa et del tardar si pente;
forse or parla di noi, o spera o teme."   4

Poi che l'ultimo giorno et l'ore estreme
spogliar di lei questa vita presente,
nostro stato dal Ciel vede, ode et sente;
altra di lei non è rimaso speme.   8

O miracol gentile, o felice alma,
o beltà senza esempio altera et rara
che tosto è ritornata ond' ella uscio!   11

Ivi à del suo ben far corona et palma
quella ch' al mondo sì famosa et chiara
fe' la sua gran vertute e 'l furor mio.   14

296

I' mi soglio accusare, et or mi scuso,
anzi mi pregio et tengo assai più caro,
de l'onesta pregion, del dolce amaro
colpo ch' i' portai già molt'anni chiuso.   4

Invide Parche, sì repente il fuso
troncaste ch' attorcea soave et chiaro
stame al mio laccio, et quello aurato et raro
strale onde morte piacque oltra nostro uso!   8

Ché non fu d'allegrezza a' suoi dì mai,
di libertà, di vita, alma sì vaga
che non cangiasse 'l suo natural modo,   11

togliendo anzi per lei sempre trar guai
che cantar per qualunque, et di tal piaga
morir contento, et vivere in tal nodo.   14

297

Two great enemies were united, Beauty and Chastity, with so much peace that her holy soul never felt any rebellion once they had come to stay with her.

And now Death has scattered and separated them: one is in Heaven, which glories and vaunts of it; the other in the earth, which mantles the lovely eyes from which so many amorous darts used to come forth.

The gentle manner, and the wise, humble speech that came from a high place, and the sweet glance that used to wound my heart (it still shows it)

have disappeared; and if I am slow to follow, perhaps it will happen that I shall consecrate her lovely noble name with this weary pen.

298

When I turn back to gaze at the years that fleeing have scattered all my thoughts, and put out the fire where I freezing burned, and ended my laboring repose,

broken the faith of amorous deceptions, and turned all my wealth into two parts only (one is in Heaven, the other in the ground), and destroyed the profit of my losses,

I shake myself and find myself so naked that I am envious of every most extreme misfortune, such anguish and fear I have for myself.

O my Star, O Fortune, O Fate, O Death, O Day to me always sweet and cruel, how you have put me in low estate!

Day: April 6 (see poems 211 and 336).

297

Due gran nemiche inseme erano agiunte,
Bellezza et Onestà, con pace tanta
che mai rebellion l'anima santa
non sentì poi ch' a star seco fur giunte.   4

Et or per Morte son sparse et disgiunte:
l'una è nel Ciel che se ne gloria et vanta,
l'altra sotterra che' begli occhi amanta
onde uscir già tant' amorose punte.   8

L'atto soave, e 'l parlar saggio umile
che movea d'alto loco, e 'l dolce sguardo
che piagava il mio core (ancor l'acenna)   11

sono spariti; et s' al seguir son tardo,
forse averrà che 'l bel nome gentile
consacrerò con questa stanca penna.   14

298

Quand' io mi volgo indietro a mirar gli anni
ch' ànno fuggendo i miei penseri sparsi,
et spento 'l foco ove agghiacciando io arsi,
et finito il riposo pien d'affanni,   4

rotta la fé degli amorosi inganni,
et sol due parti d'ogni mio ben farsi,
l'una nel Cielo et l'altra in terra starsi,
et perduto il guadagno de' miei danni,   8

i' mi riscuoto, et trovomi sì nudo
ch' i' porto invidia ad ogni estrema sorte,
tal cordoglio et paura ò di me stesso.   11

O mia Stella, o Fortuna, o Fato, o Morte,
o per me sempre dolce Giorno et crudo,
come m'avete in basso stato messo!   14

299

Where is the forehead that with a little sign used to turn my heart this way and that? Where is the lovely brow and the two stars that gave light to the course of my life?

Where is the worth, the knowledge, and the wisdom? the skillful virtuous humble sweet speech? Where are the beauties gathered in her, which for a long time had their will of me?

Where is the noble image of the kindly face that gave refreshment and repose to my tired soul and where all my thoughts were written?

Where is she who held my life in her hand? How much the miserable world has lost, and how much my eyes have lost, which will never be dry!

300

How I envy you, greedy earth that embrace her whose sight is taken from me, and keep from me the breath of the lovely face where I found peace from all my war!

How I envy Heaven, which encloses and locks in and has so eagerly gathered to itself the spirit freed from her beautiful members, but so rarely unlocks itself for others!

How I envy those souls whose fate is now to have her sweet holy company, which (with what desire!) I have always sought!

How I envy pitiless hard Death, who, having extinguished my life in her, now stays in her lovely eyes and does not call me!

299

Ov' è la fronte che con picciol cenno
volgea il mio core in questa parte e 'n quella?
Ov' è 'l bel ciglio et l'una et l'altra stella
ch' al corso del mio viver lume denno?   4

Ov' è 'l valor, la conoscenza e 'l senno?
l'accorta, onesta, umil, dolce favella?
Ove son le bellezze accolte in ella
che gran tempo di me lor voglia fenno?   8

Ov' è l'ombra gentil del viso umano
ch' ora et riposo dava a l'alma stanca
et là 've i miei pensier scritti eran tutti?   11

Ov' è colei che mia vita ebbe in mano?
Quanto al misero mondo, et quanto manca
agli occhi miei che mai non fien asciutti!   14

300

Quanta invidia io ti porto, avara terra
ch' abbracci quella cui veder m'è tolto
et mi contendi l'aria del bel volto
dove pace trovai d'ogni mia guerra!   4

Quanta ne porto al Ciel che chiude et serra
et sì cupidamente à in sé raccolto
lo spirto da le belle membra sciolto,
et per altrui sì rado si diserra!   8

Quanta invidia a quell'anime che 'n sorte
ànno or sua santa et dolce compagnia,
la qual io cercai sempre con tal brama!   11

Quant' a la dispietata et dura Morte,
ch' avendo spento in lei la vita mia
stassi ne' suoi begli occhi et me non chiama!   14

301

O valley full of my laments, river often rising by my weeping, beasts of the forest, wandering birds, and fishes that these two banks rein in,

air warmed and cleared by my sighs, sweet path become so bitter, hill that pleased and now displeases me, where still Love leads me as he is wont:

I recognize in you your accustomed forms, not, alas, mine in myself, for I have become after such gladness the dwelling of infinite grief.

From here I used to see my love, and with these steps I come back to see the place whence she went naked to Heaven, leaving on earth her beautiful vesture.

---

valley: Vaucluse.   river: the Sorgue.

302

My thought lifted me up to where she was whom I seek and do not find on earth; there, among those whom the third circle encloses, I saw her more beautiful and less proud.

She took me by the hand and said: "In this sphere you will be with me, if my desire is not deceived; I am she who gave you so much war and completed my day before evening.

"My blessedness no human intellect can comprehend: I only wait for you and for that which you loved so much and which remained down there, my lovely veil."

Ah, why did she then become still and open her hand? for at the sound of words so kind and chaste, I almost remained in Heaven.

---

third circle: see note to poem 287.   my lovely veil: my body.

301

Valle che de' lamenti miei se' piena,
fiume che spesso del mio pianger cresci,
fere selvestre, vaghi augelli, et pesci
che l'una et l'altra verde riva affrena: 4

aria de' miei sospir calda et serena,
dolce sentier che sì amaro riesci,
colle che mi piacesti, or mi rincresci,
ov' ancor per usanza Amor mi mena: 8

ben riconosco in voi l'usate forme,
non, lasso, in me, che da sì lieta vita
son fatto albergo d'infinita doglia.   11

Quinci vedea 'l mio bene, et per queste orme
torno a vedere ond' al Ciel nuda è gita,
lasciando in terra la sua bella spoglia.   14

302

Levommi il mio penser in parte ov' era
quella ch' io cerco et non ritrovo in terra;
ivi fra lor che 'l terzo cerchio serra
la rividi più bella et meno altera.   4

Per man mi prese et disse: "In questa spera
sarai ancor meco, se 'l desir non erra;
i' so' colei che ti die' tanta guerra
et compie' mia giornata inanzi sera.   8

"Mio ben non cape in intelletto umano;
te solo aspetto, et quel che tanto amasti
et là giuso è rimaso, il mio bel velo."   11

Deh, perché tacque et allargò la mano?
ch' al suon de' detti sì pietosi et casti,
poco mancò ch' io non rimasi in Cielo.   14

303

Love, who in the happy time stayed with me along these banks so friendly to our thoughts, and used to walk talking with me and with the river, to settle our old accounts:

flowers, leaves, grass, shadows, caves, waves, gentle breezes, closed valleys, high hills, and open slopes, harbor of my amorous laborings, of my so frequent and so heavy storms:

O wandering inhabitants of the green woods, O nymphs, and you whom the fresh grassy floor of the liquid crystal shelters and feeds:

my days were so bright, now they are as dark as Death who causes it! Thus in the world each has his destiny from the day he is born.

---

these banks: the banks of the Sorgue in Vaucluse.

304

While my heart was consumed by the worms of love and burned in an amorous flame, I sought on solitary and wild hills the scattered footprints of a wandering wild creature,

and I dared, singing, to complain of Love and of her who seemed so cruel to me; but wit and rhymes came scantily at that age to my new and faltering thoughts.

That fire is dead and a little marble covers it: if it had gone on growing with time, as it does in others, into old age,

armed with the rhymes of which today I am disarmed, with a mature style I would speaking have made the very stones break and weep with sweetness.

---

hills: the hills near Vaucluse.

303

Amor, che meco al buon tempo ti stavi
fra queste rive a' pensier nostri amiche,
et per saldar le ragion nostre antiche
meco et col fiume ragionando andavi: 4

fior, frondi, erbe, ombre, antri, onde, aure soavi,
valli chiuse, alti colli, et piagge apriche,
porto de l'amorose mie fatiche,
de le fortune mie tante et sì gravi: 8

o vaghi abitator de' verdi boschi,
o ninfe et voi che 'l fresco erboso fondo
del liquido cristallo alberga et pasce: 11

i dì miei fur sì chiari, or son sì foschi
come Morte che 'l fa! così nel mondo
sua ventura à ciascun dal dì che nasce.   14

304

Mentre che 'l cor dagli amorosi vermi
fu consumato e 'n fiamma amorosa arse,
di vaga fera le vestigia sparse
cercai per poggi solitari et ermi;   4

et ebbi ardir, cantando, di dolermi
d'Amor, di lei che sì dura m'apparse,
ma l'ingegno et le rime erano scarse
in quella etate ai pensier novi e 'nfermi.   8

Quel foco è morto e 'l copre un picciol marmo
che se col tempo fossi ito avanzando
(come già in altri) infino a la vecchiezza,   11

di rime armato ond' oggi mi disarmo,
con stil canuto, avrei fatto parlando
romper le pietre et pianger di dolcezza.   14

305

Beautiful soul, freed from that knot more beautiful than any
Nature ever made: from Heaven give thought to my dark life,
turned to weeping from such glad thoughts.

Gone from your heart is the false opinion that made your sweet
face sometimes harsh and cruel toward me; now all carefree turn
your eyes to me and listen to my sighs.

Gaze at the great rock from which Sorgue is born, and you will
see there one who among the grass and the waters feeds only on
your memory and on sorrow;

he wishes you to abandon and leave your dwelling where our
love was born, in order not to see in your people what
displeased you.

---

knot: the union of body and soul.　　rock from which Sorgue is born: the
fountain of Vaucluse is at the foot of a spectacular cliff.

306

That sun which showed me the right way to go to Heaven with
glorious steps, returning to the highest Sun, has closed up in a
few stones my light and her earthly prison,

so that I have become an animal of the woods, and with wandering, solitary, and weary feet I carry about a heavy heart and
eyes wet and cast down in the world, which is for me a
mountainous desert.

Thus I go searching through every region where I saw her, and
only you who afflict me, Love, come with me and show me
where to go;

her I do not find, but I see her holy footprints all turned toward
the road to Heaven, far from the Avernian and the Stygian
lakes.

---

her earthly prison: her body.　　Avernian and the Stygian lakes: Lake
Avernus, near Naples, thought to be an entrance to the underworld, and the
Styx, mythological river of the underworld.

305

Anima bella, da quel nodo sciolta
che più bel mai non seppe ordir Natura :
pon dal Ciel mente a la mia vita oscura,
da sì lieti pensieri a pianger volta.   4

La falsa opinion dal cor s'è tolta
che mi fece alcun tempo acerba et dura
tua dolce vista ; omai tutta secura
volgi a me gli occhi e i miei sospiri ascolta.   8

Mira 'l gran sasso donde Sorga nasce,
et vedra'vi un che sol tra l'erbe et l'acque
di tua memoria et di dolor si pasce ;   11

ove giace il tuo albergo et dove nacque
il nostro amor vo' ch' abbandoni et lasce,
per non veder ne' tuoi quel ch' a te spiacque.   14

306

Quel sol che mi mostrava il cammin destro
di gire al Ciel con gloriosi passi,
tornando al sommo Sole, in pochi sassi
chiuse 'l mio lume e 'l suo carcer terrestro,   4

ond' io son fatto un animal silvestro
che co' pie vaghi, solitari et lassi
porto 'l cor grave et gli occhi umidi et bassi
al mondo, ch' è per me un deserto alpestro.   8

Così vo ricercando ogni contrada
ov' io la vidi ; et sol tu che m'affligi,
Amor, vien meco et mostrimi ond' io vada ;   11

lei non trov' io, ma suoi santi vestigi
tutti rivolti a la superna strada
veggio, lunge da' laghi averni et stigi.   14

307

I thought I was skillful enough in flight (not by my power, but by his who spreads my wings) to sing worthily of that lovely knot from which Death looses me, with which Love binds me.

I found myself much more slow and frail in operation than a little branch bent by a great burden, and I said: "He flies to fall who mounts too high, nor can a man well do what the heavens deny him."

Never could any pinion of wit, let alone a heavy style or tongue, fly so high as Nature did when she made my sweet impediment;

Love followed Nature with such marvelous care to adorn her that I was not worthy even to see her: but my good fortune willed it.

308

She for whom I exchanged Arno for Sorgue and slavish riches for free poverty, turned her holy sweetness, on which I once lived, into bitterness, by which now I am destroyed and disfleshed.

Since then I have often tried in vain to depict in song for the age to come her high beauties, that it may love and prize them, nor with my style can I incarnate her lovely face.

Still now and again I dare to adumbrate one or two of the praises that were always hers, never any other's, that were as many as the stars spread across the sky;

but when I come to her divine part, which was a bright, brief sun to the world, there fails my daring, my wit, and my art.

---

exchanged Arno for Sorgue: chose to live in Vaucluse rather than in Florence.

307

I' pensava assai destro esser su l'ale
(non per lor forza, ma di chi le spiega)
per gir cantando a quel bel nodo eguale
onde Morte m'assolve, Amor mi lega.   4

Trovaimi a l'opra via più lento et frale
d'un picciol ramo cui gran fascio piega,
et dissi: "A cader va chi troppo sale,
né si fa ben per uom quel che 'l ciel nega."   8

Mai non poria volar penna d'ingegno,
non che stil grave o lingua, ove Natura
volò tessendo il mio dolce ritegno;   11

seguilla Amor con sì mirabil cura
in adornarlo, ch' i' non era degno
pur de la vista: ma fu mia ventura.   14

308

Quella per cui con Sorga ò cangiato Arno,
con franca povertà serve ricchezze,
volse in amaro sue sante dolcezze
ond' io già vissi, or me ne struggo et scarno.   4

Da poi più volte ò riprovato indarno
al secol che verrà l'alte bellezze
pinger cantando, a ciò che l'ame et prezze,
né col mio stile il suo bel viso incarno.   8

Le lode, mai non d'altra et proprie sue,
che 'n lei fur come stelle in cielo sparte,
pur ardisco ombreggiare, or una or due;   11

ma poi ch' i' giungo a la divina parte,
ch' un chiaro et breve sole al mondo fue.
ivi manca l'ardir, l'ingegno et l'arte.   14

309

The high new miracle that in our days appeared in the world and did not wish to stay in it, that Heaven merely showed to us and then took back to adorn its starry cloisters,

Love, who first set free my tongue, wishes me to depict and show her to whoever did not see her, and therefore a thousand times he has vainly put to work wit, time, pens, papers, inks.

Poetry has not yet reached the summit, I know it in myself and anyone knows it who up to now has spoken or written of Love;

he who knows how to think, let him esteem the silent truth which surpasses every style, and then let him sigh: "Therefore blessed the eyes that saw her alive!"

310

Zephyrus returns and leads back the fine weather and the flowers and the grass, his sweet family, and chattering Procne and weeping Philomena, and Spring, all white and vermilion;

the meadows laugh and the sky becomes clear again, Jupiter is gladdened looking at his daughter, the air and the waters and the earth are full of love, every animal takes counsel again to love.

But to me, alas, come back heavier sighs, which she draws from my deepest heart, she who carried off to Heaven the keys to it;

and the singing of little birds, and the flowering of meadows, and virtuous gentle gestures in beautiful ladies are a wilderness and cruel, savage beasts.

Zephyrus: the west wind.   Procne: the swallow.   Philomena: the nightingale.   Jupiter...daughter: the planets Jupiter and Venus are in favorable relation.

309

L' alto et novo miracol ch' a' dì nostri
apparve al mondo et star seco non volse,
che sol ne mostrò 'l Ciel, poi sel ritolse
per adornarne i suoi stellanti chiostri,   4

vuol ch' i' depinga a chi nol vide e 'l mostri
Amor, che 'n prima la mia lingua sciolse;
poi mille volte indarno a l'opra volse
ingegno, tempo, penne, carte, enchiostri.   8

Non son al sommo ancor giunte le rime,
in me il conosco, et proval ben chiunque
è 'nfin a qui che d'Amor parli o scriva;   11

chi sa pensare, il ver tacito estime
ch' ogni stil vince, et poi sospire: "Adunque
beati gli occhi che la vider viva!"   14

310

Zefiro torna e 'l bel tempo rimena
e i fiori et l'erbe, sua dolce famiglia,
et garrir Progne et pianger Filomena,
et Primavera candida et vermiglia;   4

ridono i prati e 'l ciel si rasserena,
Giove s'allegra di mirar sua figlia,
l'aria et l'acqua et la terra è d'amor piena,
ogni animal d'amar si riconsiglia.   8

Ma per me, lasso, tornano i più gravi
sospiri che del cor profondo tragge
quella ch' al Ciel se ne portò le chiavi;   11

et cantar augelletti, et fiorir piagge,
e 'n belle donne oneste atti soavi
sono un deserto et fere aspre et selvagge.   14

311

That nightingale that so sweetly weeps, perhaps for his children or for his dear consort, fills the sky and the fields with sweetness in so many grieving, skillful notes,

and all night he seems to accompany me and remind me of my harsh fate; for I have no one to complain of save myself, who did not believe that Death reigns over goddesses.

Oh how easy it is to deceive one who is confident! Those two lights much brighter than the sun, who ever thought to see them become dark clay?

Now I know that my fierce destiny wishes me to learn, living and weeping, how nothing down here both pleases and endures!

312

Not wandering stars going through the clear sky, nor oiled ships through calm seas, nor armed knights through the fields, nor swift happy wild creatures in lovely woods,

nor fresh news of a hoped-for good, nor poems of love in high and ornate style, nor amid clear fountains and green meadows the sweet singing of virtuous and beautiful ladies,

nor will there ever be anything else that can reach my heart: she has so buried it who was alone the light and mirror to my eyes.

Living is such heavy and long pain, that I call out for the end in my great desire to see her again whom it would have been better not to have seen at all.

311

Quel rosigniuol che sì soave piagne
forse suoi figli o sua cara consorte,
di dolcezza empie il cielo et le campagne
con tante note sì pietose et scorte,   4

et tutta notte par che m'accompagne
et mi rammente la mia dura sorte;
ch' altri che me non ò di chi mi lagne,
che 'n dee non credev' io regnasse Morte.   8

O che lieve è inganar chi s'assecura!
Que' duo bei lumi assai più che 'l sol chiari
chi pensò mai veder far terra oscura?   11

Or cognosco io che mia fera ventura
vuol che vivendo et lagrimando impari
come nulla qua giù diletta et dura.   14

312

Né per sereno ciel ir vaghe stelle,
né per tranquillo mar legni spalmati,
né per campagne cavalieri armati,
né per bei boschi allegre fere et snelle,   4

né d'aspettato ben fresche novelle,
né dir d'amore in stili alti et ornati,
né tra chiare fontane et verdi prati
dolce cantare oneste donne et belle,   8

né altro sarà mai ch' al cor m'aggiunga:
sì seco il seppe quella sepellire
che sola agli occhi miei fu lume et speglio.   11

Noia m'è 'l viver sì gravosa et lunga
ch' i' chiamo il fine per lo gran desire
di riveder cui non veder fu 'l meglio.   14

313

The time has passed now, alas, when I lived so much refreshed amid the fire; that one has passed on for whom I wept and wrote, but she has left me still my pen and my weeping.

That face is gone, so charming and holy, but as it passed it pierced my heart with its lovely eyes, that heart once mine, which departed, following her who had wrapped it in her beautiful mantle.

She carried it off with her under the ground, and to Heaven where now she triumphs adorned with the laurel that her un-vanquished chastity has merited.

Would that I, alas, freed from my mortal veil, which keeps me here by force, were with them, beyond sighs, among the blessed souls!

314

O my mind, who, foreseeing your losses, already thoughtful and sad in the happy time, so intently in her beloved sight sought rest from the future troubles:

you could well have said, at her gestures, at her words, at her face, at her garments, at her new pity mixed with sorrow, if you had been aware of it all: "This is the last day of my sweet years."

What sweetness was it, O wretched soul, how we burned in that moment, when I saw those eyes I was never to see again,

when at parting I left in their keeping, as in that of my two most faithful friends, my noblest treasure—my dear thoughts and my heart!

313

Passato è 'l tempo omai, lasso, che tanto
con refrigerio in mezzo 'l foco vissi;
passato è quella di ch' io piansi et scrissi,
ma lasciato m'à ben la penna e 'l pianto.   4

Passato è 'l viso sì leggiadro et santo,
ma passando i dolci occhi al cor m'à fissi:
al cor già mio che seguendo partissi
lei ch' avolto l'avea nel suo bel manto.   8

Ella 'l se ne portò sotterra, e 'n Cielo
ove or triunfa ornata de l'alloro
che meritò la sua invitta onestate.   11

Così disciolto dal mortal mio velo,
ch' a forza mi tien qui, foss' io con loro
fuor de' sospir, fra l'anime beate!   14

314

Mente mia, che presaga de' tuoi danni,
al tempo lieto già pensosa et trista,
sì 'ntentamente ne l'amata vista
requie cercavi de' futuri affanni: 4

agli atti, a le parole, al viso, ai panni,
a la nova pietà con dolor mista
potei ben dir, se del tutto eri avista:
"Questo è l'ultimo dì de' miei dolci anni."   8

Qual dolcezza fu quella, misera alma,
come ardevamo in quel punto ch' i' vidi
gli occhi i quai non devea riveder mai,   11

quando a lor, come a' duo amici più fidi,
partendo in guardia la più nobil salma,
i miei cari penseri e 'l cor, lasciai!   14

315

All my flowering, green age was passing, and I already felt the fire that burned my heart becoming cool, and I had reached the place from which life declines toward the end;

my dear enemy was already beginning little by little to gain confidence against her fears, and her sweet chastity was turning into joys my bitter pains;

the time was near when Love can be reconciled with Chastity and lovers may sit down together and say what occurs to them.

Death envied my happy state, rather my hope, and she attacked it in the middle of the way like an armed enemy.

316

It was by then time to find peace or truce from so much war, and it was perhaps under way, except that those glad steps were turned back by Death, who evens out all our inequalities;

for as a cloud is dissolved in the wind, so quickly did her life pass away, hers who used to guide me with her lovely eyes, and whom I now must follow with my thoughts.

She only needed to wait a little, for years and gray hair were changing my habits, so that she would not have needed to fear my speaking to her of my ills;

with what virtuous sighs I would have told her of my long labors! which now from Heaven she sees, I am certain, and, what is more, is sorry for them with me.

315

Tutta la mia fiorita et verde etade
passava, e 'ntepidir sentia già 'l foco
ch' arse il mio core, et era giunto al loco
ove scende la vita ch' al fin cade;   4

già incominciava a prender securtade
la mia cara nemica a poco a poco
de' suoi sospetti, et rivolgeva in gioco
mie pene acerbe sua dolce onestade;   8

presso era 'l tempo dove Amor si scontra
con Castitate et agli amanti è dato
sedersi inseme et dir che lor incontra.   11

Morte ebbe invidia al mio felice stato,
anzi a la speme, et feglisi a l'incontra
a mezza via come nemico armato.   14

316

Tempo era omai da trovar pace o tregua
di tanta guerra, et erane in via, forse,
se non che' lieti passi indietro torse
chi le disaguaglianze nostre adegua;   4

ché come nebbia al vento si dilegua
così sua vita subito trascorse
quella che già co' begli occhi mi scorse,
et or conven che col penser la segua.   8

Poco aveva a 'ndugiar che gli anni e 'l pelo
cangiavano i costumi, onde sospetto
non fora il ragionar del mio mal seco;   11

con che onesti sospiri l'avrei detto
le mie lunghe fatiche! ch' or dal Cielo
vede, son certo, et duolsene ancor meco.   14

317

Love had shown me a tranquil harbor from my long and turbid storm—the years of virtuous maturity that divests itself of vice and puts on virtue and honor.

My heart and my high faithfulness were now visible to her lovely eyes and no longer displeasing to them. Ah, cruel Death, how quick you are to shatter in so few hours the fruit of many years!

If only she had lived, we would have come to where, speaking, I could have put down in those chaste ears the ancient burden of my sweet thoughts,

and she would perhaps have answered me with some holy word, sighing, though our faces were changed, and the hair of both.

318

At the fall of a tree that was uprooted as if by steel or wind, scattering on the ground its rich leaves, showing its pale root to the sun,

I saw another tree, which Love chose as his object in me, which Calliope and Euterpe chose as their subject in me; it bound my heart and made it its own dwelling, as ivy snakes along a trunk or a wall.

That living laurel, where my high thoughts used to make their nest and my burning sighs that never moved a leaf of the lovely branches,

translated to Heaven, left in that faithful dwelling its roots, whence there is one who calls out with heavy accents, but there is no one to answer.

---

fall of a tree: death of the laurel (Laura's body).   another tree: the living laurel (Laura's soul; no doubt also the laurel as poetry).   Calliope: chief of the Muses, patroness especially of love poetry and epic.   Euterpe: Muse of music.

317

Tranquillo porto avea mostrato Amore
a la mia lunga et torbida tempesta
fra gli anni de la età matura, onesta,
che i vizi spoglia et vertù veste e onore;   4

già traluceva a' begli occhi il mio core
et l'alta fede non più lor molesta.
Ahi, Morte ria, come a schiantar se' presta
il frutto de molt'anni in sì poche ore!   8

Pur vivendo veniasi ove deposto
in quelle caste orecchie avrei, parlando,
de' miei dolci pensier l'antica soma,   11

et ella avrebbe a me forse resposto
qualche santa parola sospirando,
cangiati i volti et l'una et l'altra coma.   14

318

Al cader d'una pianta che si svelse
come quella che ferro o vento sterpe,
spargendo a terra le sue spoglie eccelse,
mostrando al sol la sua squalida sterpe,   4

vidi un'altra, ch' Amor obietto scelse,
subietto in me Calliope et Euterpe,
che 'l cor m'avinse et proprio albergo felse,
qual per trunco o per muro edera serpe.   8

Quel vivo lauro, ove solean far nido
li alti penseri e i miei sospiri ardenti
che de' bei rami mai non mossen fronda,   11

al Ciel translato, in quel suo albergo fido
lasciò radici onde con gravi accenti
è ancor chi chiami, et non è chi responda.   14

319

My days, swifter than any deer, have fled like a shadow and
have seen no good any longer than an instant, and few cloudless
hours, which bitter and sweet I preserve in my memory.

Wretched world, unstable and obstinate! He is entirely blind
who puts his hopes in you! For in you my heart was taken away,
and one holds it who is dust and does not join bone to muscle.

But her better form, which still lives and shall always live up in
the highest Heaven, makes me ever more in love with her
beauties,

and I go with my hair turning, only thinking of what she is like
today and where she dwells, and what her lovely veil is to see.

---

her better form: Laura's soul (the form of her body).

320

I feel the old breeze, and I see appearing the sweet hills where the
light was born that kept my eyes full of desire and gladness,
while it pleased Heaven, and now keeps them sad and wet.

Oh short-lived hopes, oh mad cares! The grass is bereaved and
the waters troubled, and empty and cold is the nest where she
lay, where I have wished to lie living and dead,

hoping to have from her gentle footprints and her lovely glance,
which so burned my heart, some repose from my many labors.

I have served a cruel and niggardly lord: I burned as long as
my fire was before me, now I go bewailing the scattering of its
ashes.

---

breeze: in Vat. Lat. 3195 Petrarch spells this word *Laura,* emphasizing the
pun.

319

I dì miei più leggier che nesun cervo
fuggir come ombra, et non vider più bene
ch' un batter d'occhio, et poche ore serene
ch' amare et dolci ne la mente servo.   4

Misero mondo instabile et protervo!
del tutto è cieco chi 'n te pon sua spene,
ché 'n te mi fu 'l cor tolto, et or sel tene
tal ch' è già terra et non giunge osso a nervo.   8

Ma la forma miglior che vive ancora
et vivrà sempre su ne l' alto cielo,
di sue bellezze ogni or piu m'innamora;   11

et vo sol in pensar cangiando il pelo ,
quale ella è oggi e 'n qual parte dimora,
qual a vedere il suo leggiadro velo.   14

320

Sento l'aura mia antica, e i dolci colli
veggio apparire onde 'l bel lume nacque
che tenne gli occhi mei, mentr' al Ciel piacque,
bramosi et lieti, or li ten tristi et molli.   4

O caduche speranze, o penser folli!
vedove l'erbe et torbide son l'acque
et voto et freddo 'l nido in ch' ella giacque,
nel qual io vivo et morto giacer volli,   8

sperando alfin da le soavi piante
et da' belli occhi suoi, che 'l cor m'ànn' arso,
riposo alcun de le fatiche tante.   11

O' servito a signor crudele et scarso:
ch' arsi quanto 'l mio foco ebbi davante,
or vo piangendo il suo cenere sparso.   14

321

Is this the nest where my phoenix put on her gold and purple feathers, where she kept my heart beneath her wings and still wrings from it words and sighs?

O first root of my sweet harms, where is the lovely face whence came the light that kept me alive and glad though burning? You were unique on earth, now you are happy in Heaven,

and you have left me here wretched and alone, so that full of grief I return always to the place that I honor and adore as consecrated to you,

seeing dark night around the hills whence you took your last flight to Heaven and where your eyes used to make day.

---

nest where . . . feathers: Laura's birthplace.

322

Never with dry eyes or with tranquil mind shall I look at those notes in which Love seems to sparkle and which Kindness seems to have made with his very hand.

Spirit once unvanquished by earthly mourning, you who now from Heaven pour down so much sweetness that you have brought back my wandering rhymes to the style from which Death separated them:

I thought to show you some other work of my young leaves; and what cruel planet was displeased to see us together, O my noble treasure?

Who forbids and hides you from me so soon, whom in my heart I see and with my tongue I honor? And in you, sweet sighing, my soul is quieted.

A reply, using the same rhymes, to a sonnet by Giacomo Colonna, who died in September 1341 (Appendix One, p. 609). In his working papers Petrarch entitled this poem "Responsio mea. Sero valde" (My reply. Late indeed), and dated it December 5, 1366.

notes: the words of Giacomo Colonna's sonnet.   young leaves: a reference to Petrarch's crowning as poet laureate, which took place on Easter Sunday, 1341, in Rome.

321

E' questo 'l nido in che la mia fenice
mise l'aurate et le purpuree penne,
che sotto le sue ali il mio cor tenne
et parole et sospiri anco n'elice?   4

O del dolce mio mal prima radice,
ov' è il bel viso onde quel lume venne
che vivo et lieto ardendo mi mantenne?
Sol eri in terra, or se' nel Ciel felice   8

et m'ài lasciato qui misero et solo,
tal che pien di duol sempre al loco torno
che per te consecrato onoro et colo,   11

veggendo a' colli oscura notte intorno
onde prendesti al Ciel l'ultimo volo
et dove li occhi tuoi solean far giorno.   14

322

Mai non vedranno le mie luci asciutte
con le parti de l'animo tranquille
quelle note ov' Amor par che sfaville
et Pietà di sua man l'abbia construtte.   4

Spirto già invitto a le terrene lutte,
ch' or su dal Ciel tanta dolcezza stille
ch'a lo stil onde Morte dipartille
le disviate rime ài ricondutte :   8

di mie tenere frondi altro lavoro
credea mostrarte ; et qual fero pianeta
ne'nvidiò inseme, o mio nobil tesoro?   11

chi 'nnanzi tempo mi t'asconde et vieta
che col cor veggio et co la lingua onoro?
E 'n te, dolce sospir, l'alma s'acqueta.   14

323

Being one day alone at the window, where I saw so many and such strange things that from the mere seeing I was already almost tired,

a wild creature appeared to me on the right hand, with a human face such as to enamor Jove, pursued by two hounds, one black, one white,

who at both sides of the noble creature were tearing so fiercely that in a short time they brought it to the pass where, closed in a stone, much beauty was vanquished by untimely death and made me sigh for its harsh fate.

Then on the deep sea I saw a ship with ropes of silk and sails of gold, all fashioned of ivory and ebony;

and the sea was calm and the breeze gentle and the sky such as when no cloud veils it, and the ship was laden with rich, virtuous wares.

Then a sudden tempest from the East so shook the air and the waters that the ship struck a rock. Oh what heavy grief! A brief hour struck down and a small space hides those high riches second to no others.

In a young grove were flowering the holy boughs of a laurel, youthful and straight, that seemed one of the trees of Eden,

and from its shade came forth such sweet songs of divers birds and so much other delight that it had rapt me from the world.

And as I gazed on it fixedly the sky around was changed and, dark to sight, struck with lightning and suddenly tore up by the roots that happy plant, whereat my life is sorrowful, for such shade is never regained.

---

two hounds: night and day.

323

Standomi un giorno solo a la fenestra
onde cose vedea tante et sì nove
ch' era sol di mirar quasi già stanco,
    una fera m'apparve da man destra
con fronte umana da far arder Giove,
cacciata da duo veltri, un nero, un bianco,   6
    che l'un et l'altro fianco
de la fera gentil mordean sì forte
che 'n poco tempo la menaro al passo
    ove chiusa in un sasso
vinse molta bellezza acerba morte,
et mi fe' sospirar sua dura sorte.   12

    Indi per alto mar vidi una nave
con le sarte di seta et d'or la vela,
tutta d'avorio e d'ebeno contesta;
    e 'l mar tranquillo et l'aura era soave
e 'l ciel qual è se nulla nube il vela,
ella carca di ricca merce onesta.   18
    Poi repente tempesta
oriental turbò sì l'aere et l'onde
che la nave percosse ad uno scoglio.
O che grave cordoglio,
breve ora oppresse et poco spazio asconde
l'alte ricchezze a null'altre seconde!   24

    In un boschetto novo i rami santi
fiorian d'un lauro giovenetto et schietto
ch' un delli arbor parea di paradiso;
    et di sua ombra uscian sì dolci canti
di vari augelli et tant' altro diletto
che dal mondo m'avean tutto diviso.   30
    Et mirandol io fiso,
cangiossi 'l cielo intorno, et tinto in vista
folgorando 'l percosse et da radice
    quella pianta felice
subito svelse, onde mia vita è trista,
che simile ombra mai non si racquista.   36

A clear fountain in that same wood welled from a stone, and fresh and sweet waters it scattered forth, gently murmuring;

to that lovely, hidden, shady, and dark seat neither shepherds came nor kine, but nymphs and muses, singing to that burden.

There I seated myself, and when I took most sweetness from that harmony and that sight, then I saw a chasm open and carry away with it the fountain and the place, whereat I still grieve, and I am striken with fear by the very memory.

A wondrous phoenix, both its wings clothed with purple and its head with gold, I saw in the forest, proud and alone,

and at first I thought it a form celestial and immortal, until it came to the uprooted laurel and to the spring that the earth steals away.

Everything flies to its end; for, seeing the leaves scattered on the earth and the trunk broken and that living water dry, it turned its beak on itself as if in scorn, and in an instant disappeared, whereat my heart burned with pity and love.

Finally I saw walking thoughtful amid the flowers and the grass a Lady so joyous and beautiful that I never think of it without burning and trembling,

humble in herself, but proud against Love; and she wore a white garment so woven that it appeared gold and snow together,

but her highest parts were wrapped in a dark mist. Pierced then in the heel by a little snake, as a plucked flower languishes she departed happy, not merely confident: ah, nothing but weeping endures in the world!

Song, you may well say: "These six visions have given my lord a sweet desire for death."

---

fountain: see notes to poems 125 and 305.   pierced . . . snake: this vision reenacts the death of Eurydice, the wife of Orpheus.

Chiara fontana in quel medesmo bosco
sorgea d'un sasso et acque fresche et dolci
spargea soavemente mormorando;
   al bel seggio riposto ombroso et fosco
né pastori appressavan né bifolci,
ma ninfe et muse a quel tenor cantando.   42
   Ivi m'assisi, et quando
più dolcezza prendea di tal concento
et di tal vista, aprir vidi uno speco
et portarsene seco
la fonte e 'l loco, ond' ancor doglia sento
et sol de la memoria mi sgomento.   48

   Una strania fenice, ambedue l'ale
di porpora vestita e 'l capo d'oro,
vedendo per la selva altera et sola,
   veder forma celeste ed immortale
prima pensai, fin ch' a lo svelto alloro
giunse ed al fonte che la terra invola.   54
   Ogni cosa al fin vola:
ché mirando le frondi a terra sparse
e 'l troncon rotto et quel vivo umor secco,
volse in se stessa il becco,
quasi sdegnando, e 'n un punto disparse,
onde 'l cor di pietate et d'amor m'arse.   60

   Alfin vid' io per entro i fiori et l'erba
pensosa ir sì leggiadra et bella Donna
che mai nol penso ch' i' non arda et treme,
   umile in sé, ma 'ncontra Amor superba;
ed avea in dosso sì candida gonna,
sì testa, ch'or et neve parea inseme,
   ma le parti supreme
eran avolte d'una nebbia oscura.
Punta poi nel tallon d'un picciol angue
come fior colto langue
lieta si dipartio, non che secura:
ahi nulla altro che pianto al mondo dura!   72

   Canzon, tu puoi ben dire:
"Queste sei visioni al signor mio
àn fatto un dolce di morir desio."   75

324

Love, when my hope, the guerdon of so much faithfulness, was flowering, she was taken away from me from whom I expected mercy.

Ah pitiless Death, ah cruel Life! One has placed me in sorrows and has untimely extinguished my hopes, the other keeps me down here against my will, and I cannot follow her who has gone, for Death does not permit it.

But still, always present, my lady sits enthroned in the midst of my heart, and what my life is, she sees for herself.

325

Silent I cannot be, and I fear that my tongue may produce an effect contrary to my heart, which would wish to honor its lady who listens to us from Heaven. How can I, if you do not teach me, Love, with mortal words equal divine works concealed by high humility gathered into itself?

The noble soul had not long been in the lovely prison from which now she has been set free, at the time when I first saw her; and so I quickly ran, for it was the April of the year and of my years, to gather flowers in those meadows around, hoping so adorned to please her eyes.

April: see notes to poems 3 and 267.

324

Amor, quando fioria
mia spene e 'l guidardon di tanta fede,
tolta m'è quella ond' attendea mercede.   3

Ahi dispietata Morte, ahi crudel vita!
l'una m'à posto in doglia
et mie speranze acerbamente à spente;
l'altra mi ten qua giù contra mia voglia,
et lei che se n'è gita
seguir non posso, ch' ella no 'l consente.   9
    Ma pur ogni or presente
nel mezzo del meo cor Madonna siede,
et qual è la mia vita, ella se 'l vede.   12

325

Tacer non posso, et temo non adopre
contrario effetto la mia lingua al core
che vorria far onore
a la sua donna, che dal Ciel n'ascolta.
Come poss' io, se non m'insegni, Amore,
con parole mortali aguagliar l'opre
divine et quel che copre
alta umiltate in se stessa raccolta?   8
    Ne la bella pregione onde or è sciolta
poco era stato ancor l'alma gentile
al tempo che di lei prima m'accorsi;
onde subito corsi
(ch' era de l'anno et di mi' etate aprile)
a coglier fiori in quei prati dintorno,
sperando a li occhi suoi piacer sì addorno.   15

The walls were of alabaster and the roof of gold, the entrance
of ivory and the windows of sapphire whence the first sigh
reached my heart and the last shall reach it; thence the
messengers of Love came forth armed with darts and fire,
and I, thinking of them all crowned with laurel, tremble at them
as if it were now.

In the midst could be seen a proud throne of squared and
faultless diamond, where the beautiful lady sat alone; before her
was a crystalline column, and every thought written within it
appeared without so clearly that it made me often glad in my
sighing.

I saw that I had come to the piercing, burning, shining arms,
to the green ensign of victory, against which in battle Jove and
Apollo and Polyphemus and Mars lose, where weeping is
forever fresh and green again; and, unable to escape, I let myself
be captured, and I know neither the way to escape nor the art.

But as sometimes a man who departs weeping sees things that
gladden his eyes and heart, so when she for whom I am in
prison, who was the only perfect thing in her days, was standing
on a balcony, I began to gaze at her with such desire that I forgot
myself and my misfortune.

---

shining arms: the arrows of the god of love.   green ensign: the laurel.
Jove . . . Mars: victims of Cupid.

Muri eran d'alabastro e 'l tetto d'oro,
d'avorio uscio, et fenestre di zaffiro
onde 'l primo sospiro
mi giunse al cor et giugnerà l'estremo;
inde i messi d'Amor armati usciro
di saette et di foco, ond' io di loro
coronati d'alloro,
pur come or fusse, ripensando tremo.   23
   D'un bel diamante quadro et mai non scemo
vi si vedea nel mezzo un seggio altero
ove sola sedea la bella donna;
dinanzi una colonna
cristallina, et iv' entro ogni pensero
scritto et for tralucea sì chiaramente
che mi fea lieto et sospirar sovente.   30

   A le pungenti ardenti et lucide arme,
a la vittoriosa insegna verde
contra cui in campo perde
Giove et Apollo et Polifemo et Marte,
ov' è 'l pianto ogni or fresco et si rinverde,
giunto mi vidi, et non possendo aitarme
preso lassai menarme
ond' or non so d'uscir la via né l'arte.   38
   Ma sì com' uom talor che piange et parte
vede cosa che li occhi e 'l cor alletta,
così colei per ch' io son in pregione
standosi ad un balcone,
che fu sola a' suoi dì cosa perfetta,
cominciai a mirar con tal desio
che me stesso e 'l mio mal posi in oblio.   45

I was on earth and my heart in paradise, sweetly forgetting every other concern, and I felt my living form become marble and full of wonder; when a lady very swift and confident, ancient in years but young of face, seeing me so intent by the expression of my forehead and brow,

said to me: "With me, take counsel with me, for I have more power than you think, and I can gladden and make sad in an instant, lighter than the wind, and I rule and revolve all you see in the world! Keep your eyes still on that sun, like an eagle, but at the same time listen to my words.

"The day she was born, the stars that produce among you happy effects were, in high and noble places, turned one toward another with love; Venus and her father with benign aspects held the most noble and beautiful parts of the heavens, and the baneful cruel lights were almost entirely dispersed.

"The sun never opened so beautiful a day, the air and the earth were joyful, and the waters of the sea and of the rivers were at peace. Among so many friendly lights, one distant cloud displeased me, which I fear will burn to weeping, if Pity does not revolve the heavens to prevent it.

------

lady very swift: Fortune.   Venus and her father: the planets Venus and Jupiter, considered favorable.   benign aspects: aspects are the relative positions of the planets on the zodiac; favorable aspects are conjunction, trine (separation by an angle of 120 degrees), and sextile (separation by an angle of 60 degrees).   most noble. . . parts of the heavens: the *medium coeli* (the intersection of the zodiac and the meridian) and the ascendant (intersection of the zodiac and the eastern horizon).   baneful cruel lights: Mars and Saturn. dispersed: formed no harmful aspects.

I' era in terra e 'l cor in paradiso
dolcemente obliando ogni altra cura,
et mia viva figura
far sentia un marmo e 'mpier di meraviglia;
quando una donna assai pronta et secura,
di tempo antica et giovene del viso,
vedendomi sì fiso
a l'atto de la fronte et de le ciglia: 53

"Meco," mi disse, "meco ti consiglia,
ch' i' son d'altro poder che tu non credi
et so far lieti et tristi in un momento,
più leggiera che 'l vento;
et reggo et volvo quanto al mondo vedi.
Tien pur gli occhi come aquila in quel sole,
parte da' orecchi a queste mie parole.   60

"Il dì che costei nacque, eran le stelle
che producon fra voi felici effetti
in luoghi alti et eletti
l'una ver l'altra con amor converse.
Venere e 'l padre con benigni aspetti
tenean le parti signorili et belle,
et le luci impie et felle
quasi in tutto del ciel eran disperse.   68

"Il sol mai sì bel giorno non aperse,
l'aere et la terra s'allegrava, et l'acque
per lo mar avean pace et per li fiumi.
Fra tanti amici lumi
una nube lontana mi dispiacque,
la qual temo che 'n pianto si resolve
se Pietate altramente il ciel non volve.   75

"When she came down to this low life, which to tell the truth was not worthy to have her, wondrous to see, already holy and sweet although unripe, she seemed a pearl enclosed in fine gold. And, now crawling, now with trembling steps, she made trees, water, earth, or stone green, clear, or soft,

"and with her hands or feet the grass fresh and proud, and with her eyes she made the fields blossom, and with the words not yet ready of a tongue that was barely weened, she quieted winds and tempests: clearly showing the deaf, blind world how much heavenly light was in her.

"When, growing in years and in virtue, she reached her third, her blossoming age, the sun never saw, I think, so much charm and beauty, her eyes full of gladness and virtue, and her speech of sweetness and of health. All tongues are dumb to tell of her what only you know,

"so bright is her face with celestial light that your sight cannot rest on it, and because of that beautiful earthly prison of hers your heart is full of such fire that no other ever burned more sweetly; but it seems to me that her sudden departure will soon make your life bitter."

Having said that, she turned to her revolving wheel, with which she spins our thread, the sad and certain prophetess of my losses; for after not many years she on whose account I so hunger to die, my Song, was killed by untimely and cruel Death, who could not kill a more beautiful body.

---

her third... age: see note on "Three days before," poem 214.

"Com' ella venne in questo viver basso,
ch' a dir il ver non fu degno d'averla,
cosa nova a vederla,
già santissima et dolce ancor acerba,
parea chiusa in or fin candida perla.
Et or carpone, or con tremante passo,
legno, acqua, terra o sasso
verde facea, chiara, soave, et l'erba   83
    "con le palme o coi pie' fresca et superba,
et fiorir coi belli occhi le campagne,
et acquetar i venti et le tempeste
con voci, ancor non preste,
di lingua che dal latte si scompagne:
chiaro mostrando al mondo sordo et cieco
quanto lume del Ciel fusse già seco.   90

    "Poi che crescendo in tempo et in virtute
giunse a la terza sua fiorita etate,
leggiadria né beltate
tanta non vide 'l sol, credo, giamai,
li occhi pien di letizia et d'onestate,
e 'l parlar di dolcezza et di salute.
Tutte lingue son mute
a dir di lei quel che tu sol ne sai: 98
    "sì chiaro è 'l volto di celesti rai
che vostra vista in lui non po fermarse,
et da quel suo bel carcere terreno
di tal foco ài 'l cor pieno
ch' altro più dolcemente mai non arse;
ma parmi che sua subita partita
tosto ti fia cagion d'amara vita."   105

    Detto questo, a la sua volubil rota
si volse in ch' ella fila il nostro stame,
trista et certa indivina de' miei danni;
ché dopo non molt'anni
quella per ch' io ò di morir tal fame,
canzon mia, spense Morte acerba et rea,
che più bel corpo occider non potea.   112

326

Now you have done your utmost, O cruel Death, now you have impoverished the kingdom of Love, now you have extinguished the flower and the light of beauty and closed it up in a little grave;

now you have despoiled our life and shaken from it every adornment and its sovereign honor; but the fame and the worth, which never die, are not in your power: keep for yourself the naked bones,

for Heaven has the other and rejoices and glories in its brightness as in a brighter sun; and in the world she will always be remembered by the good.

In such a victory, O new angel, let pity for me vanquish your heart up there as your beauty vanquished mine here.

327

The breath and the fragrance and the coolness and the shade of the sweet laurel and its flourishing sight, the light and repose of my weary life, have been taken away by her who empties the whole world.

As the sun disappears from our sight if his sister the moon eclipses him, so my high light has disappeared. I ask Death for help against Death, with such dark thoughts Love burdens me.

You have slept, beautiful Lady, a short sleep; now you have awakened among the elect spirits, where the soul internalizes herself in her Maker;

and if my rhymes have any power, among noble intellects your name will be consecrated to eternal memory.

326

Or ài fatto l'estremo di tua possa,
o crudel Morte, or ài 'l regno d'Amore
impoverito, or di bellezza il fiore
e 'l lume ài spento et chiuso in poca fossa;   4

or ài spogliata nostra vita et scossa
d'ogni ornamento et del sovran suo onore;
ma la fama et 'l valor, che mai non more,
non è in tua forza: abbiti ignude l'ossa,   8

ché l'altro à 'l Cielo, et di sua chiaritate
quasi d'un più bel sol s'allegra et gloria;
et fi' al mondo de' buon sempre in memoria.   11

Vinca 'l cor vostro in sua tanta vittoria,
angel novo, lassù di me pietate,
come vinse qui il mio vostra beltate.   14

327

L'aura et l'odore e 'l refrigerio et l'ombra
del dolce lauro et sua vista fiorita,
lume et riposo di mia stanca vita,
tolto à colei che tutto 'l mondo sgombra.   4

Come a noi il sol, se sua soror l'adombra,
così l'alta mia luc' è a me sparita;
i' cheggio a Morte incontra Morte aita,
di sì scuri penseri Amor m'ingombra.   8

Dormit' ài, bella Donna, un breve sonno,
or se' svegliata fra li spirti eletti
ove nel suo Fattor l'alma s'interna;   11

et se mie rime alcuna cosa ponno,
consecrata fra i nobili intelletti
fia del tuo nome qui memoria eterna.   14

328

The last, alas, of my happy days (of which I have seen but few in this short life) had arrived and had turned my heart to melting snow, perhaps prophetic of these sorrowful dark days.

As one about to be assailed by tertian fever already feels his muscles, pulse, and thoughts weaken, so I felt, although I did not know how swift the end of my imperfect wealth would come.

Her beautiful eyes, now in Heaven bright and happy in the Light that rains salvation and life, leaving my eyes here wretched and poor,

with chaste, strange shining said to my eyes: "Peace be with you, dear friends; never again here, no, but we shall see each other again elsewhere."

329

O day, O hour, O last moment, O stars sworn to impoverish me! O faithful glance, oh, what did you wish to tell me when I departed, never to be happy again?

Now I know my losses, now I awake, for I believed—ah vain and groundless beliefs!—that I was losing a part, not all, in going away: how many hopes does the wind carry off!

For already the contrary had been ordained in Heaven—to extinguish the rich light on which I lived—and it was written in the sweet bitter sight of her;

but before my eyes was placed a veil that made me not see what I saw, in order to make my life suddenly more sorrowful.

328

L'ultimo, lasso, de' miei giorni allegri
(che pochi ò visto in questo viver breve)
giunto era, et fatto 'l cor tepida neve,
forse presago de' dì tristi et negri. 4

Qual à già i nervi e i polsi e i penser egri
cui domestica febbre assalir deve,
tal mi sentia, non sappiend' io che leve
venisse 'l fin de' miei ben non integri. 8

Li occhi belli, or in Ciel chiari et felici
del lume onde salute et vita piove,
lasciando i miei qui miseri et mendici, 11

dicean lor con faville oneste et nove:
"Rimanetevi in pace, o cari amici;
qui mai più, no, ma rivedremne altrove." 14

329

O giorno, o ora, o ultimo momento,
o stelle congiurate a 'mpoverirme!
o fido sguardo, or che volei tu dirme,
partend' io per non esser mai contento? 4

Or conosco i miei danni, or mi risento,
ch' i' credeva (ahi, credenze vane e 'nfirme!)
perder parte, non tutto, al dipartirme:
quante speranze se ne porta il vento! 8

Ché già 'l contrario era ordinato in Cielo—
spegner l'almo mio lume ond' io vivea—
et scritto era in sua dolce amara vista; 11

ma 'nnanzi agli occhi m'era post' un velo
che mi fea non veder quel ch' i' vedea,
per far mia vita subito più trista. 14

330

That sweet, dear, virtuous, yearning glance seemed to say:
"Take what you can from me, for you will never see me here
again, once you have moved your unwilling foot away."

O intellect swifter than the panther but slow in foreseeing your
sorrows, why did you not see in her eyes what you see now,
which destroys and burns me?

Silently, sparkling beyond their wont, they were saying: "O
friendly lights, who for a great time with such sweetness have
made us your mirrors,

"Heaven awaits us; to you it will seem early, but He who bound
us here dissolves the knot and in order to cause you sorrow
ordains that the knot of your life shall grow old."

---

knot: the union of body and soul.

331

I used to go far from the fountain of my life and search
through lands and seas, following not my will, but my star,
      and (Love gave me such help) I always went into those exiles,
as bitter ones as he had ever seen, feeding my heart on memory
and hope.
      Now, alas, I throw up my hands and surrender my weapons
to my cruel violent fortune that has deprived me of so sweet a
hope; only memory is left to me, and I feed my great desire only
with that, and so my soul is failing, frail and starving.

330

Quel vago, dolce, caro, onesto sguardo
dir parea: "To' di me quel che tu poi,
che mai più qui non mi vedrai da poi
ch' avrai quinci il pe' mosso a mover tardo."   4

Intelletto veloce più che pardo,
pigro in antivedere i dolor tuoi,
come non vedestu nelli occhi suoi
quel che ved' ora, ond' io mi struggo et ardo?   8

Taciti, sfavillando oltra lor modo,
dicean: "O lumi amici che gran tempo
con tal dolcezza feste di noi specchi,   11

"il Ciel n'aspetta; a voi parrà per tempo,
ma chi ne strinse qui dissolve il nodo,
e 'l vostro, per farv' ira, vuol che 'nvecchi."   14

331

 Solea da la fontana di mia vita
allontanarme et cercar terre et mari,
non mio voler ma mia stella seguendo,
 et sempre andai (tal Amor diemmi aita)
in quelli esilii, quanto e' vide amari,
di memoria et di speme il cor pascendo.   6
 Or, lasso, alzo la mano et l'arme rendo
a l'empia et violenta mia fortuna
che privo m'à di sì dolce speranza;
sol memoria m'avanza,
et pasco 'l gran desir sol di quest'una,
onde l'alma vien men frale et digiuna.   12

As a runner on his way, if he lacks food, must slow his pace
as the strength grows less that made him swift,
    so as my life lacks that dear nutriment that has been
devoured by Death, who denudes the world and saddens my
heart,
    sweetness becomes bitter to me and pleasure troublesome
day by day; thus I hope and fear that I shall be unable to
complete this so brief journey. A cloud or dust in the wind, I flee
in order to be no longer a traveler, and so be it if that is indeed
my destiny.

Never did this mortal life please me (Love knows it, with
whom I often speak of it) except for her who was his light and
mine;
    since, dying on earth, that spirit by which I lived has been
reborn in Heaven, my highest desire is to be permitted to follow
her.
    But I must always grieve that I was unskilled to foresee my
state, which Love showed me beneath that lovely brow in order
to give me other counsel, for many a one has died sorrowful and
unconsoled who might earlier have died happy.

In her eyes, where my heart was wont to dwell (until my
harsh fate envied it and banished it from so rich a dwelling),
    with his own hand Love had written in letters of pity what
would soon become of my long yearning.
    It would have been lovely and sweet to die then, when
though I died my life would not have died, but rather the best
part of me would have lived on: now Death has scattered my
hopes, and a little earth presses down all my wealth; and I live
on, and I never think of it without trembling.

Come a corrier tra via, se 'l cibo manca,
conven per forza rallentare il corso,
scemando la vertù che 'l fea gir presto;
   così mancando a la mia vita stanca
quel caro nutrimento, in che di morso
die' chi 'l mondo fa nudo e 'l mio cor mesto,   18
   il dolce acerbo e 'l bel piacer molesto
mi si fa d'ora in ora; onde 'l camino
sì breve non fornir spero et pavento.
Nebbia o polvere al vento,
fuggo per più non esser pellegrino:
et così vada s' è pur mio destino.   24

   Mai questa mortal vita a me non piacque
(sassel Amor con cui spesso ne parlo)
se non per lei che fu 'l suo lume e 'l mio;
   poi che 'n terra morendo al Ciel rinacque
quello spirto ond' io vissi, a seguitarlo
licito fusse è 'l mi' sommo desio.   30
   Ma da dolermi ò ben sempre, perch' io
fui mal accorto a proveder mio stato
ch' Amor mostrommi sotto quel bel ciglio
per darmi altro consiglio:
ché tal morì già tristo et sconsolato
cui poco inanzi era 'l morir beato.   36

   Nelli occhi ov' abitar solea 'l mio core
(fin che mia dura sorte invidia n'ebbe,
che di sì ricco albergo il pose in bando),
   di sua man propria avea descritto Amore
con lettere di pietà quel ch' averrebbe
tosto del mio sì lungo ir desiando.   42
   Bello et dolce morire era allor quando,
morend' io, non moria mia vita inseme,
anzi vivea di me l'ottima parte;
or mie speranze sparte
à Morte, et poca terra il mio ben preme,
et vivo, et mai nol penso ch' i' non treme.   48

If my little intellect had been with me at need, and another hunger had not driven it elsewhere and made it stray,

on my lady's brow I might have read: "You have reached the end of all your sweetness and the beginning of great bitterness."

Understanding that, and sweetly shaking off in her presence my mortal veil and this noisome heavy flesh, I could have gone on before her to watch her throne being prepared in Heaven: now I will follow her, with changed hair.

Song, if you find anyone living peacefully in love, say to him: "Die while you are happy, for timely death is no grief but a refuge; let him who can die well not seek delay."

Se stato fusse il mio poco intelletto
meco al bisogno, et non altra vaghezza
l'avesse disviando altrove vòlto,
   ne la fronte a Madonna avrei ben letto:
"Al fin se' giunto d'ogni tua dolcezza
et al principio del tuo amaro molto."   54
   Questo intendendo, dolcemente sciolto
in sua presenzia del mortal mio velo
et di questa noiosa et grave carne,
potea inanzi lei andarne
a veder preparar sua sedia in Cielo:
or l'andrò dietro omai con altro pelo.   60

   Canzon, s' uom trovi in suo amor viver queto,
dí: "Muor mentre se' lieto,
ché morte al tempo è non duol ma refugio,
et chi ben po morir non cerchi indugio."   64

332

My kind fortune and glad life,
bright days and tranquil nights,
and gentle sighs and a sweet style
that used to resound in verses and rhymes,
suddenly turned to grief and weeping,
make me hate life and yearn for death.

Cruel, untimely, inexorable Death,
you give me cause never to be glad
but to live my life ever weeping,
with dark days and sorrowing nights;
my heavy sighs cannot go into rhymes,
and my harsh torment surpasses every style.

Where has it been led, my amorous style?
to speak of sorrow, to talk about death.
Where are the verses, where are the rhymes
that a noble heart used to hear thoughtful and glad?
Where is that talking of love all the night?
Now I speak and think of nothing but weeping.

Formerly, so sweet with desire was weeping
that it seasoned with sweetness every bitter style
and made me keep watch through all the nights;
now tears are more bitter to me than death,
since I do not hope ever to see that glance, virtuous and glad,
the high subject of my low rhymes.

A clear target did Love set up for my rhymes
within those lovely eyes, and now he has set it up in weeping,
sorrowfully reminding me of that glad time,
and I go changing with my cares my style
and begging you often, pale Death,
to rescue me from such painful nights.

332

Mia benigna fortuna e 'l viver lieto,
i chiari giorni et le tranquille notti
e i soavi sospiri, e 'l dolce stile
che solea resonare in versi e 'n rime,
vòlti subitamente in doglia e 'n pianto
odiar vita mi fanno et bramar morte.   6

Crudele, acerba, inesorabil Morte,
cagion mi dài di mai non esser lieto
ma di menar tutta mia vita in pianto
e i giorni oscuri et le dogliose notti;
i mei gravi sospir non vanno in rime,
e 'l mio duro martir vince ogni stile.   12

Ove è condutto il mio amoroso stile?
a parlar d'ira, a ragionar di morte.
U' sono i versi, u' son giunte le rime
che gentil cor udia pensoso et lieto?
Ov' è 'l favoleggiar d'amor le notti?
Or non parl' io né penso altro che pianto.   18

Già mi fu col desir sì dolce il pianto
che condia di dolcezza ogni agro stile
et vegghiar mi facea tutte le notti;
or m'è 'l pianger amaro più che morte,
non sperando mai 'l guardo onesto et lieto,
alto sogetto a le mie basse rime.   24

Chiaro segno Amor pose a le mie rime
dentro a' belli occhi, et or l'à posto in pianto
con dolor rimembrando il tempo lieto,
ond' io vo col penser cangiando stile
et ripregando te, pallida Morte,
che mi sottragghi a sì penose notti.   30

Sleep has fled from my cruel nights
and their usual sound from my hoarse rhymes
that cannot treat anything but death;
thus my singing is converted to weeping.
The kingdom of Love does not have so varied a style,
for now it is as sorrowful as ever it was glad.

No one ever lived more glad than I,
no one lives more sorrowful both day and night
or, sorrow doubling, redoubles his style
that draws from his heart such tearful rhymes.
I lived on hope, now I live only on weeping,
nor against Death do I hope for anything but death.

Death has killed me, and only Death
has the power to make me see again that glad face
that made sighs pleasing to me and weeping,
the sweet wind and rain of my nights,
when I wove my noble thoughts into rhymes,
Love raising up my weak style.

Would I had so sorrowful a style
that I could win my Laura back from Death
as Orpheus won his Eurydice without rhymes,
for then I would live more glad than ever!
If it cannot be, let one of these nights
now close my two fountains of weeping.

Love, for many and many years I have been weeping
my heavy loss in grieving style,
nor from you do I ever hope to have less cruel nights;
and therefore I have turned to beg Death
to take me from here, to make me glad
where she is whom I sing and bewail in rhymes.

---

redoubles his style: a sestina usually ends at line 39; this is a double
sestina.   as Orpheus won his Eurydice: after Eurydice's death Orpheus went
to the underworld and sang so beautifully (without rhyme, because Greek
poetry did not use rhyme) that Dis, the god of the dead, permitted him to lead
her up to the world, with the proviso that if he looked at her before reaching it
she would be lost again; he looked back too soon and she dissolved like smoke.
Petrarch knew versions of the story by both Virgil (*Georgics* 4.453–527) and
Ovid (*Metamorphoses* 10.1–77).

Fuggito è 'l sonno a le mie crude notti,
e 'l sono usato a le mie roche rime
che non sanno trattar altro che morte;
così è 'l mio cantar converso in pianto.
Non à 'l regno d'Amor sì vario stile,
ch' è tanto or tristo quanto mai fu lieto.   36

Nesun visse giamai più di me lieto,
nesun vive più tristo et giorni et notti,
et doppiando 'l dolor, doppia lo stile
che trae del cor sì lacrimose rime.
Vissi di speme, or vivo pur di pianto,
né contra Morte spero altro che morte.   42

Morte m'à morto, et sola po far Morte
ch' i' torni a riveder quel viso lieto
che piacer mi facea i sospiri e 'l pianto,
l'aura dolce et la pioggia a le mie notti
quando i penseri eletti tessea in rime,
Amor alzando il mio debile stile.   48

Or avess' io un sì pietoso stile
che Laura mia potesse torre a Morte
come Euridice Orfeo sua senza rime,
ch' i' viverei ancor più che mai lieto!
S' esser non po, qualcuna d'este notti
chiuda omai queste due fonti di pianto.   54

Amor, i' ò molti et molt'anni pianto
mio grave danno in doloroso stile,
né da te spero mai men fere notti;
et però mi son mosso a pregar Morte
che mi tolla di qui per farme lieto
ove è colei che i' canto et piango in rime.   60

If they can go so high, my weary rhymes,
as to reach her who is beyond sorrow and weeping
and with her beauties now makes Heaven glad,
she will surely recognize my changed style,
which perhaps used to please her before Death
made for her bright day, for me black nights.

O you who sigh for better nights,
who listen about Love or write in rhymes,
pray that Death be no longer deaf to me,
the port of misery and the end of weeping;
let her for once change her ancient style
that makes everyone sorrowful but can make me so glad.

She can make me glad in one or a few nights,
and in harsh style and anguished rhymes
I pray that my weeping may be ended by Death.

Se sì alto pon gir mie stanche rime
ch' agiungan lei ch' è fuor d'ira et di pianto
et fa 'l Ciel or di sue bellezze lieto,
ben riconoscerà 'l mutato stile
che già forse le piacque anzi che Morte
chiaro a lei giorno, a me fesse atre notti.   66

O voi che sospirate a miglior notti,
ch' ascoltate d'Amore o dite in rime,
pregate non mi sia più sorda Morte,
porto de le miserie et fin del pianto;
muti una volta quel suo antiquo stile
ch' ogni uom attrista et me po far sì lieto.   72

Far mi po lieto in una o 'n poche notti,
e 'n aspro stile e 'n angosciose rime
prego che 'l pianto mio finisca Morte.   75

333

Go, sorrowing rhymes, to the hard stone that hides in earth my dear treasure, there call for her who answers from Heaven although her mortal part is in a place dark and low.

Tell her that I am already tired of living, of sailing through these horrible waves, but that, gathering up her scattered leaves, I still follow after her step by step,

speaking only of her both alive and dead (rather still alive and now made immortal), so that the world may know and love her.

Let it please her to pay heed to my passing, which is nearby now; let her meet me, and let her draw and call me to herself, to be what she is in Heaven.

334

If virtuous love can merit mercy and if pity still has all her wonted power, I shall find mercy, for brighter than the sun is my faithfulness to my lady and to the world.

She used to fear me; now she knows, and does not have to believe, that the very thing that I now want is what I always wanted, and if formerly she heard words and saw my face, now she sees my mind and my heart.

And so I hope that at last in Heaven there will be sorrow for my many sighs, and thus it seems, as she comes back to me so full of pity;

and I hope that when I put off these remains she will come for me with our people, the true friend of Christ and of virtue.

333

Ite, rime dolenti, al duro sasso
che 'l mio caro tesoro in terra asconde,
ivi chiamate chi dal Ciel risponde
ben che 'l mortal sia in loco oscuro et basso.   4

Ditele ch' i' son già di viver lasso,
del navigar per queste orribili onde,
ma ricogliendo le sue sparte fronde
dietro le vo pur così passo passo,   8

sol di lei ragionando viva et morta
(anzi pur viva, et or fatta immortale),
a ciò che 'l mondo la conosca et ame.   11

Piacciale al mio passar esser accorta,
ch' è presso omai; siami a l'incontro, et quale
ella è nel Cielo, a sé mi tiri et chiame.   14

334

S' onesto amor po meritar mercede
et se pietà ancor po quant' ella suole,
mercede avrò, ché più chiara che 'l sole
a Madonna et al mondo è la mia fede.   4

Già di me paventosa, or sa, nol crede,
che quello stesso ch' or per me si vole
sempre si volse; et s' ella udia parole
o vedea 'l volto, or l'animo e 'l cor vede.   8

Ond' i' spero che 'nfin al Ciel si doglia
di miei tanti sospiri; et così mostra,
tornando a me sì piena di pietate;   11

et spero ch' al por giù di questa spoglia
venga per me con quella gente nostra,
vera amica di Cristo et d'onestate.   14

335

Once I saw among a thousand ladies one who was such that amorous fear assailed my heart, seeing her, in no false imaginings, to be equal in appearance to the heavenly spirits.

There was nothing earthly or mortal in her, for she cared about Heaven, not about anything else; my soul, which burned and pined so frequently for her, yearning to go with her, opened both wings,

but she was too high for my terrestrial weight, and a little after she went entirely out of my sight, so that thinking of it I still freeze and grow torpid.

O beautiful and high and shining windows where she who makes many sorrowful found the way to enter so beautiful a body!

---

windows: Laura's eyes.   she who makes many sorrowful: Death.

336

She comes to mind (rather she is within my mind, for she cannot be banished thence by Lethe) just as I saw her in her flowering, all burning with the rays of her star;

I see her in the first encounter so chaste and beautiful, so turned inward and shy, that I cry: "That is she, she is still alive!" and I beg her for the gift of her sweet speech.

Sometimes she replies and sometimes she does not say a word; I, like one who errs and then esteems more justly, say to my mind: "You are deceived:

"you know that in 1348, on the sixth day of April, at the first hour, that blessed soul left the body."

This poem is to be correlated with poem 211.
Lethe: river of oblivion, in the underworld.

335

Vidi fra mille donne una già tale
ch' amorosa paura il cor m'assalse,
mirandola in imagini non false
a li spirti celesti in vista eguale.   4

Niente in lei terreno era o mortale
sì come a cui del Ciel, non d'altro, calse;
l'alma, ch' arse per lei sì spesso et alse,
vaga d'ir seco aperse ambedue l'ale,   8

ma tropp' era alta al mio peso terrestre,
et poco poi n'uscì in tutto di vista,
di che pensando ancor m'aghiaccio et torpo.   11

O belle et alte et lucide fenestre
onde colei che molta gente attrista
trovò la via d'entrare in sì bel corpo!   14

336

Tornami a mente (anzi v'è dentro quella
ch' indi per Lete esser non po sbandita)
qual io la vidi in su l'età fiorita
tutta accesa de' raggi di sua stella;   4

sì nel mio primo occorso onesta et bella
veggiola in sè raccolta et sì romita,
ch' i' grido: "Ell' è ben dessa, ancor è in vita!"
e 'n don le cheggio sua dolce favella.   8

Talor risponde et talor non fa motto;
i' come uom ch' erra et poi più dritto estima
dico a la mente mia: "Tu se' 'ngannata.   11

"Sai che 'n mille trecento quarantotto,
il dì sesto d'aprile, in l'ora prima
del corpo uscio quell'anima beata."   14

337

What in fragrance and color surpassed the odoriferous shining Orient and the fruits, flowers, grass, and leaves for which the Occident had the renown of every rare excellence,

my sweet laurel, where every beauty, every ardent virtue, was wont to dwell, saw in its shadow chastely sitting my lord and my goddess.

More, I placed the nest of my noble thoughts in that rich tree, and in fire and ice, trembling, burning, I was most happy.

The world was full of its perfect honors when God, to adorn Heaven with her, took her back to Himself, and she was a thing fit for Him.

Before Petrarch rearranged the last poems in Vat. Lat. 3195, poems 337–349 were numbered 339–351.

338

Death, you have left the world dark and cold without the sun, Love blind and unarmed, Charm naked, Beauty weak, me unconsoled and a heavy burden to myself,

Courtesy in exile, and Chastity in the depths; I only grieve, though I am not alone in having cause to grieve, for you have uprooted the bright seed of virtue: once the highest worth is dead, what will be the second?

The air and the earth and the sea ought to weep for the lineage of man, for without her it is like a meadow without flowers or a ring without its gem.

The world did not know her while it had her; I knew her, who remain here to weep, and Heaven, which now makes itself so beautiful by my weeping.

337

Quel che d'odore et di color vincea
l'odorifero et lucido oriente,
frutti, fiori, erbe et frondi onde 'l ponente
d'ogni rara eccellenzia il pregio avea,   4

dolce mio lauro, ove abitar solea
ogni bellezza, ogni vertute ardente,
vedeva a la sua ombra onestamente
il mio signor sedersi et la mia dea.   8

Ancor io il nido di penseri eletti
posi in quell'alma pianta, e 'n foco e 'n gielo
tremando, ardendo, assai felice fui.   11

Pieno era il mondo de' suoi onor perfetti,
allor che Dio per adornarne il Cielo
la si ritolse, et cosa era da lui.   14

338

Lasciato ài, Morte, senza sole il mondo
oscuro et freddo, Amor cieco et inerme,
Leggiadria ignuda, le Bellezze inferme,
me sconsolato et a me grave pondo,   4

Cortesia in bando, et Onestate in fondo;
dogliom' io sol né sol ò da dolerme,
ché svelt' ài di vertute il chiaro germe:
spento il primo valor, qual fia il secondo?   8

Pianger l'aer et la terra e 'l mar devrebbe
l'uman legnaggio, che senz' ella è quasi
senza fior prato, o senza gemma anello.   11

Non la conobbe il mondo mentre l'ebbe;
conobbil' io ch' a pianger qui rimasi
e 'l Ciel che del mio pianto or si fa bello.   14

339

I knew (so much did Heaven open my eyes, so much did eagerness and Love raise up my wings) things new and full of grace, but mortal, which all the stars showered on one subject.

Those many other high celestial and immortal forms, so strange and so wondrous, because they were not accommodated to my intellect, my weak sight could not endure.

Thus whatever I spoke or wrote about her, who now before God returns me prayers in exchange for praises, was a little drop from infinite depths

for one's style does not extend beyond one's wit, and though one has his eyes fixed on the sun, the brighter it is the less he sees.

---

  things new . . . but mortal: Laura's physical beauty.   those . . . forms: Laura's spiritual beauty, the soul being the form of the body.

340

Sweet, dear, and precious pledge of mine, whom Nature took from me and Heaven keeps for me: ah, how is it that your pity for me is so tardy, O accustomed sustainer of my life?

You used to make my sleep at least worthy of the sight of you, and now you suffer me to burn without any relief, and who delays it? Surely up there no anger or scorn dwells,

on account of which down here even a pitying heart sometimes feeds on another's torment so that Love is vanquished even in his own kingdom.

You who see me within and know my suffering and are the only one who can end so much sorrow, with your image quiet my laments.

339

Conobbi (quanto il Ciel li occhi m'aperse,
quanto studio et Amor m'alzaron l'ali)
cose nove et leggiadre, ma mortali,
che 'n un soggetto ogni stella cosperse.   4

L'altre tante sì strane et sì diverse
forme, altere celesti et immortali,
perché non furo a l'intelletto eguali
la mia debile vista non sofferse.   8

Onde quant' io di lei parlai né scrissi,
ch' or per lodi anzi a Dio preghi mi rende,
fu breve stilla d'infiniti abissi;   11

ché stilo oltra l'ingegno non si stende,
et per aver uom li occhi nel sol fissi,
tanto si vede men quanto più splende.   14

340

Dolce mio caro et prezioso pegno
che Natura mi tolse e 'l Ciel mi guarda:
deh, come è tua pietà ver me sì tarda,
o usato di mia vita sostegno?   4

Già suo' tu far il mio sonno almen degno
de la tua vista, et or sostien ch' i' arda
senz' alcun refrigerio, et chi 'l retarda?
Pur lassù non alberga ira né sdegno,   8

onde qua giuso un ben pietoso core
talor si pasce delli altrui tormenti,
sì ch' elli è vinto nel suo regno Amore.   11

Tu che dentro mi vedi e 'l mio mal senti
et sola puoi finir tanto dolore,
con la tua ombra acqueta i miei lamenti.   14

341

Ah, what pity, what angel was so swift to carry above the heavens my heartfelt sorrow? For again, as I am wont, I feel my lady return with that sweet chaste bearing of hers

to quiet my wretched sad heart; she is so full of humility, empty of pride, and altogether such that I draw back from death, and I live, and living is no longer painful to me.

She is indeed blessed who can make others blessed with her sight or else with her words, understood only by us two:

"My dear faithful one, I am much grieved for you, but still for our good I was cruel to you," she says, and other things fit to make the sun stand still.

342

With the food of which my lord is always generous—tears and grief—I feed my weary heart, and I often tremble and often grow pale thinking of its cruel deep wound.

But she, whom no one surpassed or even approached in her time, comes to the bed where I lie sick, so lovely that I hardly dare to look at her, and full of pity sits on the edge.

With that hand which I so much desired she dries my eyes and with her speech brings me sweetness that mortal man never felt:

"What good," she says, "is knowledge to one who despairs? Weep no longer, have you not wept for me enough? For would that you were as much alive as I am not dead!"

341

Deh, qual pietà, qual angel fu sì presto
a portar sopra 'l cielo il mio cordoglio?
ch' ancor sento tornar pur come soglio
Madonna in quel suo atto dolce onesto   4

ad acquetare il cor misero et mesto,
piena sì d'umiltà, vota d'argoglio,
e 'n somma tal ch' a morte i' mi ritoglio,
et vivo, et 'l viver più non m'è molesto.   8

Beata s'è che po beare altrui
co la sua vista, o ver co le parole
intellette da noi soli ambedui: 11

"Fedel mio caro, assai di te mi dole;
ma pur per nostro ben dura ti fui,"
dice, et cos' altre d'arrestare il sole.   14

342

Del cibo onde 'l signor mio sempre abonda,
lagrime et doglia, il cor lasso nudrisco;
et spesso tremo et spesso impallidisco,
pensando a la sua piaga aspra et profonda.   4

Ma chi né prima simil né seconda
ebbe al suo tempo, al letto in ch' io languisco
vien tal ch' a pena a rimirarl' ardisco,
et pietosa s'asside in su la sponda.   8

Con quella man che tanto desiai
m'asciuga li occhi, et col suo dir m'apporta
dolcezza ch' uom mortal non sentì mai: 11

"Che val," dice, "a saver chi si sconforta?
Non pianger più, non m'ài tu pianto assai?
ch' or fostu vivo com' io non son morta!"   14

343

Thinking back on that gentle glance which today Heaven
honors, on the bending of her golden head, on her face, on that
angelic modest voice which sweetened life for me and now
breaks my heart,

I greatly marvel that l am still alive; nor would I be, if she, who
left one in doubt as to whether she was more beautiful or more
chaste, were not so quick to help me there near the dawn.

Oh what sweet and chaste and kind greetings! and how intently
she listens to, and takes note of, the long history of my sufferings!

When bright day seems to strike her she returns to Heaven, for
she knows all the ways, her eyes and both her cheeks wet.

344

Perhaps once love was a sweet thing (not that I know when),
now it is so bitter that nothing is more so; he well knows the
truth who learns it as I have, with my heavy grief.

She who was the honor of our world, and now is of Heaven,
which she all beautifies and makes bright, in her days made my
rest short and rare; now she has deprived me of all repose.

Cruel Death has taken away my every treasure, nor can great
good fortune console my adversities for having lost that lovely
soul.

I wept and sang; I cannot change my style, but day and night I
vent through my tongue and my eyes the sorrow accumulated in
my soul.

343

Ripensando a quel ch' oggi il Cielo onora
soave sguardo, al chinar l'aurea testa,
al volto, a quella angelica modesta
voce che m'addolciva et or m'accora, 4

gran meraviglia ò com' io viva ancora;
né vivrei già, se chi tra bella e onesta
qual fu più lasciò in dubbio, non sì presta
fusse al mio scampo là verso l'aurora. 8

O che dolci accoglienze et caste et pie!
et come intentamente ascolta et nota
la lunga istoria de le pene mie! 11

Poi che 'l dì chiaro par che la percota,
tornasi al Ciel, ché sa tutte le vie,
umida li occhi et l'una et l'altra gota. 14

344

Fu forse un tempo dolce cosa amore
(non per ch' i' sappia il quando), or è sì amara
che nulla più; ben sa 'l ver chi l'impara
com' ò fatt' io, con mio grave dolore. 4

Quella che fu del secol nostro onore,
or è del Ciel che tutto orna et rischiara,
fe' mia requie a' suoi giorni et breve et rara;
or m'à d'ogni riposo tratto fore. 8

Ogni mio ben crudel Morte m'à tolto,
né gran prosperità il mio stato avverso
po consolar di quel bel spirto sciolto. 11

Piansi et cantai; non so più mutar verso,
ma dì et notte il duol ne l'alma accolto
per la lingua et per li occhi sfogo et verso. 14

345

Love and sorrow incited my evil tongue, accustomed to lamenting, toward where it should not go: to say of her for whom I sang and burned that which, if it were true, would be wrong;

for her being in Heaven ought to quiet my cruel state and console my heart, seeing that she has come so near to Him whom in her life she had always in her heart.

And I do grow calm and console myself, nor would I wish to see her again here in this hell, rather I wish to live and die alone;

for more beautiful than ever I see her with my internal eye, risen in flight with the angels to the feet of her and my eternal Lord.

346

The elect angels and blessed souls who are citizens of Heaven, the first day that my lady passed over, came around her full of wonder and reverence.

"What light is this and what new beauty?" they said to each other, "for so lovely a soul never in all this age rose from the erring world to this high dwelling."

She, glad to have changed her dwelling, is equal to the most perfect souls, and still from time to time she turns back,

looking to see if I am following her, and seems to wait; and so I raise all of my desires and thoughts toward Heaven, for I hear her even pray that I may hasten.

345

Spinse amor et dolor ove ir non debbe
la mal lingua, aviata a lamentarsi,
a dir di lei per ch' io cantai et arsi
quel che, se fusse ver, torto sarebbe;   4

ch' assai 'l mio stato rio quetar devrebbe
quella beata, e 'l cor racconsolarsi
vedendo tanto lei domesticarsi
con colui che vivendo in cor sempre ebbe.   8

Et ben m'acqueto, et me stesso consolo,
né vorrei rivederla in questo inferno,
anzi voglio morire et viver solo;   11

ché più bella che mai con l'occhio interno
con li angeli la veggio alzata a volo
a pie' del suo et mio Signore eterno.   14

346

Li angeli eletti et l'anime beate
cittadine del Cielo, il primo giorno
che Madonna passò, le fur intorno
piene di meraviglia et di pietate.   4

"Che luce è questa et qual nova beltate?"
dicean tra lor: "perch' abito sì adorno
dal mondo errante a quest'alto soggiorno
non salì mai in tutta questa etate."   8

Ella, contenta aver cangiato albergo,
si paragona pur coi più perfetti
et parte ad or ad or si volge a tergo,   11

mirando s' io la seguo, et par ch' aspetti;
ond' io voglie et pensier tutti al Ciel ergo
perch' i' l'odo pregar pur ch' i' m'affretti.   14

347

Lady, who, as your rich life deserves, are now gladly seated near our Maker in a high and glorious throne, adorned with other things than pearls or purple,

O high and rare wonder among ladies: now, in the face of Him who sees all things, you see my love and that pure faith for which I poured out so many tears and so much ink,

and you know that my heart was toward you on earth as it is toward you now in Heaven, and that I never wished anything from you but the sunlight of your eyes.

Therefore to make amends for the long war in which I turned away from the world toward you only, pray that I may soon come to be with you.

348

From the most beautiful eyes and the brightest face that ever shone, and from the most beautiful hair, which made gold and the sun seem less beautiful, from the sweetest speech and sweetest smile,

from the hands and arms that without moving would have conquered whoever was most rebellious to Love, from the beautiful light feet—from the body made in Paradise—

my spirits took life; now the heavenly King delights in them, and His winged couriers, and I have remained here naked and blind.

Only one comfort for my suffering do I expect: that she who sees all of my thoughts will win grace for me that I may be with her.

347

Donna che lieta col Principio nostro
ti stai, come tua vita alma rechiede,
assisa in alta et gloriosa sede
et d'altro ornata che di perle o d'ostro,   4

o de le donne altero et raro mostro:
or nel volto di lui che tutto vede
vedi 'l mio amore et quella pura fede
per ch' io tante versai lagrime e 'nchiostro,   8

et senti che ver te il mio core in terra
tal fu qual ora è in Cielo, et mai non volsi
altro da te che 'l sol de li occhi tuoi.   11

Dunque per amendar la lunga guerra
per cui dal mondo a te sola mi volsi,
prega ch' i' venga tosto a star con voi.   14

348

Da' più belli occhi, et dal più chiaro viso
che mai splendesse, et da' più bei capelli
che facean l'oro e 'l sol parer men belli,
dal più dolce parlare et dolce riso,   4

da le man, da le braccia che conquiso
senza moversi avrian quai più rebelli
fur d'Amor mai, da' più bei piedi snelli:
da la persona fatta in paradiso   8

prendean vita i miei spirti; or n'à diletto
il Re celeste, i suoi alati corrieri,
et io son qui rimaso ignudo et cieco.   11

Sol un conforto a le mie pene aspetto:
ch' ella che vede tutt' i miei penseri
m'impetre grazia ch' i' possa esser seco.   14

349

I seem at every moment to hear the messenger whom my lady sends calling me to her; thus within and without I go changing, and in just a few years I have been so reduced

that by now I hardly recognize myself: I have banished all my accustomed life. I would be glad to know when, but still the time ought to be near.

Oh happy that day when, going forth from my earthly prison, I may leave broken and scattered this heavy, frail, and mortal garment of mine,

and may depart from such thick shadows, flying so far up into the beautiful clear sky that I may see my Lord and my lady!

350

This brittle, frail good of ours, which is wind and shadow and is called beauty, never was, except in this age, entirely in one body, and that was to my sorrow;

for Nature does not wish, nor is it fitting, to put all others in poverty in order to make one rich; but now she poured into one all her largesses (pardon me, any who is beautiful or thinks she is).

There never was such beauty, old or new, nor will there be again, I believe; but it was so hidden that the erring world hardly noticed it.

She disappeared quickly; and so I am glad to exchange the brief sight Heaven offers me, only to please her holy eyes.

This was originally poem 337.

349

E' mi par d'or in ora udire il messo
che Madonna mi mande a sé chiamando;
così dentro et di for mi vo cangiando,
et sono in non molt'anni sì dimesso   4

ch' a pena riconosco omai me stesso:
tutto 'l viver usato ò messo in bando.
Sarei contento di sapere il quando,
ma pur devrebbe il tempo esser da presso.   8

O felice quel dì che del terreno
carcere uscendo, lasci rotta et sparta
questa mia grave et frale et mortal gonna   11

et da sì folte tenebre mi parta,
volando tanto su nel bel sereno
ch' i' veggia il mio Signore et la mia donna!   14

350

Questo nostro caduco et fragil bene,
ch' è vento et ombra et à nome beltate,
non fu giamai se non in questa etate
tutto in un corpo, et ciò fu per mie pene;   4

ché Natura non vol, né si convene,
per far ricco un, por li altri in povertate;
or versò in una ogni sua largitate
(perdonimi qual è bella o si tene).   8

Non fu simil bellezza antica o nova,
né sarà, credo; ma fu sì coverta
ch' a pena se n'accorse il mondo errante.   11

Tosto disparve, onde 'l cangiar mi giova
la poca vista a me dal Cielo offerta
sol per piacer a le sue luci sante.   14

351

Sweet rigors and placid repulses full of chaste love and pity, charming angers which (I now see) tempered my inflamed and foolish desires,

noble speech in which highest chastity brightly shone with highest courtesy, flower of virtue, fountain of beauty which uprooted from my heart every low thought,

a glance so divine as to make a man blessed, now fierce in reining in my daring mind from what is justly forbidden,

now swift to comfort my frail life: this lovely variety was the root of my salvation, which otherwise was gone.

Poems 351 and 352 were originally poems 362 and 363.

352

Happy spirit, who so sweetly governed those eyes brighter than the sun and formed the sighs and lively words that still sound in my memory:

once I saw you, burning with virtuous fire, move among the grass and the violets, not as a lady but as an angel does, the feet of her who is now more than ever present to me;

whom you then, returning to your Maker, left in earth with that soft veil that was allotted to you by high destiny.

With your departure Love left the world and Courtesy, and the sun fell from the sky, and Death began to become sweet.

351

Dolci durezze et placide repulse
piene di casto amore et di pietate,
leggiadri sdegni che le mie infiammate
voglie tempraro (or me n'accorgo) e 'nsulse,   4

gentil parlar in cui chiaro refulse
con somma cortesia somma onestate,
fior di vertù, fontana di beltate,
ch' ogni basso penser del cor m'avulse,   8

divino sguardo da far l'uom felice,
or fiero in affrenar la mente ardita
a quel che giustamente si disdice,   11

or presto a confortar mia frale vita:
questo bel variar fu la radice
di mia salute, ch' altramente era ita.   14

352

Spirto felice che sì dolcemente
volgei quelli occhi più chiari che 'l sole
et formavi i sospiri et le parole
vive ch' ancor mi sonan ne la mente: 4

già ti vid' io d'onesto foco ardente
mover i pie' fra l'erbe et le viole
(non come donna, ma com' angel sole)
di quella ch' or m'è più che mai presente,   8

la qual tu poi, tornando al tuo Fattore,
lasciasti in terra, et quel soave velo
che per alto destin ti venne in sorte.   11

Nel tuo partir partì del mondo Amore
et Cortesia, e 'l sol cadde del cielo,
et dolce incominciò farsi la Morte.   14

353

Wandering bird that go singing or else weeping for past time, seeing night and winter before you, and day and the happy months behind:

if as you know your own grievous troubles you also knew my similar state, you would come to my unconsoled bosom to share its sorrowing groans.

I do not know if our portions would be equal, for she whom you weep for is perhaps still in life, of which Death and Heaven are so stingy to me;

but the forbidding season and hour invite me with the memory of the sweet and the bitter years to speak to you with pity.

This was originally poem 365. Poem 354 was numbered 364.

354

Ah, reach your hand to my weary mind, Love, and to my tired frail style, to speak of her who has become immortal and a citizen of the heavenly kingdom;

grant, Lord, that my speech may hit the target of her praises, where by itself it cannot rise, since virtue and beauty equal to hers were never in the world, which was not worthy to have her.

He replies: "All that Heaven and I can do, and good counsel and virtuous life, all was in her whom Death has taken from us;

"there has never been a form equal to hers, not since the day when Adam first opened his eyes; and let this now suffice: weeping I say it, and do you weeping write."

Adam first opened his eyes: according to Genesis 2:21–25, God had Adam sleep while he fashioned Eve from one of Adam's ribs.

353

Vago augelletto, che cantando vai
o ver piangendo il tuo tempo passato
vedendoti la notte e 'l verno a lato
e 'l dì dopo le spalle e i mesi gai :   4

se come i tuoi gravosi affanni sai
così sapessi il mio simile stato,
verresti in grembo a questo sconsolato
a partir seco i dolorosi guai.   8

I' non so se le parti sarian pari,
ché quella cui tu piangi è forse in vita,
di ch' a me Morte e 'l Ciel son tanto avari ;   11

ma la stagion et l'ora men gradita,
col membrar de' dolci anni et de li amari,
a parlar teco con pietà m'invita.   14

354

Deh, porgi mano a l'affannato ingegno,
Amor, et a lo stile stanco et frale
per dir di quella ch' è fatta immortale
et cittadina del celeste regno ;   4

dammi, Signor, che 'l mio dir giunga al segno
de le sue lode, ove per sé non sale,
se vertù, se beltà non ebbe eguale
il mondo che d'aver lei non fu degno.   8

Responde : "Quanto 'l Ciel et io possiamo,
e i buon consigli e 'l conversar onesto,
tutto fu in lei di che noi Morte à privi ;   11

forma par non fu mai dal dì ch' Adamo
aperse li occhi in prima ; et basti or questo,
piangendo il dico, et tu piangendo scrivi."   14

355

O time, O revolving heavens that fleeing deceive us blind and wretched mortals, O days more swift than wind or arrows! Now through experience I understand your frauds.

But I excuse you and I reproach myself, for Nature gave you wings to fly with, to me she gave eyes; but I still fixed them on what harmed me, whence I am ashamed and sorrowful;

and it would be time, and the time is past, to turn them to a safer place and put an end to my infinite woes.

Not from your yoke, Love, does my soul depart, but from my harms, with what effort, you know; virtue is not by chance, rather it is a subtle art.

This was originally poem 338. Poems 356–365 were numbered 352–361.

356

My sacred breeze breathes so often for my repose in weariness that I become bold to tell her the ills I have felt and feel, which I would not have dared to do while she was alive.

I begin with that love-inspiring glance that was the beginning of so long a torment, then I follow with how, wretched and happy, day by day, hour by hour, Love has gnawed at me.

She is silent, her face the color of pity, and still looks fixedly at me; sometimes she sighs and adorns her face with virtuous tears;

and so my soul, overcome by sorrow, as, weeping, it grows angry with itself, shaken from sleep returns to itself.

355

O tempo, O ciel volubil che fuggendo
inganni i ciechi et miseri mortali,
O dì veloci più che vento et strali!
ora *ab experto* vostre frodi intendo.   4

Ma scuso voi et me stesso riprendo:
ché Natura a volar v'aperse l'ali,
a me diede occhi; et io pur ne' miei mali
li tenni onde vergogna et dolor prendo,   8

et sarebbe ora, et è passata omai,
di rivoltarli in più secura parte
et poner fine a l'infiniti guai.   11

Né dal tuo giogo, Amor, l'alma si parte,
ma dal suo mal, con che studio tu 'l sai:
non a caso è vertute, anzi è bell'arte.   14

356

L'aura mia sacra al mio stanco riposo
spira sì spesso ch' i' prendo ardimento
di dirle il mal ch' i' ò sentito et sento,
che vivendo ella non sarei stat' oso.   4

I' incomincio da quel guardo amoroso
che fu principio a sì lungo tormento,
poi seguo come misero et contento
di dì in dì, d'ora in ora, Amor m'à roso.   8

Ella si tace et di pietà depinta
fiso mira pur me; parte sospira
et di lagrime oneste il viso adorna;   11

onde l'anima mia dal dolor vinta,
mentre piangendo allor seco s'adira,
sciolta dal sonno a se stessa ritorna.   14

357

Every day seems to me more than a thousand years, until I may follow my faithful, dear guide who led me in the world and now leads me by a better way to a life without troubles;

and the deceits of the world cannot hold me back, for I know them, and so much light shines within my heart all the way from Heaven that I begin to count up the time and my losses.

Nor do I fear the threats of death, which the King suffered with worse pain in order to make me constant and strong in following Him,

and which recently entered each vein of her who was allotted to me, and did not cloud her clear brow.

King: Christ.

358

Death cannot make her sweet face bitter, but her sweet face can make Death sweet; what need is there of any other guides for my dying? She guides me from whom I learn every good,

and He who was not stingy of His blood, who broke with His foot the Tartarean gates, with His death seems to strengthen me. Come therefore, Death, your coming is dear to me,

and do not delay, for it is surely time by now, and if it were not, it was time in that instant when my lady passed from this life.

From then on I have never lived a day; I was with her in life, and with her I have reached the end, and I have completed my day with her steps.

Tartarean gates: according to traditional belief, after His death Christ battered down the gates of Hell, brought forth the souls of the patriarchs, prophets, and other believers who had been imprisoned there, and led them up to Heaven.

357

Ogni giorno mi par più di mill'anni
ch' i' segua la mia fida et cara duce
che mi condusse al mondo, or mi conduce
per miglior via a vita senza affanni;   4

et non mi posson ritener l'inganni
del mondo, ch' i' 'l conosco; et tanta luce
dentro al mio core infin dal Ciel traluce
ch' i' 'ncomincio a contar il tempo e i danni.   8

Né minacce temer debbo di morte,
che 'l Re sofferse con più grave pena
per farme a seguitar constante et forte,   11

et or novellamente in ogni vena
intrò di lei che m'era data in sorte,
et non turbò la sua fronte serena.   14

358

Non po far Morte il dolce viso amaro,
ma 'l dolce viso dolce po far Morte:
che bisogn' a morir ben altre scorte?
quella mi scorge ond' ogni ben imparo;   4

et quei che del suo sangue non fu avaro,
che col pe' ruppe le tartaree porte,
col suo morir par che mi riconforte.
Dunque vien, Morte, il tuo venir m'è caro,   8

et non tardar, ch' egli è ben tempo omai;
et se non fusse, e' fu 'l tempo in quel punto
che Madonna passò di questa vita.   11

D'allor inanzi, un dì non vissi mai;
seco fui in via, et seco al fin son giunto,
et mia giornata ò co' suoi pie' fornita.   14

359

When my gentle, faithful comforter, to give repose to my weary life, sits on the left side of my bed with that sweet, skillful talk of hers,

all pale with anguish and fear, I say: "Where do you come from now, O happy soul?" A little palm branch and a laurel branch she draws from her lovely bosom and says: "From the cloudless empyrean Heaven and from those holy places I have come, and I come only to console you."

With gestures and words I thank her humbly and then I ask: "Now how do you know of my state?" And she: "The sad waves of weeping with which you are never sated,

"with the breeze of your sighs, through so much distance pass to Heaven and disturb my peace. Does it displease you so much that I have left this misery and have come to a better life? It ought to please you, if you loved me as much as you showed by your looks and your words!"

I reply: "I do not weep for anything but myself who have remained in darkness and torment, for I have been as certain that you had risen to Heaven as a man is of a thing he sees close by.

"How could God and Nature have put in a youthful heart so much virtue, if eternal salvation had not been destined for your good works? O one of the rare souls who lived nobly here among us and quickly flew up to Heaven afterward!

---

left side: see note to poem 88.

359

Quando il soave mio fido conforto
per dar riposo a la mia vita stanca
ponsi del letto in su la sponda manca
con quel suo dolce ragionare accorto,   4
    tutto di pièta et di paura smorto
dico: "Onde vien tu ora, o felice alma?"
Un ramoscel di palma
et un di lauro trae del suo bel seno,
et dice: "Dal sereno
Ciel empireo et di quelle sante parti
mi mossi, et vengo sol per consolarti."   11

    In atto et in parole la ringrazio
umilemente, et poi demando: "Or donde
sai tu il mio stato?" Et ella: "Le triste onde
del pianto di che mai tu non se' sazio,   15
    "coll'aura de' sospir', per tanto spazio
passano al Cielo et turban la mia pace.
Sì forte ti dispiace
che di questa miseria sia partita
et giunta a miglior vita?
che piacer ti devria, se tu m'amasti
quanto in sembianti et ne' tuoi dir mostrasti."   22

    Rispondo: "Io non piango altro che me stesso
che son rimaso in tenebre e 'n martire,
certo sempre del tuo al Ciel salire
come di cosa ch' uom vede da presso.   26
    "Come Dio et Natura avrebben messo
in un cor giovenil tanta vertute,
se l'eterna salute
non fusse destinata al tuo ben fare?
O de l'anime rare
ch' altamente vivesti qui tra noi
et che subito al Ciel volasti poi!   33

"But what can I do except always weep, wretched and alone, who without you am nothing? Would I had died as a suckling and in my cradle, so as not to experience the temperings of love!"

And she: "Why still weep and untune yourself? How much better it would have been to raise your wings from earth and to weigh with an accurate balance mortal things and these sweet deceptive chatterings of yours, and to follow me (if it is true that you love me so much), gathering at last one of these branches!"

"I wanted to ask," I reply then: "what do those two leaves mean?" And she: "Answer yourself, you whose pen so honors one of them;

"the palm is victory, and I when still young conquered the world and myself; the laurel means triumph, of which I am worthy, thanks to that Lord who gave me strength. Now you, if another is overpowering you, turn to Him, ask help from Him, so that we may be with Him at the end of your race."

"Is this the blond hair and the golden knot," say I, "that still binds me, and those beautiful eyes that were my sun?" "Do not err with fools, nor speak," she says, "or believe in their manner:

"I am a naked spirit, and I rejoice in Heaven: what you seek has been dust for many years now. But to help you from your troubles it is given to me to seem such, and I shall be so again, more beautiful than ever, and more loving to you, once so wild and kind, saving at once your salvation and my own."

I weep, and she dries my face with her hands and then sighs sweetly and grows angry with words that could break the stones; and after this she departs, as does my sleep.

"Ma io che debbo altro che pianger sempre
misero et sol, che senza te son nulla!
ch' or fuss' io spento al latte et a la culla,
per non provar de l'amorose tempre!"   37
    Et ella: "A che pur piangi et ti distempre?
Quanto era meglio alzar da terra l'ali,
et le cose mortali
et queste dolci tue fallaci ciance
librar con giusta lance,
et seguire me (s' è ver che tanto m'ami),
cogliendo omai qualcun di questi rami."   44

    "I' volea demandar," respond' io allora:
"che voglion importar quelle due frondi?"
Et ella: "Tu medesmo ti rispondi,
tu la cui penna tanto l'una onora.   48
    "Palma è vittoria, et io giovene ancora
vinsi il mondo et me stessa; il lauro segna
triunfo, ond' io son degna
mercé di quel Signor che mi die' forza.
Or tu, s' altri ti sforza,
a lui ti svolgi, a lui chiedi soccorso
sì che siam seco al fine del tuo corso."   55

    "Son questi i capei biondi et l'aureo nodo,"
dich' io: "ch' ancor mi stringe, et quei belli occhi
che fur mio sol?" "Non errar con li sciocchi,
né parlar," dice, "o creder a lor modo.   59
    "Spirito ignudo sono e 'n Ciel mi godo;
quel che tu cerchi è terra già molt'anni.
Ma per trarti d'affanni
m'è dato a parer tale, et ancor quella
sarò più che mai bella,
a te più cara, sì selvaggia et pia,
salvando inseme tua salute et mia."   66

    I' piango; et ella il volto
co le sue man m'asciuga, et poi sospira
dolcemente, et s'adira
con parole che i sassi romper ponno;
et dopo questo si parte ella e 'l sonno.   71

360

Having cited my old sweet cruel lord before the queen who holds the divine part of our nature and is enthroned at its summit, there, like gold being refined in the fire, I make my plaint, laden with pain, fear, and horror, like a man who fears death and begs for justice.

And I begin: "Lady, when I was young I placed my left foot in his kingdom, whence I have never had anything but sorrow and scorn; and I have suffered there so many and such strange torments that at the end that infinite patience of mine has been vanquished and I have hated life.

"Thus my time until now has been passed in flame and suffering; and how many virtuous paths did I disdain, how many joys, to serve this cruel flatterer! And what wit has such ready words that it can express my unhappy state and my grave and just complaints against this ingrate?

"O little honey, much aloes with vinegar! To how much bitterness has he trained my life with his false sweetness, which drew me to the amorous flock! For, if I am not deceived, I was of a nature to raise myself high above earth; he took me from peace and placed me in war.

---

queen: Reason.   my left foot: see poem 214.

360

Quel antiquo mio dolce empio signore
fatto citar dinanzi a la reina
che la parte divina
tien di nostra natura e 'n cima sede,
ivi com' oro che nel foco affina
mi rappresento carco di dolore,
di paura et d'orrore,
quasi uom che teme morte et ragion chiede.   8
    E 'ncomincio: "Madonna, il manco piedo
giovenetto pos' io nel costui regno,
ond' altro ch' ira et sdegno
non ebbi mai; et tanti et sì diversi
tormenti ivi soffersi
ch' alfine vinta fu quell'infinita
mia pazienzia, e 'n odio ebbi la vita.   15

    "Così 'l mio tempo infin qui trapassato
è in fiamma e 'n pene; et quante utili oneste
vie sprezzai, quante feste,
per servir questo lusinghier crudele!
Et qual ingegno à sì parole preste
che stringer possa 'l mio infelice stato
et le mie d'esto ingrato
tante et sì gravi et sì giuste querele?   23
    "O poco mel, molto aloe con fele,
in quanto amaro à la mia vita avezza
con sua falsa dolcezza,
la qual m'atrasse a l'amorosa schiera!
che, s' i' non m'inganno, era
disposto a sollevarmi alto da terra;
e' mi tolse di pace et pose in guerra.   30

"He has made me love God less than I ought and be less concerned for myself; for a lady I have equally disregarded all cares. In that, he alone has been my counselor, always sharpening my youthful desire with his wicked whetstone, and I hoped for rest under his harsh fierce yoke.

"Wretch! Why were that dear high intellect and the other gifts given to me by Heaven? For my hair is turning, but I cannot turn from my obstinate will: thus this cruel one whom I accuse despoils me of all liberty and has turned bitter living into sweet habit.

"He has made me search among wildernesses, wild beasts, rapacious thieves, bristling dunes, hard peoples and customs, and every wandering that entangles travelers, among mountains, valleys, marshes, and seas and rivers, a thousand snares spread everywhere, and winter in unaccustomed months, with present peril and labor:

"neither did he or that other enemy of mine whom I fled leave me for a single instant; therefore, if I have not come before my time to unripe cruel death, heavenly pity cares for my salvation, not this tyrant who feeds on my sorrow and on my loss.

"Questi m'à fatto men amare Dio
ch' i' non deveva, et men curar me stesso;
per una donna ò messo
egualmente in non cale ogni pensero.
Di ciò m'è stato consiglier sol esso,
sempr'aguzzando il giovenil desio
a l'empia cote, ond' io
sperai riposo al suo giogo aspro et fero.   38
    "Misero, a che quel caro ingegno altero
et l'altre doti a me date dal Cielo?
ché vo cangiando 'l pelo,
né cangiar posso l'ostinata voglia.
Così in tutto mi spoglia
di libertà questo crudel ch' i' accuso,
ch' amaro viver m'à vòlto in dolce uso.   45

    "Cercar m'à fatto deserti paesi,
fiere et ladri rapaci, ispidi dumi,
dure genti et costumi,
et ogni error che' pellegrini intrica;
monti valli paludi et mari et fiumi,
mille lacciuoli in ogni parte tesi,
e 'l verno in strani mesi
con pericol presente et con fatica.   53
    "Né costui né quell'altra mia nemica
ch' i' fuggia mi lasciavan sol un punto;
onde s' i' non son giunto
anzi tempo da morte acerba et dura,
pietà celeste à cura
di mia salute, non questo tiranno
che del mio duol si pasce et del mio danno.   60

"Since I have been his I have not had a tranquil hour, nor do I expect any, and my nights have banished sleep and cannot draw it back to themselves by herbs or by charms; by treachery and force he has made himself master of my spirits, and since then no bell has struck, when I have been in some town, that I have not heard. He knows that I am speaking the truth,

"for no worm ever gnawed old wood as he gnaws my heart, where he makes his nest and menaces it with death. Hence come my tears and sufferings, my words and my sighs, with which I go wearing myself out and perhaps others. Do you judge, who know me and him."

My adversary with sharp reproaches begins: "O Lady, hear the other side, for it shall tell the truth entirely, which this ingrate departs from. In his first age this fellow was given to selling words or rather lies; nor does he seem to be ashamed, after having been taken from that harm to my delights,

"to complain of me, who have kept him pure and clean (and now he grieves) against the desire that often wishes its own ill, and have kept him in a sweet life, which he calls wretchedness, risen to some fame only through me, who have raised up his intellect to where it could never have raised itself.

"Poi che suo fui non ebbi ora tranquilla
né spero aver, et le mie notti il sonno
sbandiro, et più non ponno
per erbe o per incanti a sé ritrarlo;
per inganni et per forza è fatto donno
sovra miei spirti, et non sonò poi squilla
ov' io sia in qualche villa
ch' i' non l'udisse. Ei sa che 'l vero parlo,   68
    "ché legno vecchio mai non rose tarlo
come questi 'l mio core, in che s'annida
et di morte lo sfida.
Quinci nascon le lagrime e i martiri,
le parole e i sospiri,
di ch' io mi vo stancando et forse altrui.
Giudica tu, che me conosci et lui."   75

Il mio adversario con agre rampogne
comincia: "O Donna, intendi l'altra parte
che 'l vero (onde si parte
quest'ingrato) dirà senza defetto.
Questi in sua prima età fu dato a l'arte
da vender parolette (anzi menzogne);
né par che si vergogne,
tolto da quella noia al mio diletto,   83
    "lamentarsi di me, che puro et netto
contra 'l desio, che spesso il suo mal vole,
lui tenni (ond' or si dole)
in dolce vita, ch' ei miseria chiama,
salito in qualche fama
solo per me, che 'l suo intelletto alzai
ov' alzato per sé non fora mai.   90

"He knows that the great Atrides and high Achilles and Hannibal, so bitter to your country, and another—the brightest of all both in virtue and in fortune—as for each his stars ordained I let fall into the base love of a slave: and for this fellow out of a thousand excellent, choice ladies I chose one

"such that her like will never be seen under the moon even though Lucretia were to return to Rome; and I gave her such sweet speech and such soft singing, that no low or heavy thought could ever endure in her presence. These were my deceptions with this fellow,

"this was the wormwood, these the scorn and the anger, much sweeter than the all of any other woman! From good seed I reap ill fruit, and that is the reward one receives for helping an ingrate. I had so carried him under my wings that his speech pleased ladies and knights; and I made him rise so high that among brilliant wits

"his name shines, and in some places collections are made of his poems; who now would perhaps be a hoarse murmurer of the courts, one of the mob! I exalt him and make him known by what he learned in my school and from her who was unique in the world.

Atrides: Agamemnon, Achilles' rival for the slave girl Briseis.   Hannibal: said to have fallen into debauchery after the battle of Cannae.   another: Scipio Africanus.   Lucretia: see note on "lovely Roman," poem 260.

"Ei sa che 'l grande Atride et l'alto Achille,
et Anibàl al terren vostro amaro,
et di tutti il più chiaro—
un altro et di vertute et di fortuna—
com' a ciascun le sue stelle ordinaro
lasciai cader in vil amor d'ancille;
et a costui di mille
donne elette eccellenti n'elessi una,   98
"qual non si vedrà mai sotto la luna
benché Lucrezia ritornasse a Roma;
et sì dolce idioma
le diedi et un cantar tanto soave
che penser basso o grave
non potè mai durar dinanzi a lei.
Questi fur con costui l'inganni mei,   105

"questo fu il fel, questi li sdegni et l'ire,
più dolci assai che di null'altra il tutto!
Di bon seme mal frutto
mieto, et tal merito à chi 'ngrato serve.
Sì l'avea sotto l'ali mie condutto
ch' a donne et cavalier piacea il suo dire;
et sì alto salire
il feci che tra' caldi ingegni ferve   113
"il suo nome, et de' suoi detti conserve
si fanno con diletto in alcun loco;
ch' or saria forse un roco
mormorador di corti, un uom del vulgo!
I' l'esalto et divulgo
per quel ch' elli 'mparò ne la mia scola
et da colei che fu nel mondo sola.   120

"And, to tell finally my greatest service, from a thousand vicious acts I have drawn him back, for low things could never please him in any way (a young man shy and shamefast in act and in thought) once he had become the vassal of her who impressed a deep mark upon his heart and made him similar to herself.

"Whatever is exceptional or noble in him, he has from her and from me of whom he complains. Never was a nocturnal phantasm so full of error as he is toward us; for since he has known us he has God's and people's graces—and that the proud fellow laments and regrets!

"Again, and this is all that remains, I gave him wings to fly above the heavens through mortal things, which are a ladder to the Creator, if one judges them rightly: for, if he looked fixedly at how many and how great virtues were in that hope of his, from one likeness to the next he could have risen to the high First Cause,

"and he has said it several times in rhyme. Now he has forgotten me along with that lady whom I gave him as the support of his frail life." At this I raise a tearful cry, and shout: "He gave her to me indeed, but he soon took her back!" He replies: "Not I, but One who desired her for Himself."

Finally, both turning to the seat of justice, I with trembling, he with high and cruel voice, each of us concludes for himself: "Noble Lady, I await your sentence." She then, smiling: "It pleases me to have heard your pleas, but more time is needed for so great a lawsuit."

"Et per dir a l'estremo il gran servigio,
da mille atti inonesti l'ò ritratto,
ché mai per alcun patto
a lui piacer non poteo cosa vile
(giovene schivo et vergognoso in atto
et in penser) poi che fatto era uom ligio
di lei ch' alto vestigio
l'impresse al core et fecel suo simile.   128
    "Quanto à del pellegrino et del gentile,
da lei tene et da me, di cui si biasma.
Mai notturno fantasma
d'error non fu sì pien com' ei ver noi,
ch' è in grazia, da poi
che ne conobbe, a Dio et a la gente:
di ciò il superbo si lamenta et pente.   135

    "Ancor, et questo è quel che tutto avanza,
da volar sopra 'l ciel li avea dat' ali
per le cose mortali,
che son scala al Fattor, chi ben l'estima:
ché mirando ei ben fiso quante et quali
eran vertuti in quella sua speranza,
d'una in altra sembianza
potea levarsi a l'alta cagion prima,   143
    "et ei l'à detto alcuna volta in rima.
Or m'à posto in oblio con quella donna
ch' i' li die' per colonna
de la sua frale vita." A questo un strido
lagrimoso alzo, et grido:
"Ben me la die', ma tosto la ritolse!"
Responde: "Io no, ma chi per sé la volse."   150

    Alfin ambo conversi al giusto seggio,
i' con tremanti, ei con voci alte et crude,
ciascun per sé conchiude:
"Nobile Donna, tua sentenzia attendo."
Ella allor, sorridendo:
"Piacemi aver vostre questioni udite,
ma più tempo bisogna a tanta lite."   157

361

My faithful mirror, my weary spirit, and my changing skin and diminished agility and strength often say to me: "Do not pretend anymore, you are old;

"to obey Nature in all is best, for time takes from us the power to oppose her." Quickly then, as water puts out fire, I awake from a long and heavy sleep,

and I see well that our life flies and that one cannot be alive more than once; and in the midst of my heart there sounds a word

of her who is now freed from her beautiful knot but in her day was so unique in the world that, if I do not err, she has deprived all others of fame.

362

I fly with the wings of thought to Heaven so often that it seems to me I am almost one of those who there possess their treasure, leaving on earth their rent veils.

Sometimes my heart trembles with a sweet chill, hearing her for whom I grow pale say to me: "Friend, now I love you and now I honor you, because you have changed your habits and your hair."

She leads me to her Lord; then I incline myself, humbly begging that He permit me to stay to see their two faces.

He replies: "Your destiny is certain, and a delay of twenty or thirty years will seem much to you, but it will be little."

361

Dicemi spesso il mio fidato speglio,
l'animo stanco, et la cangiata scorza
et la scemata mia destrezza et forza:
"Non ti nasconder più, tu se' pur veglio;   4

"obedir a Natura in tutto è il meglio,
ch' a contender con lei 'l tempo ne sforza."
Subito allor, com' acqua 'l foco amorza,
d'un lungo et grave sonno mi risveglio;   8

et veggio ben che 'l nostro viver vola
et ch' esser non si po più d'una volta;
e 'n mezzo 'l cor mi sona una parola   11

di lei ch' è or dal suo bel nodo sciolta
ma ne' suoi giorni al mondo fu sì sola
ch' a tutte, s' i' non erro, fama à tolta.   14

362

Volo con l'ali de' pensieri al Cielo
sì spesse volte che quasi un di loro
esser mi par ch' àn ivi il suo tesoro,
lasciando in terra lo squarciato velo.   4

Talor mi trema 'l cor d'un dolce gelo,
udendo lei per ch' io mi discoloro
dirmi: "Amico, or t'am' io et or t'onoro
perch' à' i costumi variati e 'l pelo."   8

Menami al suo Signor; allor m'inchino,
pregando umilemente che consenta
ch' i' stia a veder et l'uno et l'altro volto.   11

Responde: "Egli è ben fermo il tuo destino,
et per tardar ancor vent'anni o trenta
parrà a te troppo, et non fia però molto."   14

363

Death has extinguished the sun that used to dazzle me, and my eyes though whole and sound are in darkness; she is dust from whom I took chills and heat; my laurels are faded, are oaks and elms,

in which I see my gain but am still pained. There is no one to make my thoughts fearful and bold, nor to freeze and scorch them, no one to fill them with hope and overflow them with sorrow.

Out of the hands of him who pierces and heals, who once made of me such a long torture, I find myself in bitter and sweet liberty;

and to the Lord whom I adore and whom I thank, who governs and sustains the heavens with His brow, I return, weary of life, not merely satiated.

---

oaks and elms: deciduous rather than evergreen trees.

364

Love held me twenty-one years gladly burning in the fire and full of hope amid sorrow; since my lady, and my heart with her, rose to Heaven, ten more years of weeping.

Now I am weary and I reproach my life for so much error, which has almost extinguished the seed of virtue; and I devoutly render my last parts, high God, to You,

repentant and sorrowing for my years spent thus, which ought to have been better used, in seeking peace and fleeing troubles.

Lord who have enclosed me in this prison: draw me from it safe from eternal harm, for I recognize my fault and I do not excuse it.

363

Morte à spento quel sol ch' abagliar suolmi,
e 'n tenebre son li occhi interi et saldi;
terra è quella ond' io ebbi et freddi et caldi,
spenti son i miei lauri, or querce et olmi,   4

di ch' io veggio 'l mio ben et parte duolmi.
Non è chi faccia et paventosi et baldi
i miei penser, né chi li agghiacci et scaldi,
né chi gl'empia di speme et di duol colmi.   8

Fuor di man di colui che punge et molce,
che già fece di me sì lungo strazio,
mi trovo in libertate amara et dolce;   11

et al Signor ch' io adoro et ch' i' ringrazio,
che pur col ciglio il ciel governa et folce,
torno stanco di viver, non che sazio.   14

364

Tennemi Amor anni ventuno ardendo
lieto nel foco et nel duol pien di speme;
poi che Madonna e 'l mio cor seco inseme
saliro al Ciel, dieci altri anni piangendo.   4

Omai son stanco, et mia vita reprendo
di tanto error che di vertute il seme
à quasi spento; et le mie parti estreme,
alto Dio, a te devotamente rendo   8

pentito et tristo de' miei sì spesi anni,
che spender si deveano in miglior uso,
in cercar pace et in fuggir affanni.   11

Signor che 'n questo carcer m'ài rinchiuso:
tramene salvo da li eterni danni,
ch' i' conosco 'l mio fallo et non lo scuso.   14

365

I go weeping for my past time, which I spent in loving a mortal thing without lifting myself in flight, though I had wings to make of myself perhaps not a base example.

You who see all my unworthy and wicked sufferings, invisible, immortal King of Heaven: help my strayed frail soul and fill out with your grace all that she lacks,

so that, though I have lived in war and in storm, I may die in peace and in port, and if my sojourn has been vain, my departure at least may be virtuous.

To what little life remains to me and to my dying deign to be present: You know well that I have no hope in anyone else.

366

Beautiful Virgin who, clothed with the sun and crowned with stars, so pleased the highest Sun that in you He hid His light: love drives me to speak words of you, but I do not know how to begin without your help and His who loving placed Himself in you.

I invoke her who has always replied to whoever called on her with faith. Virgin, if extreme misery of human things ever turned you to mercy, bend to my prayer; give succor to my war, though I am earth and you are queen of Heaven.

---

clothed with the sun and crowned with stars: an echo of Apocalypse 12:1, "mulier amicta sole, et luna sub pedibus eius, et in capite eius corona stellarum duodecim" (a woman clothed with the sun, with the moon under her feet, and on her head a crown of twelve stars). The entire poem is a tissue of traditional epithets and phrases in praise of the Virgin.

365

I' vo piangendo i miei passati tempi
i quai posi in amar cosa mortale
senza levarmi a volo, abbiendi' io l'ale
per dar forse di me non bassi esempi.   4

Tu che vedi i miei mali indegni et empi,
Re del Cielo, invisibile, immortale:
soccorri a l'alma disviata et frale
e 'l suo defetto di tua grazia adempi,   8

sì che, s' io vissi in guerra et in tempesta,
mora in pace et in porto; et se la stanza
fu vana, almen sia la partita onesta.   11

A quel poco di viver che m'avanza
et al morir degni esser tua man presta:
tu sai ben che 'n altrui non ò speranza.   14

366

Vergine bella, che di sol vestita,
coronata di stelle, al sommo Sole
piacesti sì che 'n te sua luce ascose:
amor mi spinge a dir di te parole,
ma non so 'ncominciar senza tu' aita
et di colui ch' amando in te si pose.   6
Invoco lei che ben sempre rispose
chi la chiamò con fede.
Vergine, s' a mercede
miseria estrema de l'umane cose
giamai ti volse, al mio prego t'inchina,
soccorri a la mia guerra
ben ch' i' sia terra   et tu del Ciel regina.   13

Wise Virgin, one of the number of the blessed wise virgins,
rather the first, and with the brightest lamp, O solid shield of
afflicted people against the blows of Death and Fortune, under
which they triumph, not merely escape,

O relief from the blind ardor that flames here among foolish
mortals: Virgin, turn those beautiful eyes that sorrowing saw
the pitiless wounds in your dear Son's sweet limbs, to my
perilous state, who come dismayed to you for counsel.

Pure Virgin, whole in every part, noble daughter and mother
of your offspring, who lighten this life and adorn the other:
through you your Son, Son of the highest Father (O shining,
noble window of Heaven), came down to save us in the latter
days,

and among all earthly dwellings only you were chosen.
Blessed Virgin, who turn the tears of Eve to rejoicing again:
make me, for you can, worthy of His grace, O blessed without
end, already crowned in the kingdom above.

Vergine saggia et del bel numero una
de le beate vergini prudenti,
anzi la prima et con più chiara lampa,
o saldo scudo de le afflitte genti
contr' a' colpi di Morte et di Fortuna,
sotto 'l qual si triunfa, non pur scampa,   19
   o refrigerio al cieco ardor ch' avampa
qui fra i mortali sciocchi:
Vergine, que' belli occhi
che vider tristi la spietata stampa
ne' dolci membri del tuo caro figlio
volgi al mio dubio stato
che sconsigliato   a te ven per consiglio.   26

Vergine pura, d'ogni parte intera,
del tuo parto gentil figliuola et madre,
ch' allumi questa vita et l'altra adorni:
per te il tuo Figlio et quel del sommo Padre
(o fenestra del Ciel lucente altera)
venne a salvarne in su li estremi giorni,   32
   et fra tutt' i terreni altri soggiorni
sola tu fosti eletta.
Vergine benedetta
che 'l pianto d'Eva in allegrezza torni:
fammi, che puoi, de la sua grazia degno,
senza fine o beata,
già coronata   nel superno regno.   39

Holy Virgin, full of every grace, who through true and highest humility mounted to Heaven whence you hear my prayers: you bore the Fountain of pity and the Sun of justice, who makes bright the world though it is full of dark and thick errors.

You have gathered into yourself three sweet names: mother, daughter, and bride, O glorious Virgin, Lady of that King who has loosed our bonds and made the world free and happy, in whose holy wounds I pray you to quiet my heart, O true bringer of happiness.

Virgin unique in the world, unexampled, who made Heaven in love with your beauties, whom none ever surpassed or even approached: holy thoughts, merciful and chaste actions made a consecrated living temple of the true God in your fruitful virginity.

Through you my life can be joyous, if at your prayers, O Mary, sweet and merciful Virgin, where sin abounded grace abounds. With the knees of my mind bent, I beg you to be my guide and to direct my twisted path to a good end.

---

blessed wise virgins: the parable of the wise virgins, who provided themselves with oil for their lamps, and the foolish ones, who had no oil when the bridegroom arrived, is told in Matthew 25:1–13.

Vergine santa, d'ogni grazia piena,
che per vera et altissima umiltate
salisti al ciel ond' e' miei preghi ascolti:
tu partoristi il Fonte di pietate
et di giustizia il Sol che rasserena
il secol pien d'errori oscuri et folti.
Tre dolci et cari nomi ài in te raccolti,   45
madre, figliuola et sposa,
Vergine gloriosa,
donna del Re che' nostri lacci à sciolti
et fatto 'l mondo libero et felice,
ne le cui sante piaghe
prego ch' appaghe   il cor, vera beatrice.   52

Vergine sola al mondo, senza esempio,
che 'l Ciel di tue bellezze innamorasti,
cui né prima fu simil né seconda:
santi penseri, atti pietosi et casti
al vero Dio sacrato et vivo tempio
fecero in tua verginità feconda.   58
Per te po la mia vita esser ioconda
s' a' tuoi preghi, o Maria,
Vergine dolce et pia,
ove 'l fallo abondò la grazia abonda.
Con le ginocchia de la mente inchine
prego che sia mia scorta
et la mia torta   via drizzi a buon fine.   65

Bright Virgin, stable for eternity, star of this tempestuous sea, guide on whom every faithful helmsman relies: see in what a terrible storm I am, alone, without a tiller, and I am close to the last screams.

But still my soul relies on you, sinful though it be, I do not deny it, Virgin, but I beg you that your enemy may not laugh at my harm. Remember that our sins made God take on, to save us, human flesh in your virginal cloister.

Virgin, how many tears have I already scattered, how many pleadings, and how many prayers in vain, only for my pain and my heavy loss! Since I was born on the bank of Arno, searching in this and now this other direction, my life has been nothing but troubles;

mortal beauty, acts, and words have burdened all my soul. Holy and life-giving Virgin, do not delay, for I am perhaps in my last year; my days, more swift than an arrow, have gone away amid wretchedness and sin, and only Death awaits me.

Virgin, one is now dust and makes my soul grieve who kept it, while alive, in weeping and of my thousand sufferings did not know one; and though she had known them, what happened would still have happened, for any other desire in her would have been death to me and dishonor to her.

Now you, Lady of Heaven, you our goddess (if it is permitted and fitting to say it), Virgin of deep wisdom: you see all, and what another could not do is nothing to your great power, to put an end to my sorrow, which to you would be honor and to me salvation.

---

your enemy: Satan; see Genesis 3: 14–15.   bank of Arno: Petrarch's birth-place is Arezzo.

Vergine chiara et stabile in eterno,
di questo tempestoso mare stella,
d'ogni fedel nocchier fidata guida:
pon mente in che terribile procella
i' mi ritrovo sol, senza governo,
et ò già da vicin l'ultime strida.   71
Ma pur in te l'anima mia si fida,
peccatrice, i' nol nego,
Vergine, ma ti prego
che 'l tuo nemico del mio mal non rida.
Ricorditi che fece il peccar nostro
prender Dio per scamparne
umana carne   al tuo virginal chiostro.   78

Vergine, quante lagrime ò già sparte,
quante lusinghe et quanti preghi indarno,
pur per mia pena et per mio grave danno!
Da poi ch' i' nacqui in su la riva d'Arno,
cercando or questa et or quell'altra parte,
non è stata mia vita altro ch' affanno: 84
mortal bellezza, atti et parole m'ànno
tutta ingombrata l'alma.
Vergine sacra et alma,
non tardar, ch' i' son forse a l'ultimo anno;
i dì miei più correnti che saetta
fra miserie et peccati
son sen' andati   et sol Morte n'aspetta.   91

Vergine, tale è terra et posto à in doglia
lo mio cor, che vivendo in pianto il tenne
et de mille miei mali un non sapea;
et per saperlo pur quel che n'avenne
fora avvenuto, ch' ogni altra sua voglia
era a me morte et a lei fama rea.   97
Or tu, Donna del ciel, tu nostra Dea
(se dir lice et convensi),
Vergine d'alti sensi:
tu vedi il tutto, et quel che non potea
far altri è nulla a la tua gran vertute:
por fine al mio dolore
ch' a te onore   et a me fia salute.   104

Virgin in whom I have put all my hopes that you will be able and will wish to help me in my great need: do not leave me at the last pass, do not consider me, but Him who deigned to create me; let not my worth but His high likeness that is in me move you to help one so low.

Medusa and my error have made me a stone dripping vain moisture. Virgin, fill my weary heart with holy repentant tears, let at least my last weeping be devout and without earthly mud, as was my first vow, before my insanity.

Kindly Virgin, enemy of pride, let love of our common origin move you, have mercy on a contrite and humble heart; for if I am wont to love with such marvelous faith a bit of deciduous mortal dust, how will I love you, a noble thing?

If from my wretched and vile state I rise again at your hands, Virgin, I consecrate and cleanse in your name my thought and wit and style, my tongue and heart, my tears and my sighs. Lead me to the better crossing and accept my changed desires.

The day draws near and cannot be far, time so runs and flies, single, sole Virgin; and now conscience, now death pierces my heart: commend me to your Son, true man and true God, that He may receive my last breath in peace.

Vergine in cui ò tutta mia speranza,
che possi et vogli al gran bisogno aitarme:
non mi lasciare in su l'estremo passo;
non guardar me, ma chi degnò crearme,
no 'l mio valor, ma l'alta sua sembianza
ch' è in me ti mova a curar d'uom sì basso.   110
 Medusa et l'error mio m'àn fatto un sasso
d'umor vano stillante.
Vergine, tu di sante
lagrime et pie adempi 'l meo cor lasso,
ch' almen l'ultimo pianto sia devoto,
senza terrestro limo,
come fu 'l primo non d'insania voto.   117

 Vergine umana et nemica d'orgoglio:
del comune principio amor t'induca
miserere d'un cor contrito umile;
ché se poca mortal terra caduca
amar con sì mirabil fede soglio,
che devrò far di te, cosa gentile?   123
 Se dal mio stato assai misero et vile
per le tue man resurgo,
Vergine, i' sacro et purgo
al tuo nome et pensieri e 'ngegno et stile,
la lingua e 'l cor, le lagrime e i sospiri.
Scorgimi al miglior guado
et prendi in grado i cangiati desiri.   130

 Il dì s'appressa et non pote esser lunge,
sì corre il tempo et vola,
Vergine unica et sola,
e 'l cor or conscienzia or morte punge:
raccomandami al tuo Figliuol, verace
omo et verace Dio,
ch' accolga 'l mio spirto ultimo in pace.   137

Poems Excluded
from the *Rime sparse*

1

A lady comes often to my mind, another lady is always there; therefore I fear my ardent heart may sicken.

That lady nourishes my heart in amorous fire with a sweet suffering full of desire; this one wrings it beyond measure and inflames it so much that it must sigh doubly.

Nor does it help me to become angry and arm my heart against her, for I do not know how Love permits her this, and it offends me greatly.

This ballata was originally included in the *Rime sparse* as poem 121. Petrarch expunged it from Vat. Lat. 3195, his definitive version, and substituted another ballata.

2

When from time to time, moved with a just anger, I put aside my accustomed humility—I mean from my appearance alone, and it I arm with some small harshness, for I cannot do more—

swiftly one who is stronger comes against me, to turn me with a glance into a piece of marble similar to the one for whom Hercules put his shoulders and arms and back to the great weight.

Then, because my scattered powers return from my frontiers to my heart to console his sighs and lamentations,

my face regains its former pallor. Therefore she for shame refrains from demonstrating her utmost force on one who is dying.

Hercules: Hercules persuaded the giant Atlas to obtain the golden apples of the Hesperides for him and held the sky up in Atlas's absence. For Atlas's transformation by the head of Medusa, see note to poem 51 of the *Rime sparse*.

1

Donna mi vene spesso ne la mente,
altra donna v'è sempre;
ond' io temo si stempre   il core ardente.   3

Quella il notrica in amorosa fiamma
con un dolce martir pien de disire,
questa lo strugge oltre misura e 'nfiamma
tanto ch' a doppio è forza ch' e' sospire.   7

Né val perch' io m'adire   et armi il core,
ch' io non so come Amore,
di ch' io forte mi sdegno, gliel consente.   10

(Chigi L.V. 176)

2

Quando talor, da giusta ira commosso,
de l'usata umiltà pur mi disarmo—
dico la sola vista, et lei stessa armo
di poco sdegno, che d'assai non posso—   4

ratto mi giugne una più forte adosso
per far di me, volgendo gli occhi, un marmo
simile a que' per cui le spalle et l'armo
Ercole pose a la gran soma, e 'l dosso.   8

Allor, però che da le parti estreme
la mia sparsa virtù s'assembla al core
per consolarlo, che sospira e geme,   11

ritorna al volto il suo primo colore;
ond' ella per vergogna si riteme
di provar poi sua forza in un che more.   14

(Vat. Lat. 3196)

3   *My Reply to One Sent from Paris*

Many times a day I turn crimson and dark, thinking of the painful harsh chains with which the world involves me and holds me back so that I cannot come to you.

For to my weak distorted sight it seemed that at your hands I had some hope, and then I said: "If life sustains me, there will be time to return to the air of Tuscany."

From both those territories today I am in exile, for every smallest stream is a great obstacle to me, and here I am a slave though I dream of liberty.

Not a laurel crown, but a crown of sorbs weighs down my brow. Now I ask you if yours is not a sickness similar to mine.

The recipient of this poem has not been identified.

4   *A Reply of Mine, My Lord Commanding*

Sometimes one knight unhorses a whole squadron, when Fortune brings him to so much honor, and then later hardly defends himself against one: so time frees and imprisons valor.

Therefore perhaps he who today is prodigal of mortal blows will one day suffer for them, if I can but a little regain my breath or if Love removes the iron of his first arrow.

On this hope I feed and live, in heat and cold, at dawn and at vespers; with it I wake and sleep and read and write.

This makes my wounds so tranquil that I do not feel them, with such eagerness I come to strike him who wounded me through her beautiful eyes.

The occasion and recipient of this obscure poem are not known. "My lord" is presumably Cardinal Giovanni Colonna.

he who . . . is prodigal: Love?

3   Responsio mea ad unum missum de Parisiis

Più volte il dì mi fo vermiglio et fosco
pensando a le noiose aspre catene
di che 'l mondo m'involve et mi ritene
ch' i' non possa venir ad esser vosco;   4

che pur, al mio vedere fragile et losco,
avea ne le man vostre alcuna spene,
et poi dicea: "Se vita mi sostene,
tempo fia di tornarsi a l'aere tosco."   8

D'ambedue que' confin son oggi in bando,
ch' ogni vil fiumicel m'è gran distorbo,
et qui son servo, libertà sognando;   11

né di lauro corona, ma d'un sorbo
mi grava in giù la fronte. Or v'adimando
se 'l vostro al mio non è simil morbo.   14

(Vat. Lat. 3196)

4   Responsio mea. Domino iubente.

Tal cavalier tutta una schiera atterra
quando fortuna a tanto onore il mena,
che da un sol poi si difende a pena:
così 'l tempo apre le prodeze e serra.   4

Però forse costui ch' oggi diserra
colpi morta' ne porterà ancor pena,
s' i' posso un poco mai raccoglier lena
o se del primo strale Amor mi sferra.   8

Di questa spene mi nutrico et vivo
al caldo e al freddo, a l'alba et a le squille,
con essa vegghio e dormo et leggo et scrivo.   11

Questa fa le mie piaghe sì tranquille
ch' io non le sento, con tal voglia arrivo
a ferir lui che co' begli occhi aprille.   14

(Vat. Lat. 3196)

5   *Another Reply of Mine, My Lord Furnishing the Subject and Commanding*

Death, who strikes down the creatures of the world and reduces them to their first principle, struck that knight who fills all lands that the sea girds and locks.

But he is a basilisk that opens his eyes to give death and pain, so that no lance or chain can protect one who jousts with him.

There is but one antidote to his harmful gaze—to arm oneself with mirrors, so that when he flashes out, it may return back to him, like a river to its source;

by gazing on himself he must use up his rage. In this way both this and other cities will be saved.

Using the same rhymes as the previous poem.
  that knight: Love?   basilisk: mythological reptile, whose glance was fatal.

6   *A Reply*

If Phoebus is not a liar to his first love or has not changed his mind because of some new pleasure, never can that beautiful laurel leave his mind in whose shade I melt and burn.

This alone can make him swift or slow, glad or sorrowful, timid or bold; for at the sound of her name he seems afraid, and once against Python he was so valiant.

No other, surely, perturbed him then, when you opened your eyes on his handsome face and his changed appearance left them unharmed.

But if the one you say has indeed turned him pale, it is perhaps some resemblance of their faces: but I know well that my words will seem unlikely.

A reply, using the same rhymes, to a sonnet by Ser Dietisalvi di Siena (Appendix One, p. 607).
  Python: mythological monster serpent. According to Ovid's account, Apollo fell in love with Daphne immediately after killing it.   the one you say: Ser Dietisalvi's poem suggests that the sun was dimmed at the sight of a lady other than Laura.

5   *Alia Responsio mea.*
Domino materiam dante et iubente.

Quella che gli animai del mondo atterra
et nel primo principio gli rimena
percosse il cavalier del qual è piena
ogni contrada che 'l mar cinge et serra.   4

Ma questo è un basilisco che diserra
gli occhi feroci a porger morte et pena,
tal che giamai né lancia né catena
porian far salvo chi con lui s'afferra.   8

Un sol remedio à il suo sguardo nocivo:
di specchi armarsi a ciò ch' egli sfaville
et torne quasi a la fontana il rivo: 11

mirando sé conven che si destille
quella sua rabbia. Al modo ch' io ne scrivo
fia assicurata questa et l'altre ville.   14

(Vat. Lat. 3196)

6   *Risposta*

Se Febo al primo amor non è bugiardo
o per novo piacer non si ripente,
giamai non gli esce il bel lauro di mente
a la cui ombra io mi distruggo et ardo.   4

Questi solo il può far veloce e tardo,
et lieto et tristo, et timido et valente,
ch' al suon del nome suo par che pavente
et fu contra Fitòn già sì gagliardo.   8

Altri per certo no 'l turbava allora
quando nel suo bel viso gli occhi apriste
et non gli offese il variato aspetto.   11

Ma se pur chi voi dite il discolora,
sembianza è forse alcuna de le viste:
et so ben che 'l mio dir parrà sospetto.   14

(Vat. Lat. 3196)

7   *A Reply to Iacopo da Imola*

She who bound my youthful heart in the first time I knew love, by departing from her graceful dwelling has loosed me, to my pain, from a lovely knot.

Nor since has any new beauty seized my soul, nor has it felt any light that could make it burn, except by the memory of the worth of her who with sweet severity impelled it.

He who with her lovely eyes unlocked my soul has of course wished to try his wit again with other keys; but new nets do not entrap an experienced bird.

Yet I have been in danger between Charybdis and Scylla, and I have passed the Sirens in a deaf ship, or like a man who listens without understanding.

Iacopo da Imola's poem has been lost.

8

In heaven, in the air, on earth, in the fire, and in the sea, Love strikes and flies without any mantle; against his golden darts there is no charm; but if he wishes, he can cure with a leaden one.

In the midst of summer he makes one tremble, and burn in the dead of winter; and the more one struggles to escape and leave weeping, the more he involves one in tears.

My nurse, my swaddling clothes, and my cradle I have cursed a thousand times, and the years I have lived tasting this golden martyrdom;

but at the end I believe I can shake off these ropes and remedy my grievous troubles, if with humble patience I await the time.

7   Responsio ad Iacobum de Imola

Quella che 'l giovenil meo core avinse
nel primo tempo ch' io conobbi amore,
del suo leggiadro albergo escendo fore
con mio dolor d'un bel nodo mi scinse.   4

Né poi nova belleza l'alma strinse,
né mai luce sentì che fesse ardore
se non co la memoria del valore
che per dolci durezze la sospinse.   8

Ben volse quei che co' begli occhi aprilla
con altra chiave riprovar suo ingegno,
ma nova rete vecchio augel non prende.   11

Et pur fui in dubbio fra Caribdi e Scilla,
et passai le Sirene in sordo legno
o ver come uom ch' ascolta e nulla intende.   14

(Vat. Lat. 3196)

8

In cielo, in aria, in terra, in fuoco e in mare
Amor percuote e vola senza manto;
contra suo' strali orati non è incanto,
ma se col piombo vuol, può risanare.   4

A media state fa l'uomo tremare
et arder a gran verno, et più che quanto
se sforza di campar e uscir di pianto
in più vilupi e lacrime fa intrare.   8

La baila, le mie fascie e la mia cuna
ò biastemato mille fiate, e gli anni
onde io son vivo e gusto aureo martire;   11

m' al fin i' credo scioglier queste funa
o dar rimedio a' mie' gravosi affanni,
se tempo aspetto con umil sufrire.   14

(Casanatense 924)

9

The gold and the pearls and the lovely little flowers and the grass where Nature seems to use more than silk, the white hands and angelic fingers that reserve themselves only to noble works,

those eyes whose turning sweetens every cruelty, and the smile that forbids the air to darken, and that happy face that would humble every proud beast—

look at them, before God, look at them, noble Lord, if you have ever hoped to see on earth a sweet and very paradise:

you will see something to quiet and humble Vulcan, and Jove when he looses most thunderbolts on some condemned place down here.

The recipient of this poem has not been identified.

10

New beauty in a noble habit turned my heart to the amorous flock where pain is suffered and good is hoped for.

I must go and stand still at another's will, since on my wandering thoughts has been placed a bridle of sweet scorns and merciful glances; and the bright name and the sound of the words of my lady, and her clear face are the sparks, Love, with which you burn my heart.

I still hope for mercy, however late, for, though she show herself bitter and fierce, a humble lover overcomes a proud lady.

9

L'oro e le perle e i bei fioreti e l'erba
've par Natura aduopre più che seta,
le bianche mano e l'angelice deta
che a nobil uopre a punto se riserba,   4

quegli occhi che 'l voltar suo disacerba
ogni crudezza, e 'l riso che divieta
turbarsi l'aria, e quella faza lieta
che umil farebe ogni fera superba—   8

mirategli per Dio, signor gentile,
mitrategli, se mai bramaste in terra
veder un dolce e proprio paradiso: 11

vedrete cose d'aquetar umile
Vulcano, e Iove allor che più disserra
per fulminar qua giù luoco preciso.   14

(Casanatense 924)

10

Nuova bellezza in abito gentile
volse il mio core a l'amorosa schiera
ove 'l mal si sostene e 'l ben si spera.   3

Gir mi convene e star com' altri vole
poi ch' al vago penser fu posto un fren
di dolci sdegni e di pietosi sguardi;
e 'l chiaro nome e 'l suon de le parole
de la mia donna e 'l bel viso sereno
son le faville, Amor, di che 'l cor m'ardi.   9

I' pur spero mercé, quantunche tardi,
che, ben ella si mostre acerba e fera,
umile amante vince donna altera.   12

(Casanatense 924)

11

The amorous sparks and the sweet light of your lovely eyes, of which my memory is full, make my life always bright.

Lady, the high voyage on which I humbly exert myself to merit your grace with its difficulty would already have tired me, except that Love from your beautiful shining face is my guide and unfailing star, showing himself in the lovely black and white;
   and so my desirous heart sighs and takes on new strength that leads it upward, conquering every obstacle that hinders it.

---

black and white: the pupils of the lady's eyes.

12

Love, you that dwell in Heaven and in noble hearts and inspire whatever worth there is in the world: quiet my flaming sighs.

A haughty lady with so sweet a glance raises my heavy thought up from the earth at times, that I must praise her eyes, but I grieve for the knot on account of which I am slow to pursue my good but live in war, with my soul rebellious against your messengers.
   Lord alone omniscient and omnipotent, still I hope that You will turn my steps toward where at last I may breathe in perfect peace.

11

L'amorose faville e 'l dolce lume
de' be' vostri occhi, onde la mente ò piena,
fanno la vita mia sempre serena.   3

Donna, l'alto viaggio ond' io m'ingegno
meritar vostra grazia umilemente
con sua durezza m'averia già stanco
se non ch' Amor dal bel viso lucente
si fa mia scorta et infallibil segno,
mostrandosi nel bel nero et nel bianco;   9
onde sospira il disioso fianco
e riprende valor che 'n alto il mena,
vincendo ogni contrario che l'affrena.   12

(Casanatense 924)

12

Amor che 'n Cielo e 'n gentil core alberghi
e quanto è di valore al mondo inspiri:
acqueta l'infiammati miei sospiri.   3

Altera donna con sì dolce sguardo
leva il grave pensier talor da terra
che lodar mi conven degli occhi suoi,
ma dogliomi del nodo ond' io son tardo
'a seguire il mio bene, e vivo in guerra
coll'alma rebellante a' messi tuoi.   9
Signor che solo intendi tutto e puoi,
pur spero che' miei passi in parte giri
ove 'n pace perfetta alfin respiri.   12

(Vat. Lat. 3196)

13

Wit accustomed to profound questions, you cannot rest from your high work; but why do you not rather awaken one of those who reply without uncertainty?

My rhymes are astray elsewhere, following her for whom I grow pale, her lovely eyes and her golden tresses and her sweet speech that confounds me.

But I believe that at the same moment Love and Hope are born within the heart, and that neither can stay there without the other, in the beginning.

If the yearned-for good with its presence satisfies the soul later, then, it seems to me, Love lives on alone and his sister dies.

———

A reply, using the same rhymes, to a sonnet by Antonio da Ferrara (Appendix One, p. 603).
his sister: Hope.

14

Antonio, your city has done a thing that I never believed possible! It so moved the keys of my heart that it opened the way that reason keeps locked;

and the lord who used to war on me, secretly entering, struck me with two lovely eyes so that in my bones I carry the wound, and time does not remove the iron,

but rather kills me, and I refrain through shame from asking about the cause of my suffering, nor do I find any with whom I can share my thoughts;

and like one who is suddenly wakened as he dreams of new pleasures, so I keep thinking only who she can be.

———

Addressed to Antonio da Ferrara.

13

Ingegno usato a le question profonde,
cessar non sai dal tuo alto lavoro;
ma perché non destar anzi un di loro
ove, senz' alcun forse, si risponde?   4

Le rime mie son desviate altronde
dietro a colei per cui mi discoloro,
a' suo' begli occhi et alle trecce d'oro
et al dolce parlar che mi confonde.   8

Ma credo che 'n un punto dentro al core
nasce Amore e Speranza, e mai l'un stare senza
l'altro non possa nel principio stare.   11

Se 'l desiato ben per sua presenza
queta poi l'alma, sì come a me pare,
vive Amor solo e la sorella more.   14

14

Antonio, cosa à fatto la tua terra
ch' io non credea che mai possibil fosse!
Ella à le chiavi del mio cor sì mosse
che n'à aperta la via che ragion serra;   4

onde il signor che mi solea far guerra
celatamente entrando mi percosse
da duo begli occhi, sì che dentro all'osse
porto la piaga, e 'l tempo non mi sferra,   8

anzi m'ancide, e lasso per vergogna
di domandar de la cagion del duolo,
né trovo con chi parta i pensier miei;   11

e come suol chi nuovo piacer sogna
se di subito è desto, così solo
torno a pensar chi puote esser costei.   14

APPENDIX ONE

Poems Addressed
to Petrarch

Andrea Stramazzo da Perugia

That holy fame of which the moderns are almost entirely deprived and which now sounds only of the few, messer Francesco, attributes great worth to you as one who is rich in Apollo's treasure.

Now may it please your noble mind to be influenced by my prayers and inclined to share with me the fount of Helicon, to drink of which I derive many channels:

thinking how Cecropian Pallas, barring no man from her vessel, gives of herself even beyond one's hope;

and there is no good that is pleasing to one who appropriates it entirely to himself, as Seneca writes to Lucilius.

Petrarch's reply is poem 24 of the *Rime sparse*.

Helicon: see note to poem 7 of the *Rime sparse*.   Cecropian: Athenian.
as Seneca writes: a reference to *Epistola moralis* 6.4: "Possession of a good is never pleasant without a companion."

Antonio da Ferrara

O latter-day Tarpeia, in whom is hid that eloquent, bright treasure of the triumph of poetry, who plucked the Peneian laurel for its evergreen leaves:

open so much that your well-spoken joys may be shown to those who are waiting, and to me who yearn for them more than a thirsty stag for the clear waters.

Ah, do not wish to hide the power that Apollo grants you, for knowledge when communicated grows:

but open your eloquent style; and deign to explain to me a little, which came first, Hope or Love.

Petrarch's reply can be found on page 599.

Tarpeia: see note on "Tarpeian Mount," poem 53 of the *Rime sparse*.
Peneian laurel: see note to poem 5 of the *Rime sparse*.

Andrea Stramazzo da Perugia

La santa fama, de la qual son prive
quasi i moderni, e già di pochi sona,
messer Francesco, gran pregio vi dona,
che del tesor d'Apollo siate dive.   4

Or piaccia ch' a' mie' preghi suggestive
la vostra nobil mente renda prona
participarmi il fonte d'Elicona,
che per più berne più dilato rive: 8

pensando come Pallade Cecropia
a nessuno uomo arcando il suo vessillo,
ma oltra al disiar, di sé fa copia;   11

e non è alcun ben iocondo a quillo
che senza alcun consorte a sé l'appropia,
sì come scrive Seneca a Lucillo.   14

Antonio da Ferrara

O novella Tarpea, in cui s'asconde
quell'eloquente e lucido tesoro
del trionfo poetico, che alloro
peneio colse per le verdi fronde: 4

apri tanto che da le faconde
tue gioie si dimostrino a coloro
che aspettano, et a me ch' in ciò m'accoro
più che assetato cervo a le chiare onde.   8

Deh, non voler ascondere il valore
che ti concede Apollo, ché scienza
comunicata suol multiplicare,   11

ma apri lo stil tuo d'eloquenza,
e voglia alquanto me certificare
qual fu prima, Speranza o vero Amore.   14

Giovanni Dondi dell Orologio

I do not know if I see what I see, if I touch what I am even now
handling, if I hear what I hear, and whether lies or truth be what
I speak and what I read.

I am so troubled that I cannot stand, nor do I find a place, nor
do I know if I exist, and the more I turn my fancy about, the
more it dazzles me, nor do I correct myself.

One hope, one counselor, one support remains to me in such
deep stupor, you; in you is my health and my strength;

you have the knowledge, the power, and the wit: direct me so
that, leaving error, my wandering bark may reach port.

Petrarch's reply is poem 244 of the *Rime sparse*.

Antonio da Ferrara

Love's bow, that looses new thirst in you, slaying your reason
and all your powers, not long ago struck me also, so that my
brains are still almost buried.

Therefore, seeing how Love takes hold in a worthy mind and
how he moved your heart earlier, so that it never freed itself, I
fear that he is catching you in a close prison.

But, truly, another thought troubles me: that Love has captured you to his sweet band, driving from you all thought of me;

therefore I am getting ready to leave Bologna and come to you,
for there is nothing else I desire, as long as she keeps you there in
Ferrara.

A reply to Petrarch's "Antonio, cosa a fatto la tua terra" (p. 599).

Giovanni Dondi dell'Orologio

Io non so ben s' io vedo quel ch' io veggio,
s' i' tocco quel ch' i' palpo tuttavia,
se quel ch' i' odo oda, e sia busia
o vero e ciò che parlo e ciò ch' io leggio.   4

Sì travagliato son ch' io non mi reggio,
né trovo loco, né so s' i' mi sia,
e quanto volgo più la fantasia
più m'abarbaglia, né me ne correggio.   8

Una speranza, un consiglio, un ritegno
tu sol mi sei in sì alto stupore;
in te sta la salute e 'l mio conforto;   11

tu a' el saper, el poder e l'ingegno:
drizzami sì che tolta da l'errore
la vaga mia barchetta prenda porto.   14

Antonio da Ferrara

L'arco che in voi nova sita disserra
ragion vostra occidendo e tutte posse,
non è gran tempo che sì mi percosse
che ancora è quasi il mio pensier sotterra.   4

Onde veggendo quanto Amor s'afferra
in valorosa mente, e come mosse
già vostro core e mai non si riscosse,
temo che non vi aggiunga in stretta serra.   8

Vero è ch' un' altro pensier mi rampogna,
ch' Amor sì v'ha condotto al dolce stuolo
da voi cacciando tutti i pensier miei;   11

però m'appresto di lasciar Bologna
e vegnir presso a voi, ch' altro non golo,
pur che in Ferrara vi leghi colei.   14

Ser Dietisalvi Petri di Siena

Apollo's handsome eye, in whose gaze Juno feels a clear and amorous light, wishing to show how powerful his force is, against her who disdains all arrows,

in the hour when his gaze shines brightest, with his rays all ablaze came in array; but when he saw her luminous face, without waiting at all he fled like a coward.

Beauty and virtue that adorn her, never before seen perfectly in one person, were the cause of his high new emotion.

But which of those two united together honors Phoebus more and which her, I do not know: therefore do you fill out my lack.

Petrarch's reply can be found on page 591.
Apollo's . . . eye: the sun.   Juno: the air.   her who disdains: Ser Dietisalvi's beloved.

A Reply by My Sennuccio

Beyond her usual wont, the green laurel turns toward the place where now I sit, and more attentive; and the more I see her the more fixedly she looks in this direction,

and it seems to me now that a sorrow mixed with anger afflicts her so much that I must not be silent; therefore I call to you from her side, for she tells me that the suffering is too great.

And our lord still abounds in desire to see you sit at his table, and I have observed this in his words and in his manner;

a Column better based than him you could never find in five feasts of Saint John, on the eve of which I undertook to write to you.

A reply to poem 266 of the *Rime sparse*.
green laurel: see note to poem 5.   our lord: Cardinal Giovanni Colonna.
feasts of Saint John: Saint John was obviously Giovanni Colonna's patron saint; his feast is June 24.

Ser Dietisalvi Petri di Siena

El bell'occhio d'Apollo, dal cui guardo
sereno et vago lume Iunon sente,
volendo sua virtù mostrar possente,
contr' a colei che non apprezza dardo 4

nell'ora che più luce il suo riguardo
coi raggi accesi giunse orditamente;
ma quando vide il viso splendiente,
senza aspettar fuggì come codardo. 8

Bellezza et onestà che la colora,
perfettamente in altra mai non viste,
furon cagion dell'alto et nuovo affetto. 11

Ma qual di queste due unite et miste
più dotto Febo et qual più lei onora,
non so: dunque adempite il mio difetto. 14

(Vat. Lat. 3196)

Responsio Sennuccio nostri

Oltra l'usato modo si rigira
lo verde lauro ai qui dov' io or seggio,
et più attenta; et com' più la riveggio,
di qui in qui con gli occhi fiso mira, 4

et parmi omai ch' un dolor misto d'ira
l'affligga tanto che tacer nol deggio;
onde dal lato suo io vi richeggio,
ch' esso mi ditta ch' è troppo martira. 8

E 'l signor nostro in desire sempre abonna
di verdervi seder nelli suoi scanni,
e 'n atto et in parlar questo distinsi; 11

mei fondata di lui trovar colonna
non potreste in cinqu' altri San Giovanni,
la cui vigilia a scriver mi sospinsi. 14

(Vat. Lat. 3196)

Giacomo Colonna, Bishop of Lombez

If the parts of my body, destroyed and reduced to atoms and sparks of fire by infinite thousands, were all tongues and brought to speech,

and if all voices living and dead, that were sharper than the sword of Hector or Achilles to whoever heard them sound, all cried aloud like beaten children,

they could not recount or reach the end of telling how much my body and my limbs were delighted and how happy my mind was, hearing tell that in the Roman Forum

on the temples of the new and worthy Florentine poet there grew green a laurel wreath.

Petrarch's reply is poem 322 of the *Rime sparse.*

in the Roman Forum: Petrarch is imagined as walking around the ruins of ancient Rome wearing his laurel crown, with which he was crowned on the Capitoline Hill on Easter Sunday, 1341.

Geri Gianfigliazzi

Messer Francesco, he who sighs in love for a lady who still wills to be his enemy, and the more he cries mercy the crueler she is to him, hiding from him the two suns that he most desires,

inspired by nature or by knowledge, say what he should do who sees himself treated thus, and if he should leave her flock, though it be not without sorrow.

You speak often with Love, and I know that no condition of his is hidden from you, thanks to the high wit of your mind.

My mind, which has always been with him and understands him less now than at the beginning, do you counsel; and that will be my true excuse.

Petrarch's reply is poem 179 of the *Rime sparse.*

Iacombus de columna Lomberensis episcopus

Se le parti del corpo mio destrutte
et ritornate in athomi et faville
per infinita quantità di mille
fossino lingue et in sermon ridutte,   4

et si le voci vive et morte tutte
che più che spada de Ettor et d'Achille
tagliaron mai chi resonare odille
gridassen come verberate putte,   8

quanto lo corpo et le mie membra foro
allegre et quanto la mia mente leta,
odendo dir che nel romano foro   11

del novo et degno fiorentin poeta
sopra le tempie verdeggiava illoro,
non porian contar né porre meta.   14

(Vat. Lat. 3196)

Geri Gianfigliazzi

Messer Francesco, chi d'amor sospira
per donna ch' esser pur vuolgli guerrera,
et con' più merzé grida et più gli è fera,
celandogli i duo soli che più desira   4

qual che natura o scienza inspira,
che deggia far colui che 'n tal maniera
trattar si vede, dite, et se da schiera
partir si dee ben che non sia senza ira.   8

Voi ragionate con Amor sovente,
et nulla sua condizion so v'è chiusa
per l'alto ingegno de la vostra mente.   11

La mia che sempre mai collui è usa,
et men ch' al primo il conosce al presente,
consigliate; et ciò fia sua vera scusa.   14

(Vat. Lat. 3196)

APPENDIX TWO

Dante's *Rime petrose* and
Canzone montanina

1

I have come to that point on the wheel when the horizon
gives birth at sunset to the twinned heaven
    and the star of love is kept from us by the sun's ray that so
envelopes her transversely that she is veiled;
    and that planet which strengthens the frost shows itself to
us utterly, all along the great arc where each of the seven casts
little shadow: and nonetheless my mind casts off not one of
the thoughts of love that burden me, mind harder than stone to
hold fast an image of stone.

There arises from the sand of Ethiopia a traveling wind that
darkens the air, all because of the sun's sphere that heats it now;
    and it crosses the sea and brings us such a supply of cloud that
if some other wind does not scatter it, it shuts and solidifies all
this hemisphere;
    and then it resolves itself and falls in white flakes of cold
snow and in harmful rain, and the air becomes all grieving and
weeps: and Love, though he take down his spiderwebs from the
sky on account of the rising wind, he does not abandon me, so
beautiful a lady is this cruel one given to me as lady.

Every bird that pursues the warmth has fled the lands of
Europe, which never once lose the seven cold stars;
    and the others have posted a truce to their songs and will not
sound them again until the green season, unless it be for some
misfortune;
    and all animals that are happy by nature are released from
loving, for the cold extinguishes their spirit: and mine bears
more love; for sweet thoughts are not taken from me nor given
to me by time's turning, but a lady gives them who has lived but
a short time.

Poems 1–4 are Dante's *rime petrose* (stony rhymes), so called because the central theme is the unyielding cruelty of the lady.   The astronomical configuration described here corresponds to the position of the planets in the winter of 1296.   twinned heaven: Gemini, Dante's natal sign, which rises at sunset in December and January, when the sun rises in Capricorn.   star of love: the planet Venus.   planet which strengthens the frost: Saturn.   the great arc: the Tropic of Cancer.   each of seven: the seven planets.   seven cold stars: the constellation Ursa Major, which never sets on the northern hemisphere.

1

Io son venuto al punto de la rota
che l'orizzonte, quando il sol si corca,
ci partorisce il geminato cielo,
   e la stella d'amor ci sta remota
per lo raggio lucente che la 'nforca
sì di traverso che le si fa velo;   6
   e quel pianeta che conforta il gelo
si mostra tutto a noi per lo grand' arco
nel qual ciascun di sette fa poca ombra:
e però non disgombra
un sol penser d'amore, ond' io son carco,
la mente mia ch' è più dura che petra
in tener forte imagine di petra.   13

Levasi de la rena d'Etiopia
lo vento peregrin che l'aere turba,
per la spera del sol ch' ora la scalda;
   e passa il mare, onde conduce copia
di nebbia tal che, s' altro non la sturba,
questo emisperio chiude tutto e salda;   19
   e poi si solve, e cade in bianca falda
di fredda neve ed in noiosa pioggia,
onde l'aere s'attrista tutto e piagne:
e Amor, che sue ragne
ritira in alto pel vento che poggia,
non m'abbandona, sì è bella donna
questa crudel che m'è data per donna.   26

   Fuggito è ogne augel che 'l caldo segue
del paese d'Europa, che non perde
le sette stelle gelide unquemai;
   e li altri han posto a le lor voci triegue
per non sonarle infino al tempo verde,
se ciò non fosse per cagion di guai;   32
   e tutti li animali che son gai
di lor natura, son d'amor disciolti,
però che 'l freddo lor spirito ammorta:
e 'l mio più d'amor porta;
ché li dolzi pensier' non mi son tolti
né mi son dati per volta di tempo,
ma donna li mi dà c' ha picciol tempo.   39

The leaves have passed their limit, appointed when Aries brought them forth to adorn the world, and the grass is dead;
    every branch with green leaves is hidden from us, except in laurel, pine, fir, or other that keeps its verdure;
    and the season is so strong and bitter that it has killed the little flowers along the slopes, which cannot endure the frost: and his cruel thorn Love for all that does not draw from my heart, for I am certain to bear it ever while I am alive, though I should live forever.

The veins pour forth smoking waters because of the vapors the earth has in her belly, who draws them up from the abyss;
    therefore the path that on a fair day pleased me has now become a river and will be one as long as the great assault of winter lasts;
    it turns the ground into a surface like enamel, and the standing water changes to glass because of the cold that locks it in from without: and I in my war have not turned back one step for all that, nor do I wish to; for if the suffering is sweet, the death must surpass every other sweet.

Song, now what will become of me in that other sweet fresh season, when love rains down on the earth from all the heavens, if through these freezings love is only in me and not elsewhere? It will be with me as with a man of marble, if in a tender girl there is a heart of marble.

Aries: the sun enters Aries at the vernal equinox.   smoking waters: fountains were supposed to come forth from the earth with greater force and abundance if mixed with wind (vapors).

Passato hanno lor termine le fronde
che trasse fuor la vertù d'Ariete
per adornare il mondo, e morta è l'erba;
    ramo di foglia verde a noi s'asconde
se non se in lauro, in pino od in abete
o in alcun che sua verdura serba;   45
        e tanto è la stagion forte ed acerba
c' ha morti li fioretti per le piagge,
li quai non poten tollerar la brina:
e la crudele spina
però Amor di cor non la mi tragge;
per ch' io son fermo di portarla sempre
ch' io sarò in vita, s' io vivesse sempre.   52

    Versan le vene le fummifere acque
per li vapor' che la terra ha nel ventre,
che d'abisso li tira suso in alto;
    onde cammino al bel giorno mi piacque
che ora è fatto rivo, e sarà mentre
che durerà del verno il grande assalto;   58
        la terra fa un suol che par di smalto,
e l'acqua morta si converte in vetro
per la freddura che di fuor la serra:
e io de la mia guerra
non son però tornato un passo a retro,
né vo' tornar; ché, se 'l martiro è dolce,
la morte de' passar ogni altro dolce.   65

    Canzone, or che sarà di me ne l'altro
dolce tempo novello, quando piove
amore in terra da tutti li cieli,
    quando per questi geli
amore è solo in me, e non altrove?
Saranne quello ch' è d'un uom di marmo,
se in pargoletta fia per core un marmo.   72

2

To the shortened day and to the great circle of shade
I have come, alas! and to the whitening of the hills,
when the color is lost from the grass:
and my desire still does not change its green,
it is so rooted in the hard stone
that speaks and has sensation as if it were a lady.

So too this strange lady
stands there frozen, like snow in the shade:
for she is not moved except as a stone is
by the sweet season that warms the hills
and turns them from white to green
and clothes them with flowers and grass.

When she has on her head a garland of leaves
she drives from my mind every other lady:
because the curling yellow mingles with the green
so beautifully that Love comes to stay in the shade there,
Love who has locked me among little hills
more firmly than mortar locks a stone.

Her beauty has more power than a precious stone,
and the wound it gives cannot be healed by herbs:
for I have fled over plains and over hills
to learn to escape from such a lady;
and yet from her face there is no shade,
not of a hill, or a wall ever, or a green branch.

I saw her once dressed in green
such that she would have begotten in a stone
the love that I feel for her very shadow:
and so I have wished to have her in a fine meadow of grass,
as much in love as ever lady was,
a meadow closed in all around with high hills.

---

great circle of shade: long nights.   strange lady: *nova* may also mean
young.   in the shade there: in the shadow of her brow, that is, in her eyes.

2

Al poco giorno e al gran cerchio d'ombra
son giunto, lasso, ed al bianchir de' colli,
quando si perde lo color ne l'erba:
e 'l mio disio però non cangia il verde,
sì è barbato ne la dura petra
che parla e sente come fosse donna.   6

Similemente questa nova donna
si sta gelata come neve a l'ombra:
ché non la move, se non come petra,
il dolce tempo che riscalda i colli,
e che li fa tornar di bianco in verde
perché li copre di fioretti e d'erba.   12

Quand' ella ha in testa una ghirlanda d'erba,
trae de la mente nostra ogn' altra donna:
perché si mischia il crespo giallo e 'l verde
sì bel, ch' Amor lì viene a stare a l'ombra,
che m'ha serrato intra piccioli colli
più forte assai che la calcina petra.   18

La sua bellezza ha più vertù che petra,
e 'l colpo suo non può sanar per erba:
ch' io son fuggito per piani e per colli
per poter scampar da cotal donna;
e dal suo lume non mi può far ombra
poggio né muro mai né fronda verde.   24

Io l'ho veduta già vestita a verde,
sì fatta ch' ella avrebbe messo in petra
l'amor ch' io porto pur a la sua ombra:
ond' io l'ho chesta in un bel prato d'erba,
innamorata com' anco fu donna,
e chiuso intorno d'altissimi colli.   30

But well may the rivers climb the hills
before this moist green wood
will ever take fire (as ladies do)
for me, though I would endure to sleep on stone
all my season, and go eating grass,
so I might only see where her skirts make a shade.

Whenever the hills make blackest shade,
under a lovely green the youthful lady
makes them disappear, like a stone under the grass.

Ma ben ritorneranno i fiumi a' colli
prima che questo legno molle e verde
s'infiammi, come suol far bella donna,
di me; che mi torrei dormire in petra
tutto il mio tempo, e gir pascendo l'erba,
sol per veder do' suoi panni fanno ombra. 36

Quandunque i colli fanno più nera ombra,
sotto un bel verde la giovane donna
la fa sparer, com' uom petra sott' erba. 39

3

Love, you see perfectly well that this lady
cares nothing for your power at any time,
though you be accustomed to lord it over other ladies:
    and since she has become aware of being my lady
because of your light that shines in my face,
she has made herself Lady Cruelty
    so that she does not seem to have the heart of a woman
but of whatever beast keeps its love coldest:
for in the warm weather and in the cold
    she seems to me exactly like a lady
carved from some lovely precious stone
by the hand of some master carver of stone.

And I, who am constant (even more than a stone)
in obeying you, for the beauty of a lady,
I carry hidden away the wound from that stone
    with which you struck me as if I had been a stone
that had caused you pain for a long time,
so that the blow reached my heart, where I have turned to stone.
    And never was there found any precious stone
that from the brightness of the sun or its own light
had so much virtue or light
    that it could aid me against this stone,
that she not lead me with her coldness
to a place where I will be dead and cold.

Lord, you know that in the freezing cold
water becomes crystalline stone
under the mountain wind where the great cold is,
    and the air always turns into a cold
element there, so that water is queen
there, because of the cold:
    just so, before her expression that is all cold,
my blood freezes always, in all weather,
and the care that so shortens time for me
    turns everything into fluid cold
that issues from me through the lights
where her pitiless light came in.

---

crystalline stone: according to Pliny and other ancients, crystal is ice that has
been frozen for many years.   lights: his eyes.

3

Amor, tu vedi ben che questa donna
la tua vertù non cura in alcun tempo,
che suol de l'altre belle farsi donna;
    e poi s'accorse ch' ell' era mia donna
per lo tuo raggio ch' al volto mi luce,
d'ogne crudelità si fece donna;   6
        sì che non par ch' ell' abbia cor di donna,
ma di qual fiera l'ha d'amor più freddo:
che per lo tempo caldo e per lo freddo
    mi fa sembiante pur come una donna
che fosse fatta d'una bella petra
per man di quei che me' intagliasse in petra.   12

    E io, che son costante più che petra
in ubidirti per bieltà di donna,
porto nascoso il colpo de la petra
    con la qual tu mi desti come a petra
che t'avesse innoiato lungo tempo,
tal che m'andò al core ov' io son petra.   18
    E mai non si scoperse alcuna petra
o da splendor di sole o da sua luce,
che tanta avesse né vertù né luce
    che mi potesse atar da questa petra,
sì ch' ella non mi meni col suo freddo
colà dov' io sarò di morte freddo.   24

    Segnor, tu sai che per algente freddo
l'acqua diventa cristallina petra
là sotto tramontana ov' è il gran freddo,
    e l'aere sempre in elemento freddo
vi si converte, sì che l'acqua è donna
in quella parte per cagion del freddo: 30
        così dinanzi dal sembiante freddo
mi ghiaccia sopra il sangue d'ogne tempo,
e quel pensiero che m'accorcia il tempo
    mi si converte tutto in corpo freddo,
che m'esce poi per mezzo della luce
là ond' entrò la dispietata luce.   36

In her, beauty gathers all its light;
and so of all cruelty the cold
flows to her heart, not reached by your light:
    so beautiful into my eyes she shines
when I gaze on her, that I see her in stones
and in everything else, wherever I turn my sight.
    From her eyes comes to me the sweet light
that makes me not care about any other lady:
would that she were more merciful a lady
    toward me, for I call out night and day,
only to serve her, for place and time.
Nor for any other reason do I wish to live a long time.

    Therefore, O Power older than time,
than motion or palpable light,
take pity on me in my evil time;
    enter her heart now, for it is surely time,
and drive out the cold
that prevents me from having, like others, my time:
    for if your unavoidable time
reaches me in this state, she, noble stone,
will see me lie in little stone
    not to rise again until the end of time,
when I shall see if there was ever a lady
in the world as beautiful as this cruel lady.

    Song, I carry in my mind a lady
such that, although to me she is of stone,
still she gives me courage where all other men seem cold:
    so that I dare to make in this cold
the newness that lights up your form,
that was never conceived before in any time.

---

your unavoidable time: literally, your strong time—that of death.

In lei s'accoglie d'ogni bieltà luce;
così di tutta crudeltate il freddo
le corre al core, ove non va tua luce:
   per che ne li occhi sì bella mi luce
quando la miro, ch' io la veggio in petra,
e po' in ogni altro ov' io volga la mia luce.   42
   Da li occhi suoi mi ven la dolce luce
che mi fa non caler d'ogn'altra donna:
così foss' ella più pietosa donna
   ver' me, che chiamo di notte e di luce,
solo per lei servire, e luogo e tempo.
Né per altro disio viver gran tempo.   48

   Però, vertù che se' prima che tempo,
prima che moto o che sensibil luce,
increscati di me, c' ho sì mal tempo;
   entrale in core omai, che ben n'è tempo,
sì che per te se n'esca fuor lo freddo
che non mi lascia aver, com' altri, tempo: 54
   ché se mi giunge lo tuo forte tempo
in tale stato, questa gentil petra
mi vedrà coricare in poca petra,
   per non levarmi se non dopo il tempo
quando vedrò se mai fu bella donna
nel mondo come questa acerba donna.   60

   Canzone, io porto ne la mente donna
tal che, con tutto ch' ella mi sia petra,
mi dà baldanza, ond' ogni uom mi par freddo:
   sì ch' io ardisco a far per questo freddo
la novità che per tua forma luce,
che non fu mai pensata in alcun tempo.   66

4

So in my speech I would be harsh as in her acts this beautiful stone is, who more and more achieves greater hardness and crueler nature,

and she clothes her person with a crystal so hard that whether because of it or because she dodges, no arrow from any quiver finds her naked, ever.

And she kills and it avails no man to shield himself or gain distance from her mortal blows, which, as if they had wings, reach you and shatter any armor, and I neither know how nor have the power to protect myself from her.

I find no shield that she may not shatter nor place that may hide me from her sight, but, as a flower the tip of a plant, so of my mind she holds the summit.

Of my suffering she seems just as afraid as a ship is of a sea without waves; and the weight that is sinking me is such that no rhyme can equal it.

Ah, rasping pitiless file, silently wearing away my life, why are you not as afraid to gnaw so at my heart, layer by layer, as I am to tell who gives you your power?

4

Così nel mio parlar voglio esser aspro
com' è ne li atti questa bella petra,
la quale ognora impetra
maggior durezza e più natura cruda,
  e veste sua persona d'un diaspro
tal che per lui, o perch' ella s'arretra,
non esce di faretra
saetta che già mai la colga ignuda;   8
  ed ella ancide, e non val ch' om si chiuda
né si dilunghi da' colpi mortali
che, com' avesser ali,
giungono altrui e spezzan ciascun'arme:
sì ch' io non so da lei né posso atarme.   13

  Non trovo scudo ch' ella non mi spezzi
né loco che dal suo viso m'asconda:
ché, come fior di fronda,
così de la mia mente tien la cima.
  Cotanto del mio mal par che si prezzi
quanto legno di mar che non lieva onda;
e 'l peso che m'affonda
è tal che non potrebbe adequar rima.   21

  Ahi angosciosa e dispietata lima
che sordamente la mia vita scemi,
perché non ti ritemi
sì di rodermi il core a scorza a scorza
com' io di dire altrui chi ti dà forza?   26

For my heart, whenever I think of her in any place where others send their eyes, for fear that my care may shine through and be discovered, trembles more

than I do at the death that already chews on my every sense with the teeth that Love gives it: that is, my care wears down my powers and slows their work.

He has thrown me to the ground and stands over me with the sword with which he killed Dido—he, Love—to whom I cry out calling for mercy and humbly I beg him, and he seems set to deny all mercy.

Now and again he raises his hand and defies my weak life, this cruel one, and holds me on the earth stretched out and supine, too tired to wriggle any more:

then in my mind arise shrieks, and my blood that is dispersed through my veins fleeing rushes toward my heart, which calls it, and I turn white.

He strikes me under the left arm so fiercely that the pain rebounds into my heart; then I say: "If he lifts his arm another time, Death will have shut me up before the blow can descend."

---

sword . . . killed Dido: see note to poem 29 of the *Rime sparse*.

Ché più mi triema il cor qualora io penso
di lei in parte ov' altri li occhi induca,
per tema non traluca
lo mio penser di fuor sì che si scopra,
    ch' io non fo de la morte, che ogni sense
co li denti d'Amor già mi manduca:
ciò è che 'l pensier bruca
la lor vertù, sì che n'allenta l'opra.   34
    E' m'ha percosso in terra e stammi sopra
con quella spada ond' elli ancise Dido,
Amore, a cui io grido
merzé chiamando, e umilmente il priego:
ed el d'ogni merzé par messo al niego.   39

    Egli alza ad ora ad or la mano, e sfida
la debole mia vita, esto perverso,
che disteso a riverso
mi tiene in terra d'ogni guizzo stanco:
    allor mi surgon ne la mente strida;
e 'l sangue, ch' è per le vene disperso,
fuggendo corre verso
lo cor, che 'l chiama; ond' io rimango bianco.   47
    Elli mi fiede sotto il braccio manco
sì forte che 'l dolor nel cor rimbalza;
allor dico: "S' elli alza
un'altra volta, Morte m'avrà chiuso
prima che 'l colpo sia disceso giuso."   52

Would I might see him split her cruel heart right down the middle, for she is quartering mine. Then death would not be black for me, where I run because of her beauty!

For she shoots into the sun and into the shade indiscriminately, this homicidal thieving gangster. Ah me, why does she not bark for me, as I for her, in the hot pit?

For soon I'd shout: "I'll help you!" and I would, too, gladly, and so into her blond hair, which Love curls and gilds to destroy me, I would put my hand, and then I would please her.

If I had her blond braids grasped in my hand, that to me are become a scourge and a whip, taking hold before tierce I would pass vespers and the compline bell with them:

and I would not be pitying or courteous, I would be like a bear when it plays, and if Love whips me with them, I would take vengeance more than a thousand times.

And into her eyes, whence the sparks come forth that inflame and kill my heart, I would look from up close, fixedly, to avenge the fleeing they have done. And then I would give her lovingly the kiss of peace.

Song, go straight to that lady who has wounded my heart but steals away from me what I am most greedy for: strike her through the heart with an arrow, for to take vengeance is a lovely honor.

---

tierce . . . vespers . . . compline bell; reference to the canonical hours of prayer, held at approximately 9:00 A.M., sunset, and 9:00 P.M., respectively.   I would give her lovingly the kiss of peace: a literal translation of the Italian is "I would give her with love peace." The issue is whether the stanza as a whole concerns the act of love, as I believe it does, or only the last line.

Così vedess' io lui fender per mezzo
lo core a la crudele che 'l mio squatra;
poi non mi sarebb' atra
la morte, ov' io per sua bellezza corro:
   ché tanto dà nel sol quanto nel rezzo
questa scherana micidiale e latra.
Omè, perché non latra
per me, com' io per lei, nel caldo borro?   60
   ché tosto griderei: "Io vi soccorro!"
e fare 'l volentier, sì come quelli
che ne' biondi capelli
ch' Amor per consumarmi increspa e dora
metterei mano, e piacere'le allora.   65

   S' io avessi le belle trecce prese,
che fatte son per me scudiscio e ferza,
pigliandole anzi terza,
con esse passerei vespero e squille:
   e non sarei pietoso né cortese,
anzi farei com' orso quando scherza;
e se Amor me ne sferza,
io mi vendicherei di più di mille.   73
   Ancor ne li occhi, ond' escon le faville
che m'infiammano il cor, ch' io porto anciso,
guarderei presso e fiso
per vendicar lo fuggir che mi face;
e poi le renderei con amor pace.   78
   Canzon, vattene dritto a quella donna
che m'ha ferito il core e che m'invola
quello ond' io ho più gola,
a dàlle per lo cor d'una saetta:
ché bell'onor s'acquista in far vendetta.   83

5

Love, since I must complain aloud even though people hear me, and show myself spent of all power,
  grant me the skill to weep as I would wish to, so that as my sorrow unknots itself the words may carry it just as I feel it.
  You wish my death, and I consent: but who will excuse me if I am unable to say what you are making me suffer? Who will believe that you have finally hit me? And if you do give me speech equal to my torment, my Lord, do not let this cruel girl hear it from me before my death: for if she understood what I hear within myself, pity would make her lovely face less beautiful.

I am not able to flee her invasion of my imagination any more than I can flee my own thought that brings her there.
  My crazy soul, clever and busy to its own hurt, paints her there just as beautiful and cruel as she really is, and forms its own punishment;
  then it gazes at her, and when it is full of the great desire that it draws from her eyes, then it is angry with itself—for it has made the fire of its own wretchedness. What sharpness of reason can rein me in, when so great a tempest whirls within me? My anguish, not to be contained, breathes out through my mouth so that it can be understood, and it rewards my eyes, too.

This is sometimes referred to as the *canzone montanina* (mountain song).   My anguish . . . rewards my eyes: my anguish causes me to sob (or groan) and shed tears.

5

Amor, da che convien pur ch' io mi doglia
perché la gente m'oda,
e mostri me d'ogni vertute spento,
   dammi savere a pianger come voglia,
sì che 'l duol che si snoda
portin le mie parole com' io 'l sento.   6
   Tu vo' ch' io muoia, e io ne son contento:
ma chi mi scuserà, s' io non so dire
ciò che mi fai sentire?
chi crederà ch' io sia omai sì colto?
E se mi dài parlar quanto tormento,
fa', signor mio, che innanzi al mio morire
questa rea per me nol possa udire:
ché, se intendesse ciò che dentro ascolto,
pietà faria men bello il suo bel volto.   15

   Io non posso fuggir ch' ella non vegna
ne l'imagine mia,
se non come il pensier che la vi mena.
   L'anima folle, che al suo mal s'ingegna,
com' ella è bella e ria,
così dipinge, e forma la sua pena;   21
      poi la riguarda, e quando ella è ben piena
del gran disio che de li occhi le tira,
incontro a sé s'adira,
c' ha fatto il foco ond' ella trista incende.
Quale argomento di ragion raffrena,
ove tanta tempesta in me si gira?
L'angoscia, che non cape dentro, spira
fuor de la bocca sì ch' ella s'intende,
e anche a li occhi lor merito rende.   30

The hostile image of her is victorious and fierce, and dominates my will;

desirous of its source, it makes me go to seek her where she is real, as like always runs to like.

I see clearly that I am snow seeking the sun, but I cannot do otherwise: I am like one who is in another's power and walks on his own feet to the place where he will be killed. When I am near her I seem to hear words saying: "By and by you will see that fellow die." Then I turn about to find someone to appeal to, and at that instant she catches sight of me with the eyes that kill me wrongfully.

What becomes of me when I am so wounded, Love, you know, not I, for you are there to look on me as I lie lifeless;

and if my soul later returns to my heart, ignorance and forgetfulness have been with it in its absence.

When I stand up again and examine the wound that brought me down, I cannot gain enough strength to stop trembling all over with fear. And my face, all pale, shows what thunderbolt landed on me, for though it was sent with a sweet smile, my face long after stays dark, for my spirit has no confidence.

La nimica figura, che rimane
vittoriosa e fera
e signoreggia la vertù che vole,
   vaga di sé medesima andar mi fane
colà dov' ella è vera,
come simile a simil correr sòle.   36
   Ben conosco che va la neve al sole,
ma più non posso: fo come colui
che, nel podere altrui,
va co' suoi piedi al loco ov' egli è morto.
Quando son presso, parmi udir parole
dicer: "Vie via vedrai morir costui."
Allor mi volgo per vedere a cui
mi raccomandi; e 'ntanto sono scorto
da li occhi che m'ancidono a gran torto.   45

   Qual io divegno sì feruto, Amore,
sailo tu, e non io,
che rimani a veder me sanza vita;
   e se l'anima torna poscia al core,
ignoranza ed oblio
stato è con lei mentre ch' ella è partita.   51
   Com' io risurgo e miro la ferita
che mi disfece quand' io fui percosso,
confortar non mi posso
sì ch' io non triemi tutto di paura.
E mostra poi la faccia scolorita
qual fu quel trono che mi giunse a dosso;
che se con dolce riso è stato mosso,
lunga fiata poi rimane oscura,
perché lo spirto non si rassicura.   60

Thus you have set me up, Love, amid these mountains, in the river valley along which you are ever lording it over me:

here you probe me, alive and dead, as you please, thanks to her fierce light that lightens and shows death the way.

Alas, I see no ladies here, no people with any understanding, to whom I could complain of my suffering; if that girl lacks all concern, I cannot hope for help from others. And, like one banished from your court, Lord, she fears no arrow of yours: pride makes such a breastplate for her that it blunts them all and ends their flight, and her armored heart is never bitten.

O my mountain song, go your way: perhaps you will see Florence my city, empty of love and naked of mercy, that locks me out; if you get in there, go saying: "From now on my maker can make war on you no more; up there where I come from such a chain binds him that—even though your cruelty soften—he is no longer free to return here."

---

river valley: the valley of the Arno, probably in the Casentino, where Dante stayed in 1307–8 and in 1311.

Così m'hai concio, Amore, in mezzo l'alpi,
ne la valle del fiume
lungo il qual sempre sopra me se' forte:
    qui vivo e morto, come vuoi, mi palpi,
merzé del fiero lume
che sfolgorando fa via a la morte.   66
    Lasso, non donne qui, non genti accorte
veggio, a cui mi lamenti del mio male:
se a costei non ne cale,
non spero mai d'altrui aver soccorso.
E questa sbandeggiata di tua corte,
signor, non cura colpo del tuo strale:
fatto ha d'orgoglio al petto schermo tale
ch' ogni saetta lì spunta suo corso;
per che l'armato cor da nulla è morso.   75

    O montanina mia canzon, tu vai:
forse vedrai Fiorenza, la mia terra,
che fuor di sé mi serra,
vota d'amore e nuda di pietate;
se dentro v'entri, va' dicendo: "Omai
non vi può far lo mio fattor più guerra:
là ond' io vegno una catena il serra
tal che, se piega vostra crudeltate,
non ha di ritornar qui libertate."   84

Bibliography

The scholarly and critical literature on Petrarch is voluminous, and it continues to grow apace. Here I can list only a small selection, mostly of books and articles I myself have found useful. For bibliography before 1972, see *Petrarch: Catalogue of the Petrarch Collection in Cornell University Library*, 2nd ed. (Millwood, N.Y.: Kraus-Thomson, 1974). George Watson, *The English Petrarchans: A Critical Bibliography of the "Canzoniere,"* Warburg Institute Surveys, vol. 3 (London: The Warburg Institute, 1967), gives a nearly complete list of English translations of the individual poems, in alphabetical order. Beatrice Corrigan, "Petrarch in English," *Italica*, 50 (1973), 400–407, is a useful survey of translations and studies.

Important articles on Petrarch appeared in the journal *Studi petrarcheschi* (1948–66). For useful surveys of Renaissance and later editions see the materials appended to the Carducci-Ferrari and Chiòrboli editions listed below. The centennial year 1974 saw an outpouring of studies, papers delivered at congresses, and so forth, many still unpublished; their assimilation will take years. One of the most important commemorative collections will no doubt be the forthcoming special issue of *Italia medioevale e umanistica*, edited by Giuseppe Billanovich. This journal regularly publishes important articles on Petrarch and his circle, including a major census of manuscripts.

LIFE

Bishop, Morris. *Petrarch and His World.* Bloomington: Indiana University Press, 1963. Highly readable, but unreliable. Many of Bishop's expert translations are included, and an abridgment of the *Secretum.*

Dotti, Ugo. *Petrarca a Milano (documenti milanesi 1353–1354).* Milan: Ceschina, 1972. On Petrarch's involvement with Visconti politics.

Tatham, Edward H. R. *Francesco Petrarca, the First Modern Man of Letters, His Life and Correspondence: A Study of the Early Fourteenth Century (1304–1347)*. 2 vols. London: Sheldon, 1925–26. Translations of several dozen letters and of the *Secretum*.

Watkins, Renee Neu. "Petrarch and the Black Death: From Fear to Monuments." *Studies in the Renaissance*, 19 (1972), 196–223.

Wilkins, Ernest Hatch. *Life of Petrarch*. Chicago: Chicago University Press, 1961. The most reliable and complete biography, though based on a somewhat uncritical admiration.

ENGLISH TRANSLATIONS OF THE *RIME SPARSE*

Armi, Anna Maria, trans. *Petrarch's Sonnets and Songs*. New York: Pantheon, 1946. Complete, in the original forms, "with much straining after rhyme-words" (Watson).

Auslander, Joseph, trans. *The Sonnets of Petrarch*. London: Longmans, Green, 1931. Only the 317 sonnets, in sonnet form.

Bergin, Thomas G., ed. *The Rhymes of Francesco Petrarca: A Selection of Translations*. Edinburgh: Oliver and Boyd, 1954. Verse translations, mainly by Bergin and Morris Bishop.

————trans. *The Sonnets of Petrarch, Together with English translations*. Verona: Limited Editions, 1965.

Bishop, Morris, trans. *Love Rhymes of Petrarch*. Ithaca, N.Y.: Dragon Press, 1932. Verse translations of some sixty poems.

Flores, Angel, ed. *An Anthology of Medieval Lyrics*. New York: Modern Library, 1962. There are several fine translations by Dwight L. Durling.

MacGregor, Robert M. *Indian Leisure*. London: Smith, Elder, 1854. The first complete translation (except for poem 105).

Sonnets, Triumphs, and Other Poems of Petrarch, Now first completely translated into English verse by various hands, with a life of the poet by Thomas Campbell. London: Bohn, 1859. Not the first, but the most widely consulted translation before Armi's; several versions are given of many poems.

Synge, John Millington. *Translations*. Edited by Robin Skelton. Dublin: Dolmen, 1961. (Also in volume 1 of Synge's *Complete Works*, edited by Skelton.) Beautiful Irish prose renderings of seventeen sonnets.

ENGLISH TRANSLATIONS OF OTHER WORKS

Trionfi

Carnicelli, D. H., trans. *Lord Morley's Tryumphes of Fraunces Petrarcke: The First English Translation of the "Trionfi."* Cambridge, Mass.: Harvard University Press, 1971.

Wilkins, E. H., trans. *Triumphs.* Chicago: University of Chicago Press, 1962.

Bucolicum carmen

Bergin, Thomas G., ed. and trans. *Petrarch's Bucolicum Carmen.* New Haven: Yale University Press, 1974.

De sui ipsius et multorium ignorantia

Cassirer, Ernst; Kristeller, P. O.; and Randall, J. H., Jr.; trans. *The Renaissance Philosophy of Man.* Chicago: University of Chicago Press, 1948. This also includes *Familiares* 4.1 and passages from other letters.

De remediis utriusque fortunae

Rawski, Conrad, ed. and trans. *Four Dialogues for Scholars.* Cleveland: Press of Western Reserve University, 1966.

De vita solitaria

Zeitlin, Jacob, trans. *The Life of Solitude.* Urbana: University of Illinois Press, 1924.

Familiares

Bernardo, Aldo S., trans. *Rerum familiarum libri I-VIII.* Albany: State University of New York Press, 1975.

Cosenza, Mario Emilio, ed. and trans. *Petrarch's Letters to Classical Authors.* Chicago: University of Chicago Press, 1910. Most of book 24 of the *Familiares.*

Dotti, Ugo, ed. *Le familiari [libri I-IV].* Urbino: Argalia, 1970. The volume includes an essay on Petrarch's new definition of the role of the man of letters, from a moderate Marxian position.

————ed. *Le familiari [libri I-XI].* 2 vols. Urbino: Argalia, 1974. A revision of the 1970 translation and a new introduction.

Liber sine nomine

Zacour, P., trans. *Book without a Name*. Toronto: Toronto University Press, 1973.

Secretum

Draper, William H., trans. *Petrarch's Secret; or, The Soul's Conflict with Passion: Three Dialogues between Himself and St. Augustine*. London: Chatto & Windus, 1911. See also Tatham, Edward H. R., under Life, above, and Robinson and Rolfe, under Selections, below.

Selections

Martellotti, G.; Ricci, P. G.; Carrara, E.; Bianchi, E.; eds. *Prose*. Milan: Ricciardi, 1955. A full selection from the prose works with Italian translations and excellent annotations.

Bishop, Morris, ed. and trans. *Letters from Petrarch*. Bloomington: Indiana University Press, 1966.

Cosenza, Mario E. *Francesco Petrarca and the Revolution of Cola di Rienzo*. Chicago: University of Chicago Press, 1913. Letters and other documents on the topic.

Robinson, J. H., and Rolfe, H. W. *Petrarch: The First Modern Scholar and Man of Letters*. 2nd ed. New York: Putnam, 1914. A rich selection, including the *Secretum*.

Thompson, David B., ed. and trans. *Petrarch, a Humanist among Princes: An Anthology of Petrarch's Letters and of Selections from His Other Works*. New York: Harper & Row, 1971.

Wilkins, E. H., trans. *Petrarch at Vaucluse: Letters in Verse and Prose*. Chicago: University of Chicago Press, 1958.

————*Studies in the Life and Works of Petrarch*. Cambridge, Mass.: Medieval Academy of America, 1955. The volume includes a translation of Petrarch's coronation oration (also in *PMLA*, 68 [1953], 1241–50).

ITALIAN EDITIONS OF THE *RIME SPARSE*

Carducci, Giosue', and S. Ferrari, eds. *Le rime di Francesco Petrarca*. Florence: Sansoni, 1899. Reprinted by Sansoni with an introduction by Gianfranco Contini, 1957. The fullest and best modern commentary, including variants.

Castelvetro, Ludovico, ed. *Le rime del Petrarca*. Basel: de Sedabonis, 1582. By far the most useful of the Renaissance commentaries.

Chiòrboli, Ezio, ed. *Le "Rime sparse" e i "Trionfi."* Bari: Laterza, 1930. Included are poems addressed to Petrarch and a vaulable discussion of the development of Petrarch studies. (Chiòrboli also published an edition of the *Rime sparse* alone, with a rather emotional and romanticized but sometimes useful commentary and a full bibliography [Milan: Trevisini, 1924].)

Contini, Gianfranco, ed. *Canzoniere*. Annotated by Daniele Ponchiroli. 3rd ed. Turin: Einaudi, 1964. This is the edition most faithful to Petrarch's orthography; it includes the noted essay "Preliminari sulla lingua del Petrarca."

Griffith, T. Gwynfor, and Hainsworth, P. R. J., eds. *Petrarch: Selected Poems*. Manchester: Manchester University Press, 1971. Useful introduction and annotations.

Neri, F.; Martellotti, G.; Bianchi, E.; and Sapegno, N.; eds. *Rime, "Trionfi" e poesie latine*. Milan: Ricciardi, 1951. The most useful edition of all the Italian poetry, with brief but informative commentary; a generous selection of the Latin poetry with Italian translations.

BACKGROUNDS TO THE *RIME SPARSE*

Brown, Norman O. "Daphne, or Metamorphosis." In *Myths, Dreams, and Religion*, edited by Joseph Campbell. New York: E. P. Dutton, 1970.

———"Metamorphosis, II: Actaeon." *American Poetry Review*, 1, no. 1 (November -December 1972), pp. 38–40.

Dante Alighieri. *Rime*. Edited by Gianfranco Contini. 2nd ed. Turin: Einaudi, 1946. The most useful Italian edition.

de Boer, C., ed. *Ovide moralisé: Poème français du xive siècle*. Verhandelingen der Koninklijke Akademie van Wetenschappen te Amsterdam, 15 (1915), 21, 30, 37, 48 (1938).

Dronke, Peter. *The Medieval Lyric*. London: Hutchinson, 1968. Excellent discussions of a wide range of texts, both Latin and vernacular, including Dante's "Così nel mio parlar voglio esser aspro."

Durling, Robert M. " 'Io son venuto': Seneca, Plato, and the Microcosm." *Dante Studies*, 93 (in press). On the first of Dante's *rime petrose*.

Fenzi, Enrico. "Le rime per la Donna Pietra." In *Miscellanea di studi danteschi*, pp. 229–309. Genova: Bozzi, 1966. The best discussion to date of Dante's *rime petrose*.

Foster, Kenelm, O. P., and Boyde, Patrick, eds. *Dante's Lyric Poetry*. 2 vols. Oxford: Clarendon Press, 1967. Excellent translations facing the original, with detailed commentary.

Freccero, John. "'Medusa: The Letter and the Spirit." *Yearbook of Italian Studies*, 1972, pp. 1–18. An important interpretation of *Inferno* 9.

Fulgentius: *Fabii Planciadis Fulgentii V. C. Opera*. Edited by R. Helm. Leipzig: Teubner, 1898.

Goldin, Frederick, trans. *German and Italian Lyrics of the Middle Ages: An Anthology and a History*. Garden City, N.Y.: Doubleday, Anchor Books, 1973.

———trans. *Lyrics of the Troubadours and Trouvères: An Anthology and a History*. Garden City, N.Y.: Doubleday, Anchor Books, 1973.

———*The Mirror of Narcissus in the Courtly Love Lyric*. Ithaca, N.Y.: Cornell University Press, 1967.

Press, Alan R., ed. *Anthology of Troubadour Lyric Poetry*. Edinburgh Bilingual Library, vol. 3. Austin: University of Texas Press, 1971.

Seznec, Jean. *The Survival of the Pagan Gods*. Translated by Barbara F. Sessions. New York: Pantheon, 1953.

Sheehan, Donald. "An Interpretation of Dante's *rime petrose*." *Italica*, 44 (1967), 144–162.

Singleton, Charles S. *An Essay on the "Vita nuova."* Cambridge, Mass.: Harvard University Press, 1949.

Valency, Maurice. *In Praise of Love: An Introduction to the Love-Poetry of the Renaissance*. New York: Macmillan, 1958. A useful survey of troubador and later traditions of love poetry up to Dante.

Wilkins, E. H. *The Invention of the Sonnet, and Other Studies in Italian Literature*. Rome: Edizioni di storia e letteratura, 1959.

CRITICISM

General

Amaturo, Raffaele. *Petrarca*. Bari: Laterza, 1971. A useful annotated selection, with historical essays by Carlo Muscetta and Francesco Tateo.

Bosco, Umberto. *Francesco Petrarca*. 3rd ed. Bari: Laterza, 1965. The most influential recent full-length study.

Calcaterra, Carlo. *Nella selva del Petrarca*. Bologna: Cappelli, 1942. A classic of Petrarch criticism, this initiated many of the current critical topics.

——"Il Petrarca e il petrarchismo." In *Problemi ed orientamenti di lingua e letteratura italiana*, pp. 167–273. Vol. 3, *Questioni e correnti di storia letteraria*. Milan: Vallecchi, 1949.

Contini, Gianfranco. "Francesco Petrarca." In *Letteratura italiana delle origini*, pp. 571–694. Florence: Sansoni, 1970. An excellent introductory essay and brief anthology, including Italian translations of the Latin, and full annotations.

De Sanctis, Francesco. *Saggio critico sul Petrarca*. Edited by Ettore Bonora. Bari: Laterza, 1954. Originally published in 1869, this has been the most influential of all studies of Petrarch.

——*History of Italian Literature*. Translated by Joan Redfern. 2 vols. New York: Basic Books, 1959. Originally published in 1879, De Sanctis' Hegelian view of the secularization of Italian culture has been dominant; the chapter on Petrarch is a briefer statement of his *Saggio critico*.

Hardison, O. B., Jr. *The Enduring Monument: A Study of the Idea of Praise in Renaissance Literary Theory and Practice*. Chapel Hill: University of North Carolina Press, 1962.

Quinones, Ricardo J. *The Renaissance Discovery of Time*. Cambridge, Mass.: Harvard University Press, 1972.

Sapegno, Natalino. *Il trecento*. 3rd ed. Milan: Vallardi, 1952. The chapter on Petrarch is still the most useful brief survey of all aspects of his work.

Scaglione, Aldo, ed. *Francis Petrarch Six Centuries Later: A Symposium*. North Carolina University Studies in Philology, vol. 72, no. 5. A collection of centennial essays, many of them extremely valuable.

Tripet, Arnaud. *Pétrarque ou la connaissance de soi*. Travaux d'humanisme et renaissance, vol. 91. Geneva: Droz, 1967. A provocative study of the Latin works, of first importance.

On Petrarch's Humanism, Library, and Latin Works

Baron, Hans. *From Petrarch to Leonardo Bruni: Studies in Humanistic and Political Literature*. Chicago: University of Chicago Press, 1968. There is an important chapter on the question of Petrarch's conversion.

Bernardo, Aldo S. *Petrarch, Scipio, and the Africa*. Baltimore, Md.: Johns Hopkins University Press, 1962. On Petrarch's unfinished epic poem and its background.

Billanovich, Giuseppe. *Petrarca letterato: I., nello scrittoio del Petrarca.* Rome: Edizioni di storia e letteratura, 1947. A groundbreaking study of Petrarch's habits of work, his friendship with Boccaccio, and so forth.

———"Petrarca e il Ventoso." *Italia medioevale e umanistica,* 9 (1966), 389–401. A fundamental article on the famous letter about the climb of Mount Ventoux (*Familiares* 4.1) its late composition is established.

———"Petrarch and the Textual Tradition of Livy." *Journal of the Warburg and Courtault Institute,* 14 (1951), 137–208. On Petrarch's first triumph as a classical scholar.

Courcelle, Pierre. *Les Confessions de saint Augustin dans la tradition littéraire: antécédents et postérité.* Paris: Etudes augustiniennes, 1963. There is an important chapter on Petrarch's allusions to the *Confessions.*

de Nolhac, Pierre. *Pétrarque et l'humanisme.* 2 vols. 2nd ed. Paris: Champion, 1907. Reprinted 1965. A pioneering work, still indispensable, on Petrarch's reading, his collection of books and his annotations in them, and his allusions to classical and medieval authors.

Durling, Robert M. "The Ascent of Mt. Ventoux and the Crisis of Allegory." *Italian Quarterly,* 18 (1974), no. 69, pp. 7–28. On *Familiares* 4.1.

Martinelli, Bortolo. "Del Petrarca e il Ventoso." In *Studi in onore di Alberto Chiari,* pp. 767–834. Brescia, 1973. An important article, though from a strictly orthodox point of view.

Mommsen, Theodor E. *Medieval and Renaissance Studies.* Edited by Eugene E. Rice, Jr. Ithaca, N.Y.: Cornell University Press, 1959.

Seigel, Jerrold E. "Eloquence and Silence in Petrarch." *Journal of the History of Ideas,* 26 (1965), 147–174.

———*Rhetoric and Philosophy in Renaissance Humanism.* Princeton: Princeton University Press, 1968.

Thompson, David, and Nagel, Alan F., eds. and trans. *The Three Crowns of Florence: Humanist Assessments of Dante, Petrarca, and Boccaccio.* New York: Harper & Row, 1972.

Ullman, B. L. *Studies in the Italian Renaissance.* Rome: Edizioni di storia e letteratura, 1955. This includes the important article "Petrarch's Favorite Books."

On the Rime sparse

Appel, Carl, *Zur Entwicklungsgeschichte italienischer Dichtungen Petrarcas.* Halle a. S., 1891. A complete transcription of Vat. Lat. 3196, Casanatense 924, and Laurentian Plut. 41.14, with extensive commentary.

———"Petrarka und Arnaut Daniel." *Archiv*, 147 (1924), 212–235.

Bernardo, Aldo S. *Petrarch, Laura, and the "Triumphs."* Albany: State University of New York, 1974. On the relation of the *Rime sparse* to the *Trionfi*.

Chiappelli, Fredi. *Studi sul linguaggio del Petrarca: la canzone delle visioni.* Florence: Olschki, 1971. On poem 323.

Concordanze del "Canzoniere" di Francesco Petrarca. 2 vols. Florence: Accademia della Crusca, 1971.

Contini, Gianfranco. *Varianti e altra linguistica: una raccolta di saggi (1938–1968).* Turin: Einaudi, 1970. The volume includes the brilliant and influential essays "Preliminari sulla lingua del Petrarca," "Saggio d'un commento alle correzioni del Petrarca volgare," "Correzioni grammaticali petrarchesche," "Préhistoire de *l'aura* de Pétrarque," and "Il commento petrarchesco di Carducci e Ferrari."

Dotti, Ugo. "Petrarca: il mito dafneo." *Convivium*, 37 (1969, 9–23. An illuminating essay on the relation of the figure of Laura in the Latin poetry to that in the *Rime sparse*.

Durling, Robert M. "Petrarch's 'Giovene donna sotto un verde lauro.' " *Modern Language Notes*, 86 (1971), 1–20. On poem 30.

Dutschke, Dennis. "The Textual Situation and Chronological Assessment of Petrarch's Canzone XXIII." *Italian Quarterly*, 18 (1974), no. 69, pp. 37–69. A valuable survey of the evidence that the poem developed slowly.

Foster, Kenelm, O.P. "Beatrice or Medusa: The Penitential Element in Petrarch's *Canzoniere*." In *Italian Studies Presented to E. R. Vincent.* Cambridge: Heffer, 1962.

Freccero, John. "The Fig Tree and the Laurel: Petrarch's Poetics." *Diacritics*, 5 (1975), 34–40. A brilliant discussion in terms of semiotics.

Iliescu, Nicolae. *Il canzoniere petrarchesco e sant'Agostino.* Rome: Academia dacoromena, 1962.

McKenzie, Kenneth, ed. *Concordanza delle rime di Francesco Petrarca.* Oxford: Oxford University Press, 1912.

Martinelli, Bortolo. *"Feria sexta aprilis:* la data sacra nel canzoniere del Petrarca." *Rivista di storia e letteratura religiosa*, 8 (1972), 449–484.

Neri, Ferdinando. "Il Petrarca e le rime dantesche della pietra." *Cultura*, n.s. 8 (1929), 389–404.

Noferi, Adelia. "Note ad un sonetto del Petrarca." *Forum*

Italicum, 2 (1968), 194–205. A brilliant discussion of poem 6.
————*L'esperienza poetica del Petrarca*. Florence: Le Monnier,
1962. The emphasis is on the influence of Augustine.

Roche, Thomas P., Jr. "The Calendrical Structure of Petrarch's
Canzoniere," *Studies in Philology*, 71 (1974), 152–172. Roche
attempts to establish a close correlation between individual
poems and the individual days of 1327, 1341, and 1348. He
has many valuable numerological observations.

Phelps, Ruth Shepard. *The Earlier and Later Forms of Petrarch's
"Canzoniere."* Chicago: University of Chicago Press, 1925.

Riesz, Janos. *Die Sestine: Ihre Stellung in der literarischen Kritik
und ihre Geschichte als lyrisches Genus*. Munich: Fink, 1971.

Rigolot, François. "Nature and Function of Paranomasia in the
Canzoniere." *Italian Quarterly*, 18 (1974), no. 69, pp. 29–36.

Romano', Angelo. *Il codice degli abbozzi (Vat. Lat. 3196) di
Francesco Petrarca*. Rome: Bardi, 1955. This omits the poems
not by Petrarch; it includes the readings of Vat. Lat. 3195 and
extensive commentary on Petrarch's revisions.

Santagata, Marco. "Presenze di Dante 'comico' nel 'Canzoniere'
del Petrarca." *Giornale storico della letteratura italiana*, 146
(1969), 163–211. Although timid in its interpretations, this
article amply demonstrates that Petrarch knew the *Commedia*
by heart and echoed it on virtually every page of the *Rime
sparse*.

Scarano, Nicola. "Fonti provenzali e italiane della lirica
petrarchesca." *Studi di filologia romanza*, 8 (1900), 250–360.

Wilkins, E. H. *The Making of the "Canzoniere" and Other
Petrarchan Studies*. Rome: Edizioni di storia e letteratura,
1951. Classic discussions of the evolution of the *Rime sparse*,
of Petrarch's coronation, and other topics; of first importance. Wilkins' widely accepted theory of the pre-Chigi stages
of the *Rime sparse* (none of which exists separately) is open to
question. It rests upon the notion that "tr[anscriptum] in
or[dinem]" always refers to transcription into a version of the
Rime sparse, but it is clear that Petrarch often used the term
ordo to refer to a reference ledger: see *Le familiari*, edited by
Vittorio Rossi, vol. 1 (Florence: Sansoni, 1933), pp. XII–XIV.

Zottoli, Angelo Andrea. "Il numero solare nell'ordinamento dei
'Rerum vulgarium fragmenta.'" *La cultura*, 7 (1928), 337–348.

Index of First Lines

Ahi bella libertà, come tu m'ài, 201
A la dolce ombra de le belle frondi, 287
Al cader d'una pianta che si svelse, 497
Alma felice che sovente torni, 461
Almo sol, quella fronde ch' io sola amo, 335
Al poco giorno e al gran cerchio d'ombra, 617
Amor, che meco al buon tempo ti stavi, 483
Amor, che 'ncende il cor d'ardente zelo, 329
Amor che 'n Cielo e 'n gentil core alberghi, 597
Amor, che nel penser mio vive et regna, 285
Amor, che vedi ogni pensero aperto, 309
Amor co la man destra il lato manco, 385
Amor con sue promesse lusingando, 177
Amor, da che convien pur ch' io mi doglia, 631
Amor et io, sì pien di meraviglia, 307
Amor, Fortuna, et la mia mente, schiva, 239
Amor fra l'erbe una leggiadra rete, 327
Amor, io fallo et veggio il mio fallire, 395
Amor m'à posto come segno a strale, 271
Amor mi manda quel dolce pensero, 315
Amor mi sprona in un tempo et affrena, 325
Amor, Natura et la bella alma umile, 331
Amor piangeva et io con lui tal volta, 71
Amor, quando fioria, 507
Amor, se vuo' ch' i' torni al giogo antico, 443
Amor, tu vedi ben che questa donna, 621
Anima bella, da quel nodo sciolta, 485

647

Anima che diverse cose tante, 351
Antonio, cosa à fatto la tua terra, 599
Anzi tre dì creata era alma in parte, 369
A pie' de' colli ove la bella vesta, 43
Apollo, s' ancor vive il bel desio, 93
A qualunque animale alberga in terra, 57
Arbor vittoriosa triunfale, 425
Aspro core et selvaggio et cruda voglia, 435
Aura che quelle chiome bionde et crespe, 383
Aventuroso più d'altro terreno, 217

Beato in sogno et di languir contento, 367
Benedetto sia 'l giorno e 'l mese et l'anno, 139
Ben mi credea passar mio tempo omai, 357
Ben sapeva io che natural consiglio, 149

Cantai, or piango; et non men di dolcezza, 385
"Cara la vita, et dopo lei mi pare, 425
Cercato ò sempre solitaria vita, 421
Cesare, poi che 'l traditor d'Egitto, 205
Che debb'io far, che mi consigli, Amore, 437
"Che fai, alma? che pensi? avrem mai pace, 297
Che fai? che pensi? ché pur dietro guardi, 453
Chiare fresche et dolci acque, 245
Chi è fermato di menar sua vita, 181
Chi vuol veder quantunque po Natura, 411
Come 'l candido pie' per l'erba fresca, 311
Come talora al caldo tempo sòle, 285
Come va 'l mondo! or mi diletta et piace, 469
Conobbi (quanto il Ciel li occhi m'aperse, 537
Così nel mio parlar voglio esser aspro, 625
Così potess' io ben chiudere in versi, 199

Da' più belli occhi, et dal più chiaro viso, 545
Datemi pace, o duri miei pensieri, 453
Deh, porgi mano a l'affannato ingegno, 551
Deh, qual pietà, qual angel fu sì presto, 539
Del cibo onde 'l signor mio sempre abonda, 539
De l'empia Babilonia ond' è fuggita, 223
Del mar tirre no a la sinistra riva, 147

Dicemi spesso il mio fidato speglio, 571
Dicesette anni à già rivolto il cielo, 237
Di dì in dì vo cangiando il viso e 'l pelo, 341
Di pensier in pensier, di monte in monte, 265
Discolorato ài, Morte, il più bel volto, 463
Di tempo in tempo mi si fa men dura, 295
Dodici donne onestamente lasse, 381
Dolce mio caro et prezioso pegno, 537
Dolci durezze et placide repulse, 549
Dolci ire, dolci sdegni et dolci paci, 351
Donna che lieta col Principio nostro, 545
Donna mi vene spesso ne la mente, 587
Due gran nemiche inseme erano agiunte, 477
Due rose fresche et colte in paradiso, 407
D'un bel chiaro polito et vivo ghiaccio, 349

El bell'occhio d'Apollo, dal cui guardo, 607
E' mi par d'or in ora udire il messo, 547
È questo 'l nido in che la mia fenice, 501
Era il giorno ch' al sol si scoloraro, 39
Erano i capei d'oro a l'aura sparsi, 193

Far potess' io vendetta di colei, 419
Fera stella (se 'l cielo à forza in noi, 321
Fiamma dal Ciel su le tue treccie piova, 281
Fontana di dolore, albergo d'ira, 283
Fresco ombroso fiorito et verde colle, 405
Fu forse un tempo dolce cosa amore, 541
Fuggendo la pregione ove Amor m'ebbe, 193

Gentil mia Donna, i' veggio, 163
Geri, quando talor meco s'adira, 325
Già desiai con sì giusta querela, 373
Già fiammeggiava l'amorosa stella, 93
Giovene donna sotto un verde lauro, 87
Giunto Alessandro a la famosa tomba, 333
Giunto m'à Amor fra belle et crude braccia, 317
Gli occhi di ch' io parlai sì caldamente, 471
Gloriosa Columna in cui s'appoggia, 45
Grazie ch' a pochi il Ciel largo destina, 367

I begli occhi ond' i' fui percosso in guisa, 175
I dì miei più leggier che nesun cervo, 499
I dolci colli ov' io lasciai me stesso, 363
Il cantar novo e 'l pianger delli augelli, 375
Il figliuol di Latona avea già nove, 109
Il mal mi preme et mi spaventa il peggio, 407
Il mio adversario in cui veder solete, 111
Il successor di Carlo, che la chioma, 73
I' mi soglio accusare, et or mi scuso, 475
I' mi vivea di mia sorte contento, 387
In cielo, in aria, in terra, in fuoco e in mare, 593
In dubbio di mio stato, or piango or canto, 415
Ingegno usato a le question profonde, 599
In mezzo di duo amanti onesta altera, 223
In nobil sangue vita umile et queta, 371
In qual parte del Ciel, in quale Idea, 305
In quel bel viso ch' i' sospiro et bramo, 419
In quella parte dove Amor mi sprona, 249
In tale stella duo belli occhi vidi, 423
Io amai sempre, et amo forte ancora, 189
Io avrò sempre in odio la fenestra, 189
Io canterei d'Amor sì novamente, 269
Io mi rivolgo indietro a ciascun passo, 51
Io non fu' d'amar voi lassato unquanco, 185
Io non so ben s' io vedo quel ch' io veggio, 605
I' ò pien di sospir quest'aere tutto, 467
I' ò pregato Amor, e 'l ne riprego, 403
Io sentia dentr' al cor già venir meno, 113
Io son de l'aspettar omai sì vinto, 199
Io son già stanco di pensar sì come, 175
Io son sì stanco sotto 'l fascio antico, 185
Io son venuto al punto de la rota, 613
Io temo sì de' begli occhi l'assalto, 105
I' pensava assai destro esser su l' ale, 487
I' piansi, or canto; ché 'l celeste lume, 387
I' pur ascolto, et non odo novella, 417
Italia mia, ben che 'l parlar sia indarno, 257
Ite, caldi sospiri, al freddo core, 299
Ite, rime dolenti, al duro sasso, 531

I' vidi in terra angelici costumi, 303
I' vo pensando, et nel penser m'assale, 427
I' vo piangendo i miei passati tempi, 575

La bella donna che cotanto amavi, 195
La donna che 'l mio cor nel viso porta, 219
L'aere gravato et l'importuna nebbia, 145
La gola e 'l sonno et l'oziose piume, 43
La guancia che fu già piangendo stanca, 137
L'alma mia fiamma oltra le belle bella, 469
L'alto et novo miracol ch' a' dì nostri, 489
L'alto signor dinanzi a cui non vale, 403
L'amorose faville e 'l dolce lume, 597
L'arbor gentil che forte amai molt'anni, 139
L'arco che in voi nova sita disserra, 605
L'ardente nodo ov' io fui, d'ora in ora, 451
La santa fama, de la qual son prive, 603
Lasciato ài, Morte, senza sole il mondo, 535
La sera desiare, odiar l'aurora, 417
L'aspettata vertù che 'n voi fioriva, 207
L'aspetto sacro de la terra vostra, 149
Lassare il velo per sole o per ombra, 47
Lasso, Amor mi trasporta ov' ir non voglio, 393
Lasso, ben so che dolorose prede, 205
Lasso, che mal accorto fui da prima, 143
Lasso, ch' i' ardo et altri non mel crede, 349
Lasso me, ch' i' non so in qual parte pieghi, 151
Lasso, quante fiate Amor m'assale, 217
L'aura celeste che 'n quel verde lauro, 343
L'aura che 'l verde lauro et l'aureo crine, 409
L'aura et l'odore e 'l refrigerio et l'ombra, 515
L'aura gentil che rasserena i poggi, 341
L'aura mia sacra al mio stanco riposo, 553
L'aura serena che fra verdi fronde, 343
L'aura soave al sole spiega et vibra, 345
L'avara Babilonia à colmo il sacco, 281
Là ver l'aurora, che sì dolce l'aura, 399
La vita fugge et non s'arresta un'ora, 451
Le stelle, il cielo, et gli elementi a prova, 301

Levommi il mio penser in parte ov' era, 481
Li angeli eletti et l'anime beate, 543
"Liete et pensose, accompagnate et sole, 379
Lieti fiori et felici, et ben nate erbe, 309
L'oro et le perle e i bei fioreti e l'erba, 595
L'oro et le perle e i fior vermigli e i bianchi, 113
L'ultimo, lasso, de' miei giorni allegri, 517

Mai non fui in parte ove sì chiar vedessi, 459
Mai non vedranno le mie luci asciutte, 501
Mai non vo' più cantar com' io soleva, 209
Ma poi che 'l dolce riso umile et piano, 109
Mente mia, che presaga de' tuoi danni, 493
Mentre che 'l cor dagli amorosi vermi, 483
Messer Francesco, chi d'amor sospira, 609
Mia benigna fortuna e 'l viver lieto, 525
Mia ventura et Amor m'avean sì adorno, 347
Mie venture al venir son tarde et pigre, 135
Mille fiate, o dolce mia guerrera, 57
Mille piagge in un giorno et mille rivi, 323
Mirando 'l sol de' begli occhi sereno, 319
"Mira quel colle, o stanco mio cor vago, 405
Morte à spento quel sol ch' abagliar suolmi, 573
Movesi il vecchierel canuto et bianco, 51

Né cosi bello il sol giamai levarsi, 291
Ne la stagion che 'l ciel rapido inchina, 117
Nel dolce tempo de la prima etade, 61
Ne l'età sua più bella et più fiorita, 457
Né mai pietosa madre al caro figlio, 465
Né per sereno ciel ir vaghe stelle, 491
Non al suo amante più Diana piacque, 123
Non à tanti animali il mar fra l'onde, 395
Non da l'ispano Ibero a l' indo Idaspe, 365
Non d'atra et tempestosa onda marina, 297
Non fur ma' Giove et Cesare sì mossi, 301
Non po far Morte il dolce viso amaro, 555
Non pur quell 'una bella ignuda mano, 347
Non Tesin, Po, Varo, Arno, Adige et Tebro, 295
Non veggio ove scampar mi possa omai, 215

Nova angeletta sovra l'ale accorta, 215
Nuova bellezza in abito gentile, 595

O aspettata in Ciel beata et bella, 75
O bella man che mi destringi 'l core, 345
O cameretta che già fosti un porto, 393
Occhi miei lassi, mentre ch' io vi giro, 49
Occhi miei, oscurato è 'l nostro sole, 455
"Occhi, piangete, accompagnate il core, 187
O d'ardente vertute ornata et calda, 293
O dolci sguardi, o parolette accorte, 415
O giorno, o ora, o ultimo momento, 517
Ogni giorno mi par più di mill'anni, 555
Oimè il bel viso, oimè il soave sguardo, 437
O Invidia nemica di vertute, 319
Oltra l'usato modo si rigira, 607
O misera et orribil visione, 413
Onde tolse Amor l'oro et di qual vena, 377
O novella Tarpea, in cui s'asconde, 603
O passi sparsi, o pensier vaghi et pronti, 307
Or ài fatto l'estremo di tua possa, 515
Or che 'l ciel et la terra e 'l vento tace, 311
Orso, al vostro destrier si po ben porre, 201
Orso, e' non furon mai fiumi ne stagni, 105
Or vedi, Amor, che giovenetta donna, 235
O tempo, O ciel volubil che fuggendo, 553
Ove ch' i' posi gli occhi lassi o giri, 305
Ov' è la fronte che con picciol cenno, 479

Pace non trovo et non ò da far guerra, 273
Padre del Ciel, dopo i perduti giorni, 141
Parrà forse ad alcun che 'n lodar quella, 409
Pasco la mente d'un sì nobil cibo, 339
Passa la nave mia colma d'oblio, 335
Passato è 'l tempo omai, lasso, che tanto, 493
Passer mai solitario in alcun tetto, 383
Perch' al viso d'Amor portava insegna, 133
Perché la vita è breve, 155
Perché quel che mi trasse ad amar prima, 137
Perch' io t'abbia guardata di menzogna, 115

Per fare una leggiadra sua vendetta, 37
Per mezz' i boschi inospiti et selvaggi, 323
Per mirar Policleto a prova fiso, 177
Persequendomi Amor al luogo usato, 219
Piangete, Donne, et con voi pianga Amore, 195
Pien di quella ineffabile dolcezza, 225
Pien d'un vago penser che me desvia, 315
Piovonmi amare lagrime dal viso, 53
Più di me lieta non si vede a terra, 73
Più volte Amor m'avea già detto: "Scrivi, 197
Più volte già dal bel sembiante umano, 317
Più volte il dì mi fo vermiglio et fosco, 589
Po, ben puo' tu portartene la scorza, 327
Poco era ad appressarsi agli occhi miei, 123
Poi che la vista angelica serena, 455
Poi che 'l camin m'è chiuso di mercede, 269
Poi che mia spene è lunga a venir troppo, 191
Poi che per mio destino, 169
Poi che voi et io più volte abbiam provato, 203
Ponmi ove 'l sole occide i fiori et l'erba, 291

Qual donna attende a gloriosa fama, 423
Qual mio destin, qual forza o qual inganno, 377
Qual paura ò quando mi torna a mente, 411
Qual più diversa et nova, 273
Qual ventura mi fu quando da l'uno, 391
Quand'io mi volga indietro a mirar gli anni, 477
Quand'io son tutto volto in quella parte, 53
Quand'io veggio dal ciel scender l'Aurora, 471
Quando Amor i belli occhi a terra inchina, 313
Quando dal proprio sito si rimove, 107
Quando fra l'altre donne ad ora ad ora, 49
Quando giugne per gli occhi al cor profondo, 197
Quando giunse a Simon l'alto concetto, 179
Quando il soave mio fido conforto, 557
Quando io movo i sospiri a chiamar voi, 41
Quando io v'odo parlar sì dolcemente, 289
Quando 'l pianeta che distingue l'ore, 45
Quando 'l sol bagna in mar l'aurato carro, 379

Quando 'l voler, che con due sproni ardenti, 293
Quando mi vene inanzi il tempo e 'l loco, 321
Quando talor, da giusta ira commosso, 587
Quanta invidia io ti porto, avara terra, 479
Quante fiate al mio dolce ricetto, 461
Quanto più disiose l'ali spando, 283
Quanto più m'avicino al giorno estremo, 91
Que' che 'n Tesaglia ebbe le man sì pronte, 111
Que' ch' infinita providenzia et arte, 39
Quel che d'odore et di color vincea, 535
Quel foco ch' i' pensai che fosse spento, 133
Quella che gli animai del mondo atterra, 591
Quella che 'l giovenil meo core avinse, 593
Quella fenestra ove l'un sol si vede, 203
Quel antiquo mio dolce empio signore, 561
Quella per cui con Sorga ò cangiato Arno, 487
Quelle pietose rime in ch' io m'accorsi, 235
Quel rosigniuol che sì soave piagne, 491
Quel sempre acerbo et onorato giorno, 303
Quel sol che mi mostrava il cammin destro, 485
Quel vago, dolce, caro, onesto sguardo, 519
Quel vago impallidir che 'l dolce riso, 237
Questa anima gentil che si diparte, 91
Questa fenice de l'aurata piuma, 331
Questa umil fera, un cor di tigre o d'orsa, 299
Questo nostro caduco et fragil bene, 547
Qui dove mezzo son, Sennuccio mio, 221

Rapido fiume, che d'alpestra vena, 363
Real natura, angelico intelletto, 399
Rimansi a dietro il sestodecimo anno, 227
Ripensando a quel ch' oggi il Cielo onora, 541
Rotta è l'alta colonna e 'l verde lauro, 443

S' al principio risponde il fine e 'l mezzo, 179
S' Amore o Morte non dà qualche stroppio, 107
S' amor non e, che dunque e quel ch' io sento, 271
S' Amor novo consiglio non n'apporta, 457
Se bianche non son prima ambe le tempie, 187

Se col cieco desir che 'l cor distrugge, 135
Se Febo al primo amor non è bugiardo, 591
Se lamentar augelli, o verdi fronde, 459
Se la mia vita da l'aspro tormento, 47
Se 'l dolce sguardo di costei m'ancide, 329
Se le parti del corpo mio destrutte, 609
Se l'onorata fronde che prescrive, 71
Se 'l pensier che mi strugge, 239
Se 'l sasso ond' è più chiusa questa valle, 225
Se mai foco per foco non si spense, 115
Sennuccio, i' vo' che sapi in qual manera, 221
Sennuccio mio, ben ché doglioso et solo, 467
Sento l'aura mia antica, e i dolci colli, 499
Se quell'aura soave de' sospiri, 465
Se Virgilio et Omero avessin visto, 333
Se voi poteste per turbati segni, 143
Sì breve è 'l tempo e 'l penser sì veloce, 463
Sì come eterna vita è veder Dio, 337
Sì è debile il filo a cui s'attene, 97
S' i' fussi stato fermo a la spelunca, 313
Signor mio caro, ogni pensier mi tira, 435
S' i' 'l dissi mai, ch' i' vegna in odio a quella, 353
S' io avesse pensato che sì care, 473
S'io credesse per morte essere scarco, 95
Sì tosto come aven che l'arco scocchi, 191
Sì traviato è 'l folle mi' desio, 41
Solea da la fontana di mia vita, 519
Solea lontana in sonno consolarme, 413
Soleano i miei penser soavemente, 475
Soleasi nel mio cor star bella et viva, 473
Solo et pensoso i più deserti campi, 95
Son animali al mondo de sì altera, 55
S' onesto amor po meritar mercede, 531
Spinse amor et dolor ove ir non debbe, 543
Spirto felice che sì dolcemente, 549
Spirto gentil che quelle membra reggi, 125
Standomi un giorno solo a la fenestra, 503
Stiamo, Amor, a veder la gloria nostra, 339
S'una fede amorosa, un cor non finto, 381

Tacer non posso, et temo non adopre, 507
Tal cavalier tutta una schiera atterra, 589
Tempo era omai da trovar pace o tregua, 495
Tennemi Amor anni ventuno ardendo, 573
Tornami a mente (anzi v'e dentro quella, 533
Tranquillo porto avea mostrato Amore, 497
Tra quantunque leggiadre donne et belle, 375
Tutta la mia fiorita et verde etade, 495
Tutto 'l dì piango; et poi la notte, quando, 373

Una candida cerva sopra l'erba, 337
Una donna più bella assai che 'l sole, 227

Vago augelletto, che cantando vai, 551
Valle che de' lamenti miei se' piena, 481
Verdi panni sanguigni oscuri o persi, 83
Vergine bella, che di sol vestita, 575
Vergognando talor ch' ancor si taccia, 55
Vidi fra mille donne una già tale, 533
Vincitore Alessandro l'ira vinse, 389
Vinse Anibàl, et non seppe usar poi, 207
Vive faville uscian de' duo bei lumi, 421
Voglia mi sprona, Amor mi guida et scorge, 365
Voi ch' ascoltate in rime sparse il suono, 37
Volgendo gli occhi al mio novo colore, 141
Volo con l'ali de' pensieri al Cielo, 571

Zefiro torna e 'l bel tempo rimena, 489